Rhapsody of Philosophy

Literature and Philosophy

A. J. Cascardi, General Editor

This series publishes books in a wide range of subjects in philosophy and literature, including studies of the social and historical issues that relate these two fields. Drawing on the resources of the Anglo-American and Continental traditions, the series is open to philosophically informed scholarship covering the entire range of contemporary critical thought.

ALREADY PUBLISHED

J. M. Bernstein, *The Fate of Art: Aesthetic Alienation from Kant to Derrida and Adorno*

Peter Bürger, *The Decline of Modernism*

Mary E. Finn, *Writing the Incommensurable: Kierkegaard, Rossetti, and Hopkins*

Reed Way Dasenbrock, ed., *Literary Theory After Davidson*

David Haney, *William Wordsworth and the Hermeneutics of Incarnation*

David Jacobson, *Emerson's Pragmatic Vision: The Dance of the Eye*

Gray Kochhar-Lindgren, *Narcissus Transformed: The Textual Subject in Psychoanalysis and Literature*

Robert Steiner, *Toward a Grammar of Abstraction: Modernity, Wittgenstein, and the Paintings of Jackson Pollock*

Sylvia Walsh, *Living Poetically: Kierkegaard's Existential Aesthetics*

Michel Meyer, *Rhetoric, Language, and Reason*

Christie McDonald and Gary Wihl, eds., *Transformation in Personhood and Culture After Theory*

Charles Altieri, *Painterly Abstraction in Modernist American Poetry: The Contemporaneity of Modernism*

John C. O'Neal, *The Authority of Experience: Sensationist Theory in the French Enlightenment*

John O'Neill, ed., *Freud and the Passions*

Sheridan Hough, *Nietzsche's Noontide Friend: The Self as Metaphoric Double*

E. M. Dadlez, *What's Hecuba to Him? Fictional Events and Actual Emotions*

Hugh Roberts, *Shelley and the Chaos of History: A New Politics of Poetry*

Charles Altieri, *Postmodernisms Now: Essays on Contemporaneity in the Arts*

Arabella Lyon, *Intentions: Negotiated, Contested, and Ignored*

Jill Gordon, *Turning Toward Philosophy: Literary Device and Dramatic Structure in Plato's Dialogues*

Michel Meyer, *Philosophy and the Passions: Toward a History of Human Nature*. Translated by Robert F. Barsky

Reed Way Dasenbrock, *Truth and Consequences: Intentions, Conventions, and the New Thematics*

David P. Haney, *The Challenge of Coleridge: Ethics and Interpretation in Romanticism and Modern Philosophy*

Alan Singer, *Aesthetic Reason: Artworks and the Deliberative Ethos*

Tom Huhn, *Imitation and Society: The Persistence of Mimesis in the Aesthetics of Burke, Hogarth, and Kant*

Jennifer Anna Gosetti-Ferenci, *The Ecstatic Quotidian: Phenomenological Sightings in Modern Art and Literature*

Rhapsody of
Philosophy

Dialogues with Plato

in

Contemporary Thought

Max Statkiewicz

The Pennsylvania State University Press
University Park, Pennsylvania

Library of Congress Cataloging-in-Publication Data

Statkiewicz, Max, 1949–
Rhapsody of philosophy : dialogues with Plato in contemporary thought / Max Statkiewicz.
p. cm. — (Literature and philosophy)
Includes bibliographical references (p.   ) and index.
ISBN 978-0-271-03540-6 (cloth : alk. paper)
ISBN 978-0-271-03541-3 (pbk : alk. paper)
1. Plato. Dialogues.
2. Continental philosophy.
I. Title.

B395.S589 2009
184—dc22
2009007373

Contents

Acknowledgments   vii

A Polemic Introduction   1

1   Platonic Theater: Rigor and Play in the *Republic*
    (Genette and Lacoue-Labarthe)   35

2   *Le Beau Jeu:* The Play of Beauty and Truth in the *Phaedrus*
    (Nietzsche, Heidegger, Derrida)   70

3   The Notion of (Re)Semblance in the *Sophist*
    (Deleuze, Foucault, Nancy)   102

4   The Abyssal Ground of World and Discourse in the *Timaeus*
    (Kristeva, Irigaray, Butler, Derrida)   132

Rhapsodic Conclusion:
"The Dialogue That We Are" in Plato, Heidegger, and Nancy   162

Bibliography   197

Index   213

For Sonia

Acknowledgments

I would like to thank the teachers and friends who over the years have read earlier versions of some portions of the material included in this book: Eléanore M. Zimmermann, David B. Allison, Hugh J. Silverman, and Robert Harvey of SUNY–Stony Brook; Leon Golden of the Florida State University; and especially Pierre Aubenque of Paris-Sorbonne University (Paris IV); Edward S. Casey of SUNY–Stony Brook and Luca Somigli of the University of Toronto.

At the University of Wisconsin–Madison, I have been fortunate to have the advice and support of Mary Layoun, Maria Irene Ramalho de Sousa Santos (of the University of Coimbra), Hans Adler, and especially Sabine Gross and Próspero Saíz.

I am particularly grateful to my inspiring teacher and friend, the late Michael Sprinker, who read and commented on the initial version of this book, and to my student and friend, Valerie Reed, who read and commented on its final version.

This book is dedicated to Grażyna Sonia Wasilewska Statkiewicz, who has always been there.

A Polemic Introduction

Only a philosophical rhapsody makes possible a philosophy of rhapsody.

—JEAN-LUC NANCY

The philosophical drama of Plato . . . is a rhapsody.

—FRIEDRICH NIETZSCHE

You are poets and we are poets . . . rivals and antagonists in the noblest of dramas.

—THE ATHENIAN STRANGER

"The task of modern philosophy has been defined: to overturn Platonism."[1] Gilles Deleuze's claim expresses the sentiment of many writers, from Friedrich Nietzsche to Jean-Luc Nancy. But would they also agree with Deleuze when he ascribes to Plato himself the leading role in this task?[2] This would require a

All citations in Greek to Plato's texts are to *Platonis opera,* 5 vols., ed. John Burnet (Oxford: Oxford University Press, 1900–1907).

The first epigraph to this chapter is drawn from Nancy's "Sharing Voices," trans. Gayle L. Ormiston, in *Transforming the Hermeneutic Context: From Nietzsche to Nancy,* ed. Gayle L. Ormiston and Alan D. Schrift (Albany: State University of New York Press, 1990), 242; translation modified (French: *Le partage des voix* [Paris: Galilée, 1982], 79). The phrase itself, which in French reads "Seule une rhapsodie philosophique permet une philosophie de la rhapsodie," was probably suggested to Nancy by Friedrich Schlegel's aphorism in the *Athenaeum:* "[Humor] schwebt am liebsten über leicht und klar strömenden Rhapsodien der Philosophie oder der Poesie" ("[Humor] prefers to float above the light and clear-flowing rhapsodies of philosophy or poetry"), in Friedrich Schlegel, *Charakteristiken und Kritiken 1,* vol. 2, *Athenaeum: 1796–1801* (Munich: Ferdinand Schöningh, 1967), frag. 305, p. 217. See also Maurice Blanchot on the rhapsodic mode in his *The Infinite Conversation,* trans. Susan Hanson (Minneapolis: University of Minnesota Press, 1993), 388ff. (French: *L'entretien infini* [Paris: Gallimard, 1969], 568ff.). Cf. Roland Barthes' use of the term in reference to Proust in *The Rustle of Language,* trans. Richard Howard (1986; rpt., Berkeley: University of California Press, 1989), 281–82 (French: *Essais critiques IV: Le bruissement de la langue* [Paris: Seuil, 1984] 316-17).

The second epigraph comes from Nietzsche's posthumous fragments (in *Nachgelaßene Fragmente, 1869–1874,* in Friedrich Nietzsche, *Kritische Studienausgabe,* 15 vols., ed. Giorgio Colli and Mazzino Montinari (1967–77; rpt., Berlin: de Gruyter, 1988), 7:42; my translation. The third epigraph is from Plato, *Laws* 817, trans. Benjamin Jowett, in *The Dialogues of Plato,* 5 vols., 3rd rev. ed. (New York: Macmillan, 1892), 5:200.

1. *Difference and Repetition,* trans. Paul Patton (New York: Columbia University Press, 1994), 59 (French: "La tâche de la philosophie moderne a été définie: renversement du platonisme" [*Différence et répétition* (Paris: Presses Universitaires de France, 1968), 82]).

2. "Was not Plato to be the first to overturn Platonism, or at least to point out the direction such an overturning should take?" (Gilles Deleuze, *The Logic of Sense,* trans. Mark Lester with Charles Stivale [New York: Columbia University Press, 1990], 256; translation modified) (French: *Logique du sens* [Paris: Minuit, 1969], 295).

kind of dialogue with Plato rather than a univocal interpretation of his meaning, a play that would take into account the "rhapsodic" mode of his own dialogues, a *dia-logos* that would eventually split the dominant logos of Western
(Platonic) metaphysics rather than reversing its terms in a simple duologue.
This book argues that modern thought cannot do without such a dialogue
and such a play. Neither a mere philological analysis of Plato's texts, however meticulous, nor a summary dismissal of Platonic metaphysics suffices to
grapple with the major philosophical, political, ethical, and aesthetic problems
of our time. Legated by the tradition of Platonism, these problems must be
confronted in the very mode of their first formulation. The "closure" of the
Platonic epoch offers a unique possibility for such thought.

This epoch—"our" epoch—has been characterized as the "age of the world
picture," our world as the "world of representation," and the exacerbation of
this phenomenon as "the society of the spectacle" or the "precession of simulacra."[3] Guy Debord, for example, the prophetic analyst of the "society of the
spectacle" (and its staunch critic and enemy), implicitly refers to the Platonic,
"ideological," "theoretical" origins of the spectacle when he writes in aphorism
19 of his book that it is "heir to all the weakness of the project of Western philosophy, which was an attempt to understand activity by means of the categories of *vision* [*les categories du* voir]. Indeed the spectacle reposes on an incessant
deployment of the *rigorous* technical rationality to which that philosophical
tradition gave rise."[4] More specifically, although cautiously, Deleuze affirms
that "Plato inaugurates and initiates because he evolves within a theory of
Ideas which *will* allow the deployment of representation."[5] But it will allow
this deployment, I would like to claim, only when Plato's thought hardens into
a systematic theory, conveyed in the rigid, systematic form of a treatise.

    3. Martin Heidegger, "The Age of the World Picture," in Martin Heidegger, *The Question Concerning
Technology and Other Essays*, trans. William Lovitt (New York: Harper and Row, 1977), 115–54 (German:
"Die Zeit des Weltbildes," in *Holzwege* [1950; rpt., Frankfurt am Main: Klostermann, 1994], 69–104). Not
only do we live in the time of a certain worldview but in the time of "the world *as* picture" (134), "die Welt
als Bild" ("Weltbild, wesentlich verstanden, meint . . . nicht ein Bild von der Welt, sondern die Welt als
Bild begriffen" [90]; "daß überhaupt die Welt zum Bild wird, zeichnet das Wesen der Neuzeit aus" [89]).
Deleuze, *Difference and Repetition*, xix (French: *Différence et répétition*, 1); Guy Debord, *The Society of the
Spectacle*, trans. Donald Nicholson-Smith (New York: Zone Books, 1995) (French: *La société du spectacle*
[Paris: Gallimard, 1992]); Jean Baudrillard, *Simulacra and Simulation*, trans. Sheila Faria Glaser (Ann
Arbor: University of Michigan Press, 1994) (French: *Simulacres et simulation* [Paris: Galilée, 1981]).
    4. *The Society of the Spectacle*, 17; translation modified, my emphasis on "rigorous" (French: "Le spec-
tacle est l'héritier de toute la *faiblesse* du projet philosophique occidental qui fut une compréhension de
l'activité, dominée par les catégories du *voir;* aussi bien qu'il se fonde sur l'incessant déploiment de la ratio-
nalité technique précise qui est issue de cette pensée" [*La société du spectacle*, 23–24]).
    5. *Difference and Repetition*, 265; his emphasis (French: "Platon inaugure, initie, parce qu'il évolue
dans une théorie de l'Idée qui *va* rendre possible le déployment de la représentation" [*Différence et répétition*, 341]).

It is perhaps the opposition between the rule of representation and the freedom of the dialogic form that Debord points to when in aphorism 18 of *The Society of the Spectacle* he sets spectacle and dialogue in opposition ("the spectacle . . . is the opposite of dialogue") and when in aphorism 221 (which closes the volume) he assigns to dialogue a revolutionary function : the self-emancipation of our epoch cannot take place "until dialogue has taken up arms to impose its own conditions upon the world."[6] Thus Debord would certainly agree with Deleuze's insistence on the recourse to Plato and would link it to the importance of the dialogical form. Martin Heidegger, although quite explicit in pointing out the foundational character of Plato's text in respect to the epoch of the "world *as* picture," also points to the possibility of a confrontation/dialogue with Plato within the "closure" of our epoch. Such a dialogue would combine the necessary inscription within the rule of representation with its dialogical interruption.[7]

An authentic dialogue, in other words, would question, cut through (*dia*) the "Platonic," as well as its own *logos,* the logic of representation. Such a dialogue does take place in contemporary thought, and it is also ultimately of Platonic origin. I call this dialogue "rhapsodic," in reference to the profession, or rather *vocation,* of the rhapsode—engaged, like Ion but also Homer and Hesiod and even Plato himself, in a "chain" of magnetic, enthused "rings," transmitting voices to one another—and in reference to the very etymology of the word, the verb *rhaptein* (to stitch together, even apparently heterogeneous elements such as rigor and play, image and simulacrum, identity and difference, philosophy and poetry), as well as the noun *rhabdos* (a wand borne by the *rhapsōidos*), marking the rhythm of his performance.[8] The latter derivation, although often rejected by modern etymologists, was common in antiquity

6. *The Society of the Spectacle,* 18 (French: "[Le spectacle] est ce qui échappe à l'activité des hommes, à la reconsidération et à la correction de leur œuvre. Il est le contraire du dialogue. Partout où il y a *représentation* indépendante, le spectacle se reconstitue" [*La société du spectacle,* 23]); *The Society of the Spectacle,* 154 (French: "que le dialogue s'est armé pour faire vaincre ses propres conditions" [*La société du spectacle,* 209]).

7. "Plato's Doctrine of Truth," trans. Thomas Sheehan, in Martin Heidegger, *Pathmarks,* ed. William McNeill (Cambridge: Cambridge University Press, 1998), 155–82, esp. 181–82 (German: *Platons Lehre von der Wahrheit* [Bern: Francke, 1947]). Maurice Blanchot (in *The Infinite Conversation*) and Jacques Derrida have most clearly formulated the necessity of this closure and this interruption. Derrida developed this problematic in his work on Antonin Artaud; see especially "The Theater of Cruelty and the Closure of Representation," in Jacques Derrida, *Writing and Difference,* trans. Alan Bass (Chicago: University of Chicago Press, 1978), 232–50 (French: "Le théâtre de la cruauté et la clôture de la représentation," in *L'écriture et la différence* [Paris: Seuil, 1967], 341–68).

8. Carlo Odo Pavese, "The Rhapsodic Epic Poems as Oral and Independent Poems," *Harvard Studies in Classical Philology* 98 (1998): 63–90 (see especially his interpretation of Hesiod's *Theogony* 30 on 64); Henry George Liddell, Robert Scott, and Henry Stuart Jones, *A Greek-English Lexicon* (Oxford: Clarendon Press, 1996), s.v. I.6.

and contributed to the rapprochement between the institution of the rhapsode and the god Hermes, from whom both Plato and Heidegger playfully derive *hermēneia* and hermeneutics.[9]

Thus, "rhapsodic" here does not refer—not essentially—to a miscellaneous collection or a musical piece of irregular form, nor does it refer to the historical uses of the word in a philosophical sense (the form of thought that Immanuel Kant rejected as incompatible with the rigorous method of his analytic) or to the "philosophical rhapsody" (a relatively loose style of "rhapsodische Prosa") of Hamann, Herder, and before them, Shaftesbury.[10] Rather, it refers to the mode of thinking—Plato's mode, replayed in the texts of Nietzsche, Heidegger, Jacques Derrida, Luce Irigaray, Deleuze, Nancy, Philippe Lacoue-Labarthe— that challenges the dominance of univocal interpretation, as well as the corresponding treatise format, in the modern philosophical tradition.

Indeed, while the treatise format has become the paradigm of philosophic writing because of its "first person orientation" ("*I* write what *I* think about this or that")—that is, its sanction of the modern notion of the subject—the rhapsodic mode, both in Plato and in his contemporary "continental" readers, offers a way of questioning this notion.[11] In fact, the very notion of a text as a

9. See Harald Patzer, "ΡΑΨΩΙΔΟΣ," *Hermes* 80, no. 3 (1952): 314–25, and Andrew Ford, "The Classical Definition of ΡΑΨΩΙΔΙΑ," *Classical Philology* 83, no. 4 (1988): 300–301; cf., however, Wolfgang Schadewaldt, *Von Homers Welt und Werk* (Stuttgart: Koehler, 1965), 56, and Pavese, "The Rhapsodic Epic Poems as Oral and Independent Poems." On Plato's and Heidegger's derivation of *hermēneia* and hermeneutics from Hermes, see my "Rhapsodic Conclusion." It is perhaps this kind of play that Heidegger considers more compelling, more binding (*verbindlicher*), and even more "rigorous" than the "rigor of science" ("die Strenge der Wissenschaft" [*Unterwegs zur Sprache* (Pfullingen: Neske, 1959), 121]).

10. Kant characterizes as "rhapsodic," that is, not deduced from strict logical principles, Aristotle's list of categories. On Hamann, Herder, and Shaftesbury, see Jean-Luc Nancy and Philippe Lacoue-Labarthe, "Le dialogue des genres," *Poétique* 21 (1975): 148–75, Pat Rogers, "Shaftesbury and the Aesthetics of Rhapsody," *British Journal of Aesthetics* 12, no. 3 (1972): 244–57, and André Rudolph, "Kontinuum der Rhapsodie: Herder–Hamann–Shaftesbury," in *Der frühe und der späte Herder: Kontinuität und/oder Korrektur,* ed. Sabine Groß and Gerhard Sauder (Heidelberg: Synchron, 2007), 269–84.

11. Drew A. Hyland, *Questioning Platonism: Continental Interpretations of Plato* (Albany: State University of New York Press, 2004), 86–88; his emphasis. "Could there be a better format by which to assert, prove, refute, suggest, or call into question a philosophic position than the treatise?" asks Hyland rhetorically. Once "we" admit our commitment to a philosophical position "we" hold, "it virtually follows that the treatise format will become the paradigm of philosophic writing. And so it has." Hyland very much appreciates the other, different, almost forgotten way of writing philosophically, that of Plato. But in his view, dialogues—which best represent the "interrogative character of philosophy"—still need to be submitted to the interpretive treatment of a treatise, and he is impatient with those continental thinkers—Heidegger, Irigaray, Derrida—who have failed to recognize the need for such a nonrhapsodic interpretation.

Note that the rhapsodic does not necessarily amount to "the third way" alluded to in the title of a volume edited by Francisco J. Gonzalez on contemporary Plato studies. Ruby Blondell insists that "even direct dramatic form is always controlled by an underlying authorial and/or editorial voice," and so "the fact remains that written dialogue is never truly dialogical, in the sense that it is always controlled by a single authorial point of view, however chameleon-like that point of view may be." She refers to Plato as

stable object of study and of the self as its originator or guardian will need to be questioned: Plato "himself" will be addressed as a "mimetic gentleman" (Benjamin Jowett's translation of "mimētikos anēr") or a rhapsode. In this way, "rhapsody"—a mimetic play, a mode of discourse distinguished in the third book of the *Republic*—becomes a mode of thought as well. And Plato's dialogues that initiate it should be read neither as treatises nor as theater plays in need of interpretive treatment in a treatise, contrary to what some recent tendencies in Plato scholarship suggest.[12]

Eventually, this mode also calls into question the very possibility of simply interpreting, and either accepting or dismissing, Platonism in the history of Western philosophy. Since "Platonism," as Derrida rightly maintains, commands this history, philosophy will always be Platonic, and we shall need to "think what takes place in Plato, with Plato, what is shown there, what is hidden, so as to win there or to lose there."[13] It is for this reason as well that the reading proposed here is to be distinguished from traditional doctrinal, as well as "dramatic," interpretations.[14] Both in fact share a dogmatic stance toward the question of "Platonism": *either* acceptance *or* rejection of a determined set of theoretical presuppositions. They also share an unconditional and reverent acknowledgment of Plato's command over his "own" text, although this authority/authorship may be differently explained and supported.

To be sure, the practice of the rhapsodic mode is hardly conceivable within the existing structure of academic disciplines in which disciplines are rigorously separated from each other and favor expert knowledge rather than a questioning of their status and an interdisciplinary dialogue. This structure is not exactly Platonic, despite the name. Platonic dialogue often treats of ontology, ethics, poetics, and politics not as separate disciplines but as different

---

"puppeteer of all his characters" and argues that this role gives him "a higher level of authority than any single voice he dramatizes" (*The Play of Characters in Plato's Dialogues* [Cambridge: Cambridge University Press, 2002], 44–46).

12. See, e.g., the introductions by the editors in Charles L. Griswold Jr., ed., *Platonic Writings/Platonic Readings* (New York: Routledge, 1988), 1–15, Gerald A. Press, ed., *Plato's Dialogues: New Studies and Interpretations* (Lanham, Md.: Rowman and Littlefield, 1993), 107–27, and Francisco J. Gonzalez, ed., *The Third Way: New Directions in Platonic Studies* (Lanham, Md.: Rowman and Littlefield, 1995), 1–22.

13. "*Khōra*," trans. Ian McLeod, in Jacques Derrida, *On the Name*, ed. Thomas Dutoit (Stanford, Calif.: Stanford University Press, 1995), 121 (French: "En tant que telle . . . une philosophie serait . . . toujours 'platonicienne.' D'où la nécessité de continuer à tenter de penser ce qui a lieu chez Platon, avec Platon, ce qui s'y montre, ce qui s'y cache, pour y gagner ou pour y perdre" [*Khôra* (Paris: Galilée, 1993), 84; the original version of this text appeared in *Poikilia: Études offertes à Jean-Pierre Vernant* (Paris: EHESS, 1987)]).

14. For the clearest formulation of this alternative, see Wolfgang Wieland, *Platon und die Formen des Wissens* (Göttingen: Vandenhoeck and Ruprecht, 1982), 50ff. For a critique of the term "doctrinal," see, for example, Victorino Tejera, "The Hellenistic Obliteration of Plato's Dialogism," in *Plato's Dialogues*, 129 and n. 1. For a short summary of the long history of this controversy, see Gonzalez's introduction to *The Third Way*.

approaches to the same problem of truth, rigor, and (poetic) justice. This fact is not always noticed since modern readers of Plato are, more often than not, the readers of (not so critical) readers or anthologies, that is to say, of excerpts rather than the integral texts of the dialogues, and these excerpts are generally so distributed that there is no danger of "confusing" academic disciplines.[15] The system of rigorous academic distinctions is in fact Aristotelian, and in all rigor should be named after the *Lyceum* rather than the *Academia*.[16] It is Aristotle and his followers who "sorted out" the disciplines "confounded" in Plato's text, in particular politics, poetics, epistemology, and ontology, and thus relieved the tension between them. Even granting that Aristotle developed and systematized Socrates' own gesture, the crucial point is that this gesture became frozen when it was extracted from the rhapsodic frame of the dialogues.

Indeed, when Plato introduced—in a poetic form—his quarrel with the poets, when he rejected—in a mimetic mode—mimesis, he certainly did not think that generations of readers would take his play all too seriously (or perhaps not seriously enough!) and, beginning with his student Aristotle, would defend poetry or Plato, or both, would apologize before the court of Western philosophy and literary theory for his not conforming to the "logic of the logos."[17] It is the otherwise unquestioned presupposition of this misconceived

15. Thus, in the case of Plato's text, students of law would read, for example, the first book of the *Republic,* the political science majors books 8 and 9, the philosophers books 5, 6, and 7, and students of literature, aesthetics, and art books 2, 3, and 10. On the other hand, Plato scholars who do read the whole of Plato often confine themselves to specific problematics, such as the chronological order of the dialogues or their authenticity or the coherence of Plato's doctrine; they rarely venture into the domain of contemporary thought (but see, as a possible counterexample, Julius Moravcsik's reading of Plato and of Wittgenstein in his *Plato and Platonism* [Oxford: Blackwell, 1992]).

16. Even some very recent books on Plato and contemporary continental thought uphold the Aristotelian boundaries; Catherine Zuckert's *Postmodern Platos* (Chicago: University of Chicago Press, 1996) and Melissa Lane's *Plato's Progeny* (London: Duckworth, 2001), for example, do not question the limits of traditionally defined political thought.

17. Jean-Pierre Vernant, *Myth and Society in Ancient Greece,* trans. by Janet Lloyd (1980; rpt., New York: Zone Books, 1988), 260 (French: *Mythe et société en Grèce ancienne* [Paris: Seuil, 1974], 250). The "logic of the *logos*" ("the binary logic of yes or no" [240]) is the notion against which Vernant proposes the "logic of the myth" (165). One recent apology, explicitly labeled as such, is Mark Edmundson's *Literature Against Philosophy, Plato to Derrida: A Defence of Poetry* (Cambridge: Cambridge University Press, 1995). But the entire so-called dramatic trend in Plato scholarship may be characterized as "apologetic"; see in particular the work of Drew Hyland, Charles Griswold, and David Roochnik. Here is a typical example: "Far from being the simple-minded hater of poetry and the single-minded advocate of classical reason that the subversives typically take him to be, Plato appreciates the profound alternative poetry offers" (David Roochnik, *The Tragedy of Reason* [New York: Routledge, 1990], 182). The term "subversives" is not well defined in Roochnik's work, but it seems to include Richard Rorty as well as all those who are sensitive to the rhapsodic mode of Plato's work; it is not likely that they would recognize themselves as accusers of Plato.

series of apologies, the presupposition of a (rigorous) distinction between the rigor and stability of philosophy and science, on the one hand, and the waywardness and motility of art and play, on the other, that needs to be questioned. For does not Plato himself, or a rhapsode playing his part, proclaim play as well as seriousness to be the essence of philosophy? Indeed, the Athenian Stranger in *Epinomis* (991b–992b) suggests, both in jest and in earnest (*paizōn kai spoudazōn hama*), that a blend of serious rigor (*akribeia*) and of play (*paidia*) marks a most truly wise man (*ton alēthestata sophōtaton*). And the apparently narrow scholarly question of the "authenticity" of this dialogue might point to the "authority" of an author/pretender/rhapsode donning the mask of Plato, an imitator (*mimētēs*) of Plato, a false (*pseudos*) Plato, or "Plato," whose text, through the voice of the Athenian Stranger, integrates play, that is, mimesis and drama, into the serious business of philosophy.[18] The rhapsodic mode of reading Plato does not exclude his name from the play of quotation marks; "Plato" himself becomes a character.[19]

Thus a reconsideration of the quarrel between philosophy and poetry in the Platonic-rhapsodic rather than the Aristotelian-systematic framework has to include the problematic of the voice in/of the dialogues: ventriloquist Eurycles, rhapsode Ion, the nameless "boy" of the *Theaetetus*, and eventually Socrates "himself," speaking in the voice of another. Such an approach relinquishes the commitment to the author(ity of) Plato and his text and confronts instead a character/rhapsode like any other.[20] But in order to do that, we must not limit the dramatic interpretation to the classical form of the theater of the author.[21] Plato "himself" seems to oppose such a reading when in

18. Cf. *Laws* 688b and also the *Letter 6* 323d, where Plato "himself" calls playfulness ("παιδια") "the sister of solemnity" ("ἡ τῆς σπουδῆς ἀδελφή") (*Letter 6*, trans. Glen R. Morrow, in *Plato: Complete Works*, ed. John M. Cooper and D. S. Hutchison [Indianapolis, Ind.: Hackett, 1997], 1646). For Pierre-Maxime Schuhl, "le sérieux et le jeu sont inextricablement mêlés" in Plato, and "si le jeu n'est rien, presque tout n'est qu'un jeu" (*Platon et l'art de son temps* [Paris: Presses Universitaires de France, 1952], 63 and 62). This blend of "le sérieux" and "le jeu," of solemnity and playfulness, is, in spite of the protestations to the contrary, what is most lacking in recent Plato scholarship, including an essay whose title seems to refer to such a blend: Rosemary Desjardins' "Why Dialogues? Plato's Serious Play," in *Platonic Writing/Platonic Readings*, 110–25; once authorial intention is called for to distinguish between the serious and the playful or ironic, the play between seriousness and play is blocked.

19. Philippe Lacoue-Labarthe performs such a reading all through his essay on mimesis; see "Typography," in Philippe Lacoue-Labarthe, *Typography: Mimesis, Philosophy, Politics*, ed. and trans. Christopher Fynsk (1989; rpt., Stanford, Calif.: Stanford University Press, 1998), 43–138 (French: "Typographie," in Sylviane Agacinski et al., *Mimesis des()articulations* [Paris: Aubier-Flammarion, 1975], 165–270).

20. See Friedrich Dürrenmatt, *Turmbau, Stoffe 4–9* (Zurich: Diogenes, 1994), which includes Plato as one of its characters, and Iris Murdoch, *Acastos* (London: Chatto and Windus, 1986).

21. See Antonin Artaud's critique of such theater in *The Theater and Its Double*, trans. Mary Caroline Richards (New York: Grove Weidenfeld, 1958), 74ff. (French: *Le théâtre et son double*, in Antonin Artaud, *Oeuvres complètes*, vol. 4 [Paris: Gallimard, 1978], 72ff.).

the *Theaetetus,* he stages the "author" of the account of a dialogue between Socrates, Theodorus, and the title character and makes him intervene between the direct dialogue and its narration by Socrates, between the event and its redescription. And the "historical" Plato was apparently willing to play a rhapsode with his text: Diogenes Laertius describes his reading/performing *Lysis* and *On the Soul.*[22] One imagines Plato playing not only the role of Socrates but also those of the characters whose views would never be taken seriously by most interpreters. This mimetic, poetic performance also governs his writing, which should be understood as a dialogue/confrontation between poetry and philosophy rather than as a condemnation of the former by the latter.

This is also the case for the dialogue of modern thought with Plato, which ultimately cannot be separated from the dialogue between poetry and philosophy. What Heidegger says of the dialogue between poetry and thought—that it is long and that it has barely begun—is also true of the dialogue with Plato, because the two kinds of dialogue are essentially related; the confrontation with Platonism is the *conditio sine qua non* of the dialogue with poetry called for by Heidegger and other continental thinkers.[23] Indeed, the dialogue with poetry cannot take place in the traditional mode of univocal philosophical interpretation. And it is precisely this mode that Plato's dialogues themselves— bringing together philosophical inquiry with a rhapsodic, mimetic technique of presentation—undermine. Their challenge to such univocity results in a tension, manifested in the "quarrel" between philosophical truth and poetry or mimesis, which may in turn contain the seeds of the dialogue between poetry and thought.

The nature of rhapsodic dialogue becomes clear when it is polemically juxtaposed with the so-called dramatic reading of those who also claim to take into account the dialogic nature of Plato's work. Thus I'll take the risk of exposing myself to the objection of coming in after the war and the battle (*polemou kai makhēs*), as Callicles says to Socrates, who arrives late to Gorgias's performance.[24] Indeed, Stanley Rosen has recently declared that the "hermeneutical battle" for the recognition of reading the dialogues *as* dialogues and not as treatises "has been won and does not need to be refought."[25] Rosen refers here

22. Diogenes Laertius, *Lives of Eminent Philosophers,* 2 vols., Greek/English text, trans. R. D. Hicks (1925; rpt., Cambridge, Mass.: Harvard University Press, 1972), 309, 311.

23. "Language in the Poem: A Discussion on Georg Trakl's Poetic Work," in Martin Heidegger, *On the Way to Language,* trans. Peter D. Hertz (New York: Harper and Row, 1971), 161 (German: "Die Zwiesprache des Denkens mit dem Dichten ist lang: Sie hat kaum begonnen" ["Die Sprache im Gedicht: Eine Erörterung von Georg Trakls Gedicht," in *Unterwegs zur Sprache* (Stuttgart: Neske, 1959), 39]).

24. Plato, *Gorgias* 447a.

25. *Plato's "Republic": A Study* (New Haven, Conn.: Yale University Press, 2005), 2. Already in 1993,

to the method of reading "acknowledged by competent Plato scholars" that stresses the necessity of making a "connection between discursive argument on the one hand and the dramatic form and rhetorical elements of the text on the other" in order to "arrive at a satisfactory appreciation of his philosophical teaching."[26] Dialogue, for Rosen and most other Plato scholars attentive to the formal aspects of the text, is a literary, rhetorical, and dramatic genre particularly well suited to conveying *Plato's meaning,* for extending his invitation to philosophy—a protreptic genre.[27] In contrast to a treatise, a dialogue should obviate some of the flaws of writing, censured by Socrates in the *Phaedrus* and by Plato in "his" letters. A dialogue would be able to *imitate,* even if imperfectly, the live philosophical exchange of the type we associate with Socrates.[28] It would thus fit into Aristotle's system of mimetic arts as a "Socratic dialogue" (*Sōkratikos logos*).[29] I am insisting on this imitative character of the Socratic dialogue, and I shall insist more, because it is the question of *mimēsis* that will justify, I hope, my being not altogether late, at least for the feast (*heortē*), that is, for the play.[30] Indeed, my claim is that the notion of imitation, which dominates the so-called dramatic interpretation of Plato, needs to be challenged by rhapsodic or playful mimesis and thus that the hermeneutic *polemos* or battle does need to be "refought" or replayed.

The mimetic, imitative character of Plato's written dialogues has always been affirmed by the "dramatic" readers and sharply opposed to the "reality"

Charles Griswold was quoted on the cover of a collection of essays edited by Gerald A. Press (*Plato's Dialogues*) saying that "[t]he general argument that Plato's dialogues are to be read as philosophical *dramas* has more or less won the day" (his emphasis).

26. *Plato's "Republic,"* 1–2. Charles Griswold is another competent Plato scholar who maintains the form/content binary: "As I try to show in the following pages, the *Phaedrus* rejects the thesis just expressed that philosophy can dispense with rhetoric, although it does not reject the view that form must be suited to content" ("Style and Philosophy: The Case of Plato's Dialogues," *Monist* 63, no. 4 [1980]: 535). David Roochnik's "perfect match of form and content" refers to (Socrates' characterization of) the poets; Roochnik is quite right to maintain that "Plato *preserves* the dispute [between philosophy and poetry] and weaves it into the very fabric of his dialogue," even though he assumes that one can radically separate the philosophical and the poetic element in the *Ion* (*The Tragedy of Reason,* 184; cf. 181ff.). I return to Roochnik's reading of the *Ion* in "Rhapsodic Conclusion."

27. See, for instance, the essays collected in Gerald A. Press, ed., *Plato's Dialogues,* and Richard Hart and Victorino Tejera, eds., *Plato's Dialogues: The Dialogical Approach* (Lewiston, N.Y.: Edwin Mellen, 1997).

28. See, for instance, Dietrich Böhler, "Zu einer philosophischen Rekonstruktion der 'Handlung,'" in *Logik, Ethik, Theorie der Geisteswissenschaften,* ed. Günther Patzig, Erhard Scheibe, and Wolfgang Wieland (Hamburg: Meiner, 1977), 306–17, and Jürgen Mittelstraß, "On Socratic Dialogues," trans. Steven Gillies, in *Platonic Writings/Platonic Readings,* 126–42 (German: "Versuch über den Sokratischen Dialog," in *Das Gespräch,* ed. Karlheinz Stierle and Rainer Warning [Munich: Fink, 1984], 11–27).

29. *Poetics* 1447b11 (Greek/English: *The Poetics,* ed. and trans. W. Hamilton Fyfe [1927; rpt., Cambridge, Mass.: Harvard University Press, 1982], 7).

30. Plato, *Gorgias* 447a; without the help of Chaerephon but perhaps with that of Homer or even Euripides, to whom Chaerephon refers (447b).

of living philosophical dialogues. Drew Hyland's opinion is most consistent in this respect. One of the first to have emphasized the philosophical importance of "the dialogues as imitations," he reiterates the point more than three decades later with the same force: "Every Platonic dialogue is an *imitation* of philosophy."[31] What distinguishes Plato's dialogues from treatises is that "the dialogues are in every case the imitations of philosophy. Plato, that is, writes for a public audience always and only *mimetically.*"[32] In both of Hyland's texts, the imitation is coupled with the invitation to philosophy. The dialogues have a protreptic function, which is best performed mimetically, through the "dramatic portrayals" of "philosophical situations."[33] The term "dramatic portrayal" suggests a tableau of the neoclassical, Aristotelian theater as well as the painterly mimesis of book 10 of the *Republic*. Indeed, Hyland inscribes Plato's dialogues within the structure of representation of this book. There is a "kernel of truth" in characterizing the work of art as not being reality itself but only "an imitation of what is more real (the object painted) and ultimately of the most real thing, the Idea." Since dialogues are "philosophic works of art," their relationship to philosophy should be understood mimetically: "as imitations of philosophy, they are *not* philosophy, the reality itself."[34] There are some problems in forcing the dialogues into the representational structure of the *Republic*: Hyland's example of "secondhand accounts," such as *Parmenides, Symposium, Theaetetus*, which as "imitations of imitations" epitomize the view of art in the *Republic*, raises the question of the distinction between the dialogues.[35] Does this mean that, on the one hand, direct dialogues are closer to reality and, on the other, the most complex dialogues (the *Symposium* and *Theaetetus*) are even further removed from the truth and the king? These questions, if asked, might challenge the hermeneutics based on a simple distinction between the reality of philosophy and its "dramatic" representation in the written dialogues.

But Hyland does not consider these questions, since they do not belong to the drama proper. What does belong, for example, in the *Crito*, the dialogue he chooses to illustrate the "dramatic" reading?[36] First and most importantly, the character of Crito. He is an old friend of Socrates, he is wealthy and financially competent, and "he is *not* a philosopher."[37] Hyland gleans all this information

31. "Why Plato Wrote Dialogues," *Philosophy and Rhetoric* 1, no. 1 (1968): 43; *Questioning Platonism*, 4; his emphasis. I briefly discuss Hyland's critiques of the particular authors in the chapters devoted to them.
32. *Questioning Platonism*, 4; his emphasis.
33. *Questioning Platonism*, 4.
34. "Why Plato Wrote Dialogues," 43; his emphasis.
35. "Why Plato Wrote Dialogues," 43.
36. In the second part of his early essay. As I already indicated, Hyland repeats the general points of the essay at the outset of his *Questioning Platonism*.
37. "Why Plato Wrote Dialogues," 44; his emphasis.

from the text edited by Burnet and from Burnet's scholarly erudition. Burnet
also supports the crucial point that Crito is *not* a philosopher. In fact, all the
other dramatic elements—"the questionable status of some of the arguments,
the apparent tension between *Crito* and *Apology,* and the perplexing admission
of Socrates that not all the arguments have been considered"—cohere only
because Crito is philosophically naive ("philosophy is not for everyone").[38] We
have thus obtained a dramatic framework "in which the specific arguments of
the *Crito* must be understood and judged."[39] All of them converge in something that looks rather like an instance of ideological subject formation within
the drama, with the function of "remov[ing] from citizen Crito the dangerous
principle of civil disobedience" and "the therapeutic purpose of restoring Crito
to his status as obedient citizen."[40]

Now, this ideological/therapeutic function is not limited to the *Crito.* It
might in fact characterize most of Plato's dialogues, which would thus hang on
the rhetoric of persuasion.[41] The turning or invitation to philosophy, on this
view, consists in the comparison between the purity of philosophy, glimpsed,
for example, in the *Apology,* and the dramatically portrayed necessity of coming to terms with the multitude (*hoi polloi*), of which Crito is one of the representatives. In the words of another recent "dramatic" reader of the *Crito,* one
must take account of "the distance between what Socrates thinks and what
Kriton can understand, or that between what the philosopher is and how he
must present himself to the many (as faithfully law abiding, for example)."[42]
But can it be that it is the insistence on this distance, and on the necessity of
the ideological formation of the political subject, that "invites" readers to philosophy? Can it be, in the words of a critic of this reading, that Socrates, "like
the sophists, . . . persuades people (including his closest associates!) to embrace
doctrines that he takes to be false?"[43] Does the ideological/therapeutic function, which in this "dramatic" hermeneutics allows Socrates in the *Crito* and
elsewhere to withhold and to falsify arguments, apply to the readers of the
dialogues as well?

Hyland seems to think so, withholding as he does from his readers the
rhapsodic character of the words that he quotes from the *Crito* (they are

38. "Why Plato Wrote Dialogues," 46, 39.
39. "Why Plato Wrote Dialogues," 46.
40. "Why Plato Wrote Dialogues," 45, 47.
41. Leo Strauss, *The City and Man* (Chicago: University of Chicago Press, 1964), 60, 123, and passim;
cf. Charles L. Griswold Jr., *Self-Knowledge in Plato's "Phaedrus"* (1988; rpt., University Park, Pa.: Pennsylvania State University Press, 1996), 221.
42. Clifford Orwin, "Liberalizing the *Crito:* Richard Kraut on Socrates and the State," in *Platonic
Writings/Platonic Reading,* 176.
43. Richard Kraut, "Reply to Clifford Orwin," in *Platonic Writings/Platonic Readings,* 180.

pronounced, he says, "at a decisive point" in the dialogue), taking the passage out of the dramatic context of the speech delivered by the laws to whom Socrates only gives voice (and "face" [*prosōpon*]).[44] The speech begins at *Crito* 50a5; Socrates is addressing Crito: "Look at it this way. If, as we were planning to run away from here, or whatever one should call it, the laws and the state came and confronted us and asked: 'Tell me Socrates, what are you intending to do?'" And the address of the laws themselves continues with a few short returns to the direct dialogue between Socrates and Crito until 54c6, where the laws exhort Socrates: "Do not let Crito persuade you, rather than us, to do what he says."[45] Socrates compares the effect of the words pronounced by the laws to the effect of the music of flutes on the Corybantes and concludes with a suggestion that the voice of the laws might be the voice of the gods (54d–e). Hyland quotes the passage (51b–c) on the comparison between the allegiance to one's parents and to the laws, but he doesn't mention the figure of prosopopoeia. Why this obfuscation of the rhapsodic dimension of the *Crito*? Is it not because it would unsettle the representational schema to which the dramatic reading adheres? Indeed, the prosopopoeia raises the crucial issue of the emergence of the laws into language; "the Laws act only through being known to human beings," says Leo Strauss, referring to the *Apology* (24d–e).[46] In this sense, the laws themselves function like language, which does not easily submit to the intention of the subject/speaker. Socrates acts as a rhapsode within language and thus sets in motion the chain of messages (*hermēneiai*) that includes Plato and his text, the text that gives voice to him, Socrates, who gives voice to the laws, or to his prophetic dream, or to Homer's Achilles in his dream (44b–c), and so forth. All these voices need to be taken as the voices of the community rather than dismissed as the empty talk of the *hoi polloi* in need of political/ideological therapy.[47] Only when read rhapsodically can the dialogue be genuinely protreptic. Only then can readers—all readers—be included as the ultimate "ring" on both ends of the "chain": as the recipients of the message or as the initiators of the chain through their reading (provided, of course, that reading is not limited to an analysis of the dramatis personae).

The rhapsodic complexity of the dialogues seems to exceed Jacob Klein's "dramatic" reading as well. In the introduction to his book on *Theaetetus,* the *Sophist,* and the *Statesman,* titled *Plato's Trilogy,* he opposes Platonic dialogues

44. "Why Plato Wrote Dialogues," 46.

45. *Crito,* trans. G. M. A. Grube, in Plato, *Five Dialogues* (Indianapolis, Ind.: Hackett, 1981), 52, 56.

46. "On Plato's *Apology of Socrates* and *Crito,*" in *Studies in Platonic Political Philosophy,* 63; for Strauss, the Crito promotes "legalism" as a "wise rule of thumb" (66).

47. Kraut is right to point out that "nothing suggests that Socrates regards [Crito] as a dope who cannot really understand the highest mysteries of philosophy" ("Reply to Clifford Orwin," 179).

to treatises and promises to pay close attention to the dramatic setting of the dialogues.[48] But when it comes to *Theaetetus,* he questions the whole prologue, suggesting it is not part of the "original" dialogue. He mentions another "rather frigid" prologue, on the authority of an anonymous commentary to *Theaetetus,* but doesn't give any details or justification for dismissing a generally accepted text, and he eventually disregards both prologues in favor of an immediate consideration of the "dialogue proper."[49] The rhapsodic moment is suppressed for the sake of "dramatic unity" that in the Aristotelian mode (Klein evokes the authority of Aristotle's *Poetics*) excludes from consideration any element outside of the drama proper (*exō tou dramatos* [*Poetics* 1454b3]). What is important for Klein, just as for Hyland, is the representational structure itself, with its distinction between an imperfect imitation and reality—for Klein the "genuine and ultimate thoughts of Plato."[50] In his *Commentary on Plato's "Meno,"* Klein reaffirms the classical opposition between the reality of *ta erga* (works, deeds) and the imitation in words (*logoi*), except that here the logos itself seems to undergo a split between the "drama itself" or "dialogue proper," on the one hand, and its representation, on the other.[51] But Klein suggests reading this opposition in terms of the treatment of images in book 10 of the *Republic,* as well as in the "allegory of the cave," and he provides a series of interpretive rules for the dramatic interpretation, in particular the rules of reading the "ethological mimes"—in which the action of the speaker reveals his or her character and thought—and "doxological mimes"—in which the character of the speaker reveals the truth or falsity of his or her opinions.[52] Here as well, the representational model of the dramatic tableau seems to prevail in spite of the apparent attention to the mimetic aspect of the dialogues.[53]

48. *Plato's Trilogy: "Theaetetus," the "Sophist," and the "Statesman"* (Chicago: University of Chicago Press, 1977), 1: "A Platonic dialogue is not a treatise or the text of the lecture. . . . No Platonic dialogue can be said to represent what might be called, and has been called, the 'Platonic doctrine'; a dialogue may hint at genuine and ultimate thoughts of Plato, the thinker, but they are never set before us with complete clarity."

49. The anonymous commentary can be found in Hermann Diels and Wilhelm Schubart, *Anonymer Kommentar zu Platons "Theaetet"* (Berlin: Weidmann, 1905), 3–5; Klein, *Plato's Trilogy,* 75.

50. *Plato's Trilogy,* 1.

51. *A Commentary on Plato's "Meno"* (Chapel Hill: University of North Carolina Press, 1965), 18.

52. *A Commentary on Plato's "Meno,"* 19. This kind of "dramatic" reading based on character study that Klein offers was questioned by Josiah Gould in his 1969 critical review of Klein's book; Klein attempted to demonstrate a quasi independence of the "philosophical argument" from the characterization of the characters—Anytus, the boy, and even Meno—which seems particularly slight in this dialogue. But Gould claimed that his critique applies to most "dramatic" readings of the dialogues as "ethological mimes" ("Klein on Ethological Mimes, for example, the *Meno,*" *Journal of Philosophy* 66, no. 9 [1969]: 253–65).

53. Harry Berger has pointed out the Aristotelian character of Klein's mimetic model and the split between "the drama itself" and the written dialogue that represents it ("Levels of Discourse in Plato's Dialogues," in *Literature and the Question of Philosophy,* ed. Anthony J. Cascardi [Baltimore, Md.: Johns Hopkins University Press, 1987], 85 and passim).

In the case of *Theaetetus,* however, the distinction between the model and its image could hardly be maintained if the prologue were allowed its dramatic impact on the "dialogue proper." The prologue has a complex rhapsodic structure, complicated by the explicit use of writing. The conversation between Socrates, Theodorus, and young Theaetetus had been narrated (by Socrates himself) to Euclides from Megara, who wrote down a memoir (*hupomnēmata*) of it, and after that, every time he was in Athens, he talked to Socrates about the conversation and tried to check its accuracy. We, the readers, are participating in the dialogue between Euclides and his friend Terpsion, who had just met the old Theaetetus, dying from the wound he received at the battle of Corinth. Euclides explains that he simplified the narration by suppressing the part played by the rhapsode/narrator Socrates—in other words (the words of the Socrates in the *Republic*), he transformed the mixed mode of *diēgēsis* or narration into pure *mimēsis*.[54] Many different voices are intruding here, and they so complicate the relationship between the "dialogue proper" and the rhapsodic frame that one can understand Klein's reticence to include the latter in his reading.[55] Any attempt to save the representational structure while still reading the dramatic prologues seems doomed to failure.[56] Only a genuinely rhapsodic reading will be able to respect the integrality of the dialogue and at the same time set into play its mimetic character.[57]

Harry Berger offers an intriguing example of such a reading, which only apparently attempts to reduce the prologue to the "dialogue proper."[58] Beginning with the passage on the supposedly Protagorean theory of perception, and suggesting that it functions as "a displacement, a metonymic condensation, of the larger, more complex human relationship," Berger suggests that the fact

54. *Theaetetus* 143c; cf. *Republic* 350c–d. All these complex series of transmission also point to the possibility of distortion (cf. Plato's *Symposium:* "he didn't quite remember this or that," "he fell asleep during the argument," etc.) and thus to the unreliability of the final result, if it is to be considered a faithful (or exact) representation.

55. It seems ironic that Klein quotes the line of Friedländer on the necessity of giving due attention to both seriousness and play "beginning from the very first words of the dialogue" ("Rahmengespräch s"—literally, "framing dialogue/conversation") and expresses his debt to him on this occasion (*A Commentary on Plato's "Meno,"* 19 and n. 51; the quote is from Paul Friedländer, *Plato: An Introduction,* vol. 1 of Paul Friedländer, *Plato,* trans. Hans Meyerhoff [1958; rpt., Princeton, N.J.: Princeton University Press, 1969], 233 [German: *Seinswahrheit und Lebenswirklichkeit,* vol. 1 of *Platon* (1954; rpt., Berlin: de Gruyter, 1964), 246]).

56. On the function of dramatic frames in Plato's dialogues, see Ronna Burger, *The "Phaedo": A Platonic Labyrinth* (New Haven, Conn.: Yale University Press, 1984), 14, David M. Halperin, "Plato and the Erotics of Narrativity," in *Methods of Interpreting Plato and His Dialogues,* ed. James C. Klagge and Nicholas D. Smith (Oxford: Clarendon Press, 1992), 106–7, and William A. Johnson, "Dramatic Frame and Philosophic Idea in Plato," *American Journal of Philology* 119, no. 4 (1988): 577–98.

57. See an attempt at such reading in the conclusion to this book.

58. "Facing Sophists: Socrates' Charismatic Bondage in *Protagoras,*" *Representations* 5, no. 1 (1984): 67–68, and "Levels of Discourse in Plato's Dialogues," 8off.

that "we are bound to one another" (*allēlois dē leipetai sundedesthai* [160b]) is not an epistemological necessity but an ethical requirement. He makes this suggestion in a dialogue with Gail Fine and Willard Van Orman Quine, whose insights and terminology he then extends and displaces.[59] The postulate of the interrelatedness of all knowledge requires not only a continued circulation "within a given field" (Fine) but also an "opening up [of] the boundaries of any 'given field'" (Berger). Not only is "the total field" "underdetermined by its boundary conditions" (Quine), but also, in the dialogue, "the boundary conditions of the text are underdetermined by the boundaries and interior of the dramatic encounter" (Berger).[60] In other words, it is the "dialogue proper" that might undermine the prologue, but only when the prologue is read in the first place: "Reading may indeed be made to conform to the dynamics of an effluence theory that transmits authority and authorized meaning, for example, from Socrates to Euclides to his slave [the rhapsode/reader] to Terpsion, or from Socrates to Plato, or from Plato to us. But it need not necessarily do so. It may move in the other direction as well."[61] In the latter case, the authority of "Plato" and "his" text would be seriously undermined. The "authority" of the rhapsode/reader would be reinforced, provided it is not based on a privileged access to the "drama itself," "philosophy itself," or the "mystery of the model."[62] The kind of reading outlined by Berger depends on the rhapsodic dialogue between Socrates and his figure of Protagoras, which yields the interpreted line "we are bound to one another" in its particular dialogical sense. It is the dialogic nature of our boundness to each other that, in the dialogue with Fine and Quine, leads Berger back to the rhapsodic prologue, which cannot be dismissed as a simple boundary disturbance, and eventually opens up the text to "us," the ultimate rhapsodes/readers.

Rhapsodic reading is rare in Plato scholarship. Berger's reading is an exception to the general rule of accepting the authority of the ideal model, the author's intention, and that of the authoritative interpreter. In an influential, recently reedited, collection of essays, *Platonic Writings, Platonic Readings,* Charles Griswold emphasizes the representational principle: "Plato presents us with dramatic imitations of the practice of philosophizing."[63] And this practice can give us access to the ideal model: "The true 'forms' and 'looks' (*eidē, ideai*) of things cannot be entirely inaccessible; for even the efforts to deny their accessibility

59. Fine, "Knowledge and Logos in the *Theaetetus,*" *Philosophical Review* 88, no. 3 (1979): 368–86; Quine, *From a Logical Point of View* (New York: Harper and Row, 1963).

60. Fine, "Knowledge and Logos in the *Theaetetus,*" 385; Berger, "Levels of Discourse in Plato's Dialogues," 81; Quine, *From a Logical Point of View,* 43; Berger, "Facing Sophists," 81.

61. Berger, "Levels of Discourse in Plato's Dialogues," 82.

62. Strauss, *The City and Man,* 62–63.

63. "Plato's Metaphysics: Why Plato Wrote Dialogues," in *Platonic Writings/Platonic Readings,* 160.

or existence assume them."[64] Griswold makes his point in a debate with "deconstructionists," who "*see* their own point, as well as their opponent's point, and they do so in the light of intelligibility."[65] "Elenchic deconstruction is dialectic unaccompanied by the insight that there is a Whole"; "intelligibility and wholeness" cannot be denied even by the "antiphilosopher."[66] The "insight that there is a Whole" is, one might say, the insight possessed by the "synoptic" philosopher (*ho men gar sunoptikos dialektikos, ho de mē ou* [*Republic* 537c7]), extolled in the discussion of education that follows in the wake of the so-called allegory of the cave in the *Republic*.

But why should we read the allegory from the perspective of the one man who supposedly leaves the cave to gaze at the sun or from that of the modern philosopher who identifies with him rather than with Socrates?[67] This perspective is already a result of the major transition in Western thinking that might be detected in the "allegory of the cave" when read without an unquestioning deference to its "author's expressed intention." Heidegger gives such a reading in his *Platons Lehre von der Wahrheit,* translated as "Plato's Doctrine of Truth."[68] In fact, he is obliged to recognize that Plato's text is not explicitly about truth. In this case, one can only talk of Plato's "teaching" (*Lehre*) in terms of the "unsaid" (*das Ungesagte*).[69] It is true that the question of education and that of truth are essentially related and that the transformation of the nature of one will lead to the transformation of the other. But Plato's text needs Heidegger's voice in order to form a more explicit *Lehre*. *Lehre* will still retain its tentative character and thus perhaps shouldn't be translated as "doctrine" with its "doctrinaire," dogmatic connotations. There is no authority/authorship of Plato that would authenticate his "theory"; there is only a voice that gets heard through Heidegger's reading, which in this sense may be called rhapsodic.

But this unsaid teaching is not a speculation; it is based on what is said. Heidegger doesn't say this, but what is said in the text is not said by Plato either, not directly in the first person. It is said by Glaucon and Socrates, but, again, not directly. The dialogue between them is a reported dialogue in the long narrative of Socrates. The Socrates who presents the image of the cave and

64. "Plato's Metaphilosophy," 163.

65. "Plato's Metaphilosophy," 163; his emphasis.

66. "Plato's Metaphilosophy," 155, 163.

67. See Harry Berger Jr.'s essay "Plato's Flying Philosopher," *Philosophical Forum* 13, no. 4 (1982): 385–407, in which he argues against accepting at face value the model philosopher, the "philosophical nature," as delineated in the *Republic*.

68. On Heidegger's reading, see most recently, Maria del Carmen Paredes, "*Amicus Plato magis amica veritas:* Reading Heidegger in Plato's Cave," in *Heidegger and Plato Toward Dialogue,* ed. Catalin Partenie and Tom Rockmore (Evanston, Ill.: Northwestern University Press, 2005), 108–20.

69. "Plato's Doctrine of Truth," 155 (German: *Platons Lehre von der Wahrheit,* 5).

tells the story of the prisoners is in fact a character in Socrates' "own" story that he told to the unnamed audience. The readers might perhaps identify with this audience if they remember the beginning of the *Republic,* or with Glaucon as the immediate addressee of Socrates, or with the prisoners in the story, but not necessarily with the *one* who might have been liberated, the one who might have seen the light of intelligibility and attained the synoptic grasp of "the Whole." Is not the latter pretension a hubris somewhat incompatible not only with the rhapsodic structure of the *Republic* but also with a genuine turning to philosophizing?

"Allegory" is the most common translation of the Greek word *eikōn* (more literally "resembling image") that is used by Glaucon and Socrates in their discussion of education in the *Republic.* Socrates' well-known description of the underground world and its inhabitants comes at the outset of book 7 (514aff.): the people imprisoned at the bottom of a cavelike dwelling, chained so that they cannot move their bodies or heads, are forced to watch a spectacle of shadows on the opposite wall; the shadows are projected by the objects paraded between the prisoners and the fire as the source of light. There follows the story of one liberated prisoner's painful turning and progress toward the objects and the light of fire in the cave, then upward toward the outside world; his final look at the sun reveals the source not only of the view of the world but of the world's being. The last episode tells of the return to the darkness of the cave, when the accommodation of sight seems even more difficult than on the upward journey. This allegory/image is supposed to *illustrate* our human condition in respect to education. Indeed, Socrates asks Glaucon to *imagine* the scene when he introduces his story at the beginning of book 7: "Next, I said, *compare* the effect of education [*paideia*] and of the lack of it [*apaideusia*] on our nature to an experience like this." (514a).[70] The verb translated by Grube as "compare" is *apeikason,* which has the same root as *eikōn,* or image, "icon." Thus apparently in Plato's own text the language of representation is suggested as part of (Glaucon's and the audience's, the readers') education even before the story begins; we do not enter the world of images, we are there right from the beginning. In a sense, the turning in/from the cave has always already begun.

Heidegger does not deny an intimate connection between education and imaging; how could he? "Education" in German is *Bildung,* the root of which is *Bild* or "image." *Bildung* is a "formation" that can be understood in a double

70. *The Republic,* trans. G. M. A. Grube, rev. C. D. C. Reeve (Indianapolis, Ind.: Hackett, 1992), 208; my emphasis. Tom Griffith's translation—"If we're thinking about the effect of education—or the lack of it—on our nature, there's another comparison we can make" (*Plato: The "Republic,"* ed. G. R. F. Ferrari [Cambridge: Cambridge University Press, 2000], 220)—might suggest a treatise mode more than the Greek does in its direct address at 514a1–2: "ἀπείκασον . . . ἰδὲ" ("Compare, see—imagine").

sense: a "forming" (*Bilden*) in the sense of "the impressing of a character that unfolds" (*entfaltende Prägung*) but also in the sense of conforming to a paradigm (*Vor-bild*). It is the latter meaning that comes closer to the etymology of education (*e-* and *ducere,* or "to lead forth, guide") in Heidegger's view: a "guiding by a paradigm" (*Geleit durch ein Bild*), and it is this model of education that Heidegger associates with the notion of truth that emerges, is *e-duced,* from the "allegory."[71] In fact, it does not emerge but it appears as in a flash of light. Light of fire and of the sun and their play in shadows and reflections determine the visibility of being. It all depends on the correctness (*orthotēs*) of the gaze turned toward *idea/eidos,* or "visible form," the principle of visibility, as in Griswold's "light of intelligibility." Idea as the principle of intelligibility becomes here the "whatness" of the thing—in later, Latin terminology, *quidditas, essentia* rather than *existentia.* In order to be (real), a thing needs to pass the muster of its "whatness," an image needs to conform to its model. In ethical and theatrical terms, the model will become a "character" (*ēthos*), a place of reference. This structure necessarily refers to the notion of contemplation (*theōria*) and to its agent, the philosopher. Ideas (*ideai/eidē*) are after all "looks," "aspects," even if they are offered only to the gaze of the "eye of the soul" (*omma tēs psukhēs*).[72] Heidegger points out the interdependence between the notion of the subject—a modern notion that he traces, beyond René Descartes, to the Latin and modern reception of Plato and Aristotle—and its representation, that is, the world *as* picture.[73] In the English language of the Anglo-American tradition the word for (the philosophical, theoretical) "I" is conveniently homophonic with the organ of sight. Contemplation remains the dominant stance in the interpretation of Plato. The unity of his thought is ordinarily understood in reference to the synoptic, global view of the philosopher contemplating the "spectacle" of *ideai,* in the sense of an "ideology" of representation.

Even though the notion of truth as the correctness of images, of representation (*Vorstellung*), comes to dominate the original *alētheia,* the sense of *alētheia* as the process of unhiddenness is still present in the "allegory." The topography of the scene, an underground abode, open on its upper side, with

71. "Plato's Doctrine of Truth," 167 (German: *Platons Lehre von der Wahrheit,* 24).

72. Cf. Deleuze's characterization of Plato's world as having a structure of representation in his *Différence et répétition.* Diskin Clay confirms with a philological rigor the pictorial character of εἶδος, and he also recognizes its artistic nature (the best account of εἴδη is that of Erwin Panofsky); see Clay's *Platonic Questions: Dialogues with the Silent Philosopher* (University Park, Pa.: Pennsylvania State University Press, 2000), 213ff., esp. 227.

73. "The Age of the World Picture," 132 (German: "Daß die Welt zum Bild wird, ist ein und derselbe Vorgang mit dem, daß der Mensch innerhalb des Seienden zum Subjectum wird" ["Die Zeit des Weltbildes," 92]).

a steep, thorny path that leads there, on the one hand, and the etymology of the Greek *alētheia* (alpha privative plus *lēthē,* or "forgetfulness"), on the other, suggest a difficult process of emerging into the light of day and of struggling with the forgetfulness of *lēthē* that the term *apaideusia* only partially expresses. The continuous struggle of unhiddenness, unconcealment (*Unverborgenheit*) presupposes a more originary "hiding" nature of being, to which Heidegger seems to point in a later note to his essay, when he refers to Heraclitus's fragment 123: "Nature [or rather being] likes to hide" (*phusis kruptesthai philei*). This originary essence of truth as *alētheia* is still present in Plato, still determining his language to some extent, still resisting the enframing within a picture ("the Heraclitan world still growls in Platonism," Deleuze will say); but it needs the voice of the rhapsode/interpreter (Heidegger or Deleuze for example) in order to appear under the surface of representation.[74]

What kind of education would accompany such a notion of truth as unconcealment? Heidegger perhaps hints at it in the notion of "the impressing of a character that enfolds," but he does not develop it. Unless one considers his discussion of the dialogue between Sophocles and Hölderlin as pointing toward the "formation" of the homely status of a human being or the formation of a people in the journey through the unhomely (*das Unheimische*) or uncanny (*das Unheimliche*); after all, it is in terms of the homely that Heidegger conceives the situation of the prisoners in the *Republic* ("at home," *zu Hause*).[75] In historical terms, it is the Homeric rhapsodic tradition that brought about the unconcealment of being. Now, this reference would apparently contradict Socrates' condemnation of Homer and the tragedians. Except that Socrates "himself" acts as a rhapsode when condemning the rhapsodic tradition; he thus enters the space of play. And it is the notion of education, or *paideia,* as play, or *paidia* (both terms are derived from the Greek word for "child," *pais, paidos*), discussed in book 3 of the *Republic,* that might perhaps be able to counter the educational effects of the transformation of the essence of truth, so momentous for the "ever-advancing world history of the planet."[76]

Heidegger seems to neglect the particularity of rhapsodic mimesis when he brings together the allegory of the cave with an account of mimesis in book 10 of the *Republic,* considering the discussion of book 3 as merely "preparatory and provisional" (*vordeutend*): "On our way through these conversations, we encounter at the beginning of the seventh book the discussion of the essence of truth, based on the allegory of the cave. Only after traversing this long and

74. *Difference and Repetition,* 59 (French: "Le monde héraclitéen gronde dans le Platonism" [*Différence et répétition,* 83]).

75. "Plato's Doctrine of Truth," 164 (German: *Platons Lehre von der Wahrheit,* 19).

76. I discuss the role of play in education in chapter 1.

broad path to the point where philosophy is defined as masterful knowledge of the Being of beings do we turn back, in order to ground those statements which were made earlier in a mere provisional manner, among them the statements concerning art. Such a return transpires in the tenth and final book."[77] Indeed, his discussion of mimesis as representation avails itself of the terminology acquired in the interpretation of the "allegory," in particular the notion of the "outward appearance" (*das Aussehen*), that is, of the *idea*.[78] Such a reading brings out the "ideological" function of the spectacle of the *ideai* and the subordination of poetry and the theater to the philosophical requirements of order. This subordination, which Heidegger sees in the tenth book of the *Republic*, is also that of Aristotle's *Poetics* with its "catholic," "general" determination of poetry, "ideal" characters/types, recognition, and catharsis.

But the view of mimesis as ideological representation needs to be distinguished from the rhapsodic mimesis in the third book of the *Republic*. In this book, mimesis is discussed within the problematic of education in the sense of the formation of types (*tupoi*), the rigor (*akribeia*) of the social distinctions is opposed to the rhapsodic play (*paidia*) of mimesis, and playing an other, impersonating him or her, giving voice to another, performing a role, might lead to an actual transformation ("[The guardians] should not depict or be skilful at imitating any kind of illiberality or baseness, lest from imitation [*ek tēs mimēseōs*] they should come to be [*einai*] what they imitate" [395c–d]).[79] Thus rhapsodic play acquires a directly sociopolitical meaning. In book 10, on the other hand, there is no question of rhapsodic performance, of role-playing; mimesis consists in producing images of images, within the representational schema; it is the ontological status of images that is in question rather than the identity of the rhapsodic player.[80] Thus the "turning" of the "allegory" of the

77. *Nietzsche*, 4 vols., trans. David Farrell Krell (San Francisco: Harper and Row, 1979–87), 1:168–69 (German: "Auf dem Weg durch diese Gespräche stoßen wir zu Beginn des VII. Buches auf die Erörterung des Wesens der Wahrheit unter Zugrundelegung des Höhlengleichnisses. Erst nachdem auf diesem weiten und breiten Weg die Philosophie als das herrschaftliche Wissen vom Sein des Seienden bestimmt ist, kommt es in der Rückwendung zur Begründung der nur erst vordeutend ausgesprochenen Sätze und so auch derjenigen über die Kunst, und zwar im X. und letzten Buch" [*Nietzsche*, 2 vols. (Pfullingen: Neske, 1961), 1:171]).

78. *Nietzsche*, 1:171ff. (German: *Nietzsche*, 1:173ff.); cf. Martin Heidegger, "The Question Concerning Technology," in *The Question Concerning Technology and Other Essays*, 20 (German: "Die Frage nach der Technik," in *Vorträge und Aufsätze* [Stuttgart: Neske, 1954], 23–24) on Plato's "daring" in using the word "eidos" to designate true being; cf., in Plato scholarship sensu stricto, Klein, *A Commentary on Plato's "Meno,"* 19. Griswold makes this connection as well in his "Plato's Metaphilosophy" (161–62); Julia Annas suggests a perfect visualizing of the Cave allegory through cinematic mimesis in Bertolucci's *The Conformist* in her *Introduction to Plato's "Republic"* (Oxford: Clarendon Press, 1981), 257ff.

79. *The "Republic" of Plato*, trans. Benjamin Jowett, 3rd rev. ed. (Oxford: Oxford University Press, 1888), 80.

80. Stanley Rosen's programmatic statement should be quoted here: "The first step in reading Plato is to put aside our Aristotelian spectacles. To this extent, and in a sense that requires considerable

cave can also be read as a turning from the rhapsodic to the representational mode. In the history of Western thought, this shift occurred with Aristotle, who "seriously" responded to Socrates' challenge and integrated poetry within the representational system dominated by philosophy. The so-called dramatic interpretation of Plato's dialogues belongs to this reaction/apology initiated by Aristotle and can thus be opposed to the rhapsodic mode.

The merit of Jill Gordon's *Turning Toward Philosophy* is to dispel any doubt as to the Aristotelian character of the so-called dramatic reading.[81] Explicitly drawing on the work of Hyland and Griswold, Gordon turns directly to Aristotle: "It makes sense to consult a contemporaneous and *authoritative* work on Greek poetry to see what it might tell us about Plato's dialogues insofar as they are poetry."[82] This might indeed seem a "sensible" directive for a historical, "timely" reading. But is it even then legitimate to interpret a text using the hermeneutic system of an adversary? And the author of the *Poetics* is usually seen as Plato's adversary: F. L. Lucas, Jacqueline de Romilly, and Stephen Halliwell would certainly agree with Martha C. Nussbaum in calling the *Poetics* a "consciously anti-Platonic text."[83] Besides, the "authority" of the *Poetics* has often been questioned as to the reading of Greek tragedy; do not Plato's dialogues have in common with the tragedies the questioning of authority, the authority of *muthos* and *logos*?[84] Would not an "authoritative" poetics cancel out this function? Does not in fact the "authority" of Aristotle's text lie in the

---

modification, I prefer the dramatic to the ontological perspective" (*Plato's "Sophist": The Drama of Original and Image* [New Haven, Conn.: Yale University Press, 1983], 7). I discuss Rosen's "considerable modification" of the "dramatic perspective" and his relationship to the (phenomenological, mainly Heideggerian) "ontological perspective" on Plato's dialogues in chapters 1 and 3.

81. *Turning Toward Philosophy: Literary Device and Dramatic Structure in Plato's Dialogues* (University Park, Pa.: Pennsylvania State University Press, 1999), 76.

82. *Turning Toward Philosophy*, 76.

83. "If we remember that he [Aristotle] is answering Plato" (F. L. Lucas, *Tragedy: Serious Drama in Relation to Aristotle's "Poetics"* [New York: Collier, 1962], 39); "The quarrel with Plato could not be clearer" (Jacqueline de Romilly, *A Short History of Greek Literature*, trans. Lillian Doherty [Chicago: University of Chicago Press, 1985], 163); "The *Poetics* can indeed be described as a defense of poetry which, like so much else in Aristotle's philosophy, presupposes the existence and the provocation of his teacher's system of thought. The Platonic challenge as such goes unmentioned, but the absence of Plato's name is undisturbing: Aristotle often argues against his predecessor without drawing explicit attention to the fact" (Stephen Halliwell, *Aristotle's "Poetics"* [Chapel Hill: University of North Carolina Press, 1986], 1); Martha C. Nussbaum, *The Fragility of Goodness: Luck and Ethics in Greek Tragedy and Philosophy* (Cambridge: Cambridge University Press, 1986), 388; cf. Gerald F. Else, *Plato and Aristotle on Poetry*, ed. Peter Burian (Chapel Hill: University of North Carolina Press, 1986), 69: "It has always been acknowledged, in principle, that the *Poetics* is a reply to Plato's attacks on poetry."

84. See, for example, M. S. Silk and J. P. Stern, *Nietzsche on Tragedy* (Cambridge: Cambridge University Press, 1981), and Jean-Pierre Vernant and Pierre Vidal-Naquet, *Myth and Tragedy in Ancient Greece*, trans. Janet Lloyd (New York: Zone Books, 1990), 26, 37ff., and passim (French: *Mythe et tragédie en Grèce ancienne* [Paris: Maspero, 1979], 16, 30ff., and passim).

tradition that was able to use the *Poetics* for rendering poetry innocuous and acceptable to the powers that be, successfully meeting Socrates' challenge in the *Republic* (607b), purifying poetry and making it "philosophical" (*Poetics* 1451b5–7)? One would expect that to rely on the same authority in reading Plato's dialogues would render them rather tame.

This is precisely what Gordon shows in her book, which is not so much an attempt at a historical philological reconstruction of the missing book(s) of the *Poetics,* in the manner of Richard Janko, as a playful parody of both the *Poetics* and the "dramatic" readings of Plato.[85] Socratic dialogue would be, according to Gordon's Aristotle, "an imitation of philosophical activity which by means of language represents dialogue that aims at turning one toward the philosophical life."[86] Gordon follows this definition with a detailed comparison between the elements of tragedy as distinguished by Aristotle and those of the Socratic dialogue. She suggests the substitution of thought (*dianoia*) for plot (*muthos*) as the "soul" of the dialogue form.[87] This substitution would facilitate identification with the characters, mainly Socrates, and thus the protreptic effect of the Socratic dialogue. Reversal and recognition are also prominent in the structure of the dialogue. Recognition in particular should play an important role in the interaction with the audience or the reader, in the formation of their *identity.* It is in the context of such identification with the characters that Gordon again refers to Hyland, who seems to be outdoing Aristotle: "I understand Hyland's position to be that just what the interlocutors are portrayed as experiencing, the reader/audience is likely to experience. Comparatively, Aristotle's description of the audience's experience of pity and fear are due to a more vicarious interaction with the drama."[88] Gordon doesn't use the word "catharsis" here, but the pair "pity and fear" is an unmistakable hint that that is what she means. The over-Aristotelian reading of the dialogues thus brings Hyland, Gordon, and, as we shall see, other "dramatic" interpreters within the range of Bertolt Brecht's critique, the critique of the "Aristotelian," "cathartic" theater. Far from giving the reader/audience any choice, the identification with the hero (and Gordon explicitly presents Socrates in this role) keeps them spellbound and forces on them the dominant ideological view.[89]

---

85. She does call her adaptation of Aristotle to dialogue *Poetics 3,* coming after *Poetics 2* on comedy; cf. Richard Janko, *Aristotle on Comedy: Towards a Reconstruction of "Poetics" 2* (Berkeley: University of California Press, 1984), which is his reconstruction of the book on comedy based on the fragments of Aristotle's *On Poets* and on the *Tractatus Coisilinianus.* See also his translation of Aristotle's *Poetics* (Indianapolis, Ind.: Hackett, 1987).

86. *Turning Toward Philosophy,* 77

87. *Turning Toward Philosophy,* 79–80.

88. *Turning Toward Philosophy,* 90.

89. *Turning Toward Philosophy,* 88.

Brecht's remedy against the ideological theater of the followers of Aristotle is his own "epic," "anti-Aristotelian," "anti-cathartic" theater. He doesn't call it "rhapsodic," but he might have. The actor in the epic theater is indeed a rhapsode, not only playing a role, identifying with the character, but also taking an ironic look at both the character and him or herself in telling his or her story. Platonic theater would be rhapsodic-Brechtian rather than cathartic-Aristotelian. It is certainly for this reason that Brecht's theater has been explicitly called "Platonic"![90] In this comparison, I hope, the basic differences between the conception of the "dramatic" and "rhapsodic" dialogue are even more apparent.

Since Leo Strauss, almost no "dramatic" reader has refrained from comparing Plato to Shakespeare to make the point that it is inappropriate to identify the dramatic author's thought with that of his character, say, Hamlet or Socrates.[91] This is a remarkable comparison, but it needs to be grasped historically, that is to say, also, in an untimely way. How many Shakespeares were there, are there? Should we single out one of them—the Shakespeare from Stratford-upon-Avon or the one from the court of Elizabeth—and try to isolate his "intention"? Should we dismiss all others as inauthentic, "anti-Shakespearian"?[92] Tom Stoppard's, Heiner Müller's, or the Kabuki version of Shakespeare, for example, are perhaps no less legitimate than the versions offered by the "competent" readers supposedly privy to Plato's or Shakespeare's intentions.[93] Moreover, Plato is not a dramatist like any other, and Ruby Blondell is right to warn readers of the dialogues away from an all too easy categorization: "In the recent push to contextualize Plato's arguments with respect to both literary form and cultural milieu, it is crucial to remember that these arguments are, to an overwhelming degree, the main subject matter of his 'dramas.' 'Dramatic' criticism ignores this at its peril."[94] The truth is that, together with Plato, we his readers are engaged in the endless quarrel between philosophy and poetry, which is also an endless "dialogue of genres."[95] We

90. See chapter 1.
91. *The City and Man,* 50, 59–60, and most recently, James A. Arieti, *Interpreting Plato: The Dialogues as Drama* (Lanham, Md.: Rowman and Littlefield, 1991), 10–11, Louis A. Kosman, "Silence and Imitation in the Platonic Dialogues," in *Methods of Interpreting Plato and His Dialogues,* 74, Gordon, *Turning Toward Philosophy,* 4, and Blondell, *The Play of Characters in Plato's Dialogues,* 18.
92. Charles Griswold brands Derrida's reading of Plato in this way: "Roughly put, his [Derrida's] is in principle anti-Platonic and mine Platonic" (*Self-Knowledge in Plato's "Phaedrus,"* 235).
93. For the amazing diversity of the untimely readings of Shakespeare, see Jan Kott, *Shakespeare Our Contemporary,* trans. Boleslaw Taborski (New York: W. W. Norton, 1974), and more recently, Tadeusz Kowzan, *Hamlet; ou, Le miroir du monde* (Paris: Editions Universitaires, 1991).
94. *The Play of Characters in Plato's Dialogues,* 38.
95. See Lacoue-Labarthe and Nancy, "Le dialogue des genres," 148–75; cf., in a more restrained historical framework, Anne Wilson Nightingale, *Genres in Dialogue: Plato and the Construct of Philosophy* (Cambridge: Cambridge University Press, 1995), and, in a mode closer to the present work, Kevin Corrigan and

cannot accept, as given, the traditional Aristotelian solutions to this quarrel and this dialogue: the attribution to poetry of a dominantly philosophical character and the separation of genres.[96]

To sum up briefly: there is no alternative to the dialogue/confrontation with Plato in our—Platonic—epoch. Reading Plato's dialogues as drama might appear to be a beginning of such dialogue, but in truth, the explicit integration of the dialogue form into the Aristotelian system of mimetic genres actually blocks its dialogic potential. The "dramatic" interpretation has wound up with the Philosopher's Plato! Drama as imitation and image, with its function of identification rather than play, constitutes a powerful instrument of ideological recognition and identification. Just as with tragedy, there is a tendency in classical poetics to submit dialogue to the unity/unities. This tendency should be resisted, just as strongly as the Aristotelian/neoclassical domestication of tragedy. Rhapsodic dialogue is the mode of this resistance; hence its polemical character. But as with Socrates, and the contemporary authors discussed in this book, *polemos* is also, especially, play.

The "old quarrel" (*palaia diaphora* [*Republic* 607b5]) between philosophy and poetry is an example, perhaps the example, of *polemos*/play, if one understands it, with Socrates in the *Republic,* as *hē . . . poiētikē kai hē mimēsis* (607c5), that is, mimesis, which is play par excellence (*Sophist* 234b). Rhapsody is such mimetic play, and it constitutes not only one side of the quarrel but also its (abyssal) (play)ground, a Heraclitean "child's play" ("pais paizōn") rather than a serious well-defined game, such as an athletic competition.[97] Thus if rhapsodic reading seems to resemble "dramatic" reading, it is only in the sense that a wolf resembles a dog (*Sophist* 231a). The function of the "dramatic" reading is to control the character of the text, which it regards as univocal or at least regularly polysemic. The "dramatic" approach joins here the most traditional view of Plato scholarship in maintaining the ideal of a univocal intention. And they both achieve this goal through a strict separation of seriousness and play in their reading.

A passage from the second book of the *Republic* (375–76) gives an illustration of the convergence between these two modes of interpretation in their resistance to the free play of the rhapsodic mode. Socrates and his interlocutor

---

Elena Glazov-Corrigan, *Plato's Dialectic at Play: Argument, Structure, and Myth in the "Symposium"* (University Park, Pa.: Pennsylvania State University Press, 2004).

96. It is in this sense that Rosen's statement—"The first step in reading Plato is to put aside our Aristotelian spectacles"—is most pertinent (*Plato's "Sophist,"* 7).

97. Heraclitus, frag. 52, in Herman Diels, *Die Fragmente der Vorsokratiker,* 3 vols., 6th ed., ed. Walther Kranz (1952; rpt., Zurich: Weidmann, 1985), 1:162. See my critique of David Roochnik's view in chapter 5.

despair of finding an ideal character for a guardian that will combine two apparently opposite qualities: gentleness and ruthlessness (a guardian should be gentle to his fellow countrymen and ruthless toward the enemy). Socrates has an idea as to the model for such a character, a dog, for is it not gentle toward those whom it knows and fierce toward strangers? How amazing this "philosophical" feature in a dog is, marvels Socrates: here is an animal for whom "knowledge" is the only criterion for action. By using the quotation marks in the preceding sentence I have already suggested the traditional interpretation—that of Francis Cornford, for example—which recommends not to take seriously "the ascription of a philosophic element to dogs" because "for Plato, reason is an independent faculty, existing only in man and not developed from any animal instinct."[98] The coherence of Plato's theory is the guiding principle for Cornford here. On the other hand, for James Arieti, who does not care much for Plato's overall theoretical coherence but for "drama" alone, Socrates' argument is just a "silliness," and in the face of his interlocutor Glaucon's acquiescence, the interpreter asks rhetorically, "Doesn't even the most moderate member of Plato's audience want to go up to Glaucon and, shaking him, scold, 'Are you going to go along with everything Socrates says?'"[99] That Socrates' jest escaped Glaucon results from the drama in which both characters are engaged; that it has escaped some readers and interpreters was certainly not *intended* by Plato, according to Arieti, for whom, in general, it is safer to assume that Plato is ironic or that he is joking than that he is dead serious.[100]

Thus, Plato is bantering or making Socrates banter; the results of both the traditional "doctrinal" and the "dramatic" reading are pretty much the same as far as the notion of interpretation is concerned: the exclusion of seriousness, that is, eventually, of play that would confront the text itself and its rhapsodic mode. Plato cannot be serious or Socrates cannot be serious: it is against the accepted doctrine of Plato; it offends common sense. But are not both interpreters using precisely the criterion of *acquaintance* or *familiarity*, that is, of an agreement with the accepted theory, or common sense, which the interpreter translates into the authorial intention, the hermeneutic principle of accepted pre-judices? Philosopher or not, a watchdog would be a model of the guardian-interpreter, a guardian of the text, of its intentional and univocal understanding.

But it is perhaps not necessary (pace Cornford, Griswold, Arieti, and others) to decide in advance between the dramatic seriousness and playfulness of the

---

98. The "Republic" of Plato, trans. Francis M. Cornford (1941; rpt., London: Oxford University Press, 1961), 65–66n; cf. W. K. C. Guthrie A History of Greek Philosophy, 6 vols. (Cambridge: Cambridge University Press, 1962–81), 4:450.

99. Interpreting Plato: The Dialogues as Drama (Savage, Md.: Rowman and Littlefield, 1991), 234.

100. Interpreting Plato, 243 n. 8.

dialogues if we take "seriously" Socrates' old quarrel between philosophy and poetry and set it into play. Socrates suggests in book 10 of the *Republic* that the problem of the relationship between philosophy and poetry is not new and in fact might be eternal as the problem of philosophy's "literary" mode of presentation. There follows the famous banishment. But Socrates hastens to assure the "sweet friend and the sister arts of mimesis" that, together with the other founders of the ideal state, he will be willing to reconsider the judgment if poetry proves her political usefulness. "We are very conscious of her charms," he says, "but we may not on that account betray the truth"—"amica poesis sed magis amica veritas"! Now, Socrates' declaration should be related to the declaration of another Athenian, the Stranger in the *Laws,* who places both philosophers, the champions of truth, and poets, on a stage in a "true" play: "Best of strangers, we will say to them [the tragic poets] we [the philosophers!] also according to our ability are tragic poets, and our tragedy is the best and noblest; for our whole state is a mimesis of the best and noblest life, which we affirm to be indeed the very truth of tragedy. You are poets and we are poets . . . rivals and antagonists in the noblest of dramas" (*Laws* 817).[101] Here, the truth of tragic poetry seems to be formulated by the Athenian Stranger acting as a political philosopher. But the final decision in the matter is deferred, and the debate, the quarrel, transferred to the domain of the rhapsodic play of mimesis. Thus the passage suggests a shift from the strict opposition between poetry and philosophy, between truth and play, to the recognition of a mimetic tension between them.

To summarize briefly again: there is an urgent need for a dialogue with Plato. This is because there is always a need to come to terms with one's epoch, and ours is "Platonic," for better or worse. The "worse" is the representational structure of our thought, with the society of the spectacle at/as its "worst." The "better" is the potential for dialogic challenge, which can be found in Plato's text as well ("Was it not Plato himself who pointed out the direction for the reversal of Platonism?"[102]). The difficulties of finding it results from our own immersion in images. Even those who emphasize the dialogue form as the key to reading Plato "dramatically" understand the drama as tableau-like imitation and submit it to the ideal "form." Only the rhapsodic dialogue is able to resist the authority of the model-image structure. (The hubris of "my" claim may perhaps be mitigated by the hubris of another claim: that of the rhapsodic mode to undermine the subjectivity of the "I claim" or "I speak.")

101. *The Dialogues of Plato,* 5:200; translation modified.
102. Deleuze, *The Logic of Sense,* 256 (French: "[Ne faut-il pas dire] que Platon le premier indiquât cette direction du renversement du platonisme?" [*Logique du sens,* 295]).

The very nature of rhapsodic reading prevents a theoretical generalization of it. All of the authors discussed in this book engage in a singular confrontation/dialogue with Plato. It is thus less in terms of positive assertions than in terms of questioning, and especially a questioning of the representational character of the epoch—a questioning of modern theory and the theater, of drama theorized by a subject/spectator (*theatēs*)—that I hope to engage the reader in a serious play with what too often is taken for granted: "the author," "his or her text," "its meaning," "the world," "the self." This book accordingly does not impose a traditionally understood philosophical interpretation on the texts in question. Rather, each chapter brings together one of Plato's dialogues and a rhapsodic confrontation with Platonism by several contemporary thinkers, who draw on the dialogue in developing their own thought, displaying the play of *mimēsis,* of *pharmakon,* of *khōra,* of *hermēneia,* and of play (*paidia*) "itself."

In the book's first chapter I read the *Republic* as a play between rigor and play, and between education (*paideia*) and play (*paidia*), in the company of Gérard Genette and Lacoue-Labarthe (as well as, indirectly, Heidegger, René Girard, and Rosen). The basic claim of the whole book concerning the dialogic inseparability of philosophy and its rhapsodic, "literary" mode of presentation is here discussed in terms of rigor (*akribeia*), which is shown to be in fact the focus of the first book of the *Republic*. Rigor, the key term in the logic, ontology, and politics of the *Republic,* has to be ratified in the rigor of literary distinctions. Thus, a strict separation between terms, functions, and types—and eventually between philosophy and poetry, which underlies the famous "old quarrel" (*palaia diaphora*)—cannot be sustained in the rhapsodic interplay of, say, mimetic and diegetic modes. When Genette maintains Socrates' fundamental separation of the modes of discourse, he remains within the same ideological ("typological," "typographical") structure, even when reversing the valuation of the two modes and their corresponding genres.

But does Socrates himself not warrant the opposition between form and content in the *Republic*? Doesn't he attempt to distinguish between what is to be said (*ha lekteon*) in the myths accepted in education and the way it is to be said (*hōs lekteon*)? Yes, but "Socrates himself" is never really *himself* in the dialogue. He is a rhapsode, telling the story of a conversation concerning justice (*dikaiosunē*) in a mode that is not compatible with the very rule of justice about to be announced: one man, one job. This rule and the strict separation between classes, genders, and professions is what the "competent readers" of the *Republic* would not hesitate to call content; and yet it is also a form of discourse—a dialogue, in fact, that questions the strict delimitations of modes and genres of discourse and eventually the rule of justice itself.

At the outset of his recent commentary, Rosen recognizes the importance of the rhapsodic mode of the *Republic*, where Socrates "assumes the identities, and utters the speeches, of everyone in the dialogue, which is accordingly also mimetic," but he immediately opposes it to Plato's "invention of the entire Socratic monologue," and it is the monologue that seems to determine Plato's political thought as it is developed in the course of Rosen's book.[103] One of the great merits of Rosen's book is thus to have shown on the political level the conflict between the two modes of mimesis and the transition from rhapsodic play to (mostly visual) representation, a transition that Heidegger analyzed in his reading of the "allegory of the cave."

In conjunction with Lacoue-Labarthe's reading of Heidegger's reading and his theory of truth as *alētheia* (through Girard's notion of mimetic crisis), I argue for the necessity of the rhapsodic origin, a necessarily an-archic origin, of any rigorous order. *Akribeia* rather than *alētheia*, in its play with mimesis or play, would thus be at stake in the *Republic*—in any republic. Throughout this book, the rigor of the separation of types, classes, and genres progressively leads to a different kind of rigor, epitomized by the rhapsodic mode of the *Ion* that is also present in the *Republic*—written in a mixed rhapsodic mode and genre and as such an example of the irreducible play between mimesis and diegesis, between the truth, or at least "non-true lie" of the *muthos,* and the true lie of role (dis-)playing. Neither Socrates' rejection of dramatic mimesis nor Genette's neglect of it on the ground of its representational straightfor-wardness acknowledges the rhapsodic play in Homer, in Plato, and so forth, which consists in the constant *dia-phora* or "carrying across" between the two modes of discourse: simple narration and dramatic presentation. It is such a *dia-phora* that marks the dialogue that Lacoue-Labarthe establishes between Heidegger and Girard. His notion of "typography" brings together the rigor of types (and that of the modern "subject") with the "disinstallation" of the play of writing. One of its implications is the dependence of the subject of enunci-ation on the mode of this enunciation. Lacoue-Labarthe's own essay might be considered an instance of what we call the rhapsodic mode.

It is within the problematic of such a mode that the second chapter, "*Le Beau Jeu:* The Play of Beauty and Truth in the *Phaedrus*," asks seriously an apparently frivolous question: why the philosopher would not get the truth if she were a woman. This question might prove more serious than the famous "why Plato wrote dialogues" question and might indeed begin to answer it. It is true that Nietzsche answered the question (in fact, his own) a long time ago, but philosophers/scholars do not seem to have taken it seriously enough, that

---

103. *Plato's "Republic,"* 12.

is, playfully enough. Heidegger, for one, in his *Nietzsche: The Will to Power as Art,* addresses the opposition between art and truth, characterized by Nietzsche as a dreadful or raging discordance (*ein Entsetzen erregender Zwiespalt*), in terms of Nietzsche's intended overturning of Platonism. But Heidegger claims that there is no discordance in the *Republic,* only the hierarchical subordination of poetry or art to truth, and that the discordance of the *Phaedrus* is "felicitous," a "beglückender Zwiespalt": beauty, the domain of art, becomes a privileged site of the uncovering/unforgetting of truth. This view of poetry, or art, and truth in Plato and Nietzsche makes possible Heidegger's own characterization of art in "The Origin of the Work of Art" as the "setting into the work/to work of truth" (*das Ins-Werk-Setzen der Wahrheit*). Building on the argument of the first chapter, I attempt to substitute here the notion of *akribeia,* or rigor, for that of *alētheia,* or truth. It is indeed *akribeia* that brings play into the definition of poetry and art—in Plato as in Brecht's epic or rhapsodic theater—as a "setting into play" of the ideology of types or typography.

Here again, the so-called dramatic reading becomes a foil to the rhapsodic one. Griswold's *Self-Knowledge in Plato's "Phaedrus"* attempts a return to the representational notion of truth with its radical distinction between "literal and nonliteral truth" and its "subjection" of the latter to the former. The interpretation of the poetic palinode and the myths of the *Phaedrus* are forced into a "rhetorical framework," discovered in the "rhetoric of the palinode itself." This rhetoric is submitted to philosophy defined as "true psychotherapy," a means of enforcing the "conservative" categories and distinctions. It is Griswold's neglect of the rhaps-odic character of the palin-ode that is ultimately responsible for his obliteration of the serious play in the *Phaedrus.*

Nietzsche's quarrel with Richard Wagner concerns the same danger of *eluding* play in art. Wagner's art is false because dead serious, in spite of its theatrical character, which he uses to form an ideology rather than to question it. Nietzsche's critique is here at one with that of Socrates. And, also like Socrates, he rhapsodically gives voice to a number of dramatic characters— Socrates, Euripides, Zarathustra, the last man, the overman, "Wagner," and most importantly of all, "Nietzsche"—in displaying his thought. It is thus not an accident that Derrida brings together truth and play on the basis of Nietzsche's text in his *Spurs.* He shows that truth is necessarily included within the realm of play by woman, artist par excellence, who stands for truth as untruth, as art, as the play of dissimulation and revelation. Again, such a play can only be fully understood within the context of the opposition between the supposed rigor of scientific discourse and the rhapsodic mode of Plato's and Nietzsche's writing. Heidegger's reading of Nietzsche's overturning of Platonism, and hence, his view of both Plato and Nietzsche, doesn't do full justice to this mode, to the notion of woman-play in the relationship of art to truth. Ideal beauty, whose brilliance contributes to the recollection of the other ideas, needs art or the *pharmakon* of mimesis in order itself to appear. Socratic, rhapsodic speeches constitute such a *pharmakon,* and they belong to Plato's pharmacy/theater, just as writing as examined by Derrida does. They reveal the play between self-identity and dissimulation, between self-possession and being possessed, between logos and inspiration. The dissimulation and revelation of ideal forms may be called the truth of unconcealment (*alētheia, Unverborgenheit*), but it is also a pharmaco-logical play that challenges the rigor of a univocal logos. The play of signification, a play between the logic of rigorous definition and an irreducible ambiguity even within a single signifier (for example—and this is not an arbitrary example for Derrida—the signifier *pharmakon*), is crucial here. The playful character of writing throughout the *Phaedrus* must be taken into account, and any attempt, whether by King Thamus in Socrates' story or by Plato's interpreters, to come to a decision is frustrated in the dialogue by the logic of play that Derrida tries to carry on. The *pharmakon* will never be just a poison or just a remedy; the *beau jeu* (not exactly "fair play") will always preserve an element of risk and of play between beauty and truth, between poetry and philosophy.

The third chapter takes up a major problem of Platonism, which happens to be also a major problem of the contemporary "society of the spectacle": that of the legitimacy of representation, that is, of the distinction between images and simulacra. Plato's dialogue the *Sophist* ostensibly attempts to reduce the risk of collapsing the distinction between philosophy and its mimetic doubles, art and sophistry, precisely by maintaining the distinction between images and simulacra. I read this dialogue with Deleuze ("Plato and the Simulacrum"), Michel Foucault ("Theatrum philosophicum"), and Jean-Luc Nancy ("Le ventriloque"). I also refer to Rosen's "dramatic phenomenology," elaborated in his reading of the *Sophist,* which I claim is still governed by the rule of representation. Now, every analytical philosopher knows well that the *Sophist* is about predication rather than about Eleatic metaphysical conundrums. And the great merit of Rosen's book is rigorously to show the impasse of such a reading, the "predicationalists'" reading of the *Sophist* based on the oversimplifying translation of the verb *eoikenai* by "duplicates" or "is the same as." The Greek *eoikenai* and the modern "likeness," "similarity," or "resemblance" are slippery notions, hardly able to conform to the rigor of logical symbols.

The Elean Stranger in the *Sophist* defines the simulacrum as an image without resemblance, and on the basis of this notion—a gesture toward an overturning of Platonism—Deleuze and Foucault develop a view of modern art and philosophy of the Dionysian kind found in Nietzsche, Antonin Artaud, and others, which tends to "glorify" the world of simulacra. As attractive as it appears, the possibility of the total liberation of simulacra from the order of representation seems doubtful in general and in Plato's text in particular. An examination of René Magritte's and Francis Bacon's paintings, which should support Foucault's (*This Is Not a Pipe*) and Deleuze's (*Francis Bacon: The Logic of Sensation*) views, respectively, shows the difficulty of conceiving a simulacrum without any relation to the representational order. Paradoxically, such a liberation would require a certain mastery, a methodological rigor of separation (Plato's dialectic of *diairesis,* or division) of the kind that eventually fails in the *Sophist.* The dialogue shows a certain claim of simulacra to representational status, even through a somewhat slippery mode of resemblance. The sophist, in particular, seems to resemble the philosopher, even if only in the protean character of nonresemblance with himself. The self-referentiality of Plato's text, emphasized by Nancy, links the questioning of the notion of the subject with that of the mode of discourse on which such a notion depends. The Stranger's Eleatic belief in the possibility of a rigorous separation between being and nonbeing, as well as between the terms that designate them, is belied by the very experience with language, which always forces us to bring together what we would like rigorously to separate. This leads to the notion of the *sumplokē,* or entanglement of beings, which the Stranger develops into the "community of genres." This un-Eleatic ontology constitutes the basis for a play that attempts to deal with the conundrum of the "reality" of art, a conundrum that is displayed by notions such as "(re)semblance" and "fantastic art." Nancy's notion of "ventriloquism" playfully refers to the same experience of uncanny resemblance and helps to focus on the mode of discourse that renounces the illusion of rigor and objectivity, since it is aware of the other voice, the voice of the other, constantly present in any statement. Again, I call this mode of discourse "rhapsodic" and point to the affinity of its "stitching together" with the community of voices entangled in the Stranger's *sumplokē.*

The fourth chapter, "The Abyssal Emplacement of World and Discourse in the *Timaeus,*" proposes a reading of the *Timaeus* in dialogue with Julia Kristeva, Irigaray, Judith Butler, Elizabeth Grosz, Derrida, and John Sallis, which shows how the cosmological and discursive stage of *khōra* ("place," "space," "ground," "land," "country") becomes the un-common place for questioning the foundations of Western metaphysical, political, and aesthetic hierarchies, especially the phallogocentric—"paradigmatic," "typical," "fatherly"—repression of the feminine grounding (in all senses of the word) of emplacement. The representation of the ideal models and univocal terms in *khōra* is disturbed by *khōra's* singularizing effect. The otherness of *khōra,* its radical difference, "in a sense irreducible to a difference of sense," irreducible to the requirements of *akribeia,* undermines the efforts of Plato's demiurge to force the initial chiasm of the same and the other into an all-including circle of the same as well as the efforts of the philosopher to circumscribe his cosmo-logical discourse within a "logical" myth.[104] Thus, the *Timaeus,* the least dramatically mimetic of the Platonic dialogues, is shown here to be nevertheless the place where the rhapsodic mode of discourse (already dismissed, as we have seen in the *Republic,* because of its ontological, political, and poetical inadequacy) is again, and more radically, problematized. Chora, the third entity of the cosmological system of the *Timaeus,* is supposed to make possible the creation of a world in motion in accordance with immutable ontological, epistemological, and political oppositions, a world that would include the orderly society described in the *Republic* and invoked again in the *Timaeus.* Mimesis in the sense of resembling representation has its place in this process: the phenomenal, changing world is a copy of the ideal, unchanging paradigm.

But chora, far from performing its duty of filling the gap between these two worlds, opens an abyss, a chasm that risks undermining the entire system. Indeed, chora, which has no proper place or characteristics, has more to do with rhapsodic mimesis than with resemblance and representation. Described as "nurselike" and "motherlike," chora evokes the status of the feminine in Western thought: a "receptacle" for the creation of a (masculine) world, it is itself passive, without form, without imprint. Since it is hardly possible to banish chora, the place of support of the world and/of discourse, a (theoretical, cosmological, political, poetical) effort has to be made by the guardians of world and discourse to exorcise the disruptive, revolutionary potential of mat(t)er, of femininity, of Eros, of the semiotic, of rhapsodic mimesis, and so forth, into which the authors discussed in this chapter translate the *khōra* of the *Timaeus.* They would perhaps all agree with Sallis in comparing the liminal character of chora with the status of the Good in the *Republic:* "epekeina tēs ousias," or "beyond" ("otherwise than") being, except that the transcendence of chora would be the opposite to that of the Good; a star could never be the image of it/her but at most a planet. Chora's errancy, its/her "dispersal that holds apart from being," is inseparable from the discourse on chora. And indeed, Platonic chora can be read in terms of the discursive practice that disrupts the conservative order of a treatise, as can be seen by a comparison with a Hellenistic paraphrase of the *Timaeus* (of Timaeus)—one of the first

104. For the quote, see John Sallis, *Platonic Legacies* (Albany: State University Press of New York, 2004), 4, 42, 43; see also his *Being and Logos: Reading the Platonic Dialogues* (1975; rpt., Bloomington: Indiana University Press, 1996) and especially *Chorology: On Beginning in Plato's "Timaeus"* (Bloomington: Indiana University Press, 1999).

attempts to domesticate chora, to make it strictly cosmo-logical, orderly—
that in fact becomes a foil to the rhapsodic mode of Plato and its contemporary heirs.

My "Rhapsodic Conclusion: 'The Dialogue That We Are' in Plato, Heidegger, and Nancy" takes up the problem implicitly raised by all the preceding chapters, that of interpretation. The "interpretation of Plato" took on a
new meaning with Hans-Georg Gadamer, in whose hermeneutics Plato's dialogue and Socratic dialectic became the model for the work of interpretation.
Enforcing the priority of the question, Platonic/Socratic dialogue at the same
time, on Gadamer's view, opens up its horizon, and the state of indeterminacy
in the movement of the conversation should exclude any dogmatic abuse. But
the dialogue should also determine the direction of questioning (*Richtungssinn*),
the *sens* of the question, leading to a "correct meaning" (*richtiger Sinn*). The
continuum of meaning (*Sinnkontinuum*) in history marks the tradition embedded in language itself and its prejudices. Gadamer's reading of poetry
follows these hermeneutic directives in an attempt always to secure a precise
and definite meaning. It is perhaps this requirement of rigor that makes some
modern readers, such as David Roochnik, despair of a common language
between poetry and philosophy. Plato's *Ion* is hardly a model of the dialogue
on this account.

My reading develops, on the contrary, the notion of *hermēneia,* broached
in this dialogue, in Heidegger's "Dialogue on Language," and in Nancy's
"Sharing Voices" as radically different from philosophical ("hermeneutical")
interpretation as instantiated by Gadamer's work. It points to the necessarily
rhapsodic nature of any theoretical attempt to dominate poetry and mimesis, and thus to its necessary failure. A logically rigorous theory will always
need to examine its own language, will always need to question the authority/
authorship of its concepts, will always need to split and share its logos through
the dialogue of singular voices, ultimately through their writing. Thus, such
an attempt, as I hope to have shown, in the end defeats its own purpose, since
it opens the way for a dialogue (*dia-logos*) rather than hermeneutic mastery.
In Nancy's notion of *partage* (sharing), such a dialogue offers a chance (a divine
but finite *theia moira*) for a communal space of a radically different kind than
the one presented in the most common interpretations of Plato's *Republic*.

I have suggested that the dialogue between poetry and thought depends
on the dialogue of contemporary thought with Plato. But the progress of this
book, and especially this final chapter, suggests that the latter dialogue might
also depend on the dialogue between poetry and thought, as the example
of Heidegger's reading of Hölderlin and Trakl—and of the other thinkers discussed in this book, who also enter the dialogue with poetry—suggests. This

is because it is in the dialogue with poetry, in the experience with language that it makes possible, that the conditions of our being-with (*sun-einai, Mit-sein*) are most conspicuously manifested. The dialogue between Plato, Heidegger, and Nancy is thus the culmination of the readings traced throughout this book, revealing the full scope of the mode that we have discerned both in Plato and in his most astute contemporary readers.

Platonic Theater
Rigor and Play in the *Republic*
(Genette and Lacoue-Labarthe)

"Let me make a prediction," [Adeimantus] said. "You are going to ask whether or not we should allow tragedy and comedy into our city?" "Possibly," I said. "Possibly more than that even."
—SOCRATES

What is needed above all is an absolute skepticism toward all inherited concepts (of the kind that one philosopher *perhaps* possessed already—Plato, of course—for he taught the reverse).
—FRIEDRICH NIETZSCHE

The point . . . of considerable importance for understanding the *Republic* . . . is that it is narrated by Socrates, though in such a way that he assumes the identities, and utters the speeches, of everyone in the dialogue, which is accordingly also mimetic.
—STANLEY ROSEN

The quarrel (*diaphora*) between philosophy and poetry, which was already old when Socrates announced it in the tenth book of Plato's *Republic,* has grown older and older, but it has retained its original opposition between truth as the principle of philosophy and mimesis as the (non) principle of poetry, literature, art. Nietzsche formulated this opposition most dramatically as the "dreadful, raging discordance" (*ein Entsetzen erregender Zwiespalt*) between art and truth, and it became the basis of his philosophical project of the reversal of Platonism.[1] Even though Heidegger, in his interpretation of Plato's quarrel

---

The first epigraph to this chapter comes from Plato's *Republic* 394d (trans. Tom Griffith, in *Plato: The "Republic,"* ed. G. F. R. Ferrari [Cambridge: Cambridge University Press, 2000], 83) (Greek: "Μαντεύομαι, ἔφη, σκοπεῖσθαί σε εἴτε παραδεξόμεθα τραγῳδίαν τε καὶ κωμῳδίαν εἰς τὴν πόλιν, εἴτε καὶ οὔ. Ἴσως, ἦν δ' ἐγώ, ἴσως δὲ καὶ πλείω ἔτι τούτων"). The second epigraph comes from Nietzsche's *The Will to Power,* trans. Walter Kaufmann and R. J. Hollingdale, ed. Walter Kaufmann (New York: Random House, 1967), frag. 409, p. 221 (German: "Zunächst thut die absolute Scepsis gegen alle überlieferten Begriffe noth [wie sie vielleicht schon einmal Ein Philosoph besessen hat—Plato: natürlich (hat er) das Gegentheil gelehrt]" [in *Nachgelaßene Fragmente, 1884–1885,* in Friedrich Nietzsche, *Kritische Studienausgabe,* 15 vols., ed. Giorgio Colli and Mazzino Montinari (1967–77; rpt., Berlin: de Gruyter, 1988), 11:487]). The final epigraph is drawn from Rosen, *Plato's "Republic": A Study* (New Haven, Conn.: Yale University Press, 2005), 12.

1. In *Nachgelaßene Fragmente, 1887–1889,* in *Kritische Studienausgabe,* 13:500; see the first section of chapter 2 of this book.

and of Nietzsche's discordance, questioned the terms of the *diaphora* and *Zwiespalt,* he too retained the basic reference to truth. It is the claim of this chapter, however, that in spite of Socrates' explicit formulation in book 10 of the *Republic,* it is not truth, not even truth as *alētheia,* that ultimately governs Plato's "old quarrel," but *akribeia,* or exactness, rigor. The term that apparently opposes *akribeia,* but in fact is inseparable from it, and for that reason will eventually undo the opposition, is still art, but in its specifically dramatic aspect of theatrical and rhapsodic performance, that is, the *mimēsis* of the third book of the *Republic.* I would like to call "Platonic theater" the play between *akribeia* and rhapsodic *mimēsis,* a play that, contrary to the traditional "doctrinal" and "dramatic" interpretations of Plato's dialogues, does not accept an authoritative, explicit or ulterior motive of Plato but that does acknowledge the presence of a serious force in the dialogues, a force that might lead, and in fact did lead, to the overwhelming rule of representation in our epoch, called for that reason "Platonic."[2]

Nowhere is the blend of seriousness and play better suited to the purpose than in the discussion of mimesis, which is play par excellence.[3] The broad range of the word's meaning in Plato is perhaps a result of the process of philosophical and poetic exploration rather than a mark of an early stage in the "development of the concept" characterized by the lack of methodological precision that it will later acquire with Aristotle.[4] In other words, the play between different aspects of the indefinite character of mimesis is a necessary component of its role in the debate concerning the problem of semantic and logical rigor in philosophy, politics, science, and art, not only in fifth and fourth-century BC

2. Thus, "Platonic theater" will not have been a classical theater. But is not the phrase "Platonic theater" paradoxical? Hardly anyone sees Plato otherwise than as a pitiless censor of this kind of performance art; of any art for that matter. The phrase was actually coined to characterize the epic theater of Brecht (see Stanley Mitchell, introduction, in Walter Benjamin, *Understanding Brecht,* trans. Anna Bostock [London: Verso, 1983], xv). Could it apply to Plato's own dialogues? This is what I would like to investigate.

3. On this point, see the exchange between Theaetetus and the Elean Stranger in Plato's *Sophist* 234b:

> The Stranger: Is there any more artistic or graceful form of play [παιδιᾶς] than the mimetic performance [τὸ μιμητικόν]?"
> Theaetetus: Certainly not; and you have mentioned a very important category, which includes under one class the most diverse sorts of things [εἰς ἓν πάντα συλλαβὼν καὶ σχεδὸν ποικιλιώτατον]. (trans. Benjamin Jowett, in *The Dialogues of Plato,* 5 vols., 3rd rev. ed. [New York: Macmillan, 1892], 4:361; translation modified)

Cf. section 2 in chapter 3 of this book.

4. As Gunter Gebauer and Christoph Wulf maintain; see their *Mimesis: Culture—Art—Society,* trans. Don Reneau (Berkeley: University of California Press, 1995), 31ff. (German: *Mimesis: Kultur, Kunst, Gesellschaft* [Reinbek bei Hamburg: Rowohlt, 1992], 50ff.). It has been noted that Aristotle often returns to the traditional notions that had been "defamiliarized" by his extravagant teacher (see, for example, Pierre Aubenque's study of the Aristotelian notion of *phronesis* in his *La prudence chez Aristote* [1963; Paris: Presses Universitaires de France, 1986], 14, 155ff.); "*mimēsis*" is one of them.

Greece but also in the subsequent history of Western culture. *Mimēsis* is perhaps necessarily polysemic or even disseminative in its challenge to the univocity of *akribeia* or rigor.

Akribeia and *mimēsis* are not usually related to each other in the commentaries on Plato and the ancient texts in general. They belong apparently to two distinct domains: the former—a scientific value—to epistemology and the methodology of sciences, the latter—an aesthetic principle—primarily to the theory of art. Yet these two words or *topoi*—the poetic, and in particular rhapsodic, mode of mimesis, on the one hand, and the scientific, logical value of rigor, on the other—are in fact closely related in their agon, which subtends the "old" dispute or quarrel between (rigorous) philosophy and (mimetic) art and poetry. To be sure, Plato's Socrates in the *Republic* does not rigorously (*akribōs*) separate these domains, even if he tries hard to do so.[5]

Logical and Political Rigor in "Thrasymachus"

There is no exact way to test a man's worth; for human nature has confusion in it.

—ORESTES

It is only in the tenth book of Plato's *Republic* that the "old dispute" or quarrel between philosophy and poetry is explicitly mentioned.[6] Implicitly, it is already broached in the very first book—a kind of introduction to the problem of justice and of the rigor necessary in philosophical and political discussion—by its two protagonists: Socrates, the philosopher, and Thrasymachus, the Sophist.[7] The latter is also an *amator* of the art of acting; Thrasymachus, a historical figure—a Sophist and political orator of the fifth century BC—is the only orator interested in acting mentioned by Aristotle in the third book

---

5. The separation will soon take place in the system of Aristotle, in which the *Poetics* is relatively independent from his *Metaphysics* or *Analytics*. Aristotle refers explicitly to (the historical) Socrates as his predecessor in his *Sophistical Refutations* 183a36ff. and *Metaphysics* 1078b17–33.

6. The epigraph to this section comes from Euripides' *Electra* 367–68, in *Suppliant Women; Electra; Heracles*, vol. 3 of Euripides, *Selections*, ed. and trans. David Kovacs (Cambridge, Mass.: Harvard University Press, 1998), 193 (Greek: "οὐκ ἔστ' ἀκριβὲς οὐδὲν εἰς εὐανδρίαν/ἔχοσι γὰρ ταραγμὸν αἱ φύσεις βροτῶν" [*Suppliant Women; Electra; Heracles*, 192]).

7. It is a pity that Plato scholars, who devote so much energy to stylometric counting, seem to avoid counting words that count; see, recently, David Roochnik, *Of Art and Wisdom: Plato's Understanding of "Technē"* (University Park, Pa.: Pennsylvania State University Press, 1996). That methodological rigor is what the first book of the *Republic* "is all about" might be surmised from the mere counting of the appearances of the word "ἀκριβής" and its cognates; there are at least fourteen of them in the space of a few pages in it, compared to zero in some of Plato's other dialogues (even some longer ones such as *Gorgias*) and never exceeding single digits in one dialogue, including the longest: the *Laws* and the rest of the *Republic*.

of the *Rhetoric*.[8] The presence of such a character provides a clue as to the significance of the debate on rigor in which he is made to take part. He is certainly not an extra; it would not be amiss to call the first book of the *Republic* "Thrasymachus."[9] The book is quintessentially rhapsodic, and it imparts this mode to the rest of the *Republic*.[10] It is Thrasymachus's double interest, in politics and in acting, that marks the dialogue, and not only the first book but the whole of the *Republic* might be considered a "response to Thrasymachus." His character—although it disappears, or rather is silenced, after the first book—continues to haunt the entire dialogue and is far from exorcised by the sacrificial exclusion of the mimetic artist in the third and the tenth books.[11]

The role played by Thrasymachus in the *Republic,* his challenge to the philosopher Socrates' rigor in assigning meanings to words and social roles to citizens, epitomizes the rhapsodic mode, which is for Socrates a symptom of the corruption in the community. In his view, the demagogy of theatrocracy contaminates Athenian politics. Socrates criticizes not only the popularity of the dramatic festivals and the drama of the popular gatherings that imposes a uniform ideology, but also the process of confusing the identity of the participants in a tragic mimetic play, of blurring social distinctions, through promiscuous impersonations.[12] Its embrace of impersonation is apparently the reason for the eventual banishment of rhapsodic mimesis from the perfect city-state. The guardians of such a state are not supposed to engage in a mimetic play, "lest from imitation they should come to be what they imitate" (395c–d).[13] The danger is that they will forsake their moral, professional, and social status and become just like the characters imitated: "women, whether young or old,"

8. *Rhetoric* 1404a12f.
9. If it had been one of the dialogues, the *Thrasymachus* would have rounded out the Socratic inquiry into the nature of the four virtues: courage (in the *Laches*), piety (in the *Euthyphro*), wisdom or temperance (σωφροσύνη, in the *Charmides*), and justice. The historical characterization of Thrasymachus is no less important to the interpretation of the *Republic* than is that of Laches and Nicias to the interpretation of the dialogue on courage and that of Charmides and Critias to the interpretation of the dialogue on temperance.
10. The first book originally constituted, according to Hermann, Dümmler, Friedländer, et al., the ur-*Republic*.
11. Thrasymachus's presence is forcefully reaffirmed at *Republic* 450a–b.
12. "When they [the people] meet together, and the world sits down at an assembly, or in a court of law, or a theatre, or a camp, or in any other popular resort, and there is a great uproar, and they praise some things which are being said or done, and blame other things, equally exaggerating both, shouting and clapping their hands, and the echo of the rocks and the place they are assembled redoubles the sound of the praise and blame—at such a time will not a young man's heart, as they say, leap within him? Will any private training enable him to stand firm against the overwhelming flood of popular opinion? or will he be carried away by the stream? Will he not have the notions of good and evil which the public in general have—he will do as they do, and as they are, such will he be?" (492b–c [*The "Republic" of Plato,* trans. Benjamin Jowett, 3rd rev. ed. (Oxford: Oxford University Press, 1888), 190]).
13. *The "Republic" of Plato,* trans. Benjamin Jowett, 80.

"slaves," "drunkards," "madmen," "smiths or other artificers," "oarsmen," "boat-swains," and so forth (*Republic* 395–396).[14] Far from producing a stable member of a well-defined social structure—a so-called composed character—rhapsodic poetry promotes a rebellious character, a character that does not adhere to any well-defined position.[15] This Thrasymachean, literally "hypocritical" mimesis, will constitute the foil against which Socrates' methodology of rigorous argumentation will develop. It is this methodology that will attempt to classify the world philosophically and morally, to justify it, and to make it appear fair toward the just and the unjust.

It has been argued that Plato's ideal of methodological rigor was a natural consequence of the transition from oral to written culture; that Plato "fully exploit[ed] the potential opened up to thought by the gradual introduction of writing over the preceding centuries."[16] The written language developed by Plato was "a highly cultivated means of expression, a precision instrument that did not exist prior to his work."[17] Mimesis, as an "element of the pre-written, obsolete culture, now in the course of being overtaken by the new literate culture," was to be transformed and "subjected . . . to theoretical, conceptual, and essentialist philosophical thought," a thought using a "conceptual language constructed on the basis of definitions," on which Plato himself conferred an "unsurpassable precision and rigor."[18] It is as an artisan of this transition from oral to written culture, from the spell of the rhapsodic mode to a new mode of theory and writing, that Plato "occupies a key position in the history of mimesis."[19]

This view—typical of so many narratives of intellectual history inspired by Milman Parry, Albert B. Lord, and Eric Havelock—is a good example of what has been denounced as the imprudence of forcing a text into a schema that is itself put into question by that text.[20] Mimetic and rhapsodic dialogue, unambiguously placed by Gunter Gebauer and Christoph Wulf on the side of orality, seems to be in fact a potent element of such questioning, even if

---

14. *The "Republic" of Plato,* trans. Benjamin Jowett, 80–81; translation modified.

15. See *Republic* 604e.

16. Gebauer and Wulf, *Mimesis,* 45 (German: *Mimesis,* 69).

17. *Mimesis,* 46 (German: *Mimesis,* 70).

18. *Mimesis,* 45, 48 (German: *Mimesis,* 69, 73).

19. *Mimesis,* 45 (German: *Mimesis,* 69).

20. In the methodological remarks to Derrida's readings of classical texts. Let us mention here the essay that questions directly the univocity of "writing" and that subtends Gebauer and Wulf's analysis: "Plato's Pharmacy," in Jacques Derrida, *Dissemination,* trans. Barbara Johnson (Chicago: University of Chicago Press, 1981), 61–171 (French: "La pharmacie de Platon," in *La dissémination* [Paris: Seuil, 1972], 79–213). P. Christopher Smith's critical reading of "Plato's Pharmacy" ("Orality and Writing: Plato's *Phaedrus* and the *Pharmakon* Revisited," in *Between Philosophy and Poetry: Writing, Rhythm, History,* ed. Massimo Verdicchio and Robert Burch [New York: Continuum, 2002], 73–92) takes for granted the writing/speech opposition that is precisely at stake in both Derrida and Plato.

"Platonism" may be pointed to as the very source of the orality/literacy opposition.[21] Mimesis is called by Socrates in the *Republic*—just as writing is in the
myth of the *Phaedrus*—a *pharmakon* (a remedy or a poison, potentially both),
and it might well be that it functions as one, not only in Plato's text but in any
republic, in any political structure and in any text supposedly sustained by the
rigor of writing.[22]

Thus the first book, the most "dramatic" in the *Republic,* stages a real agon
between Socrates and Thrasymachus. Although the latter can be considered a
man of the theater, theatrical matters are not openly discussed in this book;
justice is.[23] Thrasymachus initiates one of the hottest debates in all of Plato's
dialogues by offering a rigorous and rather provocative definition of the concept. Justice, he says, is "the interest of the stronger" (*to tou kreittonos sum-
pheron* [338c]), a phrase often paraphrased by English commentators as "might
makes right."[24] Thrasymachus himself makes his initial definition more
specific, claiming justice is the interest of the established authority (*kathestē-
kuias arkhēs [sumpheron]* [339a]). The statement could be understood in the
sense of juridical (legal) positivism if one were to identify the interest of the
ruling authority with its expression in existing laws and ordinances.[25] Since,
however, Thrasymachus refuses to interpret it that way, the statement remains
paradoxical and provocative for all followers of Socrates: Polemarchus, Glaucon, Adeimantus, as well as most interpreters of the dialogue, indeed most
readers. In fact, Thrasymachus's later speech would support the interpretation
of the formula as the expression of a simple truth—conveyed, in a sense, by all
nurses to all children—namely, that it is power that determines the sense of
(legal, political) justice, that, in other (modern) terms, law, politics, and political and juridical philosophy are ideologically conditioned.

The initial questioning of Thrasymachus regarding the exact meaning of his
thesis is the most spectacular moment of the entire dialogue, marked dramatically by the joint intervention of the protagonists (Socrates and Thrasymachus)

21. Derrida, "Plato's Pharmacy," 98.

22. See chapter 2.

23. On Thrasymachus's interest in justice, see Herman Diels, *Die Fragmente der Vorsokratiker,* 3 vols.,
6th ed., ed. Walther Kranz (1952; rpt., Zurich: Weidmann, 1985), 2:326.

24. *The "Republic" of Plato,* trans. Benjamin Jowett, 15.

25. Modern interpreters at least would like thus to understand Thrasymachus's phrase, and they are
grieved by his explicit refusal. In fact, the doctrine of juridical positivism is clearly formulated by one of
Thrasymachus's supporters, Cleitophon, as a way out of the difficulty of determining the real interest of
the stronger (the ruling party): "[Thrasymachus] meant by the interest of the stronger," says Cleitophon,
"what the stronger thought to be his interest [ὃ ἡγοῖτο ὁ κρείττων αὐτῷ συμφέρειν],—this is what the
weaker has to do; and this was affirmed by him to be justice [τὸ δίκαιον]" (340b [*The "Republic" of Plato,*
trans. Benjamin Jowett, 15]).

and of their supporters (Polemarchus and Cleitophon). Modern interpreters are right to focus on Thrasymachus's strong-mindedness but perhaps wrong to blame Thrasymachus for depriving them of the Socratic discussion of the legal positivist thesis.[26] Indeed, Thrasymachus's dismissal of that thesis is the price to be paid for the opening of a debate that will extend through the entire *Republic* and beyond, until the last dialogues of Plato's career (*Timaeus, Critias,* and the *Laws*), namely, the debate between the rigor of philosophical and political distinctions and the play of mimesis.

Thrasymachus's answer gives an important indication as to the meaning of *akribeia.* There cannot be any question of a ruler mistaking his own interest, he maintains, because qua ruler he is never mistaken (340d–e). In a general way, "according to a strict logic [*kata ton akribē logon*], no craftsman [*demiourgos*] is ever mistaken" (340e).[27] A ruler is here conceived as an ideal craftsman flawlessly performing his own proper task or function or work (*ergon*).[28] He is exactly what an essential definition authorizes him to be. Any departure from the ideal is fatal for his right to carry the name of ruler. There is plenty of evidence, not only in Plato's dialogues but in other texts perpetuating the legend of Socrates, that this argument is Socratic (rather than Thrasymachean).[29] That it is, nevertheless, generally attributed to Thrasymachus in the commentaries on the *Republic* seems to result from his acting as the initiator of the argument. When Socrates says that "[Thrasymachus] came at us like a wild beast, seeking to devour us" (336b), we should perhaps think of his theatrical skill, of his art of pretense, rather than of the "brutality of Thrasymachus" (Jowett) or "*brutalité de Thrasymaque*" (Léon Robin).[30] It is a very peculiar kind

26. See, for example, R. C. Cross and A. D. Woozley, *Plato's "Republic": A Philosophical Commentary* (London: Macmillan Education, 1964), 43ff.

27. My translation.

28. For a discussion of Socrates' requirements as to τέχνη and its ἀκρίβεια, see David Roochnik, "Socrates' Rhetorical Attack on Rhetoric," in *The Third Way: New Directions in Platonic Studies,* ed. Francisco J. Gonzales (Lanham, Md.: Rowman and Littlefield, 1995), 81–94.

29. Thrasymachus is taken by Socrates, and by most interpreters of the dialogue, to be not only amoral à la Callicles or Nietzsche but also an ἀλαζών, a pretender, boasting of his knowledge, comparable to such standard Platonic characters as Euthyphro, Hippias or Ion. The refutation of his thesis is also a model of Socratic elenchus. Thrasymachus is, as Jowett puts it in one of his marginal notes, "assailed with his own weapons" and vanquished (602). In fact, Thrasymachus's "own weapon," the method of rigorously defining the terms involved, would have been associated in the mind of the first readers or listeners of the dialogue with Socrates' name. Aristophanes' *Clouds,* for example, would have justified such an association. Cf. also Aristotle's assessment of the historical Socrates' role in the development of logic (note 5 above) and Timon's reference to Socrates as an "inventor of rigorous arguments" ("ἀκριβολόγους ἀποφήνας") in Diogenes Laertius, *Lives of Eminent Philosophers,* 2 vols., Greek/English text, trans. R. D. Hicks (1925; rpt., Cambridge Mass.: Harvard University Press, 1925), 1:150–51. Were there any doubt, Thrasymachus "himself" dispels it by his "since your method is so rigorous [ἐπειδὴ καὶ σὺ ἀκριβολογῇ]" (340e [my translation; Jowett gives "since you are such a lover of accuracy," 18]).

30. *The "Republic" of Plato,* trans. Benjamin Jowett, 12 and 12n; Plato, *Oeuvres Complètes,* trans. Léon Robin and M.-J. Moreau (Paris: Gallimard, 1950), 882 n. 1.

of pretense: not only a pretense not to pretend, to be genuinely himself, but a pretense to foster a method that would exclude pretending altogether. A pretense to end all pretenses.

Is Thrasymachus's play really devoid of seriousness, though? It is certainly tempting to take it as a serious questioning of the philosophy of justice, a critique of any attempt to define exactly the concept of justice and thus a critique of the ideology of political theory.[31] Does not, indeed, an attempt to define the notion of justice in an abstract way often amount to an indifference toward actual injustice, formally condemned but actually condoned because it falls short of the ideal and is hence "unreal"? Thrasymachus is almost certainly sarcastic both in his definition and in his praise of the rigorous method of discussion. His mock-rigorous definition of justice and his argumentation attempt to show that there is no justice in the actual world of political praxis and that it is futile to require a logical precision in dealing with that world.[32]

The method of the strict semantic definition of analyzed terms is most willingly taken over by Socrates and hammered at relentlessly until Thrasymachus's thesis is demolished, that is, proven to be self-contradictory (and eventually the formal definition of justice is forged in the fourth book). In the structure of the city-state, a strict semantic rule commands the rigid separation between different professions such as physician and businessman. It is "just" for a ruler in the *polis* to "minister" to all citizens, because such ministering is what properly determines the function (*ergon*) of a politician and distinguishes it from all others. This law stems directly from the general rule of semantic accuracy, that is, from the rejection of any ambiguity in naming. Logic and ontology seem to have precedence here over moral, political, or legal matters. All things, claims Socrates with the approbation of all listeners, including the reticent Thrasymachus, are defined in their being by their proper *ergon*. They do not properly exist if they do not conform to their self-identical nature. A knife, for instance, is a knife only to the extent that it can perform the function of

---

31. W. K. C. Guthrie does recognize Thrasymachus's concern with the problem of justice, but he interprets his behavior not as a playful critique of the theory of justice but as an expression of genuine anger with the actual state of affairs in contemporary politics (*A History of Greek Philosophy*, 6 vols. [Cambridge: Cambridge University Press, 1962–81], 3:91ff., 297–98).

32. Aristotle might have been thinking of Thrasymachus when in the first book of the *Nicomachean Ethics* (1094b23–27; cf. 1097a26–28) he disputed the requirement of a mathematical precision in moral and political, that is, practical, "rhetorical" matters: "For the educated person seeks exactness in each area to the extent that the nature of the subject allows; for apparently it is just as mistaken to demand demonstrations from a rhetorician as it is to accept [merely] persuasive arguments from a mathematician" (*Nicomachean Ethics*, trans. Terence Irwin, 2nd ed. [Indianapolis, Ind.: Hackett, 1999], 2 [Greek: "πεπαιδευμένου γάρ ἐστιν ἐπὶ τοσοῦτον τἀκριβὲς ἐπιζητεῖν καθ' ἕκαστον γένος, ἐφ' ὅσον ἡ τοῦ πράγματος φύσις ἐπιδέχεται· παραπλήσιον γὰρ φαίνεται μαθηματικοῦ τε πιθανολογοῦντος ἀποδέχεσθαι καὶ ῥητορικὸν ἀποδείξεις ἀπαιτεῖν"]).

cutting. A bad doctor is not a doctor at all; only as an effective healer can he pretend to that name. A shepherd is a shepherd by his function of guardian-ship, the function of caring for sheep. By the same token, a politician, a ruler, a (wo)man in power—"the stronger" in Thrasymachus's idiom—cannot but tend to the interest of the ruled to the exclusion of her or his own interest. Thus, Thrasymachus's definition of justice as the interest of the stronger col-lapses once its key term, "the stronger," which distinguishes it from Socrates' own definition, is *rigorously* understood.[33]

The result of the discussion in the first book seems totally negative: no work-able definition of justice has been reached. Socrates underscores this in his conclusion. However, the agreement concerning the requirement of semantic and ontological rigor in a philosophical inquiry, established in the agon with Thrasymachus, already points to the positive definition of justice that will eventually be formulated in the fourth book. This definition will be but an application of the general principle of *akribeia* to the political structure of the state and to the division of the human soul. Politics and psychology will be inscribed into the logic of self-identical terms, expressed in rigorous defini-tions.[34] Justice, the cardinal virtue in the state as well as in the soul, will be vir-tually identified with the virtue of formal reasoning.

But before the rule of *akribeia* is reformulated in the fourth book of the *Republic* as the principle of identity and the rule of justice, a long detour is made into the art Thrasymachus is particularly interested in, that of the actor and rhapsode. In fact, the famous investigation into the nature of the cardi-nal virtues in the state is launched by Glaucon's *advocatus diaboli* argument, in which the advantages of "hypocrisy," or acting in politics, are depicted. To defend justice against clear injustice is relatively easy, says Glaucon, joined soon by his brother Adeimantus; to defend it against injustice that successfully *pretends* to be justice is another matter. A vexed ontological question of being and seeming here joins the issue of the truth of moral judgment. Socrates' task, imposed on him by Glaucon and Adeimantus, will be to show the superiority of the just life independently of appearances, as well as the *eudaimonia* or hap-piness of a truly just (wo)man.

The word that will designate henceforth the rhapsodic appearance, preten-sion, make-believe—*mimēsis*—associated with Thrasymachus appears for the first time in the discussion of the so-called luxurious city-state in the second book (372dff.). The increase of wealth and the growing complexity of social

33. See *Republic* 339a.
34. The "logic of the logos" in Jean-Pierre Vernant's sense (*Myth and Society in Ancient Greece,* trans. Janet Lloyd [New York: Zone Books, 1990], 260 [French: *Mythe et société en Grèce ancienne* (Paris: François Maspero, 1974), 250]).

life require, in distinction to a simple "city of pigs," a system of protection against the enemy from the outside and against "rebellious characters" inside the luxurious city. Education, especially the education of guardians—soldiers, policemen, rulers—is to be the cornerstone of such a system of protection. The problem of the role of mimesis and play arises here, since a host of hypocritical imitators (*mimētai*), "poets and their assistants—reciters-rhapsodes, actors, dancers, producers" (373b), is thriving in the luxurious city.[35] They are the traditional educators of the Greeks but also, in Socrates' view, pretenders and teachers of pretense; they seem to further the supreme injustice described by Glaucon and Adeimantus in their opening address. The dilemma is serious not only because of a possible conflict with the tradition but especially because of the theoretical difficulties involved in the task of separating education (*paideia*) from mimesis as play (*paidia*).

Paid(e)ia: Rigor and Play in Education

As a matter of fact we, it would seem, do not find in war, either as existing or as likely to exist, either real play or education worthy of the name, which is what we assert to be in our eyes the most serious thing.

—ATHENIAN STRANGER

Callistos: Did you like the play, Plato?—Deximenes: Did you like it?—Mantias [the politician]: No, I never do.—Deximenes: Why do you go then?—Mantias: One must keep an eye on the theatre, it's an influence.

—IRIS MURDOCH

The words *paideia* and *paidia* differ little: by one letter only (the resemblance owes, of course, to their common etymology).[36] It is rigorous knowledge that distinguishes the program of philosophical education crafted in Plato's *Republic* from the traditional Athenian *paideia*. The latter relies too much, for Socrates' taste, on the rhapsodic play of mimesis. Mimesis is, indeed, play par excellence, according to the Elean Stranger in Plato's *Sophist;* no other play is "more artistic" or "graceful."[37] In the *Republic* it is the possession of knowledge, the knowledge of ideal models or types, that qualifies the founders of the city-state, and subsequently the ruler-philosophers, to regulate the role of mimesis

35. *Plato: The "Republic,"* trans. Tom Griffith, 56; translation modified.
    36. The first epigraph to this section comes from Plato's *Laws* 803d (vol. II of Plato, *Works,* trans. R. G. Bury [Cambridge, Mass.: Harvard University Press, 1926], 55 [Greek "τὸ δ᾽ ἦν ἐν πολέμῳ μὲν ἄρα οὔτ᾽ οὖν παιδιὰ πεφυκυῖα οὔτ᾽ αὖ παιδεία ποτὲ ἡμῖν ἀξιόλογος, οὔτε οὖσα οὔτ᾽ ἐσομένη, ὃ δή φαμεν ἡμῖν γε εἶναι σπουδαιότατον"]). The second epigraph is from Murdoch's "Art and Eros: A Dialogue about Art," in Iris Murdoch, *Acastos: Two Platonic Dialogues* (London: Chatto and Windus, 1986), 11–12.
    37. *Sophist* 234b (*The Dialogues of Plato,* trans. Benjamin Jowett, 4:361).

or play in education (378e–379a).[38] The guardians of the ideal state are permitted a restricted exercise of dramatic mimesis only if they are able to distinguish in reality various types of citizens according to their social status. In
other words, they should not transgress the limits of play, or rather of the
game, and its rules. The impersonation of characters that depart from the
model of a guardian may be allowed exceptionally, in jest—only as a playful
supplement to the otherwise serious business of the formation and preservation
of the guardians' own virtuous character (396c–e). The phrase "in jest" (*paidias
kharin*) implies, nevertheless, that there can be such a thing as a "serious" imitation of other, improper characters and consequently a serious play.

This possibility of a serious play (*mimeisthai spoudēi* [397a]) alarms Socrates,
for at this point in the discussion (the middle of the third book) he probably
has a good idea of what the final definition of justice will be: a strict separation of faculties in the soul and of professions and classes in the state. This
stress on the principle of methodological, semantic, and political rigor (*akribeia*),
laboriously established in the debate with Thrasymachus in the first book
and referred to several times in books 2 and 3 (e.g., 370b–c, 374a, 395b–c,
397e), does not leave any doubt as to Socrates' concerns. It is a nightmare
for him to see the very principle of justice questioned daily by poets, actors,
sophists and their pupils, the politicians. He fears that mimesis might be taken
all too seriously, not "only in jest." But is such a thing as "mere play" or "proper
play" possible in the first place? Does not play always threaten to "degen-
erate" into seriousness? Is not "more at stake" (some languages employ the
word "play" explicitly here, e.g., the French "être en jeu" or the German "auf
dem Spiel stehen") whenever the status of rhapsodic or theatrical mimesis is
in question? And would not this be the difference between education combined with play and simple indoctrination combined with the illusion (obliv-
ious of its *ludic* etymology) of being able to keep play strictly, and safely,
circumscribed?

Philosophical *paideia* in Plato is apparently not (mere) play (*paidia*) and
always has to be taken "seriously." The education of children (*hē paidōn tro-
phē*) in particular should never become, according to the Athenian in Plato's
Laws (766a), a secondary (*deuteron*) or merely supplementary issue (*parergon*).
His fellow countryman, Socrates, would not disagree, of course. *Paideia* is certainly not considered to be a *parergon* in the *Republic,* although it might seem
so, given the way it is introduced in the second book: "How are the guardians to
be reared and educated?" asks Socrates, "and would the answer to this question

---

38. The possession of knowledge is also supposed to reduce the danger of mimesis in general (*Republic* 595b).

contribute [*prourgou estin*] to the success of the principal inquiry into the origin of justice and injustice in the State?" (376c–d).[39] The answer to the second question is an unequivocal "yes." The examination of *paideia* is useful and important—"functional" (*prourgou*)—to the problem of political justice. The expression *prourgou* (= *pro-ergou*, "as an essentially contributing factor"), which appears twice in this context, is not equivalent to *par-ergon*. Although it indicates, just as the *parergon* does, a relation to the essential function, expressed in a rigorous definition—here the foundation of the ideal political order—it does not connote marginality, and it also does not suggest the possibility of challenging the main issue, that is, the order of the *ergon*, which always belongs, even if it is not always premeditated, to the logic of the *parergon*.[40] The rigorous, "ergonal" character of the ideal philosophical education of the guardians is confirmed later in the dialogue when Socrates criticizes traditional Athenian *paideia* because of its treatment of philosophy as a *parergon* (498a).

The first task of philosophical *paideia*, as Socrates presents it in the second and third books of the *Republic*, seems to be the reassertion of "ergonal" rigor and the suppression of any possible manifestation of "parergonality," especially in the extreme form of dramatic mimesis or play that might jeopardize the proper functioning of the state. Indeed, *parergon* is the word used by Socrates when describing the violation of the rule "one man, one job," ratified later in the dialogue as the rule of justice. No citizen of an ideal city-state should divide her or his attention between different tasks (*erga*), lest they all become neglected as *parerga* (370b), as additional, supplementary occupations: "The work [will] be more easily and better done, when every man is set free from all other occupations to do, at the right time, the one thing for which he is naturally fitted" (370c; cf. 374b–c and 397e).[41] Paradoxically, even play needs some rigorous specialization. No one can become a good player of draughts or dice, if she or he treats her or his discipline as *parergon* (*parergōi khrōmenos* [374c]). Thus, the experience of "professional players"—those who make a living out of mimesis (poets, rhapsodes, actors)—seems to support the rule "one citizen, one *ergon*"; they too tend to specialize in their otherwise parergonal work:

> "Doesn't the same argument also hold for imitation—the same man isn't able to imitate many things as well as one?"

39. My translation.
40. See Jacques Derrida, "Parergon," in Jacques Derrida, *The Truth in Painting*, trans. Geoff Bennington and Ian McLeod (Chicago: University of Chicago Press, 1987), 15–147, esp. 73–80 (French: *La vérité en peinture* [Paris: Flammarion, 1978], 21–168).
41. *The "Republic" of Plato*, trans. Francis M. Cornford (1941; rpt., London: Oxford University Press, 1961), 57.

"No, he isn't."

"Then," I said, "he'll hardly pursue any of the noteworthy activities while at the same time imitating many things and being a skilled imitator. For even in two kinds of imitation that seem close to one another, like writing comedy and tragedy, the same men aren't capable of producing good imitations in both at the same time . . . Nor are they able to be rhapsodes and actors at the same time."

"True."

"Nor are the same actors, you know, able to do both comic and tragic imitations."

(394e–395a)[42]

There is even a further specialization within a particular genre; for example, the same actor will not successfully represent many characters.[43] In order to succeed, even actors and playwrights—who should apparently avoid any restriction of their range and preserve their mimetic versatility—in practice limit themselves to one mode, thespic or rhapsodic, to one genre, tragedy or comedy, to one *emploi,* or feature, and make of it their only art, their *ergon.*[44]

The rule of the division of labor becomes the rule of justice when an *ergon* becomes the mark of a class distinction, for example, the art of war, the proper occupation of the guardians (*to tōn phulakōn ergon* [374d–e]). Warfare apparently requires from the guardians a total commitment in order to be well performed. In fact, the profession of a soldier in an ideal city-state is also to *be* the *ergon,* the basic function of a member of the dominant class. Thus, the opposition *ergon/parergon* will not only be a consequence of the principle of a division of labor resulting from a simple empirical observation but also, or rather *principally* (in the intrinsic logical system of the *Republic*), the repercussion of the theory of onto-logical and political rigor. The distinction between farmers, craftsmen, and tradesmen on the one hand and the class of warriors (from which the class of philosopher-kings will later be culled) on the other hand appears as a politically crucial corollary of the *ergon/parergon* polarity of *akribeia.* And *akribeia* and *mimēsis,* two notions that have pointed to each other ever since Thrasymachus's "performance" at the outset of the *Republic's* conversation, are explicitly brought together in Socrates' effort to set apart from all the others the dominant class of the state: "If, then, we are to preserve the first argument—that our guardians must give up all other crafts and become

---

42. *The "Republic" of Plato,* trans. Allan Bloom, 2nd ed. (New York: Basic Books, 1991), 73; translation modified.

43. Cf. Cornford's translation-interpretation of this passage in his *The "Republic" of Plato,* 82.

44. Cf. Socrates' playful variation on this theme at the end of Plato's *Symposium.*

craftsmen of the State's freedom in a rigorous sense [*panu akribeis*], and engaging in no work which does not bear on this end—they also must not do [*prattein*] or imitate [*mimeisthai*] anything else" (395b–c).[45] Since, however, imitating one's own character and function is hardly an imitation, the guardians will always *do* their job. The strict separation of classes in the well-governed state, especially the formation of the ruling class of guardians, leads necessarily to the dismissal of mimesis as harmful to their *ergon* and hence to their status.

Education is called for to guarantee the ideological recognition of the theoretical—professional and sociopolitical—order. Indeed, the responsibility of *paideia* consists in the formation of perfectly distinct characters (*ēthē*), that is, of pure models or "impresses" (*tupoi*) corresponding to the distinct groups of society: women and men, slaves and free citizens, farmers, craftsmen, warriors and rulers, that is, the "types" necessary for making gender, trade, and especially class distinctions.[46] This responsibility may be described as the production of "ideology," or, more precisely, the impression of types, that is, "typography."[47] The members of each class and profession must be prepared for the task (*ergon*) they are to accomplish for the commonwealth. This task will define the type of social activity they are to engage in and distinguish it from all others. Once "engraved," a type or character will have a tendency to last forever.[48] The emphasis on the education of young children is justified by this durability of the *tupos* "stamped" in the beginning:

> "Don't you know that the beginning [*arkhē*] is the most important part of every work [*ergon*] and that this is especially so with anything young and tender? For at that stage it is most plastic, and each thing assimilates itself to the model [*tupos*] whose stamp anyone wishes to give to it."
> "Quite so," he said.
>
> (377a–b)[49]

In the traditional process of education, this *arkhē*, which also means "principle," is constituted by fables and legends (*muthoi*), which are responsible for

---

45. *The "Republic" of Plato*, trans. Allan Bloom, 73–74; translation modified.

46. The "typical" character of gender will be, however, questioned in book 5 of the *Republic* (451b–457b). On class distinctions, see in particular *Republic* 377a–b, 379a and *Republic* 398b, 400d–402d, and passim.

47. The term adopted by Philippe Lacoue-Labarthe in "Typography," in his *Typography: Mimesis, Philosophy, Politics*, ed. and trans. Christopher Fynsk (1989; rpt., Stanford, Calif.: Stanford University Press, 1998), 43–138 (French: "Typographie," in Sylviane Agacinski et al., *Mimesis des()articulations* [Paris: Aubier-Flammarion, 1975], 165–270).

48. "Engraving" is, in fact, the primary meaning of the Greek χαρακτήρ.

49. *The "Republic" of Plato*, trans. Allan Bloom, 54.

implementing and sanctioning the political structure of the state. The ideological function of myths is to be preserved in the philosophical education of
children in the ideal republic; the awareness of its importance will lead to state
control over education and in particular to the censorship of literary production. It is the knowledge of ideal models (*to tous tupous eidenai*) that will enable
one to become a censor: "You and I aren't poets right now but founders of the
city," says Socrates to his companions, and "[it] is appropriate for founders *to
know the models* according to which the poets must tell their tales" (378e–379a).[50]
Socrates assumes here the possession of "typographical knowledge." In the
ideal city-state, this knowledge will be deposited in a special class of experts
who will be able to recognize both the proper models of social behavior and
the educational tools appropriate to producing and enforcing them. The special concern of the designers of the ideal constitution with the *tupos* of the
guardian, both warrior and lover of learning (*philomathēs*) or lover of wisdom
(*philosophos*), is the consequence of her or his position as a guarantor of the
tradition, a guarantor of the political structure perpetuated through the state-
controlled mythology.

The overall *formal pattern* of Greek *paideia,* its division, its hierarchical
order, the general use of myths, and so forth is highly praised by Socrates:
"What is this education to be, then? Perhaps we shall hardly invent a system
better than the one which long experience has worked out, with two branches
for the cultivation of the mind [*mousikē*] and of the body [*gumnastikē*]"
(376e).[51] But what role will the play of mimesis play in the philosophical education of the ideal city-state? Is mimesis not an important part of traditional
Athenian education, not so much because of the Dionysian theatrical festivals
but mainly because of the institution of rhapsodes "performing" the poems they
read and the general dramatizing of educational texts? Is mimesis not, on the
other hand, the "quintessentially parergonal" activity challenging the rule of
"one citizen, one *ergon*"? Does it not threaten to produce not only the appearance of justice but injustice "itself"? Does it not threaten to create a "rebellious
character," ready to imperil the stability of the state? "Thus, the one—I mean
the rebellious character [*to aganaktētikon*]—thrives on countless disparate
impersonations [*pollēn mimēsin kai poikilēn ekhei*], whereas the wise and composed character, always coinciding almost perfectly with himself, is not easy
to imitate or to appreciate when imitated, especially at a public festival when
a promiscuous crowd is assembled in a theater" (604e).[52]

50. *The "Republic" of Plato,* trans. Allan Bloom, 56; my emphasis.
51. *The "Republic" of Plato,* trans. Francis M. Cornford, 68.
52. *The "Republic" of Plato,* trans. Benjamin Jowett, 319; translation modified.

A promiscuous and unruly crowd assembled in a theater and, on the stage, a rhapsodic, "hypocritical" play defying the rigorous hierarchy of types—this is, of course, a potentially anarchic situation threatening to promote the sophistic, Thrasymachean understanding (and possibly critique) of justice as the function of the established power ("the interest of the stronger").

Socrates' Rhapsodic Mode: Literary Genres and Political Types

What Plato catches a glimpse of, but immediately reduces to a "literary" problem, is that discourses would not have any fictioning power if dramatization were not inscribed in discoursing as a constant possibility (indeed, as its very pre-supposition), thus opening the space of "subjective" exchange and substitution—the entire space of mimetism.

—PHILIPPE LACOUE-LABARTHE

Socrates is certainly aware of the danger mimesis poses to "typographical" education, and so he attempts to reduce it.[53] Remarkably, it is a theory of literature—a classification of modes and genres—that founds the constitutional stipulations meant to guarantee the seriousness and rigor of ideal education. Socrates distinguishes three modes of expression or style (*lexeis*) and three corresponding genres: simple narration (*haplē diēgēsis*), characteristic of a dithyramb; (dramatic) *mimēsis*, proper to tragedy and comedy; and the rhapsodic mixture of the two, which is the style of the Homeric epics.[54] The apparently simple grammatical opposition between indirect and direct discourse (the priest Chryses said he wanted his daughter back; he said, "I want my daughter back") becomes, in the context of the theory of justice in the *Republic*, the all-important opposition between respect and disrespect for the established political structure. Indeed, simple diegesis maintains a distance between the speaker and the hero of his or her narrative, whereas impersonation, in particular the impersonation of a member of another order or class, say, a priest or a king, opens up the possibility of "simulating" any social type (*pan panti homoioun* of Plato's *Phaedrus* 261e) and thus questioning the religious and secular hierarchy.[55] Literary theory and in particular the restricting of narrative to the

53. The epigraph to this section comes from "Typography," 133; translation modified (French: "Ce que Platon entrevoit, mais réduit immédiatement à un problème 'littéraire,' c'est que les discours n'auraient aucun pouvoir fictionnant, si la dramatisation ne se marquait pas dans le discourir comme une possibilité constante (voire comme sa présupposition même), ouvrant par là l'espace de l'échange et de la substitution 'subjectifs,' qui est tout l'espace du mimétisme" ["Typographie," 264]).

54. An analysis developed in Aristotle's *Poetics* 1448a19–23 and in modern studies of narratology; see, for example, Gérard Genette, *Narrative Discourse: An Essay in Method*, trans. Jane E. Lewin (Ithaca, N.Y.: Cornell University Press, 1980), 162ff. (French: "Discours du récit," in Gérard Genette, *Figures 3* [Paris: Seuil, 1972], 184ff.).

55. On the play of the sophistic, mimetic "assimilation," see Martin Heidegger, *Plato's "Sophist,"* trans. Richard Rojcewicz and André Schuwer (Bloomington: Indiana University Press, 1997), 226–27, 263–64

indirect style have a definite political function: to support the theory and practice of social justice and to guide philosophical, "typographical" education.[56]

The discussion of literary genres in the third book of the *Republic* is often considered incidental to the main development of the argument—a part of the appraisal of contemporary Greek education. It is also read independently, as Plato's contribution to the study of literary style and linguistic expression (*lexis*) in general, and then usually compared to the apparently similar considerations in Aristotle's *Poetics*. Such is, for example, Genette's approach to this text in his provocative essay "Boundaries of Narrative."[57] The essay is provocative because it questions the meaning of Socrates' basic distinction between simple narration and mimesis, or play. The latter, considered by Socrates a source of troubles in the education of guardians, is limited and eventually excluded from the ideal republic. Now, for Genette it is precisely narration—*diēgēsis*—that is "mimetic" in a true sense, in other words, troublesome (and hence "interesting") because it involves the problem of the relationship between two levels of reality: the linguistic and the extralinguistic ("thingly"). Dramatic mimesis, on the other side, constitutes a perfect reproduction, a simple repetition of the words actually or supposedly pronounced.[58] There is no gap between what has been said, or is imagined to have been said, and its exact quotation. This is possible because the medium of representation is, exceptionally, homogeneous with what is represented: both belong to language. In the case of simple diegesis, however, there is no such homogeneity and hence a gap is unavoidable. In Genette's theory, this gap is precisely the phenomenon of imitation: "If poetic imitation is considered to be the verbal representation of a nonverbal reality, and in certain cases of a verbal reality . . . , then imitation must be found in the five narrative verses [Homer, *Iliad,* I, 12–16] but not in the five dramatic verses [*Iliad,* I, 17–21]. These dramatic verses consist simply of interpolating in the middle of a text representing events another text drawn directly from these events."[59] The words called "mimetic" by Socrates are in fact an exact replica of the priest Chryses's words as imagined by Homer; they

---

(German: *Platon: "Sophistes,"* in *Gesamtausgabe,* 102 vols. to date [Frankfurt am Main: Klostermann, 1975–], 19:326–28, 380–81).

56. At the outset of the tenth book Socrates points to this theory as the most valuable result of the whole discussion (595a).

57. "Boundaries of Narrative," trans. Ann Levonas, *New Literary History* 8, no. 1 (1976): 1–13 (French: "Frontières du récit," in Roland Barthes et al., *L'analyse structurale du récit* (1966; rpt., Paris: Seuil, 1981), 158–69).

58. "Boundaries of Narrative," 1– 2 (French: "Frontières du récit," 160).

59. "Boundaries of Narrative," 3–4 (French: "Frontières du récit," 160–61). In comparing the narrative to the dramatic verses, Genette reinterprets the example taken by Socrates in the third book of Plato's *Republic*.

are perfectly identical. But perfect identity is not imitation at all, says Genette; it is "the thing itself" (*la chose même*). Hence the paradoxical conclusion that "the only imitation is the imperfect one. *Mimesis* is *diegesis* [*Mimēsis c'est diēgēsis*]."[60] Thus, having begun his essay with Aristotle's neutral theoretical distinction in the *Poetics* between two kinds of imitating (*mimeisthai*)—through narration (*apangellonta*) and through direct representation of acting characters (*hōs prattontas kai energountas tous mimoumenous* [1448a19–23])—Genette, by opposing radically simple diegesis and mimesis and excluding the latter, concludes as dramatically as Socrates in the third book of the *Republic*. The reason for exclusion is, however, exactly the reverse: it is narration which is troublesome, mysterious (this is the sense of *mimēsis* in the final formula) and hence theoretically interesting; dramatic mimesis or direct speech, on the other hand, as an exact copy (facsimile) of the real, does not present any interest for the literary theory of representation.

Genette's argument rests on a strict opposition between the pure modes of literary expression: mimesis and simple diegesis. In fact, however, this polarity is difficult to maintain, as is the distinction between linguistic and extralinguistic reality that founds it, which Genette takes over from Aristotle without discussing its foundations and its implications. Plato's Socrates does not himself, in fact, uphold the opposition between mimesis and simple diegesis with Aristotle's or Genette's rigor. He immediately mitigates it by introducing the mixed mode of expression (a notion practically cast aside by Genette, as his correction of Socrates—"a mixed mode, or more precisely an alternating mode"— indicates) and the corresponding genre (epic).[61] And, although Socrates and his interlocutors accept the narrative mode and the corresponding genre, dithyramb, they do not devote much time to discussing them at length; nor do they consider the mimetic mode as such or the genres of tragedy and comedy, which are in principle rejected. They examine in detail only the rhapsodic mode of expression and the literary genre of epic. Dramatic mimesis is discussed in the framework of this analysis. The avoidance of the "extreme" cases clearly marks Plato's preference for the rhapsodic mode and mixed genre, in which the purest genres and modes interact—*play, interplay*—with each other.

Indeed, the whole operation of setting the limits of literary modes and genres in the framework of political constitution and education takes place in a dialogue that is itself an example of a rhapsodic mode and mixed genre.[62] In

60. "Boundaries of Narrative," 5 (French: "Frontières du récit," 162).
61. "Boundaries of Narrative," 2 (French: "Frontières du récit," 159).
62. Cf. Diskin Clay's notion of the "open dialogue" with its quasi-rhapsodic rings in the *Republic* ("Reading the *Republic*," in *Platonic Writings/Platonic Readings*, ed. Charles L. Griswold Jr. [New York: Routledge, 1988], 19–33).

a way, the theoretical division and its evaluation are not only stated but also performed. Socrates, the narrator, is not an impassive reporter but rather a rhapsode: a *metteur en scène* and a character in a performance that calls into question the very distinctions it introduces. In the first book, for example, having made Thrasymachus speak in the direct style of dramatic mimesis ("Yes," "it seems so," "it looks like it," etc.), Socrates declares that the report was actually inexact: "[Thrasymachus] conceded all these points, but not in the engaging way I have just described" (350c–d).[63] The assertions did not change, but they are now included in the problematic realm of rhapsodic play, and the reader realizes that they have always been problematic. Upon rereading, she or he considers them differently, and so it is with all other apparently "citational" assertions. Pure mimesis has been marked by diegesis and vice versa. The rigorous categories and distinctions of the theory of literature reinforced in the state constitution prove untenable in the literary praxis of the *Republic*. The awareness of the danger of a reciprocal "contamination" between the two modes of literary expression is perhaps the reason for Socrates' eventual dismissal of all poetry and mimesis, dramatic or not (606–608). Thus, the "imperfection" mentioned by Genette ("the only imitation is the imperfect one") would consist, rather, in the impossibility of isolating a pure citation of the "real" ("*res ipsa,* la chose même").[64]

The final decision of the *Republic* does not cancel the drama of the dialogue. Socrates, the champion of the "justice" of rigorous separation between "types," is in fact himself a rhapsode, a "pantomimic gentleman" (398a), impersonating all the characters of the dialogue: Cephalus, Polemarchus, Thrasymachus, Cleitophon, Adeimantus, Glaucon, and "himself."[65] He is at the same time the leading character and the narrator, giving "voice" to all the others, including "Thrasymachus" and "Plato."[66] He *does* his job in the sense of *prattein,* or practicing, but also in the sense of *poiein,* or contriving, fabricating (395c), and *plays* with the polarity playful/serious in order to distinguish "good" (or at least "accepted") from "bad" mimesis. Later in the dialogue, when Socrates apologizes for not having been playful enough in his discussion of education

63. *Plato: The "Republic,"* trans. Tom Griffith, 31.

64. "Boundaries of Narrative," 5 (French: "Frontières du récit," 162). Bertolt Brecht's "Platonic theater" will question precisely such a notion of the character's statement as "the thing itself"; the Brechtian actor will at once narrate (*erzählen*) and represent, impersonate, play (*darstellen*) a character ("A Short Organum for the Theatre," in *Brecht on Theatre,* ed. and trans. John Willett [New York: Hill and Wang, 1964], 194 [German: "Kleines Organon für das Theater," in Bertolt Brecht, *Schriften zum Theater* 2: *Gesammelte Werke,* vol. 16 (Frankfurt am Main: Suhrkamp, 1963–64), 684–85]).

65. For the phrase "pantomimic gentleman," see *The "Republic" of Plato,* trans. Benjamin Jowett, 83 (Greek: "ἀνὴρ δυνάμενος ὑπὸ σοφίας παντοδαπὸς γίγνεσθαι καὶ μιμεῖσθαι πάντα χρήματα").

66. Lacoue-Labarthe discusses the question of the subject (of literary expression) in "Typography," 121–22 (French: "Typographie," 252).

(536c)—we could also say "as education," given the role played by the *Republic* in Plato's Academy and more generally in the Western academy—he explicitly asserts the importance of the ludic element, that is, of dramatic mimesis, in raising children (*paizontas trephein* [537a]). Indeed, the theoretical distinction between simple narration and mimesis does not obtain in practice since one of its terms, mimesis (or play), permeates all literary practice, all ideological practice, for that matter. Elements of dramatic mimesis are found even in an apparently pure narrative, since the narrator himself may be considered a character, a fictional voice—a typographical, ideological character. How different the *Republic* would have been if it had been told by the rhapsode Thrasymachus instead of the rhapsode Socrates![67]

Since strict formal criteria (*hōs lekteon*) are insufficient to discriminate between modes and genres, much less rigorous considerations of the content (*ha lekteon*) of literary texts have to supplement them (398b). Thus, in order to determine a program of ideal philosophical education, a detailed censorship has to be enforced. The subtle theoretical considerations of literary modes and genres fail to account for the play of mimesis because mimesis is inherently ambivalent. Both that which makes it "bad" and that which makes it "good" fall on the same side of apparently clear dichotomies such as that between the dramatic and the narrative or between the playful and the serious. No one can deny the ideological power of a serious imitation; nothing is better suited to the task of shaping the characters and social types required for the functioning of a particular political system than playing the hero, the role model. At the same time, however, mimesis always threatens to become truly dramatic and rhapsodic, both playful and serious, questioning the legitimacy of established—moral, religious, and sociopolitical—hierarchies.[68]

To be sure, a rigorous classification of the modes of expressions and of literary genres was particularly difficult to ascertain in the Greek system of education where, even at the historical stage of dominant literacy, the transmission of culture was essentially performed by professional readers-performers, rhapsodes (*rhapsōidoi*), who determined the usual, also "private," way of reading literary texts. However, this rhapsodic mode of ancient Greek education in fact illustrates particularly well the ideological character of any culture.[69] The

67. Even the "I" of an author cannot be exempted from dramatic, mimetic interpellation; see, for example, Aryeh L. Kosman, "Acting: Drama as the *Mimēsis* of *Praxis*," in *Essays on Aristotle's "Poetics,"* ed. Amélie Oksenberg Rorty (Princeton, N.J.: Princeton University Press, 1992), 56.

68. As, for example, in Euripides' *Electra* 367–400, where a break of an assumed hierarchical difference between kings and peasants leads to the questioning of the possibility of a rigorous standard (ἀκριβές) in the matter of moral and social values (εὐανδρία).

69. See Althusser's characterization of ideology as "eternal" and "theatrical" in his "Ideology and Ideological State Apparatuses," in Louis Althusser, *Lenin and Philosophy and Other Essays,* trans. Ben Brewster

production of the dominant social types can hardly avoid the mimetic process of imitating role models, of emulating the outstanding members of the same class, or those of another class considered higher in a serious play. To the extent that it is dramatic, poetic creation (*poiēsis*) reflects this mechanism, making it remarkable and astounding (*thaumaston* [398a]). Despite Socrates' ostensible effort to keep them apart in the (ideal) republic, education and the play of mimesis appear inextricably interwoven in the process of philosophical and political rhapsodic *paid(e)ia*.

The Fictioning of the Subject and the Mimetic Crisis

> However, read "Plato": you will see that writing *works.*
> —PHILIPPE LACOUE-LABARTHE

It is truth that should set apart *paideia* from *paidia.*[70] But we can hardly refer to an unquestioned notion of truth after Heidegger's work in this domain, in particular, his claim about the radical transformation of the notion of truth in Plato's *Republic.*[71] Heidegger's definition of (the work of) art as the setting-itself-to-work of truth (*das Ins-Werk-Setzen der Wahrheit*) constitutes the most radical questioning of Socrates' opposition between philosophy/truth and poetry/mimesis in the *Republic.*[72] But Heidegger's study is based on the ontology of the so-called allegory of the cave at the beginning of book 7 in the *Republic* and that of book 10.[73] He does not refer either to the rhapsodic mimesis of book 3 or to the psychology of books 4 and 9. On the other hand, Girard's thesis of the connection between the mimetic crisis of desire and religious as well as political violence recalls the threat of mimetic impersonation in the *Republic,* even though Girard refuses to credit Plato for his insight. What is more, neither Heidegger nor Girard refers to mimesis or the rhapsodic mode of Plato's own text, thus neglecting a mutual implication of truth and mimesis in their views on poetry and art.[74]

(New York: Monthly Review Press, 1971), 161, 177, and passim (French: "Idéologie et appareils idéologiques d'état," in Louis Althusser, *Sur la reproduction,* ed. Jacques Bidet [Paris: Presses Universitaires de France, 1995], 295, 307, originally published in 1970 in the journal *La Pensée*).

70. The epigraph to this section comes from "Typography," 136 (French: "Cependant, lisez 'Platon,' l'écriture *travaillé*" ["Typographie," 268]).

71. See the introduction to this book.

72. "The Origin of the Work of Art," in Martin Heidegger, *Off the Beaten Track,* ed. and trans. Julian Young and Kenneth Haynes (Cambridge: Cambridge University Press, 2002), 16, 19, and passim (German: "Der Ursprung des Kunstwerkes," in *Holzwege* [1950; rpt., Frankfurt am Main: Klostermann, 1994], 25, 28, and passim).

73. For Heidegger's reading of Plato's *Phaedrus* and the *Sophist,* see chapters 2 and 3 of this book.

74. See Julia Annas, "Plato on the Triviality of Literature," in *Plato on Beauty, Wisdom, and the Arts,*

If nevertheless we have a dialogue between these two thinkers, a dialogue that opens up a space of rhapsodic play between various ancient and modern texts, we owe it to Lacoue-Labarthe. To be sure, he does not call this dialogue rhapsodic but assimilates it under Heidegger's method of tracing the "unsaid" (*das Ungesagte*) in Heidegger and Girard; but perhaps it is the rhapsodic mode that constitutes the unsaid of his own text. The formulation of his procedure is "telling" in this regard. He professes to "play off against Girard, against his treatment of Platonism and his hope for a revelation of mimesis[,] . . . Heidegger. But not the Heideggerian interpretation of Plato. Something else in Heidegger; let us say—in order to illustrate a bit what this is all about— a Heidegger who would himself be read in the light of a suspicion coming from . . . Girard."[75] This might appear oversophisticated (*sophistiquée*), but "in truth" it is not: dramatic/rhapsodic mimesis, "highlighted" in Girard's mimetic crisis, reclaims its rights to the archaic and Heideggerian determination of truth as *alētheia*.[76]

In Heidegger's view, which is the point of departure of Lacoue-Labarthe's analysis, Plato's introduction of *eidos/idea* as the determination of being inaugurates the history of Western metaphysics as onto-ideo-logy, or better "onto-typo-logy," which best expresses the formation of the citizen in the Platonic republic as well as the modern, Cartesian and Hegelian, formation of the subject, which Lacoue-Labarthe, following Heidegger, calls the "metaphysics of subjectivity." This metaphysics of form, or *Gestalt,* is ultimately inscribed in the framework of the *Ge-stell,* which establishes being as the site of stability, as state (*Stand, Staat*), as *Bestand,* or "standing reserve," as *Stellung,* or position, as *Gegenstand,* or object, and in general as *Stelle,* or the spatial condition of any stable presence.[77] Thus "installation of being" as a stable *idea,* or *Gestalt,* denotes

ed. Julius Moravcsik and Philip Temko (Totowa, N.J.: Rowman and Littlefield, 1982), 1–28, and Alexander Nehamas, "Plato on Imitation and Poetry in *Republic* 10," in *Plato on Beauty, Wisdom, and the Arts,* 47–78.

75. "Typography," 120–21 (French: "Faire jouer contre lui, Girard, contre son traitement du platonisme et son espoir d'une révélation de la mimesis . . . Heidegger. Mais non l'interprétation heideggerienne de Platon. Quelque chose d'autre dans Heidegger, et disons plutôt—pour illustrer un peu ce dont il s'agit–, un Heidegger qui serait lui-même déjà travaillé d'un soupçon venu de . . . Girard" ["Typographie," 251]).

76. "Sophistic," translates Fynsk ("Typography," 121), thus raising the problem of the origin of the rhapsodic mode.

77. "Typography," 62, 67–68 (French: "Typography," 189, 195–96). See "Concerning 'The Line,'" in Martin Heidegger, *The Question of Being,* trans. Jean T. Wilde and William Kluback (Albany, N.Y.: NCUP, 1958), 62–65 (German: "Über 'Die Linie,'" in *Freundschaftliche Begegnungen: Festschrift für Ernst Jünger zum 60. Gerburtstag,* ed. Armin Mohler [Frankfurt am Mein: Klostermann, 1955], 23–24), referred to in "Typography," 57 (French: "Typographie," 184); cf. Martin Heidegger, "The Question Concerning Technology," in Martin Heidegger, *The Question Concerning Technology and Other Questions,* trans. William Lovitt (New York: Harper and Row, 1977), 17ff. (German: "Die Frage nach der Technik," in *Vorträge und Aufsätze* [Stuttgart: Neske, 1954], 20ff.).

the process that establishes being in its place of truth, that is, of unconcealed erection (Aufstellung).

It is in this context of aletheic installation that the "Heideggerian decon-struction" (as Lacoue-Labarthe calls it) of the traditional opposition between poetry and philosophy, or art and truth, takes place. Indeed, the idea as a sta-ble figure or "statue" can only be formed (fashioned) through "the poetizing essence of human reason" (*das dichtende Wesen der Vernunft*), which imposes on the original chaos schemas, categories, ideas, or types.[78] As in the case of Plato's characters, the "production [*Herstellung*] and erection [*Aufstellung*] of the stable (of the Same), without which nothing can be grasped or thought," consists in fictioning (Heidegger's *Ausdichten,* Plato's *to plattein*).[79] Thus, the theoretical, philosophical determination of being as stable presence has in the last analysis a *fictioning, poietic* essence.

It is the notion of the fictioning nature of human reason that determines Heidegger's position on the quarrel between philosophy and poetry and his decision in favor of poetry. Thus Heidegger chooses to comment mainly on book 10 of the *Republic* (mimesis as the production of images and reflections) rather than on book 3 (mimesis as rhapsodic play), which has for him only a preliminary character. And the final decision concerning *poiēsis* and philoso-phy is reached only after the ontological excursus of the allegory of the cave at the outset of book 7 is accomplished. It is in this book, as Heidegger points out in his essay *Plato's Doctrine of Truth,* that the encounter of the archaic con-ception of truth as *alētheia* (*Unverborgenheit,* unconcealment) is combined with the conception of truth as *homoiosis* (*adequatio,* correspondence), and this par-ticular state of the theory of truth allows Plato to reach the decision in book 10 of the *Republic. Mimēsis* as fall from the stele is subordinated to *alētheia* as *Unverstelltheit,* or nondissimulation, literally nondisplacement, nondisinstalla-tion. Of his list of the *stellen* words that refer to this *Unverstelltheit,* Heidegger chooses *Herstellen* as most pertinent to the characterization of the fictioning installation, and he neglects in particular *Darstellen,* with its dramatic, rhapsodic connotations. In "The Question Concerning Technology," *Darstellung,* or re-presentation, is coupled with *Herstellung,* or production (in the sense of *poiēsis*), and almost immediately suppressed in favor of the latter. It is, indeed, *Herstel-lung* rather than *Darstellung* that characterizes *technē* as *poiēsis,* that is, as a bringing into presence, as a disclosive establishing ("installing"), of beings in the sense of *alētheuein.* The most striking result of this neglect of the performative,

78. *Nietzsche,* 4 vols., trans. David Farrell Krell (San Francisco: Harper and Row, 1979–87), 3:149 (German: *Nietzsche,* 2 vols. [Pfullingen: Neske, 1961], 1:584).

79. "Typography," 72 (French: "la production (*Herstellung*) et l'érection (*Aufstellung*) du stable (*du Même*), sans quoi il n'y a rien de saisissable ou de pensable" ["Typographie," 199]).

dramatic, or rhapsodic *Darstellung* in Heidegger's interpretation is the con-
comitant loss of the destabilizing potential of the play of mimesis.

Rosen's reading of Plato in terms of the quarrel between philosophy and
poetry, especially in his discussion of the *Republic,* shows Heidegger's influence
as to the preponderance of the fictioning, *poietic,* demiurgic nature of human
intellectual activity, including that of philosophy.[80] But Rosen's reading is also
insightful concerning the crucial role played by the relationship between rigor
and play in Plato's view of philosophy and poetry and their respective roles in
politics and education. The insight is particularly striking in someone who
doesn't refer to the discussion of *akribeia* in the first book of the *Republic* at all
and who, like Heidegger, presents Plato's Socrates as subordinating poetry to
philosophy and sees the rhapsodic mimesis of book 3 through the representational lens of book 10.[81] In both claims, however, Rosen's "political" reading
distances itself from the "ontological" or "ideological" reading of Heidegger:
"The contemporary defense of poetry, for example by Heidegger, attributes
to the poetic art the manifestation or unveiling of that which Plato would call
an 'Idea' or *ousia.* But the Socratic critique does not say that the poet 'veils' the
Ideas. The accusation is 'political.'"[82] Rosen refers here to the beginning of book
10, where the critique of mimesis seems to be suspended in the case of philosophers possessing the *pharmakon,* or remedy of knowledge (595b).[83] Indeed, for

80. Rosen "protests too much" to be believed in his rejection of Heidegger; see especially his *Plato's
"Sophist": The Drama of Original and Image* (New Haven, Conn.: Yale University Press, 1983) and *The
Question of Being: A Reversal of Heidegger* (South Bend, Ind.: St. Augustine's Press, 2002).

81. "Socrates does not actually, despite his explicit statement to that effect, expel poetry from his city
but rather subordinates it to philosophy" (*The Quarrel Between Philosophy and Poetry* [New York: Routledge, 1988], 14). The quote that serves as one of the epigraphs to this chapter appears only in the introduction to his latest book, in the paragraph launching a "trial balloon" (*Plato's "Republic,"* 12). Regarding
using book 10 as the means to understanding book 3, Rosen says, "One must connect the critique of Book
Three with that of Book Ten. The latter is an illustration of the more general thesis that *all* types of mimesis (τοὺς ἄλλους 'πάντας τοὺς μιμητικούς) are an outrage or destruction of the discursive intellect of those
who listen to them (τῆς τῶν ἀκουόντων διανοίας), if they do not possess the remedy (*pharmakon*):
namely, knowledge of what mimetic art actually is (595b3–7)" (*The Quarrel Between Philosophy and Poetry,*
8). There is a long debate in Plato scholarship concerning the relationship between the two books and
eventually the two types of mimesis. See, for example, J. Tate, "Imitation in Plato's *Republic,*" *Classical
Quarterly* 22, no. 1 (1928): 16–23, and J. Tate, "Plato and 'Imitation,'" *Classical Quarterly* 26, nos. 3–4
(1932): 161–69; cf. R. C. Cross and A. D. Woozley, *Plato's Republic: A Philosophical Commentary* (London:
Macmillan, 1964), and more recently Julia Annas, "Plato on the Triviality of Literature," and Alexander
Nehamas, "Plato on Imitation and Poetry in *Republic* 10." Nehamas's essay contains an extensive bibliog-
raphy on the subject.

82. *The Quarrel Between Philosophy and Poetry,* 8; see also *Plato's "Republic,"* 209, 354, and passim.

83. In Paul Friedländer's view, Plato's own dialogues would on this account be allowed in Socrates'
city: "Shortly before the great concluding myth, there follows, like a forced intrusion, the episode of the
'imitating' poet and the opposition of Plato's state to the latter. Why is this topic so important to Plato
that he assigns it such an unexpected place? Had he not previously treated this subject while discussing
the musical education of the guardians (394 et seq.)? Why, then, return to something that apparently has

the philosopher-kings, mimesis would be not only permitted but obligatory, given the necessity of noble, medicinal lies, the essence of Socrates' view of politics on Rosen's reading being that it is founded in lies.[84] Nor is there anything astounding in the necessarily mimetic nature of philosophy, since "'god' is himself on Socrates' account a poet or demiurge."[85] Both "god" and the philosopher are painters as well, the "poet-god" contemplating his own "Idea" in producing nature as a *phytourgon,* the poet-philosopher contemplating the city in the sky (*en ouranōi*) in founding the *kallipolis.*

On this account, however, a sharp distinction between the theoretical and the poetic domain might be difficult. "Plato gives us a poetic portrait of philosophy, not a theoretical one," says Rosen, although in a sense it is both a theoretical and a poetic portrait, and Rosen is right in calling it ("an appropriate anachronism") "ideological," referring not only to *ideai* but also to rhetorical devices and especially medicinal lies.[86] Rosen's analysis of the notion of *akribeia,* or rigor, in *Philebus* refines this view but doesn't change it. It confirms the triumph of poetry over a possible alternative: a discursive intellect (*dianoia*) based on exact calculation (*logismos*).[87] The divinely pure, perfectly rigorous arithmetic is of great formal beauty but can make nothing, is "non-productive par excellence."[88] From the demiurgic, poetic point of view, the impure, non-rigorous "measure, moderation, and fitness" (*metron kai to metrion kai kairion* [*Philebus* 66a]) is more appropriate to the production of the mixture of the good life. Rosen calls this measure "political and prudential," thinking of the notion of *phronēsis* as practical wisdom.[89] Yet this critique of the ontological/ideological and diaeretic/analytical reading of the dialogues, pertinent as it is, does not seem to be capable of undermining the representational structure into which Rosen inscribes the quarrel between poetry and philosophy. Indeed, he rejects both endeavors when taken separately because of their failure to attain the original and their willingness to be satisfied with an image. The quarrel thus cannot be resolved, though it can be "sublated into a demiurgic discourse that

---

already been disposed of? There would be no point in this if Plato did not have in mind the writing of his own dialogues [*die eigene Dialogdichtung*] and did not wish to secure for them an appropriate place in the new state" (1958; rpt., *Plato: An Introduction,* vol. 1 of Paul Friedländer, *Plato,* trans. Hans Meyerhoff [Princeton, N.J.: Princeton University Press, 1969], 118–19 [German: *Seinswahrheit und Lebenswirklichkeit,* vol. 1 of *Platon* (1954; rpt., Berlin: de Gruyter, 1964), 125]). It goes without saying that the dialogues read in the rhapsodic mode would not be allowed anywhere near the city commonly ascribed to Socrates' vision.

84. *The Quarrel Between Philosophy and Poetry,* 5–6.
85. *The Quarrel Between Philosophy and Poetry,* 7.
86. *The Quarrel Between Philosophy and Poetry,* 11.
87. *The Quarrel Between Philosophy and Poetry,* 22.
88. *The Quarrel Between Philosophy and Poetry,* 21.
89. *The Quarrel Between Philosophy and Poetry,* 24.

is neither poetry nor philosophy but philosophical poetry."[90] The notion of this demiurgic *Aufhebung*, however, hardly seems satisfying on the political level, as Rosen himself shows clearly in his more recent commentary on Plato's *Republic*.[91]

Rosen is not unaware of the particular literary mode of the *Republic*, as the opening remarks of his *Plato's "Republic": A Study* show: "The point . . . of considerable importance for understanding the *Republic* is that it is narrated by Socrates, though in such a way that he assumes the identities, and utters the speeches, of everyone in the dialogue, which is accordingly also mimetic."[92] But this dialogic rhapsodic mode, which he diagnoses as a blatant manifestation of injustice, is immediately opposed here to the monologic nature of Socrates' political theory, which defines the standard of justice by which the rhapsodic mode is to be judged: "This *polupragmosunē*, or minding of everyone's business, the opposite of justice as defined in the *Republic*, is exceeded only by Plato's silent invention of the entire Socratic monologue."[93] This apparent inconsistency is not fully developed in Rosen's commentary itself. The crucial text of book 3 is largely neglected in favor of the representational structure of book 10. Indeed, the political problematic of the *Republic* is discussed mostly in terms of the choice of rulers. Philosopher-kings are those who have a particular insight (achieved through dialectics) into the world of Ideal Forms: "Justice depends upon the rule of those who see the pure Ideas in their original heavenly form."[94] However, the split in the soul that is at the origin of the mimetic threat in book 3, and that is reflected in the rhapsodic mode of the dialogue, also threatens the souls of the rulers. Yet their *polupragmosunē*, minding everyone else's business, does not lead to a rhapsodic community but to its opposite. The tyrannical desire of the rulers forces all diversity of the community into the representation of the unique model of the *kallipolis*, which would eventually require the use of more than just philosophical/ideological state apparatuses.[95]

The split emphasized by Rosen results from the incompatibility between a relative unity of the soul identified with a particular class of citizens (the courageous soul of soldiers, e.g.) and the necessarily complex structure of a singular soul, in particular that of the philosopher. The dramatic aspect of this aporia

---

90. *The Quarrel Between Philosophy and Poetry*, 26.
91. *Plato's "Republic,"* 353ff.
92. *Plato's "Republic,"* 12.
93. *Plato's "Republic,"* 12.
94. *Plato's "Republic,"* 390.
95. "There are very few philosophers, and the intelligence is not capable of regulating the desires without the mediation of spiritedness (police and soldiers)" (*Plato's "Republic,"* 395). On καλλίπολις and γεωμετρία, see the *Republic* 527c2.

is perhaps best brought to light by Girard's "psychological" and "anthropolog-ical" reading of Plato as intervening in the situation of the "mimetic crisis," that is, the general confusion of social roles, literary genres, modes of presen-tation, and so forth. Indeed, Girard's vision of the mimetic crisis as the pro-liferation of doubles and simulacra forces readers of the *Republic* to return to the problematic of theatrical and rhapsodic representation, that is, to the role playing of book 3, neglected by both Heidegger and Rosen. The image of the dramatic poet in this book is that of a sacrificial victim, an ambiguous fig-ure chosen to appease a general fear and Plato's fear, in particular, of mimetic confusion. The "sacrifice" of the poet, actor, and rhapsode would from this point of view be an instance in the chain of violence directed toward a scape-goat in the effort to break away from the "undifferentiated" (*indifférencié*), in Girard's terminology, or "homo sacer" and "whatever being" (*qualunque essere*), in Giorgo Agamben's.[96] The very opposition between philosophy and poetry could be inscribed in this model of mimetic rivalry and thus would refer the decision of book 10 (banishment of the poets) back to the more original mime-sis of book 3. The rhapsodic mode would thus recover its historically crucial position in the quarrel between philosophy and poetry. After all, was not Plato initially an author of tragedies, and does not Socrates introduce himself as a lover of Homer? Doesn't he recite the *Iliad* and the *Odyssey* on any occasion, just like the rhapsode Ion does?

Lacoue-Labarthe's reading of Plato through the double, mimetic play be-tween Heidegger and Girard gives full credit to Plato's own rhapsodic play. Plato's Socrates "knows" the importance of building and of "fictioning" in the process of education, and he craves the stability founded on the "theoretical view" of the Ideas. But Plato also "knows" that "*alētheia* and *mimēsis* resemble each other and are, literally, *in homoiōsis.*"[97] When he stages the sacrifice of the poet, it is not as a random act in the chain of violence but as the very principle of indifferentiation. And he suspects that the play of sacrifice will not work, that a decision will have to be indefinitely postponed. In other words, the writer "Plato" "knows" himself and his text to be always already inscribed in the movement of originary writing.[98] Lacoue-Labarthe's notion of

96. See, for example, Giorgio Agamben's *Homo Sacer: Sovereign Power and Bare Life,* trans. Daniel Heller-Roazen (Stanford, Calif.: Stanford University Press, 1998), 8, 71–72, and passim (Italian: *Homo sacer: Il potere sovrano e la nuda vita* [Torino: Einaudi, 1955], 11–12, 79–80, and passim) as well as his *The Coming Community,* trans. Michael Hardt (Minneapolis: University of Minnesota Press, 1993), 85–86 (Italian: *La comunità che viene* [1990; rpt., Torino: Bollati Boringhieri, 2001], 68).

97. "Typography," 121 (French: "Typographie," 252).

98. See Jacques Derrida, "Writing Before the Letter," in Jacques Derrida, *Of Grammatology,* trans. Gayatri Chakravorty Spivak (Baltimore, Md.: Johns Hopkins University Press, 1976), 3–93 (French: "L'écri-ture avant la lettre," in *De la grammatologie* [Paris: Minuit, 1967], 11–144). Cf. Harry Berger's discussion

typographie brings out this interplay between the ideology of types and writing in the formation of the subject.[99] At the same time, his own text performs such a play in a rhapsodic manner: it is marked by the consistent placement of the "I" and, eventually, his "own" name within quotation marks, at the end of the essay:

> But in a certain sense, in any case, "I" "here" *decline* all responsibility—all authority in the matter. I simply wanted to see, "me" too.
>
>   "Philippe Lacoue-Labarthe"[100]

If this gesture resembles a "spec(tac)ular" formation of the subject in the structure of representation, it is because these two functions of rhapsodic mimesis are in fact inseparable. One has to be aware of performing one's "own" identity in order to be able to set it into play. One has to write one's "own" character(s) in order to be able to erase it/them at the same time. The rigor of the character(s) is played out or written, in the sense given to this notion by Derrida. For "Plato," just as for any citizen in "his" *Republic,* and any subject in the modern "Platonic" state, "Lacoue-Labarthe" and "I," among others, are "always and without knowing it, already fabricated by fiction. That is to say, 'written.'"[101] In the Platonic language of *Protagoras,* she or he is educated by following the pattern of the letters, and in the myth of metals in the *Republic,* she or he is assigned to a class according to the particular metal from which she or he has been shaped.

But Protagoras's speech and the myth of metals are always already inscribed in the drama of Plato's dialogues. And writing embodies the questioning potential of this rhapsodic mimesis. If the citizen of the Platonic republic—and the modern subject in the "Platonic" West—is from the start and by principle inscribed in the ideological hierarchy of types, she or he is also—even though imperceptibly—"hollowed out, corroded, undermined by an unassignable gap, a kind of hiatus or gaping hole, that nothing can ever close or fill up since it is anterior to any opening, any virtuality, any potency and any energy,

---

of the opposition between the "dramatistic" and "textual" readings of Plato in his "Levels of Discourse in Plato's Dialogue," in *Literature and the Question of Philosophy,* ed. Anthony J. Cascardi (Baltimore, Md.: Johns Hopkins University Press, 1987), 75–100.

99. Genette's evocative "mimo(typo)graphy," which he invokes to describe Francis Ponge's poetics, would here be superfluous since for Lacoue-Labarthe the impression of types is always already mimetic; see Gérard Genette, *Mimologics,* trans. Thaïs E. Morgan (Lincoln: University of Nebraska Press, 1994), 299 (French: *Mimologiques: Voyage en Cratylie* [Paris: Seuil, 1976], 380).

100. "Typography," 138 (French: "Typographie," 270).

101. "Typography," 136 (French: "toujours à l'avance—et à son insu—fictionné. C'est-à-dire 'écrit'" ["Typographie," 268]).

any possible reception of a future presence."[102] This is the always already present danger of mimesis, the danger of the disinstallation of the subject and, in some cases that Lacoue-Labarthe attempts to analyze, the danger of madness, especially philosophical madness, which might have been a factor in the very definition of philosophy in the Western tradition.[103] On the other hand, the presence of mimetic danger also offers a chance to undermine all political construction based on the law of the proper type or the subject (such as the ideal republic or the modern state).

One might suggest a modification of this rhapsodic, Heideggerian and Girardian, reading of Plato's text and propose a detour, which might reveal itself to be in fact a shortcut and to remedy even the appearance of "oversophistication" in Lacoue-Labarthe's interpretation. Indeed, as our reading of the first book of the *Republic* showed, it is the notion of *akribeia,* rather than that of *alētheia,* that is at play with *mimēsis* in the *Republic;* unless of course we define truth in terms of *akribeia.* In any case, it is *akribeia* that participates, together with dramatic *mimēsis,* in the definition of the proper types (*tupoi*) or functions (*ergoi*), and it is "parergonal (in)competence" (*parergōi khrōmenos*), in other words, rhapsodic play, that is in fact sacrificed in book 3 under the name of *mimēsis.* It might be objected that *akribeia* is close to *saphēneia,* or clarity, and as such belongs to the sphere of the "theoretic" *alētheia.* This is what Lacoue-Labarthe seems to suggest when he brings together accuracy, exactitude, and "e-vidence."[104] However, this is a modern view of exactitude (the Cartesian "notions claires et distinctes"), which has only slowly emerged from the Platonic *theōria.* In Plato himself there is still present, as we tried to show in the reading of books 1 and 3, a model of exactitude or *akribeia* that is practically, that is, politically and, as we shall see in a moment, ritually determined, ritually determined precisely through the social, political, and religious, as well as "literary," distinctions between the functions assigned to the citizens and modes of discourse in the constitution of the republic (*politeia*). Indeed,

102. "Typography," 137 (French: "échancré, rongé, miné par un écart inassignable, une sorte de hiatus ou de béance que rien ne pourra fermer ni saturer puisque cela précède toute ouverture, toute virtualité, toute puissance et toute énergie, tout accueil possible d'une future présence" ["Typographie," 268]).

103. "In the long run, the question posed here is that of philosophical madness. What can be said, for example, about Rousseau's madness—or Nietzsche's? Indeed, what about Hegel (who 'believed he was going mad') or even Kant? Or Comte? Or probably others still, even if they have not passed as mad, or if it is not entirely customary for us to consider them fully as 'philosophers'?" ("Typography," 44 [French: "À long terme, la question ici posée est celle de la 'folie philosophique.' Qu'en est-il, *par exemple,* de la folie de Rousseau—ou de Nietzsche? Voire de Hegel (qui 'crut devenir fou') ou même de Kant ou de Compte? Ou de quelques autres encore, c'est probable, les ignorerait-on plus ou moins comme tels ou ne serait-il pas tout à fait dans l'usage qu'on les considérât à part entière des 'philosophes'?" ("Typographie," 170)]).

104. "Typography," 85, and esp. 121 (French: "Typographie," 214, and esp. 251).

the constitution of the proper type is not only a question of theoretical exactness of observation but also, especially, of the practical, that is, political and ritual, action of persuasion and education (within the stage of the "return to the cave") and of purification meant to supplement them (with all the risks of such a dangerous supplement).

Philosophical Catharsis as *Pharmakon*

Plato's *pharmakon* is like Aristotle's *katharsis.*
—RENÉ GIRARD

Without meaning to, we have purged the city.
—SOCRATES

Purification was a ruse!
—A MESSENGER

Logical, sociopolitical, and aesthetic rigor has usually been expressed in terms of purity and cleansing: pure judgment, pure nation, pure art.[105] Also in this respect "Platonism" seems to be paradigmatic in the history of Western culture. The philosophical framing of mimesis in the *Republic* is certainly of a purifying nature. The purity of logical and social "types" is the objective of the ideal constitution and education as well as of the theory of the poetic modes and genres as their *conditio sine qua non*. Toward the end of the chapter on education, Socrates refers to his and Adeimantus's decisions concerning the organization of philosophical *paideia* as catharsis or purification:

> "And so, by the dog of Egypt," I said, "unawares we've been purifying [*lelēthamen diakathairontes*] the State that a while ago we termed luxurious."
> "And we have done wisely," he said.
> "Come, then," I said, "let's purify [*kathairōmen*] the rest."
>
> (399e)[106]

---

105. The first epigraph to this section comes from Girard's *Violence and the Sacred,* trans. Patrick Gregory (Baltimore, Md.: Johns Hopkins University Press, 1977), 296 (French: "Il en est de *pharmakon* dans Platon comme de *katharsis* dans Aristotle" [*La violence et le sacré* (Paris: Grasset, 1972), 411]). The second comes from Plato's *Republic* 399e (*Plato: The "Republic,"* trans. Tom Griffith, 90 [Greek: "λελήθαμέν γε διακαθαίροντες . . . πόλιν"]). The third comes from Euripides, *Iphigenia Among the Taurians* 1316 (*Trojan Women, Iphigenia Among the Taurians, Ion,* vol. 4 of *Selections,* 297 [Greek: "δόλια δ᾽ ἦν καθάρματα" (*Trojan Women, Iphigenia Among the Taurians, Ion,* 296)]).

106. *The "Republic" of Plato,* trans. Benjamin Jowett, 95; translation modified.

There is no reason to restrict this conclusion to the immediately preceding and immediately following considerations of sung poetry (*melos*). Sung poetry, composed of speech, harmonic modes, and rhythms, is subject to the same typological rules that were established in the part devoted to poetic expression. Speech (*logos*) must be "spoken according to the same models [*tupoi*] we prescribed a while ago and in the same way."[107] As to the harmonic mode (*harmonia*) and rhythm, they must follow speech (398d). Both spoken and sung poetry are directed toward the task of producing the character of a guardian: courageous, firm and patient, moderate (399a–c)—we might call him a guardian in the most rigorous sense of the word (*ho akribestatōi logōi phulax* [cf. 341, 345]).

Why this introduction of "catharsis," a religious, "sacred" word, toward the end of an argumentation conducted in the quasi-scientific terms of laymen? Does it mark the failure of applying rigorous methodology in political and aesthetic matters? Apparently the political theory of social types and the aesthetic theory of modes of representation and of poetic genres was in need of supplementation by a more evocative and traditionally ingrained, mystical terminology of ritual purification. Mimesis, however, the object of intended catharsis, can hardly be separated from the cathartic process itself. In general, as a religious purification, catharsis is associated with doubling, that is, ultimately with a role-playing by a "victim" (*pharmakos*). This is apparent in the religious sacrificial rites where mimesis governs the process of substitution of a victim for the "guilty party" (an individual or a social group): a mimetic resemblance in the eyes of the community is necessary for the effectiveness of such substitution.[108] In a secular state, this religious "mimesis" has to be in its turn imitated by a judge, an executioner—in a sense, a rhapsode. Catharsis—the crowning of the process of philosophical education as an ultimate cure against mimetic violence—seems itself unable to elude the play of mimesis.

The Platonic term that renders this ambivalence of mimesis is *pharmakon*, at once "poison" and "cure." The cathartic *pharmakon* should prevent the danger of pollution and contamination. The pronouncement against mimesis in the third book of the *Republic* refers, for example, to the danger of contaminating being with seeming: "[Our guardians] should not make up or be skilful at imitating any kind of illiberality or baseness, lest from mimesis [*ek tēs mimēseōs*] they should come *to be* [*einai*] what they imitate" (395c–d).[109] The

---

107. *The "Republic" of Plato*, trans. Allan Bloom, 77.

108. See the analyses of cathartic sacrifices in René Girard, *Violence and the Sacred*, 11ff. (French: *La violence et le sacré*, 26ff.), which retain their pertinence even if one does not entirely subscribe to Girard's conception of mimesis.

109. *The "Republic" of Plato*, trans. Benjamin Jowett, 80; my emphasis.

possible confusion between acting a part and becoming the character one plays, that is, between being and seeming, results from the lack of a rigorous means of distinguishing between what certainly is and what only seems to be, an il-lusion. If there were such a means, mimesis would be ineffective, but also harmless. But knowledge, which could be thought of as providing a certain criterion for judging mimesis, is (or seems to be?) "itself" a *pharmakon*. Indeed, it is knowledge that Socrates explicitly calls a *pharmakon* at the outset of the tenth book of the *Republic,* when referring to the previous discussions of mimesis (595a–b).[110] The term is translated, for example, as "antidote" by Jowett and Griffith (as "remedy" by Bloom), which then makes its object— mimesis—a poison. However, "poison" is *pharmakon* as well; the logic of *pharmakon* is not the logic of *akribeia,* and thus allows for the possibility that knowledge might be in need of a cure. The *Timaeus*—the mytho-logical sequence to the *Republic*—will present a case of such need for supplementation; and it will then be a mimetic myth that will perform the function of remedy.[111]

In the *Republic* as well, a mytho-logical form of mimesis seems to supplement knowledge in its theoretical typo-logical distinctions. At the end of the second book, Socrates characterizes the so-called other lie, a lie not accompanied by ignorance, as an imitation (*mimēma*) of a "true lie" (382b).[112] Such a form of lie is not particularly harmful as long as it does not affect the soul of the "liar," that is, as long as it remains circumscribed in the sphere of "play"; it can even be useful in certain cases as a *pharmakon* (*hōs pharmakon khrēsimon gignetai* [382c]) against enemies, and even for the benefit of friends in need of persuasion. This kind of imitation is not incompatible with the rigorous onto-logical and political distinctions operated by the philosophically minded *mimētēs,* who thus does not cease to be a philosopher.[113] And the rulers of an ideal state will have recourse to noble lies (*gennaia pseudea* [414b–c]) as *pharmaka.*[114] In particular the so-called Phoenician tale, the myth of metals at the end of the third book (414c–415d), might be considered a model of an ideological lie, apparently combining the virtues of *mimēsis* and *akribeia.* The myth is false but it reinforces the philosophically "true" notion of rigorous social distinctions; thus mimesis, which had been considered disease and madness, emerges here clearly on the side of the cure—and then again, it paradoxically "testifies" against itself.

110. Cf. Plato, *Critias,* 106a–b.

111. The myth of *Timaeus* is analyzed in terms of theatrical mimesis in chapter 4 of this book.

112. *The "Republic" of Plato,* trans. Benjamin Jowett, 65.

113. In Rosen's view there is a political necessity for this identification; see *Plato's "Republic,"* 98, 126, 396, and passim.

114. Rosen calls them "noble and medicinal lies" (*Plato's "Republic,"* 8).

The logic of the *pharmakon* is such that a sharp distinction between cure and poison cannot in fact be drawn.[115] Curative poison, poisonous cure—the chiasm of *pharmakon* evokes an abyss of catharsis, the sacrifice of a victim (*pharmakos*), a hero and a monster who oversteps ideological, that is, natural and/or cultural boundaries.[116] The rigorous method of onto-logical clarification and the typographical *paideia* might indeed be characterized, both in traditional religious terminology and in Aristotelian poetic terminology (adopted by the "dramatic" interpreters), as cathartic: they both strive toward a configuration of perfectly distinct types and characters and resort to a rite of purification in the form of sacrifice.[117] In fact, the purification of the logical procedure as the basis of philosophical education pertains to the play of mimesis and is perforce "pharmaco-logical," governed by the logic of the *pharmakon* rather than by the rigorous "acribo-logic" of exclusive notions or types.

The banishment of mimesis and its representatives—the actor, the rhapsode, the poet—is a perfect example of the sacrifice of a victim revered and abhorred at the same time. In the third book, one of these rhapsodes or "pantomimic gentlemen, who are so clever that they can imitate anything," is dismissed, but only after having been worshipped "as a sweet and holy and wonderful being," having been "anointed . . . with myrrh" and crowned with "a garland of wool" (398a).[118] The reason for this ambiguous treatment is said to be, on the one hand, an amazement (*thaumaston*) before the uncanniness of the illusion and admiration for the illusionist's skill and, on the other hand, the necessity of safeguarding the "truth," that is, the certainty of basic distinctions and types: genders, professions, classes, and so forth in the city-state.[119] The problem with mimetic illusion in Socrates' view is that the illusionist does not respect "those models [*tupoi*] which we prescribed at first when we began the education of the guardians" (398b).[120] The sacrifice of mimesis thus appears as the negative side of the educational process directed toward the impression of types and characters. It consists of the elimination of the elements supposedly transgressing the principle of rigorous self-sameness and ideo-logical justice.[121]

One might object that the cathartic rite of the third book, with its necessary mimetic component—the rhapsode representing not only all mimetic arts but all dissensions from and all "plays" with(in) the ideo-logical system of the

---

115. See my discussion of Derrida's essay "Plato's Pharmacy" in chapter 2.

116. A "bottomless chasm of violence" in René Girard's words (*Violence and the Sacred*, 8ff. [French: *Le violence et la sacré*, 26ff.]).

117. See the introduction to this book.

118. *The "Republic" of Plato,* trans. Benjamin Jowett, 83.

119. See also Plato, *Republic* 398; cf. Plato, *Sophist* 236d and passim.

120. *The "Republic" of Plato,* trans. Benjamin Jowett, 83; translation modified.

121. See the explicit coupling of rigor and catharsis in *Republic* 504e: "ἀκριβέστατα καὶ καθαρώτατα."

state—is only the consequence of the principle of *akribeia* established in a rational, scientific manner. However, a last glance at the first book of the *Republic* suggests that the principle of *akribeia* has been "contaminated" by mimesis and its principle (the principle of similitude) from the very beginning. In the heart of Socrates' debate with Thrasymachus, an argument *a simile*—concluding the identical from the resembling—was introduced. Thus the supposedly rigorous argument—the one that will eventually lead to the rejection of dramatic mimesis—was itself impure, that is, mimetic. The essential concern of the ruler—the man in power, the "stronger," in Thrasymachus's language—with the interest of the governed was implied by analogy with the attitude of a physician, a captain of a ship, a shepherd, caring for those over whom they have the authority (341c–342e). And the value of this *a simile* argument was explicitly asserted in the part of the discussion that proved the wisdom and goodness of the just. It was Thrasymachus—in Socrates' rhapsodic voice—who could not help expressing the ontological relevance of similitude to his own argument for the wisdom and goodness of the stronger, commonly considered "unjust":

> —And does not the unjust *resemble* [*eoike*] the wise and good, and the just not resemble [*ouk eoike*]?
> —How wouldn't he who is of a certain nature [*ho toioutos ōn*], he asked, resemble those of a certain nature [*eoikenai tois toioutois*], and he who is not, not do so?
> —Each of them, I said, is such as his like are [*toioutos estin hoisper eoiken*].
> —Certainly, he replied.
>
> (349d)[122]

The argumentation will prove fatal for Thrasymachus's thesis precisely because of the principle of resemblance. And Socrates will repeat it with jubilation, in "his own" voice, that is, the voice of the rhapsode-narrator, when restating his thesis of the superiority of the just man over the unjust: "But we agreed that each of them had the qualities of the person he was like" (*Hōi ge homoios hekateros eiē, toiouton kai hekateron einai*) (350c).[123]

This use of an *a simile* argument, striking as it is in the discussion of *akribeia,* is far from being exceptional in the dialogues. Resemblance (*homoiōsis, eikasia*), which is the principle of mimesis and of catharsis, often governs Socrates' apparently rigorous argumentation. Likeness is, however, a most slippery

122. *The "Republic" of Plato,* trans. Benjamin Jowett, 28; translation modified.
123. *Plato: The "Republic,"* trans. Tom Griffith, 31.

kind (*olisthērotaton gar to genos*) according to the Elean Stranger in the *Sophist* (231a), and as such it necessarily marks the principles that it helps to establish—the principles of logical, aesthetic, and political rigor—with the slippage and ambiguity of resemblance.[124]

The principle of resemblance—the basis of both mimesis and catharsis and that which proved necessary to Socrates' own philosophical argumentation—determines the ambiguous role played by mimesis and catharsis in the context of the ideological education entrusted to philosophers. Each is appealing as a supplement to the educational process of "typography" based on knowledge, as a completion of the ideological segregation between genders, professions and classes. The language of purification in particular perfectly expresses the ideal of moral, aesthetic, and political distinctions based on semantic and logical rigor (*akribeia*) that was elaborated in the debate with the Sophist and man of theater Thrasymachus in the first book of the *Republic*. But just as the presence of the character of Thrasymachus was essential to this elaboration, so the rhapsodic mimesis in which he takes part is essential to the workings of *akribeia* and of *katharsis* and thus calls them both into question by bringing them into the sphere of the play of resemblance and mimesis.[125] Such staging of the process through which the philosophical foundations of moral, aesthetic, and political systems are laid down must necessarily affect the apparently compelling results of that process, even if Socrates "himself," the Socrates of the *Republic,* does not seem to take the measure, the *exact* measure, of this fact.

But perhaps the Socrates of the *Phaedo* does see the need for a "poetic" mode of philosophizing when, in prison, awaiting the *pharmakon* of death which he calls extreme purification, he has a recurring dream urging him to practice music (*mousikēn poiei kai ergazou* [*Phaedo* 60e]).[126] He had thought that philosophy was in fact true music, although he also attempted to write a prelude to Apollo and to set Aesop's fables into verse. Nietzsche, who refers to this passage in his *Birth of Tragedy*, detects here a possible recantation and the birth of an "artistic Socrates."[127] Perhaps both are right, and Socrates' actual practice (*poiein kai ergazein*) of music—in the Greek sense of *mousikē* as everything that falls under the patronage of the Muses—combines philosophy and poetry, truth and mimesis, rigor and play, in a rhapsodic mode.

124. I discuss the notion of likeness and resemblance further in chapter 3.

125. See Adeimantus's association of the cathartic rite with play (364–365).

126. On music and philosophy, see Babette E. Babich, "*Mousikē Technē*: The Philosophical Practice of Music in Plato: Nietzsche, and Heidegger," in *Between Philosophy and Poetry. Writing, Rhythm, History,* ed. Massimo Verdicchio and Robert Burch (New York: Continuum, 2002), 171–80.

127. *The Birth of Tragedy,* in *Basic Writings of Nietzsche,* trans. Walter Kaufmann (1966; rpt., New York: Modern Library, 1992), §14, p. 92 (German: *Die Geburt der Tragödie,* in *Kritische Studienausgabe,* 1:96).

2

Le Beau Jeu
The Play of Beauty and Truth
in the *Phaedrus*

(Nietzsche, Heidegger, Derrida)

[Plato] lets the rough edges poke through the joints of his dialogue. Let us not struggle too hard, then, to unify the *Phaedrus;* for the real struggle is elsewhere.

—G. R. F. FERRARI

Nothing here is of a single piece and the *Phaedrus* also, in its own writing, plays at saving writing—which also means causing it to be lost—as the best, the noblest play. Is Plato playing fair?—some fair play!

—JACQUES DERRIDA

This chapter turns to the initial idea of the overturning of Platonism (*Umdrehung des Platonismus*) presented in the writings of Nietzsche. Nietzsche's confrontation with Platonism and with Western metaphysics in general will be seen here both in his own work and also in Heidegger's and Derrida's reformulations of the Platonic and Nietzschean opposition that underlies this metaphysics, namely, the "old dispute" (*palaia diaphora*) between philosophy and poetry and the "raging discordance" (*ein Entsetzen erregender Zwiespalt*) between art and truth, the forgetfulness of which, in the form of the modern *adiaphora*,

The first epigraph to this chapter is drawn from Ferrari's *Listening to the Cicadas: A Study of Plato's "Phaedrus"* (Cambridge: Cambridge University Press, 1987), 232. The second comes from Derrida's "Plato's Pharmacy," in Jacques Derrida, *Dissemination*, trans. Barbara Johnson (Chicago: University of Chicago Press, 1981), 67; translation modified (French: "Rien n'est ici d'une pièce et le *Phèdre* joue aussi, dans son écriture, à sauver—ce qui est aussi perdre—l'écriture comme le meilleur, le plus noble jeu. Du beau jeu que se donne ainsi Platon" ["La pharmacie de Platon," in *La dissémination* (Paris: Seuil, 1972), 89]). "Beau jeu" is admittedly not "beautiful" or "fair" play, but this translation might still be better than the apparently idiomatic "stunning hand," which gives to Plato much of the mastery that Derrida questions, and, if it still indirectly refers to "jeu," does so in the sense of a game (of cards) rather than that of a deconstructive play of dissemination ("As for the stunning hand Plato has thus dealt himself, we will be able to follow its incidence and its payoff later on" ["Plato's Pharmacy," 67]). I discuss the problem of (this) translation in the last section of this chapter.

Nietzsche dreaded.[1] It is remarkable that both Heidegger's and Derrida's versions of the overturning of Platonism take their cue not only from Nietzsche but also from Plato himself, and especially from his dialogue *Phaedrus*. Deleuze was right: even before Nietzsche, Plato himself had shown the way to the overturning of Platonism and hence of the traditional interpretation of Socrates' old dispute. And a major step toward this overturning seems to be made in the *Phaedrus*, in the rhapsodic play of the famous palinode or recantation. Unfortunately, the *rhaps-ōidic* aspect of the *palin-ōidia*, crucial to this overturning, has been ignored by most ancient and modern readers of the dialogue.

Although the chronological status of the *Phaedrus* among Plato's dialogues has never been ascertained by those who base their reading of the dialogues on the notion of Plato's development as a philosopher, there used to be a kind of consensus among scholars as to its low artistic and philosophical value.[2] Two apparently contradictory reasons accounted for this estimation: its low quality was due to either Plato's youthful inexperience (e.g., Friedrich Schleiermacher) or his senility (e.g., Hans Raeder).[3] In the twentieth century, this opinion was reversed, and another consensus established itself: the *Phaedrus* is a "great" dialogue both artistically (e.g., Robin) and philosophically (e.g., Emmanuel Lévinas).[4] These favorable judgments, however, seem to depend on the assumption

1. To be sure, "diaphora" is often translated in the context of Plato's quarrel with the poets as precisely "quarrel," "dispute," or "debate." But it commonly means "a difference." Etymologically, the word consists of the prefix "δια-" ("through," "across") and the stem "-φόρα (from "φέρειν," "to bear," "to carry"); trans-latio. For *adiaphora*, see Friedrich Nietzsche, *The Will to Power*, ed. Walter Kaufmann, trans. Walter Kaufmann and R. J. Hollingdale (New York: Random House, 1967), frag. 435, p. 239 (German: in *Nachgelaßene Fragmente, 1887–1889*, in Friedrich Nietzsche, *Kritische Studienausgabe*, 15 vols., ed. Giorgio Colli and Mazzino Montinari [1967–77; rpt., Berlin: de Gruyter, 1988], 13:272); for *Zwiespalt*, see *Nachgelaßene Fragmente, 1887–1889*, in *Kritische Studienausgabe*, 13:500.

2. For updates on the state of research in Platonic chronology, see E. N. Tiegerstedt, *Interpreting Plato* (Uppsala: Almqvist and Wiksell International, 1977), Wolfgang Wieland, *Platon und die Formen des Wissens* (Göttingen: Vandenhoeck and Ruprecht, 1982), Holger Thesleff, "Platonic Chronology," *Phronesis* 34, no. 1 (1989): 1–26, and Jacob Howland, "Re-reading Plato: The Problem of Platonic Chronology," *Phoenix* 45 no. 3 (1991): 189–214.

3. Schleiermacher, *Introductions to the Dialogues of Plato*, trans. William Dobson (1836; rpt., New York: Arno Press, 1973), 68 and passim; Hans H. Raeder, *Platons Philosophische Entwicklung* (Leipzig: Druck and Teubner, 1905), 267, 57: "Ganz mit Unrecht hat man . . . in der fehlerhaften Komposition des *Phaedros* einen Beweis für die Jugendlichkeit seines Verfassers gesehen . . . Viel wahrscheinlicher ist die entgegengesetzte Annahme, Platon habe bei zunehmendem Alter die künstlerische Form immer mehr vernachlässigt und sich mehr durch sachliche Rücksichten leiten lassen" (cited by Derrida, "Plato's Pharmacy," 67 [French: "La pharmacie de Platon," 83]).

4. According to Robin, "L'unité de la composition du *Phèdre* ne me paraît pas pouvoir être mise en doute. L'art avec lequel elle est réalisée est d'une légèreté subtile et d'une incomparable souplesse; on en alourdit nécessairement le libre jeu dans l'effort qu'on fait pour suivre ce jeu dans ses mobiles articulations" ("Notice," in Plato, *Œuvres complètes: Phèdre*, vol. 4, pt. 3, trans. Paul Vicaire, ed. Claudio Moreschini [Paris: Société d'Édition "Les Belles Lettres," 1985], lxxi–lxxii). According to Lévinas, it is "one of the finest [books in the history of philosophy] among four or five others" (*Ethics and Infinity: Conversations*

of the unity of the dialogue, and there has never been a consensus among the readers of Plato as to the *Phaedrus*'s main topic. Already the first editors of the dialogues and the organizers of Plato's corpus of writings hesitated between several subtitles supposed to indicate what the dialogue was about. And readers of all periods have rarely concurred as to what constitutes its topic. Is it beauty or love or both, rhetoric or philosophy or both, soul, ideas, *logos,* or writing? The recorded subtitles include *peri tou kalou,* or *On the Beautiful, peri tou erōtos,* or *On Love, peri psukhēs,* or *On the Soul* (or, in a more restricted, modern, Heideggerian sense, *Selbsterkenntnis,* or self-knowledge, à la Burger and Griswold]). And one might consider others, just as pertinent: *peri tekhnēs,* or *On Art, peri logous,* or *On Discourse, peri manias,* or *On Madness, peri ideōn,* or *On Ideas.*[5] One could argue, as Plato scholars have, for any of these topics as the dominant one in the dialogue.

How then could we determine the "true" and unique topic (topos) of the *Phaedrus?* Perhaps it is the problematic of "unity" or "truth" itself, or more exactly the place (topos) "itself" of truth, even though *peri alētheias* does not figure among the traditional subtitles of the dialogue. Understood as the play between forgetfulness and remembering, between hiding and appearing, between presence and absence, and eventually between poetry and philosophy, the problematic of truth might eventually question the requirement of a univocal logos in this and perhaps other dialogues. It is also truth that might bring together the two major readings of the *Phaedrus* in our time, that of Heidegger and that of Derrida. At first sight they do not have much in common, and this also seems to be the opinion of Derrida himself who, writing some ten years after the publication of Heidegger's interpretation of the *Phaedrus* in his *Nietzsche,* does not address it in his long essay "Plato's Pharmacy."[6] Both authors focus on relatively short passages, the close reading of which yields a general view of the dialogue and of Plato's thought. Derrida's "unfolding" seems larger here, but it does not include the problematic of beauty or art and truth per se, which is taken up in Heidegger's essay together with the nature

with Philippe Nemo, trans. Richard A. Cohen [Pittsburgh: Duquesne University Press, 1985], 37 [French: *Ethique et infini: Dialogues avec Philippe Nemo* (Paris: Fayard, 1982), 27–28]).

   5. See, e.g., Hermeias, *In platonis phaedrum scholia,* ed. Paul Couvreur (Hildesheim: Olms, 1971); cf. *Plato's "Phaedrus,"* trans. Reginald Hackforth (Cambridge: Cambridge University Press, 1952), 8–9, and Martin Heidegger, *Nietzsche,* 4 vols. trans. David Farrell Krell (San Francisco: Harper and Row, 1979–87), 1:191 (German: *Nietzsche,* 2 vols. [Pfullingen: Neske, 1961], 1:194).

   6. Heidegger's book was published more than twenty years after the lecture course on which it was based; Heidegger's lectures on Plato's *Sophist* from 1923, which also deal with *Phaedrus,* were published much later (*Plato's "Sophist,"* trans. Richard Rojcewicz and André Schuwer [Bloomington: Indiana University Press, 2003] [German: *Platon: "Sophistes,"* vol. 19 of Martin Heidegger, *Gesamtausgabe,* 102 vols. to date (Frankfurt am Main: Klostermann, 1975–)]). Derrida's essay "La pharmacie de Platon" has been included in the recent edition and translation of Plato's *Phaedrus* by Luc Brisson, *Phèdre* (Paris: Flammarion, 1989).

of human Dasein.[7] On the other hand, Heidegger seems to ignore the rhapsodic, poetic, half-playful and half-serious character of the *Phaedrus* and in particular of the speech that contains the view of the beautiful (and of poetry and art) and its role in making other *ideai* appear. In other words, Heidegger does not pay enough attention to the dramatic setting of the dialogue, the performance of the characters of Socrates and Phaedrus and the written characters in the mise en scène and mise en abyme (staging and ungrounding) of the play of the true and the beautiful in the human soul.

We shall thus attempt to bring together these two readings on the basis of the notion of truth, but truth understood, in the Nietzschean fashion, as multiple: "'All truth is simple.' This is a double lie. Everything simple is merely imaginary, is not 'true.' But whatever is real, whatever is true, is neither one nor even reducible to one."[8] Truth is thus always multiple, contradictory, and in motion—in other words, there *is* no truth ("There are many kinds of 'truths,' and consequently there is no truth").[9] We shall confront Nietzsche's position with respect to Plato and Platonism in the matter of truth and poetry with Heidegger's reading of the *Phaedrus* and then with Derrida's notion of play in order to argue that the "unity" of the *Phaedrus* might reside in its rhapsodic mode, constantly replaying and recanting the old quarrel between philosophy and poetry.

The Ambiguity of the Quarrel and of the Discordance: Heidegger's Notion of "Felicitous Discordance"

Because Being opens itself only to the view upon Being, and because the latter must always be snatched from oblivion of Being, and because for that reason it needs the most direct radiance of fleeting appearances, the opening up of Being must occur at the site where, estimated in terms of truth, the *mē on* (*eidōlon*), i.e., nonbeing, occurs. But that is the site of beauty.

—MARTIN HEIDEGGER

Heidegger reflects on Plato's *Phaedrus* in his lecture on Nietzsche from 1936–37 entitled *The Will to Power as Art.*[10] At first sight, this reflection seems a

---

7. Beauty and art are closely associated in Heidegger's analysis; see, for instance, *Nietzsche,* 1:198 (German: *Nietzsche,* 1:201).

8. *The Will to Power,* frag. 536, p. 291; translation modified (German: "'Alle Wahrheit ist einfach': das ist ein zwiefache Lüge. Alles, was einfach ist, ist bloß imaginär, ist nicht 'wahr.' Was aber wirklich, was wahr ist, ist weder Eins, noch auch nur reduzierbar auf Eins" [in *Nachgelaßene Fragmente, 1884–1885,* in *Kritische Studienausgabe,* 13:478]). Cf. Nietzsche, *The Gay Science,* trans. Walter Kaufmann (New York: Vintage, 1974), §143, pp. 191–92 (German: *Die fröhliche Wissenschaft,* in *Kritische Studienausgabe,* 3:490–91).

9. *The Will to Power,* frag. 540, p. 291 (German: in *Nachgelaßene Fragmente, 1884–1885,* in *Kritische Studienausgabe,* 11:498).

10. The epigraph to this section comes from *Nietzsche,* 1:198 (German: "Weil das Sein nur im Seinsblick sich eröffnet und dieser immer aus der Seinsvergessenheit herausgerissen werden muß und es dazu

digression from the main theme of the lecture course, which attempts to situate Nietzsche's position on art within the history of Western aesthetics and within the realm of modern nihilism. Heidegger had already placed Nietzsche in the last period of his schematic development of aesthetics, which begins with Plato and Aristotle, before characterizing Nietzsche's view as the reversal of the relation between art and truth. In the fifth of the theses on art and the artist, as systematized by Heidegger, Nietzsche affirms the superiority of art over truth: "Die Kunst ist mehr wert als 'die Wahrheit'" ("Art is worth more than 'the truth'").[11] This assertion requires, however, grounding (*Begründung*). And here, proclaiming the question of truth—already included in the guiding and the grounding question of being(s)—to be "the primal question of philosophy" (*die Vorfrage der Philosophie*), Heidegger proceeds to analyze the notion of truth and its relation to art.[12] Nietzsche himself characterizes this relationship as a "discordance" (*Zwiespalt*) and confesses his lifetime "dread" (*Entsetzen*) before it: "Very early I became seriously preoccupied with the relation of Art to Truth—and even now I stand in holy dread before this discordance. My first book was devoted to it; *The Birth of Tragedy* believes in Art on the background of another conviction: that *it is impossible to live with Truth;* that the 'Will to Truth' is already a symptom of degeneration."[13]

The "even now" in this text points to the early summer of 1888—the last year of Nietzsche's creative life. He does not explicitly evoke Socrates and his formulation of the old quarrel in the *Republic,* but the reference to *The Birth of Tragedy* indicates that the formulation of the dilemma and the suggestion of its solution is an *Auseinandersetzung,* a thoughtful and clarifying confrontation, with Plato, all the more so since Nietzsche has called his philosophy the reversal of Platonism.[14] In this context, Heidegger's consideration of both Nietzsche's discordance and Plato's *diaphora* belongs to his own confrontation with the tradition of Western metaphysics.[15]

---

des nächsten Scheinens des Anscheins bedarf, muß die Eröffnung des Seins dort geschehen, wo, von der Wahrheit aus geschätzt, das μὴ ὄν (εἴδωλον), das Nichtseiende west. Dies ist jedoch der Ort der Schönheit" [*Nietzsche,* 1:201]).

11. *Nietzsche,* 1:75 (German: *Nietzsche,* 1:73).

12. *Nietzsche,* 1:141 (German: *Nietzsche,* 1:143).

13. My translation (German: "Über das Verhältniß der Kunst zur Wahrheit bin ich am frühesten ernst geworden: und noch jetzt stehe ich mit einem heiligen Entsetzen vor diesem Zwiespalt. Mein erstes Buch [war] ihm geweiht; *Die Geburt der Tragödie* glaubt an die Kunst auf dem Hintergrund eines anderen Glaubens: daß es *nicht möglich ist mit der Wahrheit zu leben;* daß der 'Wille zur Wahrheit' bereits ein Symptom der Entartung ist" [in *Nachgelaßene Fragmente, 1887–1889,* in *Kritische Studienausgabe,* 13:500]).

14. "Meine Philosophie umgedrehter Platonismus" (in *Nachgelaßene Fragmente, 1869–1874,* in *Kritische Studienausgabe,* 7:199).

15. Brigitte Schillbach writes, in the 1998 edition of *Nietzsche,* that the lectures constitute Heidegger's "seinsgeschichtliche Auseinandersetzung mit der Metaphysik" (2:449).

In his foreword to the first complete edition of his Nietzsche lecture series in 1961, Heidegger chooses the word *Aus-einander-setzung* ("confrontation," "dialogue," "coming to terms"; literally, "setting apart from one another," Heidegger's hyphenation) in order to characterize the thing, the matter (*Sache*) of thinking, the lectures were supposed to prepare. A rigorous setting apart of the concepts of thought, conducted in a thoughtful dialogue—this might be a fair paraphrase of *Auseinandersetzung*. One could relate this method, this way of thought, to the rhapsodic mode. Yet we have seen that one important aspect of this mode seemed to be missing from Heidegger's account of Plato. Does his confrontation with Nietzsche take account of rhapsodic play? The weight given to *Thus Spoke Zarathustra* in Heidegger's reading seems to suggest an affirmative answer; yet, as we shall see, it does not display the same blending of philosophical rigor and mimetic play as Nietzsche's own text.[16]

Although Heidegger's immediate objective in this lecture series is thus the "confrontation with the 'Nietzsche matter,'" the confrontation with Plato is implicitly announced in the same short foreword, through the reference to the lecture "Plato's Doctrine of Truth," which originated in 1930–31 and which Heidegger considers a major text in the development of his thinking.[17] And we have seen that the confrontation with Plato turned out to be a reconsideration of the "old quarrel" between philosophy and poetry first announced in the *Republic*. But can we consider Nietzsche's discordance between art and truth to be his version of the Platonic old quarrel between poetry and philosophy? And would Plato accept such a reformulation? Heidegger answers both questions with a decisive "no" when he explicitly distinguishes Plato's *diaphora* from Nietzsche's *Zwiespalt*. Indeed, discordance requires a parity of rank between the two terms and their derivation from a more original common term, comparable to a bifurcated tree trunk (*Zwiesel*).[18] But in the *Republic*, "poetry and mimesis" belong, together with truth and philosophy, to a hierarchical

---

16. Heidegger's 1953 essay "Who is Nietzsche's Zarathustra?" (trans. Bernd Magnus, in *The New Nietzsche: Contemporary Styles of Interpretation*, ed. David B. Allison [1977; rpt., Cambridge, Mass.: MIT Press, 1985], 64–79; also in Heidegger, *Nietzsche*, 2:211–33 [German: "Wer ist Nietzsches Zarathustra?" in Martin Heidegger, *Vorträge and Aufsätze* (Stuttgart: Neske, 1954), 97–122]) is more rhapsodic in this regard, and the 1954 "A Dialogue on Language (Between a Japanese and an Inquirer)" (in *On the Way to Language*, trans. Peter D. Hertz [New York: Harper and Row, 1971], 1–57 [German: "Aus einem Gespräch von der Sprache (Zwischen einem Japaner und einem Fragenden)," in Martin Heidegger, *Unterwegs zur Sprache* (Pfullingen: Neske, 1959), 83–156]) both thematizes and practices this mode. I take up "A Dialogue on Language" in the concluding chapter.

17. *Nietzsche*, 1:xl (German: "Aus-einander-setzung mit der 'Sache Nietzsches'" [*Nietzsche*, 1:12]); cf. William J. Richardson, *Heidegger: Through Phenomenology to Thought*, 4th ed. (1963; rpt., New York: Fordham University Press, 2003), 301–8.

18. See *The Principle of Reason*, trans. Reginald Lilly (Bloomington: Indiana University Press, 1991), 104 (German: *Der Satz vom Grund* [Stuttgart: Neske, 1957], 173).

ontological and epistemological system and are not radically separated from
them but rather *distanced* ("thrice removed from the king and the truth" [*Republic* 597e]).[19] Distance (*Abstand*), not being a separation (*Spaltung*), cannot
lead to discordance (*Zwiespalt*).[20]

Nietzsche's discordance could refer, however, to the relationship between philosophy and art (or more exactly the one between truth and beauty) in Plato's
Phaedrus, says Heidegger. And it is in this context that he points to a genuine
Zwiespalt between *alētheia* and *kallos* in that dialogue. Both phenomena are
related to Being as *Idea:* truth as its ultimate unveiling in its proper realm (possibly in philosophy) and beauty as the medium of its appearance and supreme
shining (*to ekphanestaton*). In fact, the latter leads directly to the former: "The
beautiful elevates us beyond the sensuous and bears us back into the true."[21]
Even though truth and art seem to be separated and opposed to one another
as the intelligible is opposed to the sensible, they both strive to bring about the
openness of the nonsensuous realm of Being: "Truth and beauty are in essence
related to the selfsame, to Being; they belong together in one, the one thing
that is decisive: to open Being and keep it open."[22] Thus there is a discordance
between truth and beauty, or art, in Plato's *Phaedrus,* but it is far from being
dreadful. On the contrary, from the ontological, epistemological, and aesthetic
point of view, it is a harmonious, "felicitous discordance" (*ein beglückender
Zwiespalt*). To put it differently, the discordance sensu stricto, the opposition
between the sensible and the intelligible, beauty and truth, art or poetry and
philosophy, is circumvented: "But it belongs to the essence of Platonism that
it is able to get out of the way of (*ausweichen*) that discordance by positing
Being in such a way that it can do so without this circumvention becoming
visible as such."[23] Thus the harmonious character of the discordance might in
fact result from the concealment of its dreadful aspect. In Heidegger's commentary, this possibility and this danger is hinted at by the use of the same
word (*Abstand,* or "distance") to characterize the relationship between art and
truth in *Phaedrus*—art, residing in the sensuous, finds itself "far removed from

19. *The "Republic" of Plato,* trans. Benjamin Jowett, 3rd rev. ed. (Oxford: Oxford University Press, 1888),
310.

20. *Nietzsche,* 1:198 (German: *Nietzsche,* 1:202).

21. *Nietzsche,* 1:198 (German: "Das Schöne hebt über das Sinnliche hinweg und trägt in das Wahre
zurück" [*Nietzsche,* 1:202]).

22. *Nietzsche,* 1:198 (German: "Wahrheit und Schönheit sind in ihrem Wesen auf das Selbe, das Sein,
bezogen; sie gehören in dem Einen, Entscheidenden zusammen: das Sein offenbar zu halten und offenbar zu machen" [*Nietzsche,* 1:201]).

23. *Nietzsche,* 1:198–99 (German: "Aber es ist das Wesen des Platonismus, daß er diesem Zwiespalt
ausweicht, indem er das Sein so ansetzt, daß er ausweichen kann und dieses Ausweichen nicht als ein
solches sichtbar wird" [*Nietzsche,* 1:202]). Krell's translation of "ausweichen" as "effacing" risks obliterat-
ing the difference between the *Phaedrus* and the *Republic.*

truth" (*im weiten Abstand von der Wahrheit*)—and in the *Republic*—art as *mimēsis* "stands far below truth in Plato's metaphysics; we encounter here a distance [*einen Abstand*]."[24]

In order to avoid the danger of ultimately placing poetry and art "under the guidance of philosophy as knowledge of the essence of beings," it would be helpful to reread the *Phaedrus,* and especially Socrates' so-called palinode, in a rhapsodic mode.[25] Even before the passage on beauty's particular role in the disclosure of the realm beyond sky/heaven (the passage discussed by Heidegger), a crucial interplay between poetry and truth, the truth of poetry, the poetry of truth, takes place. Indeed, Socrates' first, rhetorical-philosophical speech is interrupted by poetry in the form of a quote from Ibycus—"for offending the gods I am honored by men" (242d)—the remembrance of which made him uneasy when delivering the speech.[26] This evocation of Ibycus is followed by a quasi-mythical story of another poet, Stesichorus, who supposedly went blind after slandering the divinely beautiful Helen in his poem.[27] But as soon as he composed his recantation (*palinōidia*)—"There's no truth to that story [*Ouk est' etumos logos houtos*]/You never sailed that lovely ship,/You never reached the tower of Troy"—he recovered sight.[28] His fault was a disrespect of both beauty and truth, of true *logos,* of "etymology" (*etumos logos*). That the true *logos* here is in fact still part of *muthos,* the "true" version of the myth of Helen and of Troy, should not surprise; in Plato's dialogues, *muthos* is sometimes identified with *logos.*[29] The significance of this poetic truth of myth in the context of the debate over the discordance between art and truth and the quarrel between philosophy and poetry lies in its questioning the simple opposition of both pairs of opposites. It is, indeed, poetry in its relation to myth that is here taken as the model for a speech that apparently contains many theses of the "Platonic" philosophy, such as the ontology of the Ideas and the epistemology of anamnesis.

In his speech, Socrates repeats verbatim Stesichorus's line when he evokes the preceding speech on love and madness: "'There's no truth to that story' [*Ouk*

---

24. *Nietzsche,* 1:187, 198 (German: *Nietzsche,* 1:190, 202).

25. *Nietzsche,* 1:187 (German: "Doch Abstand ist nicht Zwiespalt, dies vor allem dann nicht, wenn die Kunst . . . unter die Leitung der Philosophie als des Wissens vom Wesen des Seienden gestellt wird" [*Nietzsche,* 1:190]).

26. *Phaedrus,* trans. Alexander Nehamas and Paul Woodruff, in *Plato: Complete Works,* ed. John M. Cooper and D. S. Hutchison (Indianapolis, Ind.: Hackett, 1997), 521.

27. See, for example, *Greek Lyrics,* trans. Richmond Lattimore (Chicago: University of Chicago Press, 1955), 37, and *Early Greek Lyric Poetry,* trans. David Mulroy (Ann Arbor: University of Michigan Press, 1992), 103, for the possible poem that required the famous παλινῳδία.

28. *Greek Lyrics,* 37; *Early Greek Lyric Poetry,* 101; Plato, *Phaedrus* 243a–b.

29. See, for example, Plato, *Gorgias* 523a and *Timaeus* 27c and 29d.

est' etumos logos houtos]—that when a lover is available you should give your favors to a man who doesn't love you instead, because he is in control of himself while the lover has lost his head. That would have been fine to say [*kalōs an elegeto*] if madness were bad, pure and simple; but in fact the best things we have come from madness, when it is given as a gift of the god" (244a).[30]

Even though "fine" is here a fair translation of the adverb *kalōs,* the word also points to its other form, *to kalon,* or the beautiful, which will play the crucial role in the epistemology of the palinode. The reference to the authority of the poet Stesichorus might appear remarkable here as well, since in the hierarchy that accompanies Plato's "psychology" of madness later in the dialogue (where Socrates elucidates the theory of the immortality of the soul and of metempsychosis), the poet (*poiētikos*) occupies a rather low place—sixth (248e). Here, however, the poet is not a *mimētēs,* an imitator trice removed from the truth, but an inspired "follower of the Muses" (*mousikos*), a term reserved for one of the highest forms of madness (243a), which also includes the love of beauty (*philokalia*) and love of wisdom (*philosophia*) (248d) in the category of sources of the "best things" (244a).[31] Stesichorus's temporary blindness and his poetic insight into beauty and truth foreshadow the insight of Socrates' lover in the later passage on anamnesis through the sight of bodily beauty.

Indeed, it is ostensibly Stesichorus who is "singing" the *palinōidia;* Socrates only gives him his voice.[32] *Palinōidia* is a *rhapsōidia,* the one that, as a limit case, grounds all others—the series in the midst of which it is situated. If the earlier logos or speech of Socrates was in fact that of Phaedrus, the lover of speeches, the next one is by Stesichorus, the poet.[33] And it is, as we have seen,

30. *Phaedrus,* trans. Alexander Nehamas and Paul Woodruff, 528.
31. *Phaedrus,* trans. Alexander Nehamas and Paul Woodruff, 521, 522.
32. "Στησιχόρου τοῦ Εὐφήμου, Ἱμεραίου," or founder or initiator of χορός (a round dance or chorus), "son of Good Speaker, from the Land of Desire" (*Phaedrus* 244a, trans. Nehamas and Paul Woodruff, 522 n. 21). The etymology is of course part of the play here; there is an ancient anecdote, reported by Ammianus Marcellinus, that Stesichorus's song was one of the last things Socrates desired to learn when he overheard it in his prison. When asked why, Socrates replied: "In order that I may know something more before I depart from life [*ut aliquid sciens amplius e uita discedam*]" (*The Surviving Books of History,* 3 vols., Latin/English text, trans. John C. Rolfe [Cambridge, Mass.: Harvard University Press, 1950], 3:147 [Latin: *Rerumgestarum libri qui supersunt,* 3:146]). The story should be related to Socrates' dream in prison and the injunction to "make music" ("μουσικὴν ποίει καὶ ἐργάζου" [Plato, *Phaedo* 60e6–7]).
33. Toward the end of the palinode, there is a prayer (257a): "So now, dear Love, this is the best and most beautiful palinode we could offer as payment for our debt; some of its language, in particular, was perforce poetical, to please Phaedrus" (*Phaedrus,* trans. Alexander Nehamas and Paul Woodruff, 533; translation modified [Greek: "Αὕτη σοι, ὦ φίλε Ἔρως, εἰς ἡμετέραν δύναμιν ὅτι καλλίστη καὶ ἀρίστη δέδοταί τε καὶ ἐκτέτεισται παλινῳδία, τά τε ἄλλα καὶ τοῖς ὀνόμασιν ἠναγκασμένη ποιητικοῖς τισιν διὰ Φαῖδρον εἰρῆσθαι"]). There is a hesitation here as to the authorship of the palinode, even though, in the English translation, neither Hackforth ("Thus then, dear God of Love, I have offered the fairest recantation and

a reference to another poet, Ibycus, that actually initiated the reversal of the attitude toward love and the resulting poetic recantation. The turn to passionate love is here unambiguously associated with the turn to poetry. And thus the reversal of the attitude toward Eros and madness may also signal the rethinking of the old quarrel and raging discordance, or at least that of their common, philosophical or rhetorical, settlement.

One of the latest attempts at a solution, both to the problematic relationship between poetry and philosophy in general and to the problem of the unity of the *Phaedrus* in particular, is Griswold's *Self-Knowledge in Plato's "Phaedrus."*[34] The attempt seems paradoxical, since it arrives at the result dreaded by Nietzsche through an ostensible interest in the "literary" devices of the dialogues and especially those of the *Phaedrus*. Palinode, for example, plays a prominent role in Griswold's reading, but the extension of its model and its supposed ubiquity in the dialogue will eventually lead to the obliteration of the only true "poetic palinode" under discussion here. Noticing the "strange" rhapsodic mode of the palinode, Griswold plays it down as a simple "conceit" and explains it allegorically: "Socrates' first speech corresponds to Stesichorus' original ode. . . . The war fought over Helen corresponds to the contest between Socrates and Lysias"; all this "fits nicely" with the passage in the *Republic*, where Socrates evokes Stesichorus's palinode in the context of the war fought over an *eidōlon* of Helen.[35] Since *eidōlon* is opposed to truth (*to alēthes*), Griswold marvels that the palinode, ostensibly reverting to the truth, will have recourse to an image as well. But he doesn't pause to investigate the relationship between poetry and truth, whether "dreadful" or "felicitous." He simply proclaims poetic language "suitable to articulating the fantasies of love"; hence it is quite natural that "Socrates' palinode is suitably poetic."[36] And poetry and myth are not incompatible with truth provided we distinguish

fullest atonement that my powers could encompass; some of its language, in particular, was perforce poetical, to please Phaedrus" [*Plato's "Phaedrus," 110*]) nor Nehamas/Woodruff ("especially in view of the rather poetical choice of words Phaedrus made me use" [533]) seems to preserve it. Without reaffirming Stesichorus's authorship, however, Socrates does reaffirm the poetic character of the palinode, and the text doesn't specify its author; Socrates says "our" palinode, and Phaedrus figures as its instigator.

34. *Self-Knowledge in Plato's "Phaedrus"* (1988; rpt., University Park, Pa.: Pennsylvania State University Press, 1996): "A major thesis of this book is that when the *Phaedrus* is interpreted with the form-and-content maxims in mind, the dialogue comes to light as a whole unified by the theme of self-knowledge" (2). The rhetoric of Socrates' palinode will play the crucial role in cementing this unity: "The unity of the *Phaedrus* will become still clearer, however, if we pause to reflect on the first question just mentioned, that is, on the rhetoric of the palinode itself" (137). Another, less radically unifying, attempt to read the Phaedrus rhetorically is that of Ronna Burger (*Plato's "Phaedrus": A Defence of a Philosophic Art of Writing* [Alabama: University of Alabama Press, 1980], 63, 69, 107, and passim).

35. See *Republic* 586c; *Self-Knowledge in Plato's "Phaedrus,"* 73.

36. *Self-Knowledge in Plato's "Phaedrus,"* 73.

between "literal and nonliteral truth," which Griswold claims Socrates does: "Socrates' demand that myth serve his effort to know himself means that the myths must be *subjected* to *interpretation,* as is evident from his use at the start of the *Phaedrus* of the figure of Typhon."[37] As is evident from Griswold's own use of the figure of Typhon at the start of his book, however, it is ultimately the dramatic interpretation that "subjugates" the poetic images of the text, forcing them into his "rhetorical framework"—the expression that governs Griswold's reading of the palinode.[38] The speech is "primarily about the soul; it is a psychology first and a cosmology second."[39] At the end both poetry and philosophy are subjugated to rhetoric, and it is in the last analysis not so much self-knowledge that unites the *Phaedrus*—G. R. F. Ferrari is right to point out that this could be a unified theme of nearly all the dialogues—as an all-encompassing rhetoric of persuasion.[40] This rhetorical unity of the *Phaedrus* can be "clearly" seen in the "rhetoric of the palinode itself," writes Griswold.[41] Indeed, it is the rhetoric of the palinode that connects the rhetorical speeches of the first part with the discussion on rhetoric in the second part.

On this account, the "rhetoric of the palinode," exclusive of its rhapsodic play between poetry and truth, ultimately leads to a "therapeutic" view of both philosophy and rhetoric; philosophy is characterized as "true psychotherapy," supposed to heal the sick soul of Phaedrus by turning him in the right direction.[42] Griswold extends this therapeutic reading to other dialogues of Plato,

37. *Self-Knowledge in Plato's "Phaedrus,"* 141; his emphasis on "interpretation," my emphasis on "subjected."

38. *Self-Knowledge in Plato's "Phaedrus,"* 74.

39. *Self-Knowledge in Plato's "Phaedrus,"* 75.

40. "'Self-knowledge' as Griswold sometimes seems to take the term—roughly, a salutary understanding of what it is to be human (2–6)—could be judged the ultimate theme of almost all Platonic dialogues" (G. R. F. Ferrari, review of *Self-Knowledge in Plato's "Phaedrus,"* by Charles L. Griswold Jr., *Philosophical Review* 97, no. 3 [1988]: 109). Cf. Ferrari's book on *Phaedrus, Listening to the Cicadas,* written against the scholarly and philosophical assault on its poetry; the last words seem to address Griswold in particular: "[Plato] lets the rough edges poke through the joints of his dialogue. Let us not struggle too hard, then, to unify the *Phaedrus;* for the real struggle is elsewhere" (232). Heidegger does recognize the importance of the passion of self-knowledge in Plato's *Phaedrus* ("Leidenschaft zur Selbst-Erkenntnis") but doesn't understand it in Griswold's rhetorical fashion (*Plato's "Sophist,"* 219 [German: *Platon: "Sophistes,"* 316]).

41. *Self-Knowledge in Plato's "Phaedrus,"* 137.

42. See a critique of this kind of reading among the "dramatic" readers of Plato, and in particular Drew Hyland, in the introduction to this book. Gadamer's warning against taking a therapeutic conversation for an authentic dialogue might be "salutary" here (*Truth and Method,* trans. Joel Weinsheimer and Donald G. Marshall [1975; rpt., New York: Continuum, 2002], 363 and 385 [German: *Wahrheit und Methode: Grundzüge einer philosophischen Hermeneutik* (Tübingen: Mohr, 1960), 345 and 363]). For philosophy as "true psychotherapy," see Griswold, *Self-Knowledge in Plato's "Phaedrus,"* 77; cf. a more nuanced view of the Socratic θεραπεία τῆς ευχῆς in *Plato's "Phaedrus,"* trans. Reginald Hackforth, 9ff. See the critique of this reading by G. J. de Vries, review of *Self-Knowledge in Plato's "Phaedrus,"* by Charles L. Griswold Jr., *Mnemosyne* 41, nos. 1–2 (1988): 161–64.

which "are medicinal in that they vary the treatment with the patient."[43] Indeed, Plato was "not a revolutionary," and his "medicine" was to be "conservatively applied" in maintaining the existing structure of social distinctions, especially the one between the philosopher-rulers and "non-philosophical people."[44] Phaedrus, the character, belongs to the latter category. Neither Socrates nor Plato would bother to talk to him in "the course of life."[45] Phaedrus is wrong to imagine himself a friend of Socrates.[46] Indeed, Socrates ultimately cares only about his own self-medication of "spiritual self-motion."[47] It would perhaps be beneficial in this reading to retranslate all these terms ("therapy," "antidote," "medicine," etc.) into Socrates' language of *pharmakon,* but Griswold would certainly consider such a gesture "anti-Platonic," that is, contrary to Plato's clear intentions.[48]

Griswold's therapeutic rhetoric is "philosophical." And somewhat perversely again, the poetic rhapsodic palinode is made into a model, and reduced to a stage, in an all-encompassing dialectic. The poetic, literary aspect is not what really counts: "The issue of the unity of the *Phaedrus* signals not so much a literary as a deeply philosophical problem."[49] And it is this "deeply philosophical

43. *Self-Knowledge in Plato's "Phaedrus,"* 221.

44. *Self-Knowledge in Plato's "Phaedrus,"* 221.

45. *Self-Knowledge in Plato's "Phaedrus,"* 225. One wonders what kind of teaching Griswold had in mind in an earlier passage of his book: "Since the central division in the hierarchy is between the philosophers and nonphilosophers, the problem of rhetoric is especially exhibited by the problem of the ability for the former to communicate with—and teach—the latter" (103).

46. *Self-Knowledge in Plato's "Phaedrus,"* 227.

47. *Self-Knowledge in Plato's "Phaedrus,"* 229. Just like love, friendship is only a means to the all-encompassing goal of self-knowledge; see G. R. F. Ferrari, review of "*Self-Knowledge in Plato's "Phaedrus,"* 408–11, and G. J. de Vries, review of *Self-Knowledge in Plato's "Phaedrus,"* 161–64.

48. *Self-Knowledge in Plato's "Phaedrus,"* 201. Here again, the rhapsodic reading is best displayed in contrast to the dramatic, mirror-based interpretation, which tends to reformulate the terms of Socrates' quarrel. Griswold, for example, acknowledges that "the really fundamental debate is 'the ancient quarrel between philosophy and poetry,'" but he maintains that "Plato understands that his fundamental argument is not with other philosophers . . . but with the hordes of antiphilosophers" ("Plato's Metaphilosophy: Why Plato Wrote Dialogues," in *Platonic Writings/Platonic Readings,* ed. Charles L. Griswold Jr. [New York: Routledge, 1988], 152). Griswold mentions the poets, sophists, and popular rhetoricians, but he is more interested in modern "antiphilosophers," and one knows from his *Self-Knowledge in Plato's "Phaedrus"* that Derrida and Rorty are his prominent examples of the latter (I suspect that all contemporary authors discussed in the present book would share this honor). The "anti-" argument seems particularly "rigorous" in Griswold's comparison of his own and Derrida's interpretation of the *Phaedrus:* "Roughly put, his [Derrida's] is in principle anti-Platonic and mine Platonic" (*Self-Knowledge in Plato's "Phaedrus,"* 235). And what if Derrida's playful style resembled that of Socrates? "Like a wolf resembles a dog," Griswold would retort, but without the Elean Stranger's playful irony; indeed, he does have a sure criterion to distinguish them—a good intention: "There is ruse and dissembling in Socratic and Platonic irony as well, but with the opposite intention from Derrida's" (291 n. 9). All this sounds rather dogmatic for a professedly antidogmatic philosopher.

49. *Self-Knowledge in Plato's "Phaedrus,"* 200.

problem" that will require a sublation of the rhapsodic palinode by rhetorical *tekhnē*. Now, *tekhnē* is itself "subordinated to telos," and this subordination is itself "a kind of palinode."[50] Thus the dialogue is understood as a series of odes and palinodes: "The repeated movement from an 'ode' to 'palinode' (the latter serving as an 'ode' for a further 'palinode') is a recovery of a larger context that is 'already there.'"[51] The dialogue is ultimately defined as "the living self-motion of thought."[52]

I have devoted so much attention to Griswold's reading of the *Phaedrus* because it seems now to be a largely accepted "dramatic" reading, one that ostensibly respects the dialogue form and yet ends up framing the *Phaedrus* in terms of a monologic, quasi-Hegelian dialectic that dissolves the rhapsodic-poetic *palinōidia* in a series of philosophical-rhetorical movements.[53] Indeed, Griswold's repression of dialogue results from his neglect of the rhapsodic nature of Plato's text, as epitomized in the palinode.[54] Socrates should not be identified as the only author and "user" of the palinode, just as Plato should not be considered a transcendent author of "his" text. The palinode presents a vision that restructures the relationship between art or poetry and truth, and it does so through the particular role played by beauty and passionate love in the recollection of the being of other ideas. This goal can only be achieved because of the rhapsodic/mimetic character of the palinode. It is not a philosopher or a rhetorician who "uses" poetic images in order to achieve his immediate or ulterior purposes. It is a poet who sings the *palinōidia* and thus opens up the world, including the world of the self. And for that reason there is only one palinode in the *Phaedrus*. Its character is poetic and singular.

A palinode is an inspired speech, different from all the others that might be controlled by *tekhnē;* as the palinode itself says of poetry: "If anyone comes to the gates of poetry and expects to become an adequate poet by acquiring expert knowledge or competence [*ek tekhnēs*] without the Muses' madness, he will fail, and his self-controlled verses will be eclipsed [outshined *ēphanisthē*] by the poetry of men who have been driven out of their minds [*mainomenoi*]" (245a).[55] The word *ēphanisthē* in this passage, paraphrased by Reginald Hackforth as "is

---

50. *Self-Knowledge in Plato's "Phaedrus,"* 201.

51. *Self-Knowledge in Plato's "Phaedrus,"* 218.

52. *Self-Knowledge in Plato's "Phaedrus,"* 219.

53. See the terminology of "cancellation or negation," "preservation," and "progress," as well as of "synthesis" in Griswold, *Self-Knowledge in Plato's "Phaedrus,"* 153; cf. an explicit, and nuanced, comparison between the Platonic and Hegelian dialectic in David Roochnik, *Beautiful City: The Dialectical Character of Plato's "Republic"* (Ithaca, N.Y.: Cornell University Press, 2003), 147–48.

54. See Takis Poulakos's critique of Griswold's dogmatism in his review of *Self-Knowledge in Plato's "Phaedrus"*: "It is unfortunate that a book about dialogue does not promote the perpetuation of dialogue" (*Quarterly Journal of Speech* 75, no. 2 [1989]: 231).

55. *Phaedrus*, trans. Alexander Nehamas and Paul Woodruff, 523.

nowhere to be found," has the same root as the word *ekphanestaton* or the most brilliant ("the most manifest to sense" [Hackforth], "the most clearly visible" [Alexander Nehamas/Paul Woodruff]), which characterizes beauty in contradistinction to other ideas such as wisdom or justice in the climax of the palinode.[56] It is this characteristic that allows for the privileged role of beauty in the recovery of the forgotten perception of being. The fact that poetry is also characterized with a word akin to "shining" and "appearing" (*phainesthai*) is important for the recognition of the essential link between the poetry of the palinode itself and beauty as crucial to the unconcealment of being, that is, *alētheia,* or truth.

If we are attentive to the rhapsodic, poetic character of the palinode, we can no longer include it in the continuous series of arguments (Griswold's "palinodes"). In fact, the poetry of the palinode *interrupts* the series of speeches and arguments. In other words, the quarrel or (dreadful) discordance is reaffirmed even though the particular role assigned to beauty (*kallos*) in the palinode might suggest the possibility of a "felicitous discordance." What is problematic in Heidegger's reading of the *Phaedrus* in light of Nietzsche's discordance is the association of beauty with art or poetry. Only if we take the palinode to be a rhapsodic performance of a poem, a unique and singular manifestation of beauty, can the potentiality for a "felicitous" relationship between art (as poetry) and truth be inscribed into the—otherwise dreadful—discordance.[57] In this sense, the credibility of the palinode's philosophical vision would in fact depend on its rhapsodic performance.

One might ask, though, whether any reconciliation between art and truth does not necessarily lead to the obliteration of the poetic resistance to philosophical recuperation and whether Heidegger's view (which makes him single out the thought of the *Phaedrus;* it is, he claims, "the most accomplished" dialogue of Plato, belonging to "the *akmē* of Plato's creative life") does not call into question the very possibility of a definite reconciliation in Plato.[58] Indeed, when in the conclusion of his lecture on Plato's *Phaedrus* Heidegger emphasizes the danger of evading the discordance between beauty or art and truth and of veiling this very evasion, it is to Platonism, not to Plato himself, that he ascribes the concealment of the *Zwiespalt*.[59] Although some of Plato's texts (such as the *Phaedrus, Symposium,* or even parts of the *Republic*) may have

56. *Plato's "Phaedrus,"* trans. Reginald Hackforth, 57; *Phaedrus,* trans. Alexander Nehamas and Paul Woodruff, 528; *Plato's "Phaedrus,"* trans. Reginald Hackforth, 93.

57. John Sallis seems to suggest the same problematic in his insistence on the radical separation "from being" that can only be "mitigated" through the contemplation of "earthly" images (*Being and Logos: Reading the Platonic Dialogues* [Bloomington: Indiana University Press, 1996], 156–57).

58. *Nietzsche,* 1:190 (German: *Nietzsche,* 1:194).

59. *Nietzsche,* 1:198–99 (German: *Nietzsche,* 1:202).

suggested such a concealment, other texts (such as those discussed in this book) can hardly be taken as concealing discordance's irreducible character. Is not, in fact, the banishment of the poets the most striking feature of the last book of the *Republic?* And the same gesture is repeated in the last of Plato's dialogues, the *Laws,* where the Athenian, a philosopher, clearly addresses the tragic poets as those who belong to the opposite side of an (equally irreducible) opposition: they are at the same time his peers and contenders on the same field.[60] Nietzsche's so-called reversal of Platonism would then reaffirm and even accentuate this antagonism and rivalry between philosophers, the champions of truth, and tragic poets, an antagonism proclaimed in the *Laws* by Plato's Athenian. The "reversal" would consist in revealing the concealment (considered "Platonist") of the subordination of poetry or art to truth or philosophy. In Heidegger's words: "When Platonism is overturned everything that characterizes it must also be overturned; whatever it can cloak and conceal, whatever it can pronounce felicitous[,] . . . must out, and must arouse dread."[61]

Perhaps the most important aspect of the confrontation between Plato, Nietzsche, and Heidegger in respect to beauty or art and truth, the possibility of their dreadful or felicitous discordance (*Zwiespalt*), is the disclosure of the "ambivalence" of the term *Zwiespalt* itself.[62] Besides its common sense meaning of "antagonistic discordance" or "abscission" (*Zerrissenheit*), the word *Zwiespalt* may signify a simple severance, "breaking in two" (*Entzweiung*), not incompatible with a "concordance" (*Einklang*), which is the case of the relationship between beauty and truth in the *Phaedrus:* "Accord prevails in the severance, because the beautiful, as radiant and sensuous, has in advance sheltered its essence in the truth of Being as supersensuous."[63] Nor is the ambivalence to be limited to the idiom of the German language. Rather, it is only a particularly striking expression of the nature of the relationship between truth and beauty or art, the latter being always in danger of succumbing to the rule of the former. Heidegger's own rejection of the "old dispute" in Plato's *Republic* as a possible case of Nietzsche's discordance perhaps results from such an ambivalence and from the tendency to favor the *Einklang* acceptation of the discordance. In the same vein, Socrates' *diaphora*—originally a problem—might

60. See Plato, *Laws* 817, trans. Benjamin Jowett, in *The Dialogues of Plato,* 5 vols., 3rd rev. ed. (New York: Macmillan, 1892), 5:200.

61. *Nietzsche,* 1:199 (German: "Wo aber der Platonismus umgedreht wird, muß auch alles, was ihn kennzeichnet, sich umdrehen und, was sich verbergen und verschleiern ließ und als beglückend in Anspruch genommen werden konnte, muß . . . heraustreten und Entsetzen erregen" [*Nietzsche,* 1:202]).

62. Indeed, "ambivalence" is a possible rendering of "Zwiespalt."

63. *Nietzsche,* 1:198 (German: "In der Entzweiung überwiegt der Einklang, weil das Schöne als das Scheinende, Sinnliche im voraus sein Wesen in der Wahrheit des Seins als des Obersinnlichen geborgen hat" [*Nietzsche,* 1:202]).

well contain the seeds of the two traditional means of its solution: on the one hand, the exclusion of all art from the ideal philosophical and political structure and, on the other hand, the subordination of art to philosophy and politics, historically accomplished in Neoplatonic and Aristotelian poetics.[64]

Tragedy and Philosophy:
The "New Opposition" Between the Dionysian and the Socratic

Profound aversion to reposing once and for all in any one total view of the world. Fascination of the opposing point of view: refusal to be deprived of the stimulus of the enigmatic character.
—FRIEDRICH NIETZSCHE

What is remarkable in Heidegger's interpretation of the Nietzschean "overturning of Platonism" is the lack of any reference to the historical context of the death of tragedy, which in Nietzsche's view coincided with the birth of what he initially called "Socratism" (*Sokratismus*).[65] Yet it is this context that is the setting of Nietzsche's confrontation with Plato in the text that first marked the "dread" in face of the discordance, *The Birth of Tragedy*. And one of Nietzsche's contributions to the understanding of the "old dispute" is to have shown it to be historical. The adjective *palaia* used by Socrates in the *Republic* suggests the persistence of the dispute. To be sure, Socrates promised to reconsider his verdict of banishment if someone—"poet or not"—managed to prove the public utility of poetry and mimesis, and Aristotle is generally believed to have successfully done just that. However, it is doubtful that true poetry and tragedy would be willing to return from exile on Aristotle's terms—at least Nietzsche doubts it when in *The Birth of Tragedy* he attributes the death of Attic tragedy to circumstances very similar to those created by Aristotelian poetics. Tragedy would have died by the excess of logos in the sense of the rational element, by becoming not only "more philosophical than history" but *too* philosophical in general.

---

64. Even if a strict distinction between the hierarchical subordination of art to the system of Ideas in the *Republic*, on the one hand, and the harmonious discordance between beauty and truth in the *Phaedrus*, on the other hand, is difficult to draw—for example, the systematic integration is far from being smooth in the *Republic* and the beauty in the *Phaedrus* can hardly be associated with art without further ado—Heidegger's reading has the merit of pointing out the "Platonic" origin of the tension (emphasized by Nietzsche in his short "History of an Error" [*Twilight of the Idols*, trans. Duncan Large (Oxford: Oxford University Press, 1998), 20 (German: *Götzen-Dämmerung*, in *Kritische Studienausgabe*, 6:80; cf. *The Will to Power*, frag. 567, pp. 305–6)]) between Neoplatonic and especially Christian "Platonism" and Plato himself (*Nietzsche*, 1:202–5 [German: *Nietzsche*, 1:205–8]).

65. The epigraph to this section comes from *The Will to Power*, frag. 470, p. 262 (German: "Tiefe Abneigung, in irgend einer Gesammt-Betrachtung der Welt ein für alle Mal auszuruhen; Zauber der entgegengesetzten Denkweise; sich den Anreiz des änigmatischen Charakters nicht nehmen lassen" [in *Nachgelaßene Fragmente, 1885–1886*, in *Kritische Studienausgabe*, 12:142]).

If it is true that Plato formulated the controversy and that Aristotle ratified the decision to end it, both the controversy and the decision were already
at stake at least one generation earlier. In the twelfth section of *The Birth of
Tragedy*, Nietzsche refers to this fateful event when he opposes the Aeschylean
and Sophoclean "noble" (*edle*), even though "unconscious" (*bewusstlose*), art-
istry (*Künstlerschaft*) to the conscious critical production of Euripides.⁶⁶ It is
also in this section that, discussing the so-called suicide of tragedy, Nietzsche
corrects the direction of his attack (the object of which, in this and in the preceding section of the book, was the last of the great tragedians): "Euripides
was, in a sense, only a mask: the deity that spoke through him was neither
Dionysus nor Apollo, but an altogether newborn demon, called *Socrates*. This
is the *new opposition* [*neuer Gegensatz*]: the Dionysian and the Socratic—and
the art of Greek tragedy was wrecked on this."⁶⁷

The opposition is *new* in respect to the Apollo/Dionysus polarity, which
governs the poetics of tragedy and art in general as presented in the first half
of *The Birth of Tragedy*. The substitution of the Socratic for the Apollonian
here is not a simple exchange of one symbolic figure for another in the same
realm. Indeed, the Apollonian and the Dionysian were in Nietzsche's view
the two exclusive aesthetic principles, and the intrusion of an alien element
must have had disastrous consequences for the equilibrium that governed the
tragedy of Euripides' predecessors.

Whereas the "Platonic" ("Socratic") version of the *diaphora* establishes a
timeless relationship that could be equitably solved only by the intervention
of a transcendent, ideal realm, Nietzsche sees the opposition as historically situated in the second half of fifth-century Greece: the *neue Gegensatz* was an
effect of the intervention of sophistic ratiocination and Socratic philosophy in
the difficult balance of forces that the Apollonian and the Dionysian attained
in Hellenic culture and in particular in Attic tragedy. Attic tragedy was the
effect of reconciliation, of the treaty of peace or rather truce in the struggle
between the two original, vital, and artistic, principles: "This reconciliation is
the most important moment in the history of the Greek cult: wherever we turn
we note the revolutions resulting from this event. The two antagonists were
reconciled; the boundary lines to be observed henceforth by each were sharply

66. *The Birth of Tragedy*, in *Basic Writings of Nietzsche*, trans. Walter Kaufmann (1966; rpt., New York: Modern Library, 1992), §12, pp. 84–85 (German: *Die Geburt der Tragödie*, in *Kritische Studienausgabe*, 1:86).

67. *The Birth of Tragedy*, §12, p. 82; translation modified, my emphasis; "neue Gegensatz" can also mean "new discord" (German: "Euripides war in gewissen Sinne nur Maske: die Gottheit, die aus ihm redete, war nicht Dionysus, auch nicht Apollo, sondern ein ganz neugeborner Dämon, genannt *Sokrates*. Dies ist der neue Gegensatz: das Dionysische und das Sokratische, und das Kunstwerk der griechischen Tragödie ging an ihm zu Grunde" [*Die Geburt der Tragödie*, in *Kritische Studienausgabe*, 1:83]).

defined, and there was to be a periodical exchange of gifts of esteem. At bottom, however, the chasm was not bridged over."[68]

Indeed, the tension persisted and commanded the development of Greek art. Attic tragedy did not suppress it; in particular it did not suppress the danger of the uncontrolled release of Dionysian energies. Euripides' own play the *Bacchae* brings to light the possibility of an irrepressible tide of Dionysian flow submerging all Apollonian boundaries set to contain it. And instead of reading the *Bacchae,* with Nietzsche, as a belated recantation of the poet, we might consider this tragedy to be Euripides' justification for his rejection of the tragedies of his predecessors, tragedies that maintained the dangerous tension. The offense to the philosophical sense of justice attains in this tragedy such a degree of disorder (*adikia* as *Unfug,* in Heidegger's terminology) that the old balance of power between Dionysus and Apollo is threatened. This balance had been challenged and eventually suppressed in Euripides' other plays, by his "conscious insight" (*die bewusste Einsicht*).[69] This effect was achieved through the alliance between Euripides and Socrates, that is, in a sense, between poetic art and philosophy. It was, in Nietzsche's words, the historical victory of aesthetic and logical Socratism.[70]

"Aesthetic Socratism," an oxymoron on the traditional reading of Plato's text, was, according to Nietzsche, the result of the "dubious enlightenment" of the age of the Sophists, which led to the progressive surrender of the "old Marathonian stalwart fitness of body and soul."[71] It is, however, Socrates and Euripides, rather than the usually chastised Sophists—Protagoras, Gorgias, or Hippias—that are the object of Nietzsche's prosecution and condemnation. And it is true that the names of the two men are sometimes mentioned in the same breath in documents from Greek antiquity. Both are, for instance, juxtaposed in the famous Delphic oracle record: Socrates is pronounced the wisest man living, with Euripides closely behind.[72] They are coupled in the raillery of Aristophanes' comedy; they could have actually met in the theater, Euripides'

68. *The Birth of Tragedy,* §2, p. 39 (German: "Diese Versöhnung ist der wichtigste Moment in der Geschichte des griechischen Cultus: wohin man blickt, sind die Umwälzungen dieses Ereignisses sichtbar. Es war die Versöhnung zweier Gegner, mit scharfer Bestimmung ihrer von jetzt ab einzuhaltenden Grenzlinien und mit periodischer Uebersendung von Ehrengeschenken; im Grunde war die Kluft nicht überbrückt" [*Die Geburt der Tragödie,* in *Kritische Studienausgabe,* 1:32]).

69. *The Birth of Tragedy,* §12, pp. 85–86 (German: *Die Geburt der Tragödie,* in *Kritische Studienausgabe,* 1:83).

70. *The Birth of Tragedy,* §§12 and 13, p. 86 and 89 (German: *Die Geburt der Tragödie,* in *Kritische Studienausgabe,* 1:87 and 91).

71. *The Birth of Tragedy,* §13, p. 87 (German: *Die Geburt der Tragödie,* in *Kritische Studienausgabe,* 1:88).

72. Sophocles would have been a *distant* third if he were to fit Nietzsche's argument (*The Birth of Tragedy,* §13).

tragedies having reportedly been the only ones honored by Socrates' presence.[73] There are even insinuations in Diogenes Laertius (quoting Mnesilochus, Callias, and Aristophanes) that Socrates gave a hand to Euripides in writing tragedies.[74] But more significant than these anecdotal indications of the collusion between Socratic philosophy and Euripidean tragedy is the actual structure of Euripides' plays, with their principle of *logos:* pro-logue, dia-logue (with its rhetorical speeches), and epi-logue. The characters in Euripides' plays, although bearing the same names as the heroes of Aeschylus and Sophocles, are no longer half gods, figures of the god Dionysus. They are, rather, incarnations of the spectator, the man on the street or more precisely the man at the Athenian agora in the late fifth-century BC: a lover of argument, schooled by the Sophists and by Socrates. The spectator is subjugated not by the power of fabulous vision, by the evocation of heroic deeds and celebration of memorable events, but by the compelling force of the arguments dealt by the familiar characters, the likes of himself (or herself?[75]). To be properly appreciated, a scene of rhetorical exchange must be free of an immediate interest in the development of plot, free of any suspense. The Euripidean prologue serves the purpose of excluding any enigma; it presents the spectator with the entire schema to be fleshed out progressively by individual scenes. Not so much the marvelous, the astounding (*thaumaston*), as the rationally plausible (*eikos*) and rigorous (*akribes*) is now appreciated in the theater. Euripides' tragedy integrated a new philosophy of the Greek enlightenment and thus announced the victory of philosophy in its dispute with tragedy, a victory that eventually led to the death of tragedy. A couple of generations later, Aristotle theoretically ratified this victory and began a long tradition in the history of Western philosophy and art, maintained especially through neoclassical, "Academic" rules that were still governing the bourgeois theater of Nietzsche's own time.[76] When in 1888 Nietzsche spoke of the discordance between art and truth, he referred to his first book and thus, implicitly, to the "new opposition" between the Dionysian and the Socratic—the beginning of the "dreadful" (*entsetzlich*) development.

73. See Diogenes Laertius, *Lives of Eminent Philosophers,* 2 vols., Greek/English text, trans. R. D. Hicks (1925; rpt., Cambridge, Mass.: Harvard University Press, 1972), 2:162–63.

74. *Lives of Eminent Philosophers,* 2:148–49.

75. The presence of women in the Athenian theater is debated among the historians.

76. In his *Poetics,* Aristotle required the presence of "consistent" (or "consistently inconsistent") characters subordinated to plot and understandable to the audience because of their "familiarity" ("τὸ ὅμοιον" [1453a5–6; 1454a23; 1454b10–11]), and he made λόγος or μῦθος "the first principle and as it were the soul of tragedy" (1450a38–39 [Greek/English text: *The Poetics,* ed. and trans. W. Hamilton Fyfe (1927; rpt., Cambridge, Mass.: Harvard University Press, 1982), 26]), allowing only for a limited play of the θαυμαστόν, when it does not exceed the logical sequence of the events ("δι' ἄλληλα" [1452a4–5]).

Nietzsche's puzzlement at the Greek institution of the rhapsode is significant in this context. In the eighth section of *The Birth of Tragedy*, he attempts to explain the tragic chorus as dramatic proto-phenomenon through an opposition with the rhapsodic artist. The rhapsode does not become fused with the images he contemplates, and he is not actually metamorphosed into another character, as is the case with the tragic satyr who surrenders his own identity. A rhapsode is able, like a painter, to contemplate the images he helps to produce.[77] In section 12, Nietzsche interprets Euripides' drama in light of what he calls "dramatized epos," which belongs to the Apollonian form of art. The actor in such a drama is never fully an actor; he remains a rhapsode (*Der Schauspieler in disem dramatisirten Epos bleibt im tiefsten Grunde immer noch Rhapsode*), contemplating the images of the Apollonian dream.[78] Euripides, however, is linked not to the archaic epic rhapsode but to its modern version. Nietzsche evokes Plato's *Ion* as the portrait of such a rhapsode: he is no longer absorbed in mere appearance but is now also impressed by fiery affects and by thoughts "copied very realistically [*höchst realistisch nachgemachte*] and in no sense dipped into the ether of art."[79] I reconsider this interpretation of *Ion* in my concluding chapter. Here let us notice that Nietzsche "himself" might have eventually become an epic rhapsode, giving voice to the character "Nietzsche" and observing, for example, his confrontation with Wagner (within his confrontation with Plato and the Western metaphysical tradition) in "Nietzsche contra Wagner" or his play of hyperboles in *Ecce Homo*. It seems that after dismissing Wagner as a champion of the modern revival of the tragic, Nietzsche himself remained the only candidate to perform the role of the protagonist in the *agon* between philosophy and tragedy, but again as a Platonic rhapsode, watching from time to time the effect of his play on the audience. Thus the old quarrel and the new opposition took, in the words of Werner Dannhauser, the form of "[Nietzsche's] quarrel with Socrates." It was "part of a vast historical drama which [Nietzsche] recounts [in his work] and which features Socrates as the first villain and Nietzsche himself as the final hero."[80]

---

77. *The Birth of Tragedy*, §8, p. 64 (German: *Die Geburt der Tragödie*, in *Kritische Studienausgabe*, 1:61).

78. *The Birth of Tragedy*, §12, p. 83 (German: *Die Geburt der Tragödie*, in *Kritische Studienausgabe*, 1:84).

79. *The Birth of Tragedy*, §12, p. 83 (German: *Die Geburt der Tragödie*, in *Kritische Studienausgabe*, 1:84).

80. *Nietzsche's View of Socrates* (Ithaca, N.Y.: Cornell University Press, 1974), 272; cf. Hermann Josef Schmidt, *Nietzsche und Socrates* (Meisenheim: Anton Hain, 1969).

"Rhapsodic Woman": The Play of Art and Truth

The reading or writing supplement must be rigorously prescribed, but by the necessities of a *game,* by the logic of *play,* signs to which the system of all textual powers must be accorded and attuned.

—JACQUES DERRIDA

Derrida's reading of Plato's *Phaedrus* in "Plato's Pharmacy" ("La pharmacie de Platon" [1968]) does not refer either to Heidegger's reading of the same dialogue or to Nietzsche's texts on the "raging discordance," which prompted Heidegger's reconsideration of the Platonic view on art.[81] But Derrida does reflect on the Plato-Nietzsche-Heidegger *Auseinandersetzung,* or confrontation, on the subject of art and truth—read in terms of "woman" as the incarnation of both—in a later text, *Spurs: Nietzsche's Styles* (*Éperons: Les styles de Nietzsche* [1978]).[82] This text is an excellent introduction to Derrida's take on the problematic of the old quarrel and of the raging discordance, both of which are ultimately at stake in "Plato's Pharmacy." On the other hand, "Plato's Pharmacy" provides *Spurs* with the key notion of the *pharmakon.* The two texts should be read together as a supplement to Heidegger's commentary, which not only *contourne la femme* ("skirts the woman") but at the same time *contourne,* goes around, evades *play*—which, on Derrida's reading of Nietzsche, "belongs" to "woman's nature," that is to say, to the "nature" of both art and truth.[83]

The phrase "woman's nature" or "woman's essence" can only appear within quotation marks, since woman as an artist par excellence (*das Weib ist so artistisch*) is a "concealer of naturalness" (*dissimulat[rice] de la nature, Verhehler[in] der Natürlichkeit*); there is no essence of woman because "woman distances, and distances herself from herself" (*la femme écarte et s'écarte d'elle-même*).[84] Now, within the conventionally conceived structure of the old quarrel, the place of (essentially mimetic) woman would be at the far end of essence and of truth. Derrida does not accept this simple binary schema, however, and shows that Nietzsche as an author is far from adhering to it either. Both "woman" and "Nietzsche" incarnate truth and dissimulation at the same time—incarnate the truth of dissimulation and the dissimulation of truth. The femininity of truth is not limited to an erotic image for an unveiling philosopher but indicates,

81. The epigraph to this section comes from "Plato's Pharmacy," 64 (French: "Le supplément de lecture ou d'écriture doit être rigoureusement prescrit mais par la nécessité d'un *jeu,* signe auquel il faut accorder le système de tous ses pouvoirs" ["La pharmacie de Platon," 80]).

82. Published in a French/English edition as Jacques Derrida, *Éperons: Les styles de Nietzsche/Spurs: Nietzsche's Styles,* trans. Barbara Harlow (Chicago: University of Chicago Press, 1979).

83. *Éperons/Spurs,* 84/85.

84. Friedrich Nietzsche, *The Gay Science,* §361, p. 317 (German: *Die fröhliche Wissenschaft,* in *Kritische Studienausgabe,* 3:609); *Éperons/Spurs,* 46/47; Derrida, *Éperons/Spurs,* 50/51; translation modified.

rather, a constant play with veils as the truth of both truth and play, for example, the play of writing. Nietzsche's writing belongs in the space of this play of truth, play with genders and genres. His text does not follow the rules of a philosophical treatise, with its stable authorial position, but rather enters the mimetic space of the rhapsodic mode.

"Supposing truth is a woman—What then?" Derrida quotes Nietzsche. "Is the suspicion not justified that all philosophers, insofar as they were dogmatists, have had little understanding of women (*sich schlecht auf Weiber verstanden*, have been mishearing [*mal entendu*] as to women)?"[85] And he blames, with Nietzsche, a dreadful seriousness (*le sérieux effroyable, der schauerliche Ernst*) for the philosophers' incapacity to deal with truth, that is, woman. For truth belongs to the realm of the play of dissimulation and revelation (*le jeu des voiles*), and it is woman, artist par excellence, who brings truth within this realm.[86] Woman is "a non-identity, a non-figure, a simulacrum, the abyss of distance, the out-distancing of distance," or in the Heideggerian terminology of *Entfernung*, "the veiled enigma of proximation."[87] Truth takes place in the opening of this distancing, in the frustration of identity, when woman "distances herself there of/from herself" (*la femme s'y écarte d'elle-même*).[88] If there is no truth or essence of woman, it is because this "abyssal distancing of/from truth" (*de la vérité*) is "truth" as untruth and because a name of this truth is, precisely, woman. Art is another name for this "non-truth of truth," and both are united in Nietzsche and Derrida through the notion of dissimulation.[89]

In the role of this nontruth of truth, both woman and art reveal the "beautiful potentialities" (*belles possibilités*) of life but only in a form that is veiled, and thus all the more seductive.[90] Dogmatic philosophers cannot understand woman or art precisely because they believe in truth without veil, truth of full presence. Woman, on the other hand, like art, "*is* truth, she knows that there is no truth, that the truth does not take place, and that no one possesses the truth."[91] Like a Brechtian artist, woman distances herself from the truth she is

85. *Éperons/Spurs*, 54/55; translation modified; cf. Friedrich Nietzsche, *Beyond Good and Evil*, trans. Walter Kaufmann, in *Basic Writings of Nietzsche*, 192 (German: "Vorausgesetzt, dass die Wahrheit ein Weib ist–, wie? ist der Verdacht nicht gegründet, dass alle Philosophen, sofern sie Dogmatiker waren, sich schlecht auf Weiber verstanden?" [*Jenseits von Gut und Böse*, in *Kritische Studienausgabe*, 5:11]).

86. *Éperons/Spurs*, 40/41.

87. *Éperons/Spurs*, 48/49–50/51.

88. *Éperons/Spurs*, 50/51; translation modified.

89. As for example, in the fragment "We Artists!" ("Wir Künstler!") from *The Gay Science*, which Derrida takes up (*Éperons/Spurs* 44/45–46/47).

90. *The Gay Science*, §339, pp. 271–72 (German: *Die fröhliche Wissenshaft*, in *Kritische Studienausgabe*, 3:568–69).

91. "Si la femme est vérité, elle sait qu'il n'y a pas la vérité, que la vérité n'a pas lieu et qu'on n'a pas la vérité" (*Éperons/Spurs*, 52/53); translation modified.

pretending and is believed to incarnate. It is this dissimulative play with models of truth that makes of woman and art "an affirmative power" (*une puissance d'affirmation*). Nietzsche even identifies life with woman: *vita femina.*[92]

Does this apparent ambiguity as to play and woman require a modification of Heidegger's view of Nietzsche's attempt to overturn Platonism and to reconfigure the relationship between art and truth? In *Spurs,* Derrida does address Nietzsche's discordance in its Heideggerian interpretation, although he does not directly refer to the chapter on Plato's *Phaedrus* but to the following one, "Nietzsche's Overturning of Platonism."[93] It is in this chapter that Heidegger analyses the famous text from the *Twilight of the Idols:* "How the 'True World' Finally Became a Fable: The History of an Error."[94] The second of Nietzsche's six phases of the history of Platonism marks the passage from Plato to Platonism, and it is here that the progress of the idea ("more cunning, insidious, ungraspable") is characterized as feminine: "*It becomes woman*" (*sie wird Weib*).[95] These three words are emphasized by both Nietzsche and Heidegger, but Heidegger does not draw all the consequences from Nietzsche's text. Heidegger "skirts the woman"; in other words, he "skirts" play in Nietzsche's view of truth and perhaps in Plato's view as well. How does Derrida's reading of Heidegger, Nietzsche, and Plato in light of this skirting affect the understanding of the dreadful discordance and of the old quarrel?

Derrida's Mise en Scène of Plato's Theater

This pharmacy is also, we begin to perceive, a theater.
—JACQUES DERRIDA

"Supposing truth is a play? What then?"[96] Is this not a legitimate transposition of Nietzsche's question both in his own and in Derrida's view, especially in Derrida's reading of Plato's *Phaedrus?* Play, in all the ambiguity of *jeu* and *paidia,* rhapsodic play, may be considered "the single theme" of "Plato's Pharmacy." Derrida's deconstruction of Platonism in this essay, like Nietzsche's historical account in *The Birth of Tragedy,* refers to the event of the sophistic and Socratic intervention in the culture of fifth-century Greece, the emergence

---

92. *Éperons/Spurs,* 66/67; Nietzsche, *The Gay Science,* § 339, pp. 271–72 (German: *Die fröhliche Wissenschaft,* in *Kritische Studienausgabe,* 3:568–69).

93. *Éperons/ Spurs,* 72/73ff.

94. *Nietzsche,* 1:200–210 (German: *Nietzsche,* 1: 202–13).

95. Nietzsche, *Twilight of the Idols,* 20 (German: *Götzen-Dämmerung,* in *Kritische Studienausgabe,* 6:80); Heidegger, *Nietzsche,* 1:205 (German: *Nietzsche,* 1:207); Derrida, *Éperons/ Spurs,* 84/85).

96. The epigraph to this section comes from "Plato's Pharmacy," 142 (French: "Cette pharmacie est aussi, nous l'avons senti, un théâtre" ["La pharmacie de Platon," 78]).

of the power of logos—rhetorical-sophistic and Socratic—and their ambiguous *agōn*. It is this event, rather than the supposed felicitous discordance between beauty and truth, or more specifically between (tragic) art and philosophy, that determines in Derrida's view the structure of Plato's dialogue. And he sees in the text of Plato, which gives the most thorough account of this intervention, the seeds of the dissemination of the dominant logocentric tradition of Western thought. Here lies, it seems, a major difference between Derrida's deconstruction of Plato in general—and in particular his reading of *Phaedrus*—and Heidegger's *Destruktion* of Western aesthetics, in which the reading of *Phaedrus* also plays a crucial role.

The most important side effect of Heidegger's reinterpretation of Plato's *Republic* and *Phaedrus* in his *Nietzsche* is the neutralization—in the form of the felicitous discordance—of the dramatic character of both the "old quarrel" and the raging discordance. Poetry or art (*poiēsis*) is not dignified enough to match philosophy or truth in the *Republic,* and it is so exalted in the *Phaedrus*—through its relation to truth—that it again *eludes* any tension or play of opposition. Beauty, the site of poetry and art, becomes the site of truth as an opening to being through remembrance. But, as we have seen, such a relation between beauty and truth was in danger of becoming instrumental, was in danger of subordinating the former to the latter. On the other hand, is the felicitous discordance of the *Phaedrus* really as harmonious as Heidegger suggests? Should not the exalted moment of the *sun-ergeia* of beauty to truth be *inscribed* in the par-ergonal, dramatic frame of the dialogue as a whole?[97] This is the point of Derrida's reading of *Phaedrus* in "Plato's Pharmacy." It is the *pharmakon* of writing and the play between the double valence of the Greek *pharmakon* or drug, at once remedy and poison, that is the focus of the essay—but this play of *pharmakon,* in Derrida's argument, opens out into the general movement of archwriting and of deconstruction that no local rule of the game is able to control.

To be sure, Derrida himself formulates his reading as an analysis of the two forces active within Plato's dialogue as well as in the course of Western thought in general: on the one hand, what we called earlier the logic of the rigorous definition of concepts (*akribeia*) attempts to sort out the various meanings of words, in particular various meanings of the same word in order to preserve their identity; on the other hand, the logic of play (*paidia*) tends to maintain the ambiguity, the communication between meanings, in particular within the "unity of the same signifier."[98] In the *Phaedrus,* for example—a particular example—

---

97. For the notion of *parergon* as frame, especially in its opposition to *sunergon,* see Jacques Derrida, *The Truth in Painting,* trans. Geoff Bennington and Ian McLeod (Chicago: University of Chicago Press, 1987), 15–148 (French: *La vérité en peinture* [Paris: Flammarion, 1978], 19–168).

98. "Plato's Pharmacy," 98–99 (French: "La pharmacie de Platon," 122).

writing as *pharmakon* is played on by the king Thamus and the inventor
Theuth in the final myth, but only in Greek; translations tend to represent
merely the first of the forces in play: "Their discourse plays within [the unity
of the signifier *pharmakon*], which is no longer the case in translation."[99] The
translation seems to block play and thus to belong to the force of logical rigor
or *akribeia:*

> All translations into languages that are the heirs and depositaries of
> Western metaphysics thus produce on the *pharmakon* an *effect of analy-
> sis* that violently destroys it, reduces it to one of its simple elements by
> interpreting it, paradoxically enough, in the light of the ulterior devel-
> opments it itself has made possible. Such an interpretive translation is
> thus as violent as it is impotent: it destroys the *pharmakon* but at the
> same time forbids itself access to it, leaving it untouched in its reserve.[100]

The serious task (*Aufgabe*) of undertaking a semantically rigorous (in the
sense of univocal) translation would thus be a failure, a "giving up" (*Aufgabe*)
of another kind of rigor, that of play.[101] If we want to call the theme of Derrida's essay "play," it is because of this (play of) *Aufgabe;* its movement tends
to reverse the pull toward an apparent semantic rigor and thus to restore the
communication of opposing semantic valences within the same word (here
pharmakon), which is the condition of play.[102]

Is then the problematic of translation another "single theme" of the *Phaedrus* and of Derrida's essay? To some extent, yes. But we should take it as
a philosophical problematic par excellence, touching the problematic of the
foundation of Western philosophy. For the translation conundrum is not
merely a contingent, empirical difficulty of translators but rather an "irreducible difficulty of translation" that is located within the Greek language, perhaps
within language itself as manifested in poetry. It is, says Derrida, "a violent
difficulty in the transference of a nonphilosopheme into a philosopheme. With
this problem of translation we will thus be dealing with nothing less than the
problem of the very passage into philosophy."[103] The problem of translation as

99. See Michael Naas's discussion of the translation of "φάρμακον" as "drug" in his *Taking on the
Tradition: Jacques Derrida and the Legacies of Deconstruction* (Stanford, Calif.: Stanford University Press,
2003), 10–11.

100. "Plato's Pharmacy," 99 (French: "La pharmacie de Platon," 122).

101. See Walter Benjamin, "The Task of the Translator," in Walter Benjamin, *Illuminations,* trans.
Harry Zohn (New York: Schocken Books, 1969), 69–82 (German: "Die Aufgabe des Übersetzers," in
Illuminationen [Frankfurt: Suhrkamp, 1955], 56–69).

102. Benjamin's *Aufgabe* and Nietzsche's/Heidegger's *Zwiespalt* are two other cases of resistance to a
univocal semantically rigorous translation.

103. "Plato's Pharmacy," 72 (French: "La pharmacie de Platon," 89).

the passage into philosophy would thus be situated within the question of rigor that goes back to the opposition between philosophy and poetry. It is ultimately poetry's rhapsodic/mimetic play that marks language's resistance to the univocal translation into rigorous concepts.

It is worth noting that the English translation of "La pharmacie de Platon" itself performs the reductive function diagnosed by Derrida. Indeed, Barbara Johnson, in her otherwise excellent translation, most of the time suppresses the play in the French word *jeu,* a single signifier within the unity of which Derrida's text is played out. For the undecidability of play governs Derrida's text, just as it does Plato's—if, that is, they are to be considered texts in Derrida's view. Indeed, a short introduction to his essay begins with this general characterization of texts: "A text is not a text unless it hides from the first comer, from the first glance, the law of its composition and the rule of its play [*la règle de son jeu*]."[104] This rule of the concealment and perhaps suspension of all rules in a text is here immediately suspended by the decision of the translator who, following the *context,* renders *jeu* as "game." To be sure, only a game seems to have rules; the word "play" is apparently reserved for a clear case of *ludic,* playful anarchy, which the translator recognizes only in the fifth and last appearance of the word *jeu* in the introduction, where it is coupled with the notion of the supplement: "The reading or writing supplement must be rigorously prescribed, but by *the necessities of a game, by the logic of play*, signs to which the system of all textual powers must be accorded and attuned."[105] Is the decision of the translator in all these other cases (like the decision that Derrida allows for any reading—"la décision de chaque lecture") legitimate? Only if the "logic of play" affirmed in the last case is kept in mind in all the others, that is, paradoxically, only when the decision is constantly suspended. The same can be said of the "playful" character of writing in Plato's *Phaedrus;* when it is first introduced by Derrida, the translator decides to render both *jeu* and *paidia* as "game," but again the decision may be considered legitimate only if the "logic of play" is not totally concealed.

The last section of Derrida's essay returns to the notion of "beau jeu," introduced at the outset. In this section, the translator clearly distinguishes between "play" and "game," according to the supposed intention of the author—Derrida or Plato, as the case may be—helped this time, in Derrida's case, by the plural *jeux,* which seems to indicate the ordered plurality of games (the translation of "le beau jeu" by "stunning hand" is also apparently confirmed by

104. "Plato's Pharmacy," 63; translation modified (French: "La pharmacie de Platon," 79).

105. "Plato's Pharmacy," 64; the italicized passage renders the French "la nécessité d'un *jeu*" (French: "Le supplément de lecture ou d'écriture doit être rigoureusement prescrit mais par la nécessité d'un *jeu,* signe auquel il faut accorder le système de tous ses pouvoirs" ["La pharmacie de Platon," 80]).

the context, since Derrida talks about "the Platonic repression of play" ["la répression platonicienne du jeu"]).[106] But if there is certainly in Plato's text a movement toward losing play in games—"Le jeu se perd toujours en se sauvant dans les jeux," which Johnson translates as "Play is always lost when it seeks salvation in games"—there is also in Plato's language a "logic" of play (*paidia/jeu*), which escapes the rigorous logic of any game.[107]

In fact, play makes its appearance in the dialogue *Phaedrus* right at the beginning, when Socrates and Phaedrus get ready to "unpack" the *pharmakon* of writing. Socrates tells the story of the princess Oreithuia, who was abducted by Boreas, the North Wind, when playing (*paizousa*) with the nymph Pharmacia (229c), a serious and dangerous play, resulting in the death of the princess. The story triggers a discussion of the truth of myth, which is also the truth of play. Apparently, both myth and play are dismissed in the name of truth.[108] But in fact, the decision is postponed; Phaedrus's question, "Do you really believe that that legend [*muthologēma*] is true [*alēthes*]?" receives a provisional answer: Socrates saying goodbye (*khairein easas*) to myths because of a more urgent inquiry—inquiry into himself.[109] He will recall the myth, though, as soon as he considers writing and its potential beauty. The truth of writing, Derrida suggests, that is, its nontruth, cannot be an object of knowledge but only of a mythical fable; there is a "kinship of writing and myth, both of them distinguished from logos and dialectics."[110] Of course, the truth of this statement will depend first of all on the validity of the *muthos/logos* opposition, that is, on the latter's independence from play.

But the name of the nymph in this first myth in the dialogue, who before being sent away had been fully introduced, points toward the player of choice in the "jeu" of deconstruction—which, in contradistinction with the controlled game of *polysemy,* Derrida calls *dissemination* (the translator again stops this play by translating "par son jeu"—which is itself the translation of *paizousa*— as "[t]hrough her games").[111] Indeed, the movement from *Pharmakeia* (Pharmacia)—and the *pharmakon* that precedes it in the drama of *Phaedrus,* of the walks (*peripatoi*) prescribed to Phaedrus by the doctor Acoumenos and of Lysias's paradoxical but persuasive *logos,* in this case a written speech—to *pharmakeus,* or wizard, and *pharmakos,* or scapegoat, to the hemlock of *Phaedo* (another *pharmakon*), and finally to the self-erasure of the impossible "play

106. "Plato's Pharmacy, 157 (French: "La pharmacie de Platon, 195).
107. "Plato's Pharmacy," 158 (French: "La pharmacie de Platon," 197).
108. "Plato's Pharmacy," 69 (French: "La pharmacie de Platon," 85).
109. *Phaedrus,* trans. Alexander Nehamas and Paul Woodruff, 509.
110. "Plato's Pharmacy," 75 (French: "parenté de l'écriture et du mythe, l'un et l'autre distingués du *logos* et de la dialectique" ["La pharmacie de Platon," 92]).
111. "Plato's Pharmacy," 75 (French: "La pharmacie de Platon," 92).

as such" and to the "play of the other within being," that is, eventually the mimetic-theatrical play of the *diaphora* and the *Zwiespalt,* is the movement of Derrida's reading of the *Phaedrus,* a model for other texts that contain the seed for dissemination.[112]

Thus, even though writing (*grammata*) as *pharmakon* in the narrow sense is formally the main theme of Derrida's essay, it ultimately functions as a privileged example of play in general, governing writing in general, the very structure of signification or "general writing" (also *archi-écriture*), through its iterability and the eventual undecidability of its meaning.[113] However, when arguing that writing is the dominant theme of *Phaedrus,* Derrida still refers to writing sensu stricto, pointing out the central position of the critique of writers (*logographoi*) and of their works (*sungrammata*) by both Phaedrus and Socrates in the dialogue:

> At the precisely calculated center of the dialogue—the reader can count the lines—the question of *logography* is raised (257c). Phaedrus reminds Socrates that the citizens of greatest influence and dignity, the men who are the most free, feel ashamed (*aiskhunontai*) at "speechwriting" and at leaving *sungrammata* behind them. They fear the judgment of posterity, which might consider them "sophists" (257d).[114]

The reason for this fear is that both a sophist and a writer of speeches are considered to be untrue, to incarnate the falsehood of nonpresence, of quasi-rhapsodic repetition of the same, so that even though a decision concerning writing is not made in this discussion of logographers, the opposition between writing (*l'écrit*) and truth (*le vrai*) is announced and, as it were, rhapsodically performed or "staged" (*mise en scène*).[115] At the same moment, the question of the beautiful makes its appearance on the stage of the dialogue. In the absence of a categorical decision concerning the propriety of writing as such, Socrates corrects Phaedrus's assertion (and not Phaedrus himself as Derrida suggests),

112. "Plato's Pharmacy," 156, 163 (French: "La pharmacie de Platon," 195, 204).

113. See Derrida, *Of Grammatology,* trans. Gayatri Chakravorty Spivak (Baltimore, Md.: Johns Hopkins University Press, 1974) (French: *De la grammatologie* [Paris: Minuit, 1967]). Christopher Smith disregards this notion in his critique of Derrida in his "Orality and Writing: Plato's *Phaedrus* and the *Pharmakon* Revisited," in *Between Philosophy and Poetry: Writing, Rhythm, History,* ed. Massimo Verdicchio and Robert Burch (New York: Continuum, 2002), 73–89.

114. "Plato's Pharmacy," 68 (French: "Au centre très excactement calculé du dialogue—on peut compter les lignes—on se demande en effet ce qu'il en est de la *logographie* (257 c). Phèdre rappelle que les citoyens les plus puissants et les plus vénérés, les hommes les plus libres, ressentent de la honte (*aiskhunontai*) à 'écrire des discours' et à laisser derrière eux des *sungrammata.* Ils craignent le jugement de la postérité, et de passer pour des 'sophistes' (257d)" ["La pharmacie de Platon," 84]).

115. "Plato's Pharmacy," 68 (French: "La pharmacie de Platon," 85).

arguing that it is only shameful (*aischros*) to write speeches that are ugly (*aischros*), and asks what it means to write beautifully (*kalōs, de la belle façon*) (258d).[116] This question of beautiful writing—implying as it does that beauty might overcome the nontruth and nonpresence of speechwriting—is the one that, in Derrida's words, constitutes "the central nervure, the great fold that divides the dialogue" (*la nervure centrale, le grand pli qui partage le dialogue*).[117] Thus, even if it is not perhaps the primary meaning of *kalōs* that suggests itself here, the significance of the beautiful cannot be suppressed in the reading of this passage.[118] For Phaedrus's enthusiasm for speeches does not allow us to interpret the beautiful way of writing as a simple appropriateness; both Socrates and Phaedrus want *logoi,* speeches or discourses, including those written by *logographoi,* to be truly beautiful, independently of the dominant opinion. Thus this theme of the "beauty" of speeches permeates the whole dialogue through the dialectics, or rather play, between its myths and its discourses.

Not only the quasi-mythical story of the poet Stesichorus but also that of the winged souls and their journey through heaven in Socrates' "inspired" speech belong to the category of the "most beautiful play" (*pankalē paidia*) with serious matters, as opposed to the "vulgar play" (*phaulē paidia*) evoked in Phaedrus's conclusion to Socrates' argument later in the dialogue: "Socrates, you are contrasting a vulgar play with the most beautiful—with the play of a man who can while away his time telling stories [*muthologounta*] of justice and the other matters you mentioned" (276e).[119] The possibility of beautiful play with serious myths, which is affirmed here, is significant (even though Socrates still prefers the seriousness of dialectical art—*dialektikē tekhnē*) precisely in its retroactive appreciation of Socrates' inspired and "more beautiful" (*kalliō*) speech, the poetic/rhapsodic palinode (257c). Socrates "himself" aims at making his speech the "most beautiful" (257a). It is as if the conclusion of Socrates' speech points back to its poetic inauguration.

The palinode is poetical and also rhapsodic. In this Platonic theater, Socrates rehearses Phaedrus's own language, using a grand style that is most certainly a mime of sophistic, and especially Gorgian, eloquence. "This pharmacy is also . . . a theater," says Derrida, perhaps especially a theater.[120] Not Aristotelian or neoclassical theater, with its rules and unities but rather a rhapsodic

116. It is worth noting that in order to avoid tautology in this passage, one tends to translate "αἰσχρός" in two different ways, and "it is shameful to write in an ugly way" rather than "it is ugly to write shamefully," especially in view of the characterization of Socrates' speech as a "beautiful palinode."
117. "Plato's Pharmacy," 68 (French: "La pharmacie de Platon," 85).
118. As happens in the translation of "καλῶς γράφειν" as "writing well," for example, in Alexander Nehamas and Paul Woodruff's translation of Plato's *Phaedrus,* 51.
119. *Phaedrus,* trans. Alexander Nehamas and Paul Woodruff, 553; translation modified.
120. "Plato's Pharmacy," 142 (French: "La pharmacie de Platon," 178).

theater, a theater of danger, such as Plato conceived (and apparently feared) before Artaud. Indeed, Derrida's "play of writing," of arch-writing, is dangerous, disruptive of the social and political order, and cruel in its familial relationship of exposure, struggle, and parricide. Writing is dangerous because it opens up a "violent movement of surrogation": a surrogate son, a supplement to the absent living logos or speech, a reminding (*hupomnēsis*) replacing memory (*mnēmē*).[121]

Just as Derrida emphasizes the centrality of writing in the composition of *Phaedrus,* we could, in the same playful way, point out in the middle of "Plato's Pharmacy"—"the reader can count the pages"—the change of focus from *pharmakon* to *pharmakeus,* or magician, in other words (and using the terminology deconstructed here), from a seemingly objective investigation of a *substance* to the rhapsodic (self-)display of the pharmacist and writer. *Pharmakon* (remedy or poison, philter or paint, "substance") is shown to be the instrument of a magician or a sorcerer, a *pharmakeus.* Gorgias himself had presented the *pharmakon* of *logos* (discourse or speech) as the instrument (*organon*) of an orator.[122] In a mock-defense (*apologia*), he emphasized the power of persuasion that allows Paris, the orator, to bewitch Helen and render impossible any resistance on her part. For Gorgias, logos is a great lord (*logos dunastes megas estin*).[123]

It is not Gorgias, however, or any other sophist, that is for Derrida a *pharmakeus* par excellence but rather Socrates. Indeed, this is his persona in several dialogues. Perhaps the most striking of these is the quasi-biographical portrait of Socrates in Plato's *Symposium.* First, he seems to be alluded to in Diotima's description of Eros (Love), who has neither riches, nor beauty, nor delicacy but is constantly in pursuit of those things. This pursuit is the life of philosophizing (*philosophōn dia pantos tou biou*), and Eros, who guides this constant quest, is called a "magician" (*pharmakeus*) and a sophist (*sophistēs*) (203c–e). Later in the dialogue, in Alcibiades's explicit praise, Socrates is said to be a piper (*aulētēs*) who accomplishes his task without a pipe, without any instrument (*aneu organōn*), with only his own voice and body. In other words, he is his own instrument. Just like the actors (*hupokritai*) in the classification of the *Sophist,* Socrates thus uses his own body as a means of bewitching mimesis. More clearly than the sophists, who are attached to their image or opinion (*doxa*) of seriousness, Socrates, who accepts the opinion of him as a (comic) character (*eirōn*), is a rhapsode, a *mimētēs,* a participant in a play.

---

121. "Plato's Pharmacy," 109 (French: "La pharmacie de Platon," 135).
122. Gorgias, "Encomium of Helen" B. frag. 11, in Hermann Diels, *Die Fragmente der Vorsokratiker,* 6th ed., 3 vols., ed. Walther Kranz (1952; rpt,. Zurich: Weidmann, 1985), 2:288–94.
123. "Encomium of Helen" B. frag. 11. It is in fact perhaps a Heraclitean rather than rhetorical logos that is so powerful, the same poetic logos that animates Socrates' rhapsodic palinode.

The play of *Phaedrus* both looks back to the *Republic* and forward to *Timaeus* (in the common chronology). Derrida reconsiders the decision of Socrates to banish the poets and the play of mimesis and even the very formulation of the old dispute between philosophy and poetry. Even before the formulation of the *palaia diaphora* and the decision in favor of philosophy and truth, an ambivalent space of "indecision" is opened in the *Republic* by the play of the *pharmakeus/pharmakon*. Indeed, knowledge as *pharmakon* (595a) is said to be an antidote against mimesis, and mimesis is later illustrated by the activity of particularly efficient *pharmakēs*, charlatans and *thaumaturges* (602d). A kind of *pharmakon* is thus supposed to neutralize the pernicious activity of various kinds of *pharmakeus;* but given that the latter cannot function without the former, it is ultimately *pharmakon* that will have to oppose *pharmakon*. As Derrida notes: "Long before being divided up into occult violence and accurate knowledge, the element of the *pharmakon* is the combat zone between philosophy and its other. An element that is *in itself,* if one can still say so, *undecidable.*"[124] Thus, for Derrida, the quarrel, the opposition between philosophy and poetry, let alone a decision in favor of the former, is not an originary event—it is derivative of the disseminative play of which *pharmakon* is a "paradigmatic" case.

The disseminative character of play forbids its translation by (regularized) "game" or even by the suggestion of such a game. This is emphasized in "Plato's Pharmacy" by the reference to a future "penetration" into the field of cosmological, political, and linguistic play in the *Timaeus*. Indeed, the longest quotation in the essay sets the stage for the most radical deconstruction of Platonism and its rigorous oppositions as well as of the "structurality" that governs Western metaphysical discourse. An attempt to inscribe this structurality meets with resistance from the ground of inscription itself, or chora, which in the *Timaeus* reverberates within the initial suspension of a decision concerning the methodological opposition *logos/muthos* or rigor/play.[125]

But is not this suspension of a decision, this placement of *pharmakon* at the origin, a decision after all, the decision in favor of mimesis/rhapsody (a play and the poetic principle in/of the *Republic*)? The play of the mise-en-abyme is in fact the only possible answer to the question of the relationship between "philosophy and its other," both in Plato and Derrida. Like the Platonic playful rejection of play, the Derridean decision for undecidability leads to a logical aporia. Hence, recourse to methods and forms of writing that suspend but do not dissolve the appearance of logical rigor through the rigor of disseminative play. The relationship between beauty and truth, apparently so serene

---

124. "Plato's Pharmacy," 138 (French, "La pharmacie de Platon," 172).
125. I discuss the "original inscription of the world as a trace" in chapter 4.

on Heidegger's reading, can no longer ignore the vicissitudes of play on Derrida's. Neither a quarrel (*diaphora*) nor a discord (*Zwiespalt*)—whether fearful (*Entsetzen erregend*) or felicitous (*beglückend*)—is called for in order to characterize both Plato's view of philosophy and art and its Derridean deconstruction; rather, it is the rhapsodic fair play (*beau jeu*) to the movement of which no "stunning translation" would be able to put a stop.

3

The Notion of (Re)Semblance
in the *Sophist*
(Deleuze, Foucault, Nancy)

Good strategy: seem to pretend to resemble that which one truly resembles.
—JEAN-LUC NANCY

Perhaps Socrates would deny the possibility of distinguishing between icons and fantasms.
—STANLEY ROSEN

How to tell the sophist from the *Sophist?* Plato scholars acknowledge that there is no formal way to distinguish the two cases: neither capitalization nor italics are available in Greek manuscript, and there are no other formal marks that would allow us to tell the difference between the man and the text. Nevertheless, they would assure us, it is possible to determine whether Plato is talking about the man or about his own dialogue whenever he writes *ho sophistēs* (the *Sophist*/the sophist). In fact he never has his own dialogue in mind in the *Sophist:* if he did, the certainties of Plato scholarship might suffer, and in the end, philosophy would be hardly distinguishable from sophistic tricks. We should not sin against modern logic and allow self-referential statements to be taken seriously. A Sophist condemning sophists for lying should puzzle us no more than a Cretan who says that all Cretans are liars. Don't we have Bertrand Russell's set theory to protect us against such riddles? Thus, Plato, the writer, or his character—characters especially can know nothing about the dialogue they are in—never has his own dialogue in mind. One passage, however, in the *Statesman*, seems to disturb this assurance and to question the identity of the writer and of the speaker. Indeed, to whom or what does the Elean Stranger refer when in the *Statesman*, he compares his and his interlocutor's, the young

---

The first epigraph to this chapter comes from Nancy's "Le ventriloque (ou de l'authenticité du Sophiste de Platon, et, donc, du Philosophe)," in Sylviane Agacinski et al., *Mimésis des()articulations* (Paris: Aubier-Flammarion, 1975), 296; my translation (French: "Bonne *stratégie:* sembler faire semblant de ressembler à ce à quoi on ressemble vraiment"). The second is drawn from Rosen's *Plato's "Sophist": The Drama of Original and Image* (New Haven, Conn.: Yale University Press, 1983), 65.

Socrates' present conundrum with the one *en tōi sophistēi* (in the *Sophist*/with the sophist [*Statesman* 284b])? It is impossible to deny with certainty a reference to the dialogue here. C. J. Rowe, for example, translates the phrase "just as with the sophist" but immediately appends a note: "i.e., in the *Sophist,*" which completes his translation.[1]

What if we suspected the same reference to the dialogue behind any of the multiple occurrences of the word *sophistēs* in the *Sophist* itself? asks Jean-Luc Nancy. Such a procedure, drawing Plato's text into the uncertainties of the mimetic play of the sophist, would undermine the authority of Plato the author, which neither doctrinal nor "dramatic" interpreters are willing to question. It would also undermine the authority of the philosopher, whom traditional readings radically oppose to the sophist, and of the philosophical interpreter, who ultimately derives his or her own authority from that of the author. He or she would no longer be able to keep a distance from "his" or "her" text. In the terms of the *Sophist* (the sophist), a legitimate image of a thing would hardly be distinguishable from an illicit simulacrum, of which the sophist, the actor, and the rhapsode are the foremost examples.

Plato's *Sophist* is traditionally taken as a dramatic challenge to the ontology that underlies the representational system of the *Republic* and that constitutes the basis of both ancient—Aristotelian and Neoplatonic—and modern interpretations of Platonism. The dialogue questions the basic distinction between the two modes of representation, philosophy on the one side, and poetry/mimesis on the other, which is supposed to govern Plato's theory of being as *idea* and his politics of partition. But the challenge of the *Sophist* seems so radical that many contemporary thinkers turn to this dialogue in their desire to "overturn Platonism." One knows the impact of Heidegger's reading of this dialogue, in his lecture course of 1924–25, on his own thought of being and nonbeing, of truth as *alētheia,* of Dasein, and of logos as language.[2] It is no accident that *Being and Time* begins with a lengthy quotation from the *Sophist;* the forgetfulness of being is measured against the bafflement of Theaetetus and the Elean Stranger exhibited in this dialogue. Heidegger's reading of the *Sophist* and of the dialogues in general has indirectly marked contemporary thought, even though his lecture course on Plato's *Sophist* was published only

---

1. *Statesman,* trans. C. J. Rowe, in *Plato: Complete Works,* ed. John M. Cooper and D. S. Hutchison (Indianapolis, Ind.: Hackett, 1997), 327.

2. *Plato's "Sophist,"* trans. Richard Rojcewicz and André Schuwer (Bloomington: Indiana University Press, 1997) (German: *Platon: "Sophistes,"* vol. 19 of Martin Heidegger, *Gesamtausgabe,* 102 vols. to date [Frankfurt am Main: Klostermann, 1975–]). On these lectures, see, most recently, Catalin Partenie, "Imprint: Heidegger's Interpretation of Platonic Dialectic in the *Sophist* Lectures (1924–25)," in *Heidegger and Plato: Toward Dialogue,* ed. Catalin Partenie and Tom Rockmore (Evanston, Ill.: Northwestern University Press, 2005), 42–71.

in 1992, long after the publication of such texts as Deleuze's "Plato and the Simulacrum," Foucault's "Theatrum philosophicum," and Nancy's "Le ventriloque"—texts that take their cue from the *Sophist* and are crucial to the confrontation with Platonism in continental philosophy.

Two problems elude the apparently rigorous method of dialectical *diairesis* in the *Sophist:* that of the difference between image and simulacrum and that of the difference between the philosopher and the sophist. In fact, these problems are not unrelated, even though the most compelling readings of the dialogue focus mainly on the first (Deleuze, Foucault) or the second (Nancy). All three readings challenge the traditional view of Plato's "metaphysics of representation" that dominates Plato scholarship. And they resist the recuperation of mimesis as something that may be "good" provided it fits into the representational system as a kind of participation (*methexis*) of images in the being of ideas. The *Sophist* in fact problematizes this straightforward view both in its ontological considerations and in its dramatic setting, which the tradition has always tried to keep separate. The readings we are considering in this chapter show their resistance to this separation, which is at the same time a resistance to the imperial principle (*divide et impera*) of rigorous division and univocal interpretation.

Image Without Resemblance in Plato and Deleuze

If you are going to be safe, you have to be especially careful about similarities, since the type we're talking about is very slippery.

                                                                        —THE STRANGER

"Image without resemblance" is a disturbing phrase, particularly for the Greeks and their heirs, who derive the notion of image (*eikōn*) directly from the notion of "resembling" (*eoikenai*).[3] Yet, the Stranger from Elea in Plato's *Sophist* does not seem to mind the paradox when introducing the distinction between resembling and dissembling images; nor does Deleuze when he claims to develop the Platonic polarity into his own theory of simulacra, a theory that should lead to . . . the "overturning of Platonism." Indeed, for Deleuze the paradox of "dissembling images" accompanies the paradox of using Plato's own text as leverage in the attempt to fulfill the major task of modern philosophy: "to

---

3. The epigraph to this section comes from Plato, *Sophist* 231a (*Sophist,* trans. Nicholas P. White, in *Plato: Complete Works,* 251) (Greek: "τὸν δὲ ἀσφαλῆ δεῖ πάντων μάλιστα περὶ τὰς ὁμοιότητας ἀεὶ ποιεῖσθαι τὴν φυλακήν· ὀλισθηρότατον γὰρ τὸ γένος"); cf. Rosen's very literal translation of this passage in his *Plato's "Sophist,"* 131: "The man who goes securely must always be especially on guard against likenesses; this family is the slipperiest."

overturn Platonism."[4] "Was not Plato to be the first to overturn Platonism, or at least to point out the direction such an overturning should take?" asks Deleuze after having evoked the end of the *Sophist,* where the sharp distinction between the philosopher and the sophist, the true image of wisdom and the sophistic and "hypocritical" simulacrum, seems to break down.[5]

"Image without resemblance" is certainly a disturbing phrase for Rosen, who quotes Deleuze's "oversimplified" para-phrase of the Stranger, "the copy is an image endowed with resemblance; the simulacrum is an image without resemblance," and then points out the impossibility of the latter: "An image that does not resemble X cannot be an image of X. Despite its 'dissymmetry,' the fantasm looks like the original to the viewer."[6] A problem of translation is involved here. Indeed, since it would be awkward for a Greek to talk about a "nonresembling icon," the Stranger is opposing a resembling *eikōn* to a non-resembling *phantasma;* the latter only seems to resemble (*phainetai eoikenai*), say, the beautiful (*tōi kalōi*), but in fact it does not (236b–c). In this passage the word *eidōla* (in the Stranger's line at 236a) might function as a synonym of *phantasmata,* since they do not have the "real proportions" (*ousas summetrias*) that Rosen takes as the principle of the ontological ("being") versus phenomenological ("appearing") resemblance. Yet in the "pivotal discussion in the *Sophist* of the nature of an image," *eidōlon* becomes a generic term for all kinds of images, both resembling icons and nonresembling phantasms (239d–240b; cf. 266d–e).[7] Now, Rosen does not object to this terminology; he himself distinguishes between "accurate and inaccurate images."[8] What he does seem to resist is the nonresemblance of any image, including phantasm or simulacra. And this is perhaps the crucial question: is an absolute (that is, completely detached from any "original") simulacrum/phantasm possible at all? The stability of the order of representation, and, dramatically, the definitional "capture" of the sophist, will depend on it.

What could be more dangerous for Platonism as the rule of representation than confusing the philosopher, a champion of truth, with the sophist, a master of mimesis? One recalls Socrates' proclamation of the old dispute between philosophy and poetry or mimesis in the tenth book of the *Republic* and the

---

4. *Difference and Repetition,* trans. Paul Patton (New York: Columbia University Press, 1994), 59 (French: "le renversement du platonisme" [*Différence et répétition* (Paris: Presses Universitaires de France, 1968), 82]).

5. *The Logic of Sense,* trans. Mark Lester with Charles Stivale (New York: Columbia University Press, 1990), 256; translation modified (French: *Logique du sens* [Paris: Minuit, 1969], 295).

6. *Plato's "Sophist,"* 172–73; *The Logic of Sense,* 257 (French: "La copie est une image douée de ressemblance, le simulacre une image sans ressemblance" [*Logique du sens,* 297]). Deleuze refers to the *Sophist* 236b and 264c on the preceding page of his text.

7. *Plato's "Sophist,"* 190.

8. *Plato's "Sophist,"* 152, and 65.

dramatic banishment of drama, and mimesis in general, from the ideal city, a city ruled by philosophers. But mimesis is back, and again, just as in the third book of the *Republic,* it threatens to disrupt with play (*paidia*) the serious business of education (*paideia*).[9] The wild, irresponsible side of mimesis remains problematic, however, and the Stranger's distinction between images and simulacra seems to be introduced precisely in order to separate the "good" from the "bad" side of mimesis. This distinction is part of a larger project in the *Sophist,* namely, the separation of philosophy from (the "art" of) sophistry through the method of division (*diairesis*). Mimesis as such appears to be too large a category to be able to circumscribe the philosopher's other, the sophist (a player of mimesis, an artist), and too important in the process of education to be rejected as a whole. A further division, the division of mimesis itself, is necessary in order to settle the old dispute between philosophy and mimetic art.

Paradoxically, the method of division is the major Platonic characteristic to be conserved in carrying out the task of overturning Platonism, according to Deleuze.[10] This method is not only an example of dialectic in general but also the culmination of all dialectical power that might suggest a philosophy of difference, the development of which is the task of Deleuze's philosophical project. In this reading, division functions as "the measure of both Platonism and of the possibility of overturning Platonism."[11] To be sure, Deleuze does not take division in its traditional Aristotelian interpretation, namely, as a lame syllogism, lacking a middle term and thus unable to determine exactly the species of a genus to which the object of an investigation should belong. Rather, he sees in division a method of selection, of establishing "pure lines of descent" in a confused species.[12] Division is a method of arbitrating competing claims not through identification but through authentication, through a juridical rather than logical judgment. The quarrel between philosophy and poetry might well be a particular example, or even the paradigm, of such a contest of claims—which are also claims for the position of power in the city, that is, the right to legislate and to educate.

Division is not a dialectic of contradiction in Deleuze's view but a dialectic of rivalry, a dispute. In a parallel text, "Plato and the Simulacrum," Deleuze calls Platonism a "philosophical *Odyssey*" because of the preeminence of this

9. As we have seen, mimesis is play par excellence. See Plato's *Sophist* 234b and section 2 in this chapter.

10. "That this overturning should conserve many Platonic characteristics is not only inevitable but desirable" (*Difference and Repetition,* 59) (French: *Différence et répétition,* 82).

11. *Difference and Repetition,* 59 (French: "mesure à la fois le platonisme et la possibilité de renverser le platonisme" [*Différence et répétition,* 83]).

12. Heidegger's notion of "origination" (*Herkunft*) in the interpretation of the *Sophist* comes close to Deleuze's "specific" genealogy.

method of selecting rivals.[13] Another comparison, with purification, especially that of gold, displaces the Platonic method from the domain of logic, where Aristotle and his followers had confined it, to the domain of religious ritual and of alchemical experimentation. Division consists of sifting impurities in order to obtain the most precious element, pure gold, the genuine king, the unadulterated truth. Left out by the division/purification are false pretenders, simulacra. And this is exactly the paramount motivation of Platonism, according to Deleuze: to "draw a distinction between 'the thing itself' and the simulacra" (*une distinction à faire entre 'la chose même' et les simulacres*).[14] Such division is not a simple separation of different from different; it is a form of qualified separation that sifts out the impurities, a kind of ritual catharsis with all its consequences. It is exclusive and cruel: false claimants become victims (*pharmakoi*) and are sacrificed.

Division accomplishes its task by revealing the connection of *met-hexis* or participation, which Deleuze translates quite literally as "possessing in a secondary way." A pretender has to make evident his or her title to a quality that, unlike the Idea, he or she does not possess primarily. He or she has to show a rightful derivation or descent from the primary possessor, that is, a foundation. Deleuze's comparison of the model, the copy, and the simulacrum (or the Neoplatonic triad: the unparticipated, the participated quality, and the participant) to the father, the daughter, and the suitor brings out the dramatic character of the method, its function of distributing roles and claims.[15] Establishing a foundation is a family business. In order to prove his claim a suitor has to become a legitimate family member, to please the father, to resemble him. To explain the distinction between rightful claimants and false pretenders—between images/copies and simulacra—in quantitative terms, namely, as a distance from the model, the king and the truth (in other words, in accordance with the common reading of the *Republic*), is for Deleuze to miss the point. Indeed, the *essential* difference between legitimate images, that is to say, icons or copies (Deleuze's translation of Plato's *eikones* and *mimēmata*) and simulacra (*phantasmata*) is resemblance itself: "The copy is an image endowed with resemblance, the simulacrum is an image without resemblance."[16]

Resemblance (*homoiotēs*) is, however, "a very slippery kind" (*olthisthērotaton gar to genos*), as the Stranger warns in the *Sophist*, and "a cautious person should

13. *The Logic of Sense*, 254 (French: *Logique du sens*, 293).

14. *Difference and Repetition*, 66 (French: *Différence et répétition*, 91).

15. *The Logic of Sense*, 255 (French: *Logique du sens*, 294); *Difference and Repetition*, 62 (French: *Différence et répétition*, 87).

16. *The Logic of Sense*, 257 (French: *Logique du sens*, 297); cf. *Difference and Repetition*, 60–61 (French: *Différence et répétition*, 85). See page 105 above for Stanley Rosen's critique of this statement of Deleuze's.

above all be on his or her guard against resemblances" (231a).[17] Deleuze does not mention this passage of the *Sophist*, but he might have it in mind when, following in the Stranger's steps, he attempts to prevent such sliding, that is, when he attempts to render resemblance unambiguous. He is apparently more successful than Plato's character in developing the image/simulacrum polarity; it is rigorous and never questioned, but is it less "slippery"? It seems that once the resemblance with the father is verified, the legitimacy of the claim and claimant is established; once it is disproved, they are both, claim and claimant, rejected and sacrificed as *pharmakoi*/simulacra. Thus in Deleuze's reading of Plato's texts—the *Phaedrus*, the *Statesman*, the *Sophist*—a simulacrum is not a vaguely resembling figure of the father, a fading image still preserving some traits of the original/originator, but rather an absolutely dissembling counterfeit violating the principles of family resemblance.[18] Resemblance marks a profound genetic dependence, an interior kinship, and no superficial effect produced by the simulacrum can compensate for the lack of it.

Since the value of resemblance is unquestioned, and a definite test is in principle possible, the weight falls on the way to set the test. When, at the outset of "Plato and the Simulacrum," Deleuze characterizes the method of division as a combination of the power of dialectic with "another power," he certainly has the power of myth in mind. Here again his interpretation differs from the tradition of Plato scholarship. The latter usually takes Platonic myth to be an element foreign to dialectics and introduced only in order to mark its impotence, whereas Deleuze regards it as an integral part of the method of *diairesis:* "Division . . . integrates myth into the dialectic."[19] In both the *Statesman* and *Phaedrus,* two other major dialogues introducing and employing the method of division, the myth provides a foundation in the form of the standard against which competing claims are to be measured. In the *Phaedrus* the contemplation of the Ideas during the mythic journey around the world decides between the rival forms of madness; in the *Statesman* the figure of the ancient god-pastor of men arbitrates between different pretenders to the coveted role of the statesman. One might object that the *Sophist,* the third dialogue displaying the method of division, does not have a myth to support its dialectic. But this is because, as Deleuze would argue, this dialogue professes precisely to expose the false pretender par excellence, the sophist, and to examine the mode

17. *Sophist,* trans. Harold N. Fowler, in *Plato in Twelve Volumes* (Cambridge, Mass., Harvard University Press, 1921), 317; translation modified.

18. On this reading Platonic family resemblance, contrary to the Wittgensteinian notion, is logically and ontologically rigorous and inflexible.

19. *Difference and Repetition,* 61 (French: "C'est la division qui . . . intègre le mythe dans la dialectique" [*Différence et répétition,* 86]).

of (non)being of the simulacrum: thus no foundation can be established, no re-semblance found. If, at the end of the dialogue, the sophist "resembles" Socrates, it is—ironically—because they both *lack* resemblance to any mythic, founda-tional pattern.

The question of resemblance is crucial to the problem of overturning Pla-tonism because the ontological and cosmological framework of the Platonic system has the structure of representation. In the sublunary world, the thing itself is an image. It is the fact of being a legitimate image, a well-founded copy, connected to its model—the Idea—by a proper relation of resemblance, that gives a claimant the right to be called a being at all and not a false pre-tender, a simulacrum. Platonism and representation stand or fall together. For Deleuze, simulacra (*phantasmata*) result precisely from the frustration of this foundational procedure, and in their turn cause the foundation to collapse. Here lies the revolutionary potential of ab-solute simulacra. Their production and diffusion are the best means of confronting and overturning the regime of representation. Simulacra are not just false copies inside this system. By put-ting in question the very notions of copy and model, they threaten the coher-ence of representation as such. Plato is aware of this threat when he attempts to exclude the simulacra that flout the two complementary principles of the sys-tem of representation: identity and resemblance. In Deleuze's words, the most profound motivation of Platonism is "to repress [the part of becoming that remains rebellious] as deeply as possible, to shut it up in a cavern at the bottom of the Ocean" and "to keep [simulacra] completely submerged, preventing them from climbing to the surface, and 'insinuating themselves' everywhere."[20] This "image," in its nonresemblance with Homeric and Platonic mythology, com-bines the realm of Poseidon and that of Hades and, in a sense, the realm of poetry and that of philosophy.

The revolutionary task of modern thought and art consists in confound-ing the realms, countering the effort rigorously to separate them, countering the effort of repression by liberating and glorifying simulacra (*glorifier le règne des simulacres et des reflets*), which should be allowed to leave their cavern at the bottom of the ocean and to rise to the surface or, in a different and appar-ently opposed series of images (or simulacra), should be allowed to resist such an elevation from the cave.[21] Deleuze even recommends a search for "another

20. *The Logic of Sense*, 259, 257 (French: "[Il s'agit de] refouler [la part du devenir qui resterait rebelle] le plus profond possible, l'enfermer dans une caverne au fond de l'Océan" and "de maintenir [les simu-lacres] enchaînés tout au fond, de les empêcher de monter à la surface et de 's'insinuer' partout" [*Logique du sens*, 298, 296]).

21. *Difference and Repetition*, 66 (French: *Différence et répétition*, 92); *The Logic of Sense*, 262 (French: *Logique du sens*, 302).

cave beyond, always another in which to hide."[22] This refers, of course, to Plato's underground spectacle and to its Nietzschean displacement.[23] The overturning of Platonism seems to be conditioned by this displacement of the old dispute, the *palaia diaphora* of the *Republic,* into theater.[24] Instead of thinking of philosophy and poetry or mimesis as facing each other, we should rather consider there to be two kinds of the theater of philosophy: the representational (Aristotelian, neoclassical) and the fantastic (Nietzsche's "Dionysian Machine"). It is the latter that Deleuze regards as the essence of modern art, striving to become "a veritable *theater* of metamorphoses and permutations."[25]

Paradoxically—especially in the French terminology of Deleuze—"Dionysian theater" is not a theater of *représentation* ("representation" or "performance") but a theater of *répétition* ("repetition" or "rehearsal"). *Répétition,* far from preparing for and facilitating a final performance, that is, far from preparing to realize a representation, renders such a representation impossible by calling into question the notions of model and copy, of the true and the verisimilar, and thus of a definite, fixed form of theatrical production. Repetition, Deleuzian repetition, just like rereading, is always a repetition of the different, displaying the uniqueness of any gesture, of any word. Eternal return, the model of the reign of simulacra in the form of repetition, is not a return of the identical (even if Nietzsche himself occasionally gives support to such an interpretation) but of the dissimilar and different. Theater, says Artaud—whose "aesthetic

22. *Difference and Repetition,* 67 (French: *Différence et répétition,* 92–93).

23. Nietzsche's "hermit" would doubt "whether a philosopher could *possibly* have 'ultimate and real' opinions, whether behind every one of his caves there is not, must not be, another deeper cave—a more comprehensive, stranger, richer world beyond the surface, an abysmally deep ground behind every ground, under every attempt to furnish 'grounds'" (*Beyond Good and Evil,* in *Basic Writings of Nietzsche,* trans. Walter Kaufmann [1966; rpt., New York: Modern Library, 1992], 419) (German: "ob ein Philosoph 'letzte und eigentliche' Meinungen überhaupt haben könne, ob bei ihm nicht hinter jeder Höhle noch eine tiefere Höhle liege, liegen müsse—eine umfänglichere fremdere reichere Welt über einer Oberfläche, ein Abgrund hinter jedem Grunde, unter jeder 'Begründung'" [*Jenseits von Gut und Böse,* in Friedrich Nietzsche, *Kritische Studienausgabe,* 15 vols., ed. Giorgio Colli and Mazzino Montinari (1967–77; rpt., Berlin: de Gruyter, 1988), 5:234]).

24. Cf. Martin Puchner, "Theater in Modernist Thought," *New Literary History* 33, no. 3 (2002): 521–32. Puchner is right to talk about a "theatrical turn" in modern and contemporary philosophy and to connect the notion of speculative theater in Deleuze's *Difference and Repetition* to Artaud's theater of cruelty. His claim that Deleuze's model derives directly from Artaud's, however, might seem slightly exaggerated and not fully substantiated.

25. *Difference and Repetition,* 56 (French: *Différence et répétition,* 79). Cf. Michel Foucault, "Theatrum philosophicum," *Critique* 26, no. 282 (1970): 885–908 (reprinted in Michel Foucault, *Dits et écrits,* 4 vols. [Paris: Gallimard, 1994], 2:75–99). Foucault refers here to (post)modern art and philosophy as "the multiplied, polyscenic, simultaneous theater, sliced into scenes ignoring and signaling each other, and where without representing anything (to copy, to imitate) masks dance, bodies scream, hands and fingers gesticulate" (889–90). See also Sarah Kofman, *Nietzsche et la scène philosophique* (Paris: Union générale d'éditions, 1979) and Jacques Taminiaux, *Le théâtre des philosophes* (Grenoble: Millon, 1995).

of cruelty" came as close as one can get to Deleuze's ideal of Dionysian theater—"is the only place in the world where a gesture . . . can never be made
the same way twice."[26] The spectacle of the sophist at the end of Plato's dialogue is an example of such a "unique double" of the philosopher. Although
indistinguishable from Socrates (a dissembler who "in private conversations
and in short speeches forces the interlocutor to contradict himself"), the
sophist does not resemble the model of the philosopher. The "cruelty" of the
Sophist lies in the threat posed to the philosopher's identity, that is to say, to
his soul, rather than to his body, as in other dialogues of Plato, such as the
Apology, Crito, or *Phaedo.*

Art and Truth in Painting (Magritte and Foucault, Bacon and Deleuze)

If we are concerned about the likeness of our faces, we must consider whether he who speaks is a
painter, or not.

—SOCRATES

Is, however, a "cruelty" of pure simulacra, a Dionysian theater without any reference to Apollonian/Platonic Forms, possible at all?[27] Is it possible to "imagine"
an image without any resemblance to an accepted model, an aesthetic cogni-
tion without any form of recognition (*anagnōrisis*)? Is it possible strictly to separate (resembling) images and (dissembling) simulacra? Deleuze points to the
moment of Pop Art—the Eugene Ionesco of the *Bald Soprano* and the *Lesson*
would be its counterpart in theater sensu stricto and Jean-Luc Godard (e.g.,
Crazy Pete) in cinema—as a successful transformation of the "artificial" (*le fac-
tice,* that is, a copy of a copy, entangled in the web of representation) into the
simulacrum.[28] The end of Foucault's *This Is Not a Pipe* sounds like an echo
of Deleuze's "Plato and the Simulacrum": "A day will come when, by means
of similarity [*similitude*] relayed indefinitely along the length of a series, the
image itself, along with the name it bears, will lose its identity. Campbell,
Campbell, Campbell, Campbell."[29] Deleuze himself could have written this

26. Antonin Artaud, *The Theater and its Double,* trans. Mary Caroline Richards (New York: Grove
Weidenfeld, 1958), 75 (French: "Le théâtre est le seul endroit au monde où un geste fait ne se recommence
pas deux fois" [*Le théâtre et son double,* in Antonin Artaud, *Oeuvres complètes,* vol. 4 (Paris: Gallimard,
1978), 73]). It is from Artaud that Deleuze has borrowed the phrase "crown anarchy," which characterizes
the rise of simulacra.

27. The epigraph to this section comes from Plato, *Theaetetus* 144e–145a (*Theaetetus,* trans. Harold
N. Fowler, in *Plato in Twelve Volumes,* 15) (Greek: "Νῦν δέ γ', οἶμαι, εἴ τι μέλει ἡμῖν τῆς τῶν προσώπων
ὁμοιότητος, σκεπτέον εἰ γραφικὸς ὢν λέγει ἢ οὔ").

28. *The Logic of Sense,* 265–66 (French: *Logique du sens,* 306–7).

29. Michel Foucault, *This Is Not a Pipe,* trans. James Harkness (Berkeley: University of California
Press, 1982), 54 (French: "Un jour viendra où c'est l'image elle-même avec le nom qu'elle porte qui sera

sentence (with the exception perhaps of the term "similarity"). Andy Warhol's
series of soup cans is a perfect case of the metamorphosis of the most overused
commercial rhetoric into the poetry of simulacra, into an extreme manifestation of multiplicity.[30]

Foucault's use of the term "similarity" (*similitude*) should not mislead. He
is not challenging Deleuze's characterization of simulacra as images deprived
of all resemblance to a model. The two words, "similarity" and "resemblance,"
are not synonymous in *This Is Not a Pipe*. To be sure, they were synonymous
in Foucault's earlier *The Order of Things*, and it is to this book that Deleuze
refers in *Difference and Repetition* in order to support his notion of resemblance as the criterion of the Platonic distinction between images and simulacra.[31] Foucault's theory in *This Is Not a Pipe* differs, however, from the clear
picture of *The Order of Things*. The change of perspective apparently results
from a closer consideration of modern art, in particular the paintings and the
art theory of Magritte.[32] One might also hear in this new theory of images and
simulacra an echo of the Platonic Stranger's warning against resemblance, save
that Foucault seems to situate the slippery character of resemblance exclusively
on the image/representation side of the Stranger's and Deleuze's distinction.
Although not directly referring either to Plato or to Deleuze, Foucault situates
This Is Not a Pipe in the framework of the Deleuzian overturning of Platonism.[33] He begins, just like the Elean Stranger, by expressing misgivings about
the devious workings of resemblance: "Let a figure resemble an object . . . and
that alone is enough for there to slip into the [pure] play of the painting a[n
obvious] statement. . . . 'What you see is *that*.'"[34] The motivation behind this
statement questioning images and likeness in *This Is Not a Pipe* is, however,
different from, and apparently opposed to, that of the Stranger. Foucault does
not fear that likeness might allow a phenomenon to slip out of representation.
On the contrary, it is precisely the realm of representation that he would like

désidentifiée par la similitude indéfiniment transferée le long d'une série. Campbell, Campbell, Campbell, Campbell" [*Ceci n'est pas une pipe* (Montpellier: Fata Morgana, 1973), 79]).

30. Foucault, "Theatrum philosophicum," 902–3.

31. *Difference and Repetition*, 262 (French: *Différence et répétition*, 337). Indeed, resemblance/similar-
ity, dominating the episteme of the sixteenth century, was considered by Foucault one of the principles of
the classical episteme as well; see Michel Foucault, *The Order of Things* (New York: Random House, 1970),
esp. 28–29, 41, 47, 51 (French: *Les mots et les choses* [Paris: Gallimard, 1966], 44–45, 56, 61, 65).

32. See the letters of Magritte in *This Is Not a Pipe*, 57–58 (French: *Ceci n'est pas une pipe*, 83–85).

33. Cf. "Theatrum philosophicum," in particular, the definition of philosophy as any endeavor of
whatever kind to overturn Platonism ("toute enterprise, quelle qu'elle soit, pour renverser le platonisme"
[885]).

34. *This Is Not a Pipe*, 34 (French: "Qu'une figure ressemble à une chose . . . , et cela suffit pour que
se glisse dans le jeu de la peinture, un énoncé évident. . . : 'Ce que vous voyez, c'est *cela*.'" [*Ceci n'est pas
une pipe*, 42–43]).

art to escape; and he praises Magritte for having achieved just that. In order to allow for such a possibility Foucault—refining Magritte's own theory of art—turns to the same notion as the Stranger and Deleuze: "an image without resemblance." He seems to follow the suggestion of Deleuze and uses Plato's own texts, the *Sophist* in particular, in order to reverse the order of representation dominating the "Platonic" theory of art.[35] Apparently reinforcing the Stranger's distinction between images and simulacra, he assigns to each of them a positive characteristic: "ressemblant" and "similaire." Images function in the framework of representation based on *resemblance;* simulacra proliferate freely beyond that framework, according to the principle of *similarity:*

> Resemblance has a "master-model" (un"patron"), an original element that orders and hierarchizes the increasingly less faithful copies that can be struck from it. Resemblance presupposes a primary reference that prescribes and classes. The similar develops in series that have neither beginning nor end, that can be followed in one direction as easily as in another, that obey no hierarchy, but propagate themselves from small differences among small differences. Resemblance serves representation, which rules over it; similarity serves repetition, which ranges across it. Resemblance predicates itself upon a model it must return to and reveal; similarity circulates simulacrum as an indefinite and reversible relation of the similar to the similar.[36]

This is a clear formulation of Deleuze's basic distinction. But Foucault's terminology here reflects, perhaps better than that of Deleuze, the positive power that governs the proliferation of simulacra. The distinction seems to express the need for a term that would resemble, or rather be similar to, resemblance without dragging the series of simulacra back to the hierarchy of representation. But "similarity" (*similitude*), a word synonymous with "resemblance" in *The Order of Things,* can hardly fulfill this task. Rather, it seems to confirm the

35. "Theatrum philosophicum," 885–86.
36. *This Is Not a Pipe,* 44; translation modified (French: "La ressemblance a un 'patron': élément original qui ordonne et hiérarchise à partir de soi toutes les copies de plus en plus affaiblies qu'on peut en prendre. Ressembler suppose une référence première qui prescrit et classe. Le similaire se développe en séries qui n'ont ni commencement ni fin, qu'on peut parcourir dans un sens ou dans l'autre, qui n'obéissent à aucune hiérarchie, mais se propagent de petites différences en petites différences. La ressemblance sert à la représentation, qui règne sur elle; la similitude sert à la répétition qui court à travers elle. La ressemblance s'ordonne en modèle qu'elle est chargée de reconduire et de faire reconnaître; la similitude fait circuler le simulacre comme rapport indéfini et réversible du similaire au similaire" [*Ceci n'est pas une pipe,* 61]). Deleuze and Guattari's notion of the rhizome in *A Thousand Plateaus,* vol. 2 of their *Capitalism and Schizophrenia,* trans. Brian Massumi (Minneapolis: University of Minnesota Press, 1987 (French: *Mille plateaux,* vol. 2 of *Capitalisme et schizophrénie* [Paris: Minuit, 1980]) can be seen as a development of this notion of similarity.

Elean Stranger's apprehension and reveal the ambiguity—the slippery character—of *homoiotēs* (similarity/resemblance).

Thus the resemblance (or similarity) between resemblance and similarity
makes it difficult to maintain a rigorous theoretical distinction between images
and simulacra, that is, to dispose of representation completely. Magritte's painting *Représentation* gives an artistic display of this problem. Like many artists,
many painters—such as Diego Velázquez in *Las meninas* (analyzed by Foucault
in *The Order of Things*)—Magritte confronts the enigma of representation by
introducing it *into* the picture, by making it the object of painting. Thus the
opposition inside/outside, thing/image, and so forth, is now doubled, if not
actually mise en abyme, by the extension of the operation ad infinitum. What
is particularly puzzling in Magritte's *Représentation* is the maximum of resemblance between, if not the identity of, the two images of the playing field, and
the lack of a clear framing that would place them in the model/copy structure
of representation. A first guess would probably take the smaller image to be the
picture of the larger, the "real" one. But one could also consider the bigger
"image" to be a blowup photograph placed just behind the smaller one, which
would thus become the "original." For Foucault, the similarity between the two
images, or rather two simulacra, in the series disturbs a possible reference to
an exterior model and abolishes the hierarchy of representation. He acknowledges, however, that the exact similarity of the two images points toward a third
one that would function as a "paradigm" of the others (compare this to the
"third man" argument, a critique of the Platonic theory of ideal representation).
In other words, it points toward the resemblance with a model. The fact that
all efforts to order the picture according to the pattern of resemblance are frustrated does not preclude the pressure of the representational model, which thus
remains the "subject" of the painting. The field of play of representation is situated between the two images of the (soccer) field of play in Magritte's painting.
It consists in the shuttling movement between the desire and effort to resolve
the problem of resemblance and appearance—the problem of (re)semblance—
and the failure to do so. Thus the registration of the lack of any hierarchical
relationship between the two images, or rather simulacra, of the field of play,
which eventually imposes itself in Magritte's *Représentation,* is not an immediate
impression of the painting but rather the result of a careful scrutiny in which
the representational connection of resemblance has to be taken into account.

Foucault himself acknowledges the importance of mimetic play when he
credits Magritte not only with the distinction between resemblance and similarity but also with bringing them into play against each other.[37] This notion

---

37. *This Is Not a Pipe,* 44 (French: "Il me parait que Magritte a dissocié de la ressemblance la similitude et fait jouer celle-ci contre celle-là" [*Ceci n'est pas une pipe,* 61]).

of play applies to Magritte's other paintings, including the conventional figure of a pipe—as pipe as one can get, according to the conventional idea of a
pipe—with its puzzling inscription. One can usually distinguish three phases
in the experience with Magritte's paintings: an immediate impression of the
representation of a familiar scene, a shattering of this initial impression—often
caused by the image of shattered glass, picture as/or window pane—and finally
an effort to make the vision coherent again in an alternative structure of representation. The difficulty of the third phase and the eventual failure of the
effort is perhaps the most important feature of Magritte's art.

Deleuze's 1981 study of Bacon similarly focuses on the elements of play
between the structure of representation and its collapse. Bacon's method of
challenging figurative, representational composition consists mainly in the iso-
lation of an image or figure so that it cannot enter into a coherent relationship
with the other figures of the picture, with other images, other paintings.
Bacon's famous triptychs are not tri*logies;* there is no unity of composition con-
sisting of three parts, no assemblage, no logical sequence. Bacon's portraits are
not "portrait-images" in the sense of Paul Ricoeur, who valorizes them against
"simulacrum-images."[38] But, although they do not conform to the strict rule
of resemblance, they do suggest a model, which they strive precisely to de-
form. The introduction of a mirror into the picture complicates this play of
resemblance/dissemblance and again, just as in Magritte's *Représentation,* displaces the relationship of representation inside the picture. The model and the
image are now directly confronted in the picture, and the viewer is made the
judge of their resemblance. They certainly do not correspond to each other in
any ordinary way, but they do evoke, "address," the relationship of representation, which they render extraordinary. The portraits of George Dyer—"staring
into a mirror" from 1967 and "in the mirror" from 1968—are two versions of
Bacon's challenge to the conventional assumption of the specular reflection. The
second one seems more radical in its questioning of the "mirror image." The
"model" and the image in the mirror do not resemble one another in a direct
way; they are both disfigured, but differently. However, an effort is demanded
from the viewer to (re)construct the figure itself beyond the disfigurations.[39]
The *Portrait of George Dyer Staring into a Mirror* is perhaps even more disqui-
eting in its play with representation. The resemblance of the mirror image is uncanny, and its reality is so overwhelming that the ordinary specular hierarchy

38. See Paul Ricoeur, *Être, essence, et substance chez Platon et Aristote* (Paris: Société d'enseignement
supérieur, 1982), 108.

39. Cf. Andrew Benjamin's analysis of this painting and of the aesthetic and ontological aspects of the
phenomenon of the mirror in general in his *Art, Mimesis and the Avant-Garde: Aspects of a Philosophy of
Difference* (London: Routledge, 1991), 31ff.

seems reversed. In Deleuze's words, the figure is moving entirely into the mirror, together with its shadow, leaving the model (and thus the realm of representation) behind.[40] In fact, the strong figure in the mirror could be also construed as the model for the staring George Dyer, who would thus become a duplicate who has just found his real self. But in both cases, representation would still be the unavoidable point of reference for the work of specular displacement between a model, its faithful image, and a series of simulacra.

It is thus perhaps neither image nor simulacrum, but rather a play between the two, that constitutes the basic structure of Magritte's and Bacon's art. Does not Plato's *Sophist* suggest precisely such a play, the name of which would be *mimēsis*? Only a few pages after making his fateful distinction between (resembling) images and (dissembling) simulacra, the Stranger of Elea depicts *mimēsis* as play par excellence; no other play seems to him more "graceful" (*khariesteron*) and "more artistic" (*tekhnikōteron*). On this point, he elicits from Theaetetus a response more eloquent than is usual in this dialogue: "Certainly not; and you have mentioned a very important category, which includes under one class the most diverse sorts of things."[41] It is perhaps this variety, difficult to define—and eventually revealed as an irreducible ambiguity—that, rather than division, makes of mimesis "simultaneously the measure of both Platonism and the possibility of overturning Platonism." Indeed, *mimēsis* seems to be a *conditio sine qua non* of both images and simulacra, of both representation and the challenge to its reign. The Stranger might well call it "slippery"; and perhaps he does. After all, *homoiotēs*, which he explicitly calls *olisthēra*, constitutes, as (re)semblance, the "anarchic" principle of the play of *mimēsis*.

Mimontology in Plato and Nancy

Let's imitate:—What! This unheard-of science that we are, at this very moment, forced to discover, must we not give it a name that resembles its object?—But which one?—If you agree, and however ridiculous it might seem, we will call it mimontology.

—JEAN-LUC NANCY

Mimesis and play are associated with each other in the *Republic*—they are opposed to the gravity (*spoudē*) of serious men and women, soldiers, politicians, and philosophers—and are condemned for their lack of a solid epistemological

---

40. *Francis Bacon: The Logic of Sensation*, trans. Daniel W. Smith (New York: Continuum, 2003), 18 (French: *Francis Bacon: Logique de la Sensation* [Paris: Éditions de la Différence, 1981], 17–18).

41. *Sophist* 234b, trans. Benjamin Jowett, in *The Dialogues of Plato*, 5 vols., 3rd rev. ed. (New York: Macmillan, 1892), 4:361; translation modified (Greek: "Οὐδαμῶς· πάμπολυ γὰρ εἴρηκας εἶδος εἰς ἓν πάντα ξυλλαβὼν καί σχεδὸν ποικιλώτατον").

and ontological foundation (602b).[42] The serious occupation Socrates has in mind there is the guardianship of political distinctions in the constitution of the society (501a). Play can only have a limited place in political education: mimesis, the rhapsodic and theatrical ("hypocritical") mimesis of the third book, is only acceptable in the training of the guardians when circumscribed in the field of a play-game (*paidias kharin* [396d–e]). Now, the purpose of the strict separation of images and simulacra in the *Sophist* is precisely to delimit such a field for the harmless play of mimesis. If clearly circumscribed, neither resembling images nor dissembling simulacra are able to put in doubt the limits of reality. Taken as a "mere play" or game, that is, not in the least seriously, a simulacrum would be inoffensive to the order of representation based on faithful images. But the Stranger is unable to maintain a strict boundary between the two. His division of the art of making images (*eidōlopoiikē*)—in other words mimesis in the broad sense—into the production of resembling images (*eikastikē*) and that of mere appearances (*phantastikē*) is not a successful one in the dramatic scheme of the *Sophist*. And here, perhaps even more than in the *Republic,* and contrary to a powerful tradition, the doctrinal content of the dialogue, its "kernel," cannot be separated from its dramatic setting or its "shell."[43] Indeed, every theoretical decision in the dialogue, and the "capture" of the sophist in particular, is of vital interest to the being of the participants, including the readers, whose very existence is at stake in the problem of the possibility of limiting the proliferation of simulacra and, in particular, of separating philosophical from sophistic existence.

Although Heidegger's lecture course on the *Sophist* was published only in 1992, his thought contributed to undermining the interpretative principle of shell/kernel in this and other dialogues, a principle that allows one to isolate the content and to ignore the vital difficulties and aporias of the actual movement of investigation into the nature of being and language. Heidegger situates the thought of the dialogue within the history of being, as a manifestation of Greek Dasein. This position refuses in advance any interpretation of Plato that does not extend the aporia of the dialogue to Plato's authority/authorship by situating him in the development of historical thought.[44] For Heidegger,

42. The epigraph to this section comes from Nancy, "Le ventriloque," 308; my translation (French: "Imitons:—Eh quoi! Cette science inouïe que nous sommes, à cette heure, contraints de découvrir, ne faut-il pas la nommer d'un nom qui ressemble à son objet?—Mais lequel?—Si tu y consens, et quel qu'en soit le ridicule, nous l'appellerons mimontologie").

43. See, e.g., the classical work of Ulrich von Willamowitz-Moellendorff, *Platon—Sein Leben und seine Werke* (Berlin, 1929), 561, cited in Nancy, "Le ventriloque," 278.

44. Drew Hyland doesn't seem to take into account this fact and in particular Heidegger's hermeneutic of facticity in his critique of Heidegger's reading of the *Sophist* (*Questioning Platonism: Continental Interpretations of Plato* [Albany: State University of New York Press, 2004], 30ff.).

the importance of Plato's thought lies in bringing together the theory of being and nonbeing with the potential mode of Dasein, the factical existence of the sophist (*seine Faktizität*), which manifests the possibility of the "being of non-beings, i.e., the existence of deception and error."[45] Such a possibility is the fundamental condition of human being, that is, the phenomenon of being-in (*In-sein*) or being-in-a-world (*In-einer-Welt-sein*), originally permeated by *agnoia*, which is not a complete ignorance but a partial and apparent knowledge.[46] The *Sophist's* analysis of various forms of purification (*katharsis*), and its characterization of both the sophist and the philosopher as those who perform the highest form of purification, that is, *elenkhos*, or refutation, should be understood in this context of originary *agnoia;* no rigorous *ontic* knowledge (in the terminology of *Being and Time*)—be it that of the philosopher or that of the sophist—will be able to circumvent the *ontological* questioning of human Dasein and its aporia. This is the principal lesson of Plato's dialogues and particularly the *Sophist*. Heidegger quotes at length the embarrassed statement of Theaetetus at 231b–c, which he translates/paraphrases in the following way:

> *Dia to polla pephanthai,* "because so many things have now been shown" in relation to the sophist, "I can no longer find a way out," *aporō,* I do not know, *ti ontōs einai,* "what then the sophist actually [*wirklich*] is" and how he is to be determined in reality. I do not know what I am supposed to say, if I *hōs alēthē legō* (cf. c1) "if I am to speak in such a way that I present the matter at issue," and specifically *diiskhurizomenon* (c1), "on firm ground" [*gefestigt*].[47]

Heidegger presents the embarrassment of Theaetetus not as a scholarly or research difficulty that can be objectified and satisfactorily explained within

---

45. *Plato's "Sophist,"* 244 (German: *Platon: "Sophistes,"* 352). Rojcewicz and Schuwer's translation of "in seiner Faktizität" as "in his factual existence" might be misleading here; cf. Heidegger's lecture course from summer 1923, *Ontology: The Hermeneutics of Facticity*, trans. John van Buren (Bloomington: Indiana University Press, 1999), 7, 15, 21, and passim (German: *Ontologie [Hermeneutik der Faktizität]*, in *Gesamtausgabe*, 63:5, 12, 17, and passim). *Plato's "Sophists,"* 244 (German: "Das Sein des Nichtseienden, die Existenz des Truges und des Irrtums" [*Platon: "Sophistes,"* 352]).

46. *Plato's "Sophist,"* 255–56 (German: *Platon: "Sophistes,"* 369). As a source of the interpretation of the world, ἄγνοια often inhibits genuine knowledge, which it nevertheless calls for. Indeed, the ἀγνοεῖν or lack of knowledge is also a form of desire—ὁρμή—"toward an ἀληθεύειν [a disclosure] which has the potential to break through the actual ignorance" (*Plato's "Sophist,"* 256) (German: *Platon: "Sophistes,"* 369–70).

47. *Plato's "Sophist,"* 263–64 (German: "διὰ τὸ πολλὰ πεφάνθαι, 'dadurch, daß sich jetzt so Vielfaches gezeigt hat' bezüglich des Sophisten, 'finde ich überhaupt keinen Ausweg mehr,' ἀπορῶ, ich weiß nicht, τί ὄντως εἶναι, 'was denn nun der Sophist wirklich ist,' als was er wirklich bestimmt werden soll. Ich weiß nicht, was ich sagen soll, wenn ich ὡς ἀληθῆ λέγω (vgl. c1), 'wenn ich so sprechen soll, daß ich die Sache selbst gebe,' und zwar διισχυριζόμενον (c1), 'gefestigt'" [*Platon: "Sophistes,"* 381]).

the dramatic context but as an existential crisis, involving the very being of not only Theaetetus but also the reader of the dialogue. Indeed, the reality of the sophist is also that of the reader's finite Dasein, implicated in the possibility of error and deception (*to pseudos*). To be sure, Theaetetus's aporia is not final in the *Sophist* or in Heidegger's commentary. However, the stress on its essential and irreducible character in human Dasein's being-in-the-world cannot be overlooked in any reading of this or any other dialogue of Plato, which must become readers' own confrontation with history (*Auseinandersetzung mit der Geschichte*) and must be accompanied by the awareness that their reading itself is history (*daß sie selbst die Geschichte ist*).[48] This view questions both the doctrinal and the "dramatic" interpretation of Plato, even though the latter has benefited indirectly from Heidegger's insights in his reading of the *Sophist*.[49]

Nancy, in his essay "Le ventriloque," draws the most radical consequences from both Heidegger's hermeneutics and his own thorough reading of the *Sophist*. It is, indeed, Plato's text itself that confirms that in this dialogue there is "neither shell nor kernel, nor a compilation of pretexts. But a single text, that of the sophist, with all the values that this genitive will be able to have."[50] Only one text then, but multiple in the sense of valuations and references, one of the most crucial of which is the abyssal reference to itself that opens up the possibility of a truly rhapsodic mode, in which the voice of the speaker is never properly and exclusively his or her own. The author, narrator, character but also the reader is always a ventriloquist; there is always an other hidden in the text.[51] Nancy supports his thesis with a philological rigor: given the mention of the *Sophist* in another of Plato's dialogues, the *Statesman*, Nancy, as we have seen, suggests that one think of "the present dialogue" whenever one reads "the sophist."[52]

48. *Plato's "Sophist,"* 158 (German: *Platon: "Sophistes,"* 229).

49. See, for example, Rosen, *Plato's "Sophist,"* 4–6; from this point of view, again, the critique of Heidegger by Drew Hyland, the author of *Finitude and Transcendence in the Platonic Dialogues* (Albany: State University of New York Press, 1995), in his recent *Questioning Platonism,* 17–84, appears unjust.

50. Nancy, "Le ventriloque," 277; my translation (French: "Il n'y a ni coque ni fruit, ni montage de prétextes. Mais un seul texte, celui du sophiste, en toutes les valeurs que pourra prendre ce génitif").

51. John Sallis uses the word "ventriloquy" as part of his discussion, in the prologue to his *Chorology,* of the "double signature" that marks all Platonic dialogues: "For the double signature is irreducible: what is said in these texts, what is said to be said, is always signed by—that is, said to be said by—someone other than Plato. The double signature thus marks the reserve of the writer, the practice of a certain graphic ventriloquy" (*Chorology: On Beginning in Plato's "Timaeus"* [Bloomington: Indiana University Press, 1999], 1). He does not, however, develop this notion of ventriloquy; Ruby Blondell, addressing the *Sophist* in particular, notes that the Stranger in this dialogue "takes virtually all the substantive roles in the imagined conversations, ventriloquating the voices of Theaitetos, himself, and a range of imaginary opponents"; her view of the role of "ventriloquism" in Plato's dialogues, however, remains reliant upon a notion of Plato as an author in full control of the voices he creates (Blondell, *The Play of Characters in Plato's Dialogues* [Cambridge: Cambridge University Press, 2002], 348). See also the discussion of Blondell in the introduction to this book.

The consequences of this thesis are most radical in Nancy's view: the reading of the *Sophist* should bring a "violent and surreptitious perturbation that will have wrecked the Philosopher forever," even though he also agrees with Heidegger that it is with Plato and his "world-view" that "thinking about the being of beings has become—'philosophy,' because it is a matter of gazing up at the 'ideas.'"[53] Heidegger makes his comment based on the *Republic,* but the same conclusion can be drawn from his lecture course on the *Sophist.*[54] For Nancy, the paradoxical thesis of the simultaneous foundation and dismantling of "philosophy" in Plato rests on the postulation of an "unidentifiable" mimesis that corresponds to the ungraspable status of the sophist as artist, supposed to present himself or herself as the other against whom philosophy defines itself: "The philosopher will never have spoken (mastered) himself (and of himself), other than *in the mimesis of the sophist*—which implies, as at once cause and consequence, that philosophy will never have said *mimesis itself,* whether mimesis be simple or double (or that which philosophy identified under all the concepts derived from "mimesis," and under "imitation" in particular, lets itself be constantly overwhelmed [*débordée*] by *a mimesis much less identifiable*)."[55] What this text describes is a double bind of the philosopher: he or she needs to use mimesis in the process of self-identification, and yet he or she cannot master it, nor, therefore, master his or her identity. Philosophy cannot define itself without its counterpart (its other), mimesis, which necessarily compromises the definition itself. Obviously, this mimesis that is hardly identifiable (*bien moins identifiable*) refers to what we have called "dramatic or rhapsodic mimesis," which will appear to be involved in every kind of mimesis. And the abyssal play between the *Sophist* and the sophist will result in the ultimate confrontation/ dialogue between the "rigorous" philosopher and the philosopher rhapsode.

We may recall that the principle of rigor and self-sameness in the *Republic* was in the last instance established through the notion of resemblance that was

52. "Le ventriloque," 277; my translation (French: "Si par ailleurs on transporte dans ce texte l'usage du Politique, on pourra lire, chaque fois que le sophiste est nommé, 'le présent dialogue.' Chacun pourra s'exercer à cette transcription abyssale").

53. "Le ventriloque," 275; my translation (French: "Il faut lire le *Sophiste* comme la perturbation, violente et surnoise, qui aura fait avorter pour toujours le Philosophe"); "Plato's Doctrine of Truth," trans. Thomas Sheehan, in Martin Heidegger, *Pathmarks,* ed. William McNeill (Cambridge: Cambridge University Press, 1998), 180 (German: "Seit Platon wird das Denken über das Sein des Seienden—'Philosophie,' weil es ein Aufblicken zu den 'Ideen' ist" [*Platons Lehre von der Wahrheit* (Bern: Francke, 1947), 48]).

54. See, for example, *Plato's "Sophist,"* 141f (German: *Platon: "Sophistes,"* 204f).

55. "Le ventriloque," 275; my translation and emphasis (French: "Jamais le philosophe n'aura parlé (maîtrisé) lui-même (et de lui-même), sinon dans la mimesis du sophiste—ce qui implique, cause et conséquence à la fois, que jamais la philosophie n'aura dit *la mimesis elle-même,* que celle-ci soit simple ou double (ou: ce que la philosophie a identifié sous tous les concepts dérivés de 'mimesis,' et sous 'imitation' en particulier, se laisse constamment déborder par une mimesis bien moins identifiable)").

also the principle of mimesis. And we have already seen that the Stranger in the *Sophist* questions the reliability of the "slippery kind" of resemblance. The ideal of exactness does reappear in the *Sophist,* in the form of the new method of division (*diairesis*). Division is supposed to be rigorous, that is, to present a clear, exclusive dichotomy without a remainder. And the method seems to work well whenever the sophist, the master of mimesis, is not involved; as soon as the question of mimesis is at stake, however—as soon as the question of images/simulacra or of the philosopher/the sophist arises—the division breaks down and the definition, the "capture" of the sophist and the simulacrum, fails.

Since rigor is of such crucial importance to the definition of the philosopher—to definition in general—one might ask why the very word *akribeia,* the chief word for rigor and, as we have seen in the first chapter, the key word for understanding the *Republic,* appears only once in the *Sophist.* It is true that the context of this one occurrence is significant. Theaetetus and the Stranger are examining the competence of the sophist, who had been found to be an expert in disputation (*antilegein*). His claim is apparently not only to know but also to produce (*poiein*) all things (*sunapanta pragmata*) (233d). Since this can only be done in play (*paidia*), mimesis, as the most famous and apparently fitting play, is considered. The figure of the sophist thus becomes equivalent to that of the poet/rhapsode in the *Republic*—a master of mimesis, a producer of images. The division of the art of making images (*eidōlopoiikē tekhnē*) (235b), especially in words (*eidōla legomena*) (234c), into that of making resembling images (*eikastikē*) and that of producing simulacra (*phantastikē*) raises the problem of nonbeing. Is it possible to say what is not (to make a statement without reference, a fiction [*pseudē legein*], that is, to say a nonbeing ["to mēdamōs on . . . phthengesthai"] [237b])? In Greek "to say nothing" (*ouden legein, mēden legein*) also means "to say nonsense." Is it nonsense to maintain that this is possible? At 237a, Parmenides' ontology is evoked as an obstacle to admitting the being of nonbeing, and hence falsehood; it is this possibility, then, the being of the simulacrum, that is at stake. The necessity of refuting Parmenides' argument is stated in most dramatic terms: the Stranger of Elea, a disciple of Parmenides, speaks of patricide. He summarizes the development of pre-Platonic ontology, and then, at 243b, the word *akribeia,* or rigor, in its adverbial form, appears in the following sentence: "Earlier in my life I used to think I understood exactly [*akribōs*] what someone meant when he said just what we are confused about now [*to nun aporoumenon*], namely, what is not [*to mē on*]."[56] The perplexity of the Stranger might not be limited to nonbeing, yet the

---

56. *Sophist,* trans. Nicholas P. White, in *Plato: Complete Works,* 264. With its opposition between the earlier assurance and the present confusion (ἀπορία), this passage is parallel to the one quoted by Heidegger at the outset of *Being and Time.* It is in fact extracted from the *Sophist* 244a.

opposition between philosophical rigor (*akribeia*) and nonbeing (*mē on*) was perhaps the objective of the excursus into the history of ancient ontology in this passage. The incompatibility between the rigorous philosophical method and the problematic of *mē on* is here strongly emphasized.

Now, if we think of the essence of human Dasein in terms of finitude, error, and death, which are forms of nonbeing, the incompatibility in question becomes an existential rather than simply epistemological or methodological question. In other words, the Stranger might dramatically suggest here an intimate relationship between the problem of mimesis as essential to the human condition—mimesis is after all the origin of the question of nonbeing in the *Sophist*—and the problem of the mode of discourse able to articulate it. The incompatibility between philosophical rigor and mimesis would no longer be an extrinsic problem, susceptible to extrinsic measures, such as the banishment of the poets/rhapsodes in the *Republic,* but rather an internal tension within the soul of the philosopher.[57]

Toward the end of the dialogue the images of the philosopher and the sophist become inseparable in spite of the most rigorous method of *diairesis:* "One could not divide anything without bringing, to this more and more strict schema of the sophist, something of the philosopher."[58] Nancy conceives this relationship as a ventriloquism (*ventriloquie* or *gastérographie*).[59] In other words, any attempt to formulate rigorously one's thought has to take into account the presence of a "ventriloquous" mimesis of the sophist; any attempt to define the philosopher has to begin by defining the sophist as his own phantasm ("Let us recall that the sophist is looked for only as being himself the philosopher's phantasm," says Nancy[60]). Thus, the rigorous "typography" of the *Republic* becomes in the *Sophist* a rhapsodic "gasterography." Indeed, it is the philosopher who will turn out to be the ground for the definition, that is, eventually the stage for impersonation, for all the other types, especially those of the sophist and the politician, even though he will never become an eponym of a specific dialogue: "One won't be able to count the fourth dialogue, the one featuring Socrates and his homonym, Socrates and his *mimēma*. But it is carefully taken into account in the others, and if it does not follow them, it is because it is already the stage on which they are all played out."[61] The dramatic

---

57. It is true that this tension was foreshadowed by Socrates' alleged compunction in banishing the poets in the *Republic.*

58. "Le ventriloque," 332; my translation (French: "on ne saurait rien diviser sans recueillir, dans ce schéma que l'on affine du sophiste, quelque chose du philosophe").

59. "Le ventriloque," 275.

60. "Le ventriloque," 291; my translation (French: "Rappelons seulement que le sophiste n'est cherché qu'en tant qu'il est lui-même un fantasme du philosophe").

61. "Le ventriloque," 333; my translation (French: "On ne pourra pas compter le quatrième dialogue,

undecidability of the main character—the Stranger—the uneasiness as to his method, his very anonymity, all this points to the parallel between the difficulty (perhaps impossibility) of defining the sophist and that of defining the philosopher. For Nancy, this aporia is definitive: the result of the *Sophist* cannot be reversed, and the absence of the dialogue entitled the *Philosopher* (which the tradition of Plato scholarship has tried to explain through some contingency) has nothing accidental about it. Indeed, there cannot be a discussion of the philosopher separated from that of the sophist ("There will be no authentic *Joker,* nor an authentic *Philosopher*"[62]). And thus the *Sophist* is also the *Philosopher.*

Thus the failure to define the sophist entails the failure to define the philosopher and eventually the failure of a rigorous, definitional mode of thought in the matter of being and non-being. The playfulness of the procedure and the ridicule of the examples of division indicate a critique of the apparently rigorous method. To be sure, the presence of the "angler" and the "lice killer" among the examples used to illustrate the method of division does not by itself invalidate the merit of the method. It is the attempt to define mimesis and the problem of being and nonbeing that brings about the definite aporia and the failure of the rigorous method of division. It is this crucial combination of the dramatic play of mimesis (the form or the "shell" of traditional scholarship) and the questioning of the theory of being and nonbeing (its supposed content or "kernel")—but also the rhapsodic prologue to the whole "trilogy," *Theaetetus,* the *Sophist,* the *Statesman,* which draws the author philosopher "himself" into play—that justifies Nancy's term "mimontology," playfully elaborated in his reading of the *Sophist.*[63] It denotes the mutual involvement of the fundamental decisions concerning being and the mimetic rhapsodic mode of the drama of *logoi.* Mimontology consists in staging the *logoi—dia-logoi* ("without dialogue, no thought and no philosophy"); the philosopher mimes himself "who is another."[64] Mimontology as the "treatise of the altered being" (*le traité de l'être altéré*) is derivative (*de façon seconde*) and subordinated to the staging of the philosopher/ *mimētēs.* A painter—also a philosophical "painter," say, Parmenides painting being or Socrates painting an ideal city—needs a mise en scène: "Being is nothing that would get said (or, would say itself) if it were not

---

celui de Socrate et de son homonyme, de Socrate et de son mimème. Mais son compte est soigneusement établi dans les autres, et s'il ne les suit pas, c'est qu'il est déjà la scène sur laquelle tous sont joués").

62. "Le ventriloque," 333; my translation (French: "Il n'y aura pas d'authentique *Fou,* ni d'authentique *Philosophe*").

63. See the introduction to this book.

64. "Le ventriloque," 330; my translation (French: " sans dialogue, pas de pensée, et pas de philosophie. Sur la scène du dialogue, qui le philosophe mime-t-il? lui-même, toujours, qui est un autre").

staged. Parmenides immobile is nothing, but let him be set in motion, let him write and recite his poem, and there's the one who mimics—necessarily, for his myth doubles as an engastrimyth. He does not imitate being, he mimics, he stages the one who says it."[65] And the one who says it is the sophist-rhapsode-actor—an "authentic" artist, since he needs only himself to achieve the effect of mimesis.[66] In terms of the *Sophist*, he is a phantastic artist, and we might, with Nancy (and to some extent with Rosen), suspect the philosopher-Stranger of being such an artist, just as we suspected of Socrates in the *Republic*.

Phantastic Art: Between Image and Simulacrum

But I was uncertain before in which of the two [the domain of images, *eikastikē*, or that of simulacra, *phantastikē*] the sophist should be placed, and even now I cannot see clearly.
—THE STRANGER

We know at this point that the *mimēmata are*, and that an art of deception, *tekhnē apatētikē*, exists.
—JEAN-LUC NANCY

The constant evasion of the sophist and his or her "art" can function in the drama of the *Sophist* only in conjunction with the relentless pursuit of the Stranger and Theaetetus.[67] Why this determination to circumscribe "the phi-losopher's phantasm," as Nancy calls him or her? Perhaps he or she is not just a phantasm, that is, perhaps he or she has some claim to being "real." The strength of the sophist, of the art of deception, perhaps results from this impossibility of deciding between images and simulacra. Indeed, the major crisis in the dialogue results from the difficulty of proclaiming the sophist and his or her art a mere fantasy. If they were pure simulacra, would they have any reality, any relation to being at all? This is the conundrum of the Stranger and Theaetetus: how to circumscribe the sophist without rejecting his or her reality, the reality of error, of falseness, and of deception, and eventually the reality of poetic fiction. This conundrum is ours as well.

The rigid opposition of *eikōn* and *phantasma*, of resembling image and sim-ulacrum, made by the Stranger of Elea and taken up by Deleuze, belongs to

65. "Le ventriloque," 329; my translation (French: "L'être n'est rien qui se dise s'il n'est mis en scène. Parménide immobile n'est rien, mais qu'il soit mis en branle, qu'il écrive et qu'il récite son poème, et le voici qui mime—par force, car son mythe se double d'un engastrimythe. Il n'imite pas l'être, il mime, il met en scène celui qui le dit").

66. "Le ventriloque," 328; he is also self-annihilating ("auto-thentēs" [275]).

67. The first epigraph to this section comes from Plato, *Sophist* 236c (*Sophist*, trans. Harold N. Fowler, 337) (Greek: "Ὁ δέ γε καὶ τότ' ἠμφεγνόουν, <ἐν> ποτέρᾳ τὸν σοφιστὴν θετέον, οὐδὲ νῦν πω δύναμαι θεάσασθαι σαφῶς"). The second comes from "Le ventriloque," 324; my translation (French: "On sait à présent que les mimèmes *sont*, et qu'un art de tromperie, *techné apatétiké* existe").

the tradition of Parmenidean ontology that excludes any common ground between being and nonbeing (the exclusion of mimesis in the *Republic* proceeded from the same fear of contaminating being with nonbeing). It is this ontology (and this fear) that allows the master of mimesis, the sophist, to escape the accusation of producing a falsehood or fiction (*to pseudos*). A simulacrum, an image without any reference to the reality of the model, is nothing. An image without resemblance, a semblance, a mere appearance (*phantasma*) does not partake of being. A sophist, say Gorgias or Antisthenes, would object to the reality of pure semblance.[68] There is no lie, *ouk esti pseudos,* there is no "pure" simulacrum. On the other hand, the arguments based on the harmlessness of simulacra as the mere play of nonbeing (such as the nonserious mimesis, *paidias kharin,* in the *Republic*) only reinforce the sense of the "real" as ideologically accepted.[69] The conundrum is formulated—and at the same time perhaps a response initiated—in a quasi stichomythia between Theaetetus and the Stranger. The Elean pretends to maintain the strict Eleatic and sophistic position but, unexpectedly, he meets the resistance of Theaetetus. The latter, when asked to define the image in general (*eidōlon*), takes recourse to resemblance and thus seems to evoke the *resembling* image (*eikōn*). In this exchange, one can also hear our discussion of Magritte's *This Is Not a Pipe* ("it is certainly not a real pipe; however, . . ."):

> Theaetetus: Why, Stranger, what can we say an image [*eidōlon*] [of a pipe] is, except another such thing fashioned in the resemblance [*aphōmoiōmenon*] of the true [*pros talēthinon*]?—Elean Stranger: Do you mean another true [pipe], or in what sense did you say "such" [*toiouton*]?—Th.: Not a true one by any means, but only one like [*eoikos*] the true.—S.: And by the true you mean the one that really is [*ontōs on*]?—Th.: Exactly.—S.: And the not true is the opposite of the true?—Th.: Of course.—S.: The one that resembles, then, you say does not really exist [*ouk ontōs on*], if you say it is not true—Th.: But it does exist, in a way, somehow [*pōs*].—S.: But not truly [*ouk alēthōs*], you mean.—Th.: No, except that it is really a resembling image [*eikōn ontōs*] [of a pipe].— S.: Then what we call image, though not really existing, really does exist. (240a–b; cf. 236a)[70]

68. See Pierre Aubenque, *Le problème de l'être chez Aristote* (Paris: Presses Universitaires de France, 1962), 98ff., on the two kinds of the sophistic argument of the impossibility of lying.

69. They seem to perform the same ideological function as our Disneyland—see for example, Jean Baudrillard, "The Precession of Simulacra," in Jean Baudrillard, *Simulations,* trans. Paul Foss, Paul Patton, and Philip Beitchman (New York: Semiotext[e], 1983), 23–26 (French: "La précession des simulacres," in *Simulacres et Simulation* [Paris: Galilée, 1981], 24–28).

70. *Sophist,* trans. Harold N. Fowler, 349, 351; translation modified.

Thus in this exchange, a shift has occurred from *eidolon* (image in general) to *eikōn* (resembling image). It is only this "reality of resemblance" that saves the image from fading into nothingness. But resemblance, a slippery kind, does not mean here the undisputed derivation from a model. Once again, thinking of Foucault's reading of Magritte, we might say that Magritte's pipe would retain its reality even without the other pipe (the ideal one?) that appears hovering above the ostensibly painted one in the later version of this theme. For it would not do to limit the notion of resemblance in this text to the domain of *eikones*. It is clearly the art of the sophist, the art of simulacra (*phantastikē tekhnē*), which is discussed here.[71] We are thus far from the certitude of the first book of the *Republic* where Socrates effectively related resemblance to identity.[72] Identity as form of resemblance, which points ultimately toward the essential affiliation with the model, the Idea, would not need such a strong dramatic justification. But in the *Sophist* there *is* a question of the "resemblance of a pure semblance," that is, ultimately of a simulacrum.

I have already mentioned Rosen's objection to the expression "image without resemblance," that is, to the notion of "pure simulacrum," and I have already pointed out the possible difficulties of translating the Greek *eikōn* and *eidōlon*. But the issue at stake ("in play") here can hardly be resolved— if it can be resolved at all—by philological means. The long debate around the problem of a possible "theory" of predication in the *Sophist* testifies to the importance of the stakes.[73] The merit of Rosen's book in this context is its patient analysis not only of Plato's text but also of its possible interpretations. Only after a review of representative secondary texts does he return to the passage under discussion here, on the nature of image and resemblance. As to the problem of the distinction between images and simulacra, Rosen has conjectured right from the beginning—referring to Socrates' use of the verb *phantazomai* at 216c–d—that "[p]erhaps Socrates would deny the possibility of distinguishing between icons and fantasms."[74] The Stranger's relentlessness

71. *Sophist,* 239c–d and 240d.

72. "But we agreed that each of them had the qualities of the person he was like" (*Plato: The "Republic,"* trans. Tom Griffith, ed. G. F. R. Ferrari [Cambridge: Cambridge University Press, 2000], 31) (Greek: "ᾧ γε ὅμοιος ἑκάτερος εἴη τοιοῦτον καὶ ἑκάτερον εἶναι," *Republic,* 350c).

73. Rosen discusses the analyses of Francis M. Cornford, G. E. L. Owen, Michael Frede, J. L. Ackrill, Harold Cherniss, Gregory Vlastos et al. in *Plato's "Sophist,"* 29ff. and 195ff.; cf. Yvon Lafrance "Autour de Platon: Continentaux et analystes," *Dionysius* 3, (1979): 17–37. See also, more recently, Francis J. Pelletier, *Parmenides, Plato, and the Semantics of Not-Being* (Chicago: University of Chicago Press, 1990), the articles in Richard Kraut, ed., *The Cambridge Companion to Plato* (Cambridge: Cambridge University Press, 1992), and Job Van Eck, "Falsity without Negative Predication," *Phronesis* 40, no. 1 (1995): 20–47.

74. *Plato's "Sophist,"* 65.

has only confirmed this supposition, since Rosen reads the whole dialogue in terms of the dramatic contrast between the characters of Socrates and the Stranger. The problem of distinguishing images from simulacra is that of the Stranger, and it depends on the relationship between the image and simulacrum, on the one hand, and the original, on the other. "The closest we can come to analyzing 'is like'" and still preserve the distinction between original and image—a distinction compromised by the "predicationalist" translation of *eoike* as "duplicates" or "is the same as"—"is to say that the image, *qua* likeness, is and is not the original."[75] But this comes close to an aporia. Since the being of the image is resemblance, it is this last notion that remains puzzling. For Rosen, it ultimately leads to the failure of a "discursive distinction between icons and fantasms"; thus there is "no epistemic or commonly acceptable definition of the distinction between the philosopher and the sophist."[76] Was then the long effort of the Stranger and Theaetetus in vain? Perhaps it served the same purpose (played the same role) as, eventually, Rosen's own discussion of the sophisticated analysis of Plato's dialogue by modern logicians does.[77]

But such apparently rigorous analysis appears helpless when faced with the "art" of the sophist, the "phantastic art" (*phantastikē tekhnē* [239d]), which is characterized as deceptive (*apatētikē tekhnē*), with the simulacrum (*phantasma*) explicitly said to be its object (240d).[78] It seems that it is the question of the possibility of such a phantastic art that initiates the long ontological detour of the dialogue. And it is in fact the status of images in general that causes utter perplexity in the Stranger, Theaetetus, the other characters, including Socrates, and the readers. An image (*eidōlon*) and a simulacrum or semblance (*phantasma*), as opposed to the real and the true, *are not,* and yet, precisely through resembling (*eoikenai*), they somehow *are.* The slippery resemblance and the "many-headed sophist" will thus force Theaetetus, the Stranger and the readers of the dialogue to admit the being of nonbeing.[79] But they will also force them to recognize the significance of the entanglement or intertwining (*sumplokē*) of resembling and dissembling images in the "stitching" of rhapsodic mimesis.

75. Plato's "Sophist," 193; cf. Francis M. Cornford, *Plato's Theory of Knowledge* (London: Routledge and Kegan Paul, 1935), 322–23, and Lafrance, "Autour de Platon: Continentaux et analystes," 33–34.

76. Plato's "Sophist," 325.

77. Indeed, Rosen's rigorous method can appear as questionable as that of the Elean Stranger; see, for example, Lesley Brown, review of Plato's "Sophist," by Stanley Rosen, *Classical Review* 35, no. 1 (1985): 69–70.

78. I use this archaic form, which is almost a transliteration of Plato's Greek—used, for example, by Sidney—in order to avoid the common associations of "fantastic" and "phantasmagoric," as well as to keep in mind the references to appearance and appearing ("φαίνεσθαι").

79. Plato, *Sophist* 240c (trans. Benjamin Jowett, 4:369).

The ontological discussion of the *Sophist* constitutes a dramatic break (a "parricide") with the principle of Parmenides (and mutatis mutandis the rigorous understanding of the so-called theory of Ideas), which underlies the strict separation between images and simulacra. The break is facilitated by the common experience of language, which resists the formulation of this extreme ontological doctrine. There is no language without syntax, that is, without a kind of blending (*summeixis*). Those who refuse to admit any such blending refute themselves every time they use language beyond simple tautology: "They're forced to use *being* [*einai*] about everything, and also *separate* [*khōris*], *from others* [*tōn allōn*], *of itself* [*kath' hauto*], and a million other things. They cannot help linking them together in their speech. So they don't need other people to refute them, but have an enemy within, as people say, to contradict them, and they go carrying him around talking in an undertone inside them like the strange ventriloquist Eurycles" (252c).[80] The consideration of common language frustrates the efforts of the theoretician, of both the sophist and the philosopher and of the interpreter. The image of the ventriloquist, who in a playful mode constantly overrides rigorous theoretical constructions, calls for a view of language that speaks rather than is spoken in an instrumental way— a "rhapsodic" view of language. We shall see in the concluding chapter that this originary ventriloquism of language is an expression of the common character of human Dasein as *Mit-sein,* or being-with. Nancy will characterize it as a *partage des voix* or sharing (of) voices.

It is certainly not accidental that in the *Sophist* the word *sumplokē* appears for the first time in the discussion of the phantastic art. Since the entanglement of nonbeing and being as well as that of semblance and resemblance is not only the source of perplexity but also that of its overcoming or at least acceptance, the phantastic art, and perhaps art in general, is destined to play a crucial role in this *sumplokē*. A phantastic artist makes things appear (*phainesthai*) but also distorts them, simulates, produces simulacra (*phantasmata*). But to address (*ansprechen*) the other is precisely to address it "as other than what it itself is" (*als ein anderes, als es selbst ist*) and thus requires a play of

---

80. *Sophist,* trans. Nicholas P. White, 274. The name of Eurycles is familiar from Aristophanes who in *The Wasps,* through his chorus, in a remarkable parabasis, presents the poet (himself) as comparable to the famous ventriloquist; "You have wronged him much, he protests, a bard/ who had served you often and well before;/ Partly, indeed, himself unseen,/ assisting others to please you more;/ With the art of a Eurycles, weird and wild,/ he loved to dive in a stranger's breast,/ And pour from thence through a stranger's lips/ full many a sparkling comical jest" (*The Wasps* 1017–20, trans. Benjamin Bickley Rogers [Cambridge, Mass.: Harvard University Press, 1982], 69) (Greek: "μιμησάμενος τὴν Εὐρυκλέους μαντείαν καὶ διάνοιαν,/ εἰς ἀλλοτρίας γαστέρας ἐνδὺς κωμῳδικὰ πολλὰ χέασθαι" [Aristophanes, *Comoediae,* ed. F. W. Hall and W. M. Geldhart (Oxford University Press, 1906)]). Eurycles was a ventriloquist ("ἐγγαστρίμυθος"), and Nancy's neologisms are derived from this word.

masking and unmasking, in other words, of resembling/dissembling.[81] Thus in the ontology of the *Sophist*, an ontology of the community of genres (*koinōnia tōn genōn*), it is perhaps the genre (*genos*) of (re)semblance, a slippery one, that determines the relationship of being and its other and that allows the play of the other in being.

Dramatic mimesis epitomizes this phenomenon of play between masking and unmasking, the play of (re)semblance. The last series in dividing the phantastic art in the *Sophist* brings forward the notion of the sophist/simulacrum. As an artist, a *poiētēs* and a *mimētēs* in the strict sense—and unlike, say, a painter, a sculptor, or an author of a dithyramb—the sophistic "performance artist" uses his own body as a means of generating a false resemblance (*tōi heautou khrōmenos sōmati prosomoion* [267a]). Thus, he is a rhapsode—at the same time a producer and a product of mimesis. This is mimesis "in the strict sense," a rhapsodic mimesis:

> The Stranger: Let's recall that one part of image-making [*eidōlourgikēs*] is likeness-making [*eikastikon*]. The other kind was going to be simulacrum-making [*phantastikon*], if falsity [*pseudos*] appeared to be truly falsity [*ontōs on pseudos*] and by nature one of *those that are* [*tōn ontōn hen*].—Th.: Yes, it was.—S.: But falsity did turn out that way, so are we going to count likeness-making and simulacrum-making as indisputably two forms?—Th.: Yes.—S.: Then let's divide the art of simulacrum-making [*phantastikon*] in two again.—Th.: How?—S: Into one sort that's done with tools [*di'organōn*] and one that uses one's own self as the tool [*to de autou parechontos heauton organon*] of the person making the simulacrum [*phantasma*].—Th.: What do you mean?—S.: When somebody uses his own body or voice to make something similar to your body or voice, I think the best thing to call this part of simulacrum-making is "imitating" [*mimēsis touto tēs phantastikēs malista keklētai pou*].—Th.: Yes.—S.: Let's set this part off by calling it "imitation" [*Mimētikon dē touto autēs proseipontes aponeimōmetha*]. (266d–267b)[82]

Phantastic art thus becomes the quintessential art, mimesis par excellence. It involves the entire person, his or her *skhēma,* or figure, and his or her *phōnē,* or voice. Is not the Stranger, the divine (*theios*) philosopher, as suggested by Theodoros at the outset of the dialogue (216b–c), in fact an authentic

---

81. Heidegger, *Plato's "Sophist,"* 297 (German: *Platon: "Sophistes,"* 431).

82. *Sophist*, trans. Nicholas P. White, 291; translation modified. See, on this passage and its interruptive character, Seth Benardete, *The Argument of the Action: Essays on Greek Poetry and Philosophy* (Chicago: University of Chicago Press, 200), 351–52.

sophist/rhapsode, performing with his own organs the father Parmenides and the dissident son, an anonymous stage manager of the "battle of gods and giants . . . [in] their dispute with each other over being" (*gigantomachia peri tēs ousias*)?[83] Does he cease to be a philosopher for all that? Or is this not in fact the art that Socrates will require from a "phantastic philosopher" in the *Timaeus* and *Critias?* The immobile perfection of the Parmenidean being and of the ideal model of community calls for the supplement of actual staging, for rhapsody, giving voice to the heroes of the community.

But painterly mimesis, the mimesis of the icon, is not suppressed because of that (330). An image imposes itself through its resemblance (*Sans doute fallait-il aborder Mimesis par son icône*, writes Nancy) and serves as a constant reference point for the questioning of the order of representation. In the long third postscript to his essay—on staging the image of Athens and Atlantis in *Critias*—Nancy shows this process of interaction between resembling mimesis (*apeikasia*) and rhapsodic mimesis, giving "bodies, schemes, and voices" to the images in *logoi*.[84] It is now the latter that furnishes the standard of exactness, although reduced exactness in divine matters. But since immobility, as the *Sophist* shows, is no longer an ideal, the "second mimesis" will supplement the *apeikasia*, will make it alive, but also will suppress the Idea as its immobile standard of resemblance, will make it enter the domain of play and show that rigorous resemblance of the icon might be "un défaut d'illusion" rather than "un défaut de l'illusion."[85] In other words, the illusion of representative art is not illusion enough (not *ludic* enough) to enter—and to be effective in—the domain of movement and life. Only "Daedalic," rhapsodic art could achieve that crossing of the boundary between art and life.

These two aspects of mimesis (iconic and rhapsodic) reinforce the entanglement of the sophist in the aesthetic, social, political text of ideological representation. Resemblance remains one of the principles of the *sumplokē* of addressing the other in/of representation. The perplexity of the last image of the sophist—a double of Socrates, the ideal philosopher—depends on a "true resemblance."[86] One cannot avoid taking this image of the sophist for that of the philosopher, for that of Socrates "himself": one who can "maintain his insincerity [*eirōneuesthai*]" by using "short speeches in private conversation to force the person talking with him to contradict himself" (268b).[87] Indeed, one

83. *Sophist,* trans. Nicholas P. White, 267.
84. "Le ventriloque," 337; my translation.
85. "The lack of illusion" rather than "the defect of the illusion."
86. "Le ventriloque," 336; my translation. "No need to say whom he resembles," says Nancy (French: "Inutile de souligner à qui il ressemble").
87. *Sophist,* trans. Nicholas P. White, 292. A scientific imitation founded on knowledge ("ἡ μετ' ἐπιστήμης ἱστορική τις μίμησις") as a possible characterization of philosophy was excluded from the

cannot avoid confusing in these last divisions the sophist and the philosopher, and this confusion cannot be dismissed as a mere play of false resemblance, as "mere similarity" (in Foucault's terms), in which case there would be no problem for "Platonism." But the sophist *does* resemble Socrates, even if the principle of this resemblance is (dis)similarity in mimesis. Both the sophist and Socrates, like the figures in Magritte's and Bacon's paintings, are pieces and players in the play of (re)semblance, the play in and with the order of representation.

Such a play of (re)semblance is perhaps the only way to conceive art—phantastic art—and its fiction as a subversive activity. Indeed, art is always a powerful instrument of ideology when it upholds the principle of "reality" supported by a clearly defined structure of representation. Both in the case of the identification of resembling images and of the absolute detachment of simulacra, the "real" comes out reinforced. The former achieves this reinforcement by the direct control of the "iconology," the latter by discrediting a revolutionary alternative. The glorious revolution of simulacra might end up in the "simulacrum of revolution."[88] Effective subversion can result only from the shuttling movement between the two—the movement of (re)semblance. The text it creates, the *sumplokē* of images and simulacra, is able to reflect and to reflect on the model of representation, a task that no Dionysian hubris, no Parmenidean and sophistic argument, could actually perform. In fact, Plato's text itself weaves (or stitches—*rhaptei*) together such apparently incompatible epistemological, aesthetic, and ontological categories as myth and the method of division, mimesis and diegesis, being and nonbeing, and image and simulacrum in the double, questioning movement of the serious play of (re)semblance.[89]

---

discussion at 267d–e; it needs to be thought within the problematic of the φάρμακον of knowledge in the *Republic* and in the *Crito*.

   88. In the words of one of the harshest critics of Deleuze, see Jean-François Mattéi, *L'étranger et le simulacre* (Paris: Presses Universitaires de France, 1983), 436; my translation. Mattéi places himself emphatically on the philosophical side of the "old quarrel." See, on the other hand, Paul Patton, "Anti-Platonism and Art," in *Gilles Deleuze and the Theater of Philosophy*, ed. Constantin V. Boundas and Dorothea Olkowski, 141–56 (New York: Routledge, 1994).

   89. As to the mimesis/diegesis opposition, one might recall that the direct dialogic form is probably the transcription of Socrates' narrative; see the beginning of Plato's *Theaetetus*, to which the *Sophist* is apparently a sequel.

4

The Abyssal Ground of World and Discourse in the *Timaeus*

(Kristeva, Irigaray, Butler, Derrida)

> For unclear reasons
> Under unknown circumstances
> Ideal Being ceased to be satisfied.
> . . . .
> Why on earth did it start seeking thrills
> In the bad company of matter?
> What use could it have for imitators,
> Inept, ill-starred,
> Lacking all prospects for eternity?
> —WISŁAWA SZYMBORSKA

The ontological categories of the *Republic,* even in the form of their sophisti-cated redefinition in the *Sophist,* might not resist the unsettling of worldly emplacement, or the chora. Indeed, such an emplacement raises the problem of borders and marginality that necessarily accompanies any attempt to cir-cumscribe a region and that threatens to spill over and confuse all genres and categories. It is thus important to determine the place, the status of a margin, of a border, since it is only from a margin that a text or a world can be deter-mined. A margin is, however, an uncertain place, a topos of uncertainty. One is bound to lose the sense of direction and of boundaries (*margines, fines*) when entering a marginal region; one becomes an errant (*hē planetē/ho planetēs*). A margin is by definition, paradoxically, indefinite. It marks and blurs the differ-ence between the main corpus (text or body politic, a world) and its outside by dissolving the border (*margo*) of separation. Another place, a place of an other, banished but not released—an errant margin constitutes the dreadful

The epigraph to this chapter is drawn from Szymborska's poem "Plato, or Why?" trans. Clare Cavanagh and Stanisław Barańczak, *Poetry* 185, no. 5 (2005): 352 (Polish: "Z przyczyn niejasnych, / w okolicznościach nieznanych / Byt Idealny przestał sobie wystarczać. . . . // Czemu, u licha, zaczął szukać wrażeń / W złym towarzystwie materii? // Na co mu naśladowcy / niewydarzeni, pechowi, / bez widoków na wieczność?" ["Platon, Czyli Dlaczego," in Wisława Szymborska, *Chwila* (Kraków: Wydawnictwo Znak, 2002)], 17).

oxymoron of an "internal exile." A place of an other supposed to sanction the identity of the same, it is made to stand (*stehen*) against (*gegen*) the same: it is objectified. It resists precisely by refusing the status of an *object,* by not offering resistance to the (op)pression of the same, by refusing its own topicality, its *proper* place. Through its very dis-position a margin can defy the center, cause the fall of an empire. Margin is the most ex-centric of places, apparently far from the familiar and domestic.

But what if this unhomely, this uncanny, this *atopos* place of marginality were discovered to be the foundation of the system of strict oppositions? Within the structure of an established topography, it would be hardly a place at all, a nonplace; not so much topos as chora, at least the chora of Plato's *Timaeus,* a matter of creation that ceased to be a matter of course, familiar, homely and precisely because of its uncanny, *unheimlich* position, at once central and marginal (errant).

Plato's *Timaeus* has rarely been read otherwise than from the position, the place, of a central Ideal Being (and from the place of its emanation in an Ideal Republic), the position imposing the question of why on earth it started "seeking excitement in the bad company of matter," the marginal place of uncertainty, that is, of the chora. The thinkers discussed in this chapter, on the contrary, all descend to the slums of *on,* or being, and *polis,* or city, in order to reconsider their importance to the establishment of the central order.

Kristeva's *Revolution in Poetic Language,* not a detailed reading of the *Timaeus* but perhaps a suggestion for such a reading, was one of the first attempts to use the chora as a challenge to the logocentric tradition of Western thought.[1] Kristeva borrows the concept of the chora for the expression of the philosophical, linguistic, and poetical aspects of her notion of the "semiotic," an area of indetermination and potentialities, submitted to the forceful inscription of the symbolic order. Her view of the chora as an indeterminate structuration of semiosis, always accompanied by the contrary movement of destructuration, played an important role in giving the problematic of the chora a significance exceeding the limits of Plato scholarship. Irigaray's work, although for the most part not a direct reading of *Timaeus* either, intervenes more directly in the Platonic structure of Western institutions by miming its language; it is in a sense a performative "overturning of Platonism."[2] Derrida's essay "*Khōra,*" which also belongs to this most recent history of rereading Plato's text, offers a reading of Socrates as "playing" the chora and suggests that

1. *Revolution in Poetic Language,* trans. Margaret Waller (New York: Columbia University Press, 1984) (French: *La révolution du langage poétique* [Paris: Seuil, 1974]).
2. See *Speculum of the Other Woman,* trans. Gillian C. Gill (Ithaca, N.Y.: Cornell University Press, 1985) (French: *Speculum de l'autre femme* [Paris: Minuit, 1974]).

134 Rhapsody of Philosophy

Plato's text already contains the seeds of the overturning—or rather undermining, hollowing out—of Platonism.[3] Butler's and Sallis's readings of the *Timaeus* have been elaborated in dialogue with Irigaray and Derrida respectively, and this dialogue is part of their approach to the problematic of the chora, especially on the discursive level.

All the authors discussed in this chapter maintain that the threat of the chora is ultimately the threat of dramatic mimesis, the threat that proper roles and categories will be undermined by actors and rhapsodes, imitators, mimes. Such readings oppose not only the classical interpretations that, taking their cue from Proclus and the Neoplatonists in general, considered the character of Timaeus a mouthpiece of Plato's philosophy and read the dialogue mainly as a scientific treatise, but also the most recent interpretations that do take into account the dramatic mise en scène of the *Timaeus* and yet share with the tradition an almost exclusive focus on the cosmological part of the dialogue, maintaining, however, in contrast to the classical interpretations, that it is a travesty of serious science.[4] Through their insistence on a uniformly "ironic" mode of presentation, "dramatic" readings lead to the exact inversion of the Neoplatonic interpretation, becoming dogmatic themselves in their assurance of having secured Plato's "true meaning."[5] In both views, Plato's intention is supposed to be unequivocal and valid for all times, and what is more, the interpreters take on themselves the responsibility for making this intention explicit and communicating it to the reader.[6] Neither the traditional nor the "dramatic" interpretation gives full consideration to the play of the text.

3. "*Khōra*," trans. Ian McLeod, in Jacques Derrida, *On the Name,* ed. Thomas Dutoit (Stanford, Calif.: Stanford University Press, 1995), 87–127 (French: *Khôra* [Paris: Galilée, 1993]; the original version of this text appeared in *Poikilia: Études offertes à Jean-Pierre Vernant* [Paris: EHESS, 1987]). Derrida's reading has been acknowledged by Luc Brisson in the recent reedition of his classical commentary *Le Même et l'Autre dans la structure ontologique du "Timée" de Platon: Un commentaire systématique du "Timée" de Platon* (1974; rpt., Sankt Augustin: Academia, 1994).

4. For a classical interpretation, see André Jean Festugière, *Commentaire sur le "Timée" [par] Proclus,* vol. 1 (Paris: J. Vrin, 1966); for an example of the more recent interpretations, see, e.g., James A. Arieti, *Interpreting Plato: The Dialogues as Drama* (Savage, Md.: Rowman and Littlefield, 1991), 19–53.

5. Plato's text always contains the seeds of an interpretation that could be extracted from it and systematized as a doctrine. This implies the recognition of "Platonism" as one of the effects of the dialogue, as the effect of a "thetic abstraction," which Derrida characterizes as the dominant mode of Western philosophy. The "dramatic" interpreters' rejection of so-called Platonism as a misinterpretation of Plato ignores this potential of Plato's text, just like any other text, to have an effect independently of its author's supposed intention ("*Khōra*," 120–21 [French: *Khôra,* 82–84]). Cf. Derrida's consideration of Nietzsche's text in "Otobiographies," trans. Avital Ronell, in Jacques Derrida, *The Ear of the Other: Otobiography, Transference, Translation,* ed. by Christie McDonald (Lincoln: University of Nebraska Press, 1985), 3–38 (French: *Otobiographies: L'enseignement de Nietzsche et la politique du nom propre* [Paris: Galilée, 1984], 35–118).

6. Drew Hyland shows the tenacity of this "intentional fallacy" in his *Questioning Platonism: Continental Interpretations of Plato* (Albany: State University of New York Press, 2004).

To be sure, *Timaeus* is only a probable myth (*eikos muthos*), and a theatrical mimesis (*mimēsis, theatron*).[7] It is nevertheless a serious myth and a serious play. Derrida emphasizes the "rigorous" character of both the myth and the rhapsodic play into which it is woven: "On the one hand, myth derives from play; hence it will not be taken seriously. . . . But on the other hand . . . , when one cannot lay claim to a firm and stable *logos,* when one must make do with the probable, then myth is *de rigueur;* it is rigor, the only possible rigor. These two motifs are necessarily interwoven, which gives the play [*jeu*] its seriousness and the seriousness its play [*jeu*]."[8] The first condition of such a rigorous play consists in "stitching together" the scientific, cosmological content of the dialogue and its dramatic and political frame. Thus, for example, the word *khōra* in the cosmological account of Timaeus ought not to be dissociated—as a "technical" term— from the use of the same word as a geographic and political entity in the dramatic mise en scène of the conversation and in what precedes but also what follows dramatically, that is to say, the dialogue on the ideal state and the fragmentary history of ancient Athens in the *Critias.* In this context, Derrida's suggestion of a possible analogy between *khōra* and the character of Socrates should not be dismissed as fanciful, and the problematic form of Derrida's direct, dialogical address *eis khōran* must be addressed in order to question his dramatic question, *qui es-tu, khōra?* (who are you, chora?), and the related one, *qui es-tu, Socrate?* (who are you, Socrates?). How does the rhapsodic mode of these questions—Derrida's inscription in the hermeneutic chain of messages in the *Timaeus,* not unlike the rhapsodic intervention of the narrator in Homer's *Odyssey* ("Who are you, Eumaeus?")—relate to the classical Socratic question, *ti esti?* (what is?), a question that the *Timaeus* places within its mimetic topology?[9]

Plato's Mimetic Topology

Mise en abyme of the discourse on *khōra,* site of politics, politics of sites, such would be, then, the structure of an overprinting without a base.

—JACQUES DERRIDA

Is it not illegitimate to bring together two notions, two words, such as chora and character, under the pretext of a common first letter, a common character?[10]

7. *Timaeus,* 29d; Plato, *Critias,* 107b, 108d.

8. "*Khōra,*" 112; translation modified (French: "D'une part, le mythe relève du jeu. On ne le prendra donc pas au sérieux . . . Mais, d'autre part . . . quand on ne peut prétendre à un *logos* ferme et stable, quand on doit se contenter du vraisemblable, le mythe est de rigueur, il constitue la rigueur, la seule possible. Ces deux motifs s'enchevêtrent nécessairement, ce qui donne au jeu son sérieux et au sérieux son jeu" [*Khōra,* 66]). As to the translation of "jeu" sometimes by "game" and sometimes by "play," according to the context, see chapter 3.

9. See the *Odyssey* 14–16.

10. The epigraph to this section comes from "*Khōra,*" 104 (French: "*Mise en abyme* du discours sur

But the letter *chi* (χ, *khei*) is not common; it is the mark of a bringing together, twining-together (*sum-plekein*) of a particular kind, a coupling that at the same time entails a separation (*khōrismos*), a double tension by which we have characterized the rhapsodic mode of Plato's dialogues in general.[11] *Chi* perfectly "symbolizes" this mode. But it also marks the *displacement* of the logic of fixed boundaries, the rigorous topology of the center and the margins, and the political typology of assigned places and rehearsed roles.[12] As a part of the divine mimetic production of the world, the chiasm of the same (*tauton*) and the other or radically different (*thateron*) in the *Timaeus* (36b–c) apparently belongs to the realm of copies, of images. However, when (dis)placed in the context of "errant causality" or chora, it breaks the paradigm/copy opposition and reintroduces the play of mimesis into the topology of (the political) being—the place of ideology.

The ideology of places is what connects the *Timaeus* to the politics of the *Republic,* at least if we take seriously Socrates' introductory mise en scène of the former.[13] The composition of the *Timaeus* (and its sequel, *Critias*) and that of the *Republic* are not considered to be contemporaneous in Plato scholarship.[14] Dramatically, however, only two days separate one philosophical and political, but also poetical, conversation from the other, at least if one identifies the discussion summarized by Socrates at the beginning of the *Timaeus* with the one described in the *Republic.*[15] Socrates' introduction in the *Timaeus* and the conversation that follows it should be placed, I suggest, in the larger context of the old dispute between philosophy and poetry or mimesis, a context marked by Socrates' opening lines in the tenth book of the *Republic:*

khôra, lieu de la politique, politique des lieux, telle serait donc la structure d'une surimpression sans fond" [*Khôra,* 49]). "*Khōra*" ("land," "country," in general "place," and in the *Timaeus,* "region of all regions") and "*kharaktēr*" ("engraving," "impress," "distinctive mark," "personal disposition").

11. Compare Kristeva's characterization of the semiotic chora as the double movement of structuration and destructuration (*Revolution in Poetic Language,* 25ff. [French: *La révolution du langage poétique,* 22ff.]); we shall see that the same structure governs the dif-ference (*Unter-schied*) in Heidegger's view of the dialogue between poetry and thought.

12. See "*Khōra,*" 99 (French: *Khôra,* 35); cf. Jacques Derrida, *The Truth in Painting,* trans. Geoff Bennington and Ian McLeod (Chicago: University of Chicago Press, 1987), 165–66 (French: *La vérité en peinture* [Paris: Flammarion, 1978], 188–89).

13. *Timaeus,* 19b–20c.

14. See A. E. Taylor, *A Commentary on Plato's "Timaeus"* (1928; rpt., New York: Garland, 1987), 3ff., and, more recently, Paul Friedländer, *Plato: The Dialogues, Second and Third Periods,* vol. 3 of Paul Friedländer, *Plato,* trans. Hans Meyerhoff (1958; rpt., Princeton, N.J.: Princeton University Press, 1969), 447ff. (German: *Die platonischen Schriften, zweite und dritte Periode,* vol. 3 of *Platon* [1954; rpt., Berlin: de Gruyter, 1964], 415ff.).

15. To do so follows a long tradition of interpretation beginning at least with Proclus; see Festugière, *Commentaire sur le "Timée,"* 1:33–34.

"Speaking in confidence, for I should not like to have my words repeated to the tragedians and the rest of the imitative tribe [*pros . . . hapantas tous mimētik-ous*]—but I do not mind saying to you all, that all these things seem to be ruinous as to the judgment of the hearers who do not possess as an antidote [*pharmakon*] a knowledge [*to eidenai*] of how they really are" (595b).[16] The frame is provisionally closed by Timaeus's opening lines in *Critias:* "If unintentionally I have said anything wrong, I pray that [the god] will impose upon me a just retribution, and the just retribution of him who errs is that he should be set right. Wishing, then, to speak truly in the future concerning the generation of the gods, I pray him to give me knowledge [*epistēmēn*], which of all medicines [*pharmakōn*] is the most perfect and best" (106b).[17] The two passages apparently resemble each other in their appeal to knowledge as a *pharmakon against* mimesis. The nonambivalent rendering of the term *pharmakon* by modern translators seems warranted by the characters' general epistemological faith and, in the cited texts, by the opposition between ruin (*lōbē*) and knowledge in the first citation and between error and knowledge in the second. Both speakers, Socrates (in the *Republic*) and Timaeus (in *Critias*), point to knowledge (*to eidenai, epistēmē*) as a proper remedy (*pharmakon*) against the poison (*pharmakon*) of mimesis: drug against poison, drug against drug.[18]

The word *pharmakon* does not explicitly designate mimesis here. However, Socrates does use the word *pharmakon* in other passages of the *Republic* (382c and 389b) to characterize the useful, so-called nontrue lies (for example, the "myth of metals") included in the category of mimesis; and Timaeus refers to his own *mimetic* (in more than one sense) myth when speaking of a *pharmakon* in the *Critias*. The dramatic setting of the two passages marks the difference and suggests "clearly" the ambivalence of *pharmakon*. Socrates speaks the cited lines in the *Republic*—the philosopher condemning all imitators. In the *Critias,* the speaker—Timaeus—is himself an imitator, although he is at the same time a philosopher and a politician. Indeed, in his response to Timaeus, Critias maintains, with the approbation of all the participants in the discussion, that "all that is said by any of us can only be imitation and representation [*mimēsis*] by resemblance and by images [*apeikasia*]" (107b).[19] The phrase "any of us" designates—with the possible exception of Socrates—philosophers. The association of philosophy with mimesis, the possible exclusion of Socrates

16. *The "Republic" of Plato,* trans. Benjamin Jowett, 3rd rev. ed. (Oxford: Oxford University Press, 1888), 307.

17. *Critias,* trans. Benjamin Jowett, in *The Dialogues of Plato,* 5 vols., 3rd rev. ed (New York: Macmillan, 1892), 3:527.

18. See the discussion of Derrida's "Plato's Pharmacy" in chapter 2.

19. *Critias,* trans. Benjamin Jowett, 3:528; translation modified.

from the club of philosophers—this is the end of the world of the *Republic*. What happened in the meantime? The beginning of the world (of becoming) has been (dramatically) narrated by Timaeus.

It is true that in Socrates' recapitulation of the earlier conversation concerning the ideal *politeia,* the themes of the old dispute and of mimesis seem to be left out. Socrates goes through "the chief points of the *Republic*"—in Jowett's list: "separation of classes," "division of labour," "the double character of the guardians," "their education," "community of goods," "the women to share the pursuits of men," "the nuptial lots," "transposition of good and bad citizens"—without saying a thing about artists and their products, about impersonators, about the moral, political, and ontological shortcomings of mimesis.[20] It does not take long, however, for mimesis to reappear. After having evoked the "tableau" of the (ideal) Republic, Socrates points to the insufficiency of such a static picture, to the lack of life in it, lack of action, of drama, of a moving picture (a "cinema"). The deficiency of the ideal state seems to be paradoxically its "stately" perfection. In the process of catharsis (399e), the founders of the republic, the painters of the perfectly self-same tableau (500c–e), apparently purified it of all difference, of all motion and of life. Eternal and ideal, sheltered from the contingency of becoming, the *immortal* heavenly model (592b) is not *viable.* In order to live, it has to be incarnated, has to enter the region of corruptible matter, that is, paradoxically, it has to face death. Timeless and immutable being has to face the time and motion of becoming. The purpose of the rendezvous in the *Timaeus,* says Socrates, is to render motion to the picture, to prompt the republic to action, to show it functioning, rendering justice, fighting, and so forth. Socrates' hosts, the guests of yesterday, are to repay the debt of *logoi*—words, discourses—and dramatize the Republic for him and for the readers of the two dialogues.[21] Can they do this without engaging in mimesis—that is, without engaging in what was so vehemently criticized in the *Republic?*

Socrates seems to believe so when he pretends to engage in the preliminary "casting." Paradoxically, but in keeping with the principles set out in the *Republic,* he excludes professional performers, rhapsodes, actors, pretenders, imitators (*mimētai*). Surprisingly (for the readers of the *Republic* at least), Socrates also eliminates himself; and he pretends not to be surprised. He is unable to celebrate the city and her citizens in a befitting manner, but he does not say why. However, when he moves to the matter of the exclusion of the

---

20. *Republic,* trans. Benjamin Jowett, in *The Dialogues of Plato,* 3:438–39nn.

21. To all appearances the initial plan of Socrates will not be realized. The historical-mythical narrative of Critias will be first temporarily suspended by Timaeus's cosmological myth and then, in the *Critias,* definitely interrupted with the dialogue itself.

poets, he points clearly to the issue of mimesis. Although he apparently does not intend to deprecate them, Socrates calls the poets "a tribe of imitators" (19d–e).[22] They can imitate perfectly and with ease what is familiar to them from the place of their upbringing (*hois an entraphēi*), but that which is beyond the scope of familiar education (*to d'ektos tēs trophēs*) is too difficult to carry out in action and still more difficult to imitate in words (19d–e). Is Socrates restating here the terms of the old dispute that jointly rejected the poetic and mimetic? Or is he rather questioning the competence of poets, inexperienced in politics? What exactly is his own position, the place from which he pronounces his judgment? It seems that, far from explicitly taking the philosophical side of the dispute, Socrates places himself on the side of poets and rhapsodes, pretending, as it were, to be such as pretenders are. If mimesis is here related to the rule of justice in the political (anti)drama—"one man, one [social] role"—just as it was in the third book of the *Republic*, it is surprisingly a pretender (*hupokritēs*) who plays the role of a judge (*kritēs*).

The same judgment falls on the other, in a sense marginal, characters of contemporary political life, the Sophists. The Sophists cannot paint the ideal city because they are not familiar with any city, do not possess a place of habitation, a proper place (*idia oikēsis*). They wander from one city to another, not belonging to any actual social structure. Socrates calls them "errant" (*planētai* [19e]). Ontological stability—*status*—is here expressed in economic and political terms (*oikos* and *polis*). Stability, which the Sophists—and again, by association, Socrates—lack, is what in the *Republic* is thematized as type (*tupos*) or character (*ēthos*), character not so much in the sense of "moral ethos" prominent in Aristotelian ethics as in the sense of a social and dramatic type—a classical and modern notion of dramatis persona, which can be traced to Theophrastus's *Kharaktēres,* to the fifteenth chapter of Aristotle's *Poetics,* and eventually to Plato's own *Protagoras, Ion,* and *Meno.*[23] Another word that Socrates could have used here to characterize a determined social status as a necessary condition of a correct political outlook is "chora." In fact, he *had* already used this word in the sense of social status, type, or character at the beginning of the dialogue in the last heading of his summary of the prior conversation (19a). There, "chora" designated the possibility of undermining a class position, which, although theoretically and ideologically (through the myth of metals [*Republic* 414, 415]) fixed, was to be secretly "corrected" by those who established the order in the first place (the Uranian, heavenly place), the philosophers.[24] It is certainly not a matter of indifference that in the *Timaeus,*

22. *Timaeus,* trans. Benjamin Jowett, in *The Dialogues of Plato,* 3:440.
23. See chapter 1.
24. John Sallis relates this opening of the closed system in the *Republic,* recalled in the *Timaeus,* to

the concept of chora as determining social characters or types appears initially in the context of political displacement, which in the *Republic* was associated with the mimetic impersonations of characters by pretenders, actors (*hupokritai*), and rhapsodes (*rhapsoidoi*) and was condemned.[25]

It is not the problem of *dis*placement, however, but that of *em*placement that brings the chora to the foreground of Timaeus's discourse.[26] "Anything that is must needs be in some place [*en tini topōi*] and occupy some room [*khōran tina*]; what is neither on earth nor somewhere in heaven is nothing" (52b).[27] This general requirement of being is nothing new; Zeno and Gorgias had argued the point from different perspectives.[28] What is unique to the *Timaeus* is its inclusion of the requirement within the frameworks of both mimesis and of universal emplacement. A need for emplacement is translated into the need for a medium in which the images of the eternal paradigm might appear. It is thus the very structure of the mimetic/poetic mechanism that demands a material support that preexists it.

The chora is indeed a necessary medium—a mirror, a movie screen—supplementing the mimetic schema of the demiurgic (re)production of the world. As such, it has to be manageable, malleable as "plastic" (*ekmageion*), as gold, or as a perfume base (50b–c). It has to be soft, smooth, level, in "itself" characterless: "If there is to be an impress presenting all diversities of aspect, the thing in which the impress comes to be situated cannot have been duly prepared unless it is free from all those characters [*ideai*] which it is to receive from elsewhere. . . . [T]hat which is to receive in itself all kinds must be free from all characters [*eidē*]; . . . that which is duly to receive over its whole extent and many times over all the likenesses of eternal things ought in its own nature to be free of all the characters [*eidē*]" (50d–51a).[29] There is some justification for translating both *idea* and *eidos* by "character" in its most literal, bodily sense.

ἔρως as a mark of the limit to the technical manipulation of the procreative order; see "The Politics of the Χώρα," chapter 2 in his *Platonic Legacies* (Albany: State University of New York Press, 2004).

25. Compare the discussion of mimetic confusion in the *Republic* in chapter 1.

26. See Edward S. Casey, *The Fate of Place* (Berkeley: University of California Press, 1997), 34. Comparing the ancient Pelasgian, Hebraic, and Greek cosmogonies, Casey notes the common "intolerability of no-place-at-all" (6).

27. Francis M. Cornford, *Plato's Cosmology: The "Timaeus" of Plato, Translated with a Running Commentary* (1937; rpt., London: Routledge, 1966), 192; translation modified.

28. Plato made his character Parmenides question the argument at least in respect to the One (*Parmenides,* 138a–b); see Mitchell H. Miller, *Plato's "Parmenides": The Conversion of the Soul* (Princeton, N.J.: Princeton University Press, 1986), and Kelsey Wood, *Troubling Play: Meaning and Entity in Plato's "Parmenides"* (Albany: State University of New York Press, 2005); for Zeno, see Aristotle, *Physics* 4.3.209a23, 210b22; for Gorgias, see Sextus Empiricus, *Against the Logicians* 1.77 and [Aristotle], *On Melissos, Xenophanes, and Gorgias* 979a–980b.

29. Cornford, *Plato's Cosmology,* 185–86.

But can the lack of any characteristic, the radical character of the chora's passive receptivity, become a place of material resistance, which is also to be understood—by reference to the first meaning of the word in the dialogue and the associations that it will later generate—in terms of social, political, and sexual— "erotic"— resistance?

The chora of the *Timaeus* is sometimes understood as "matter" in the sense of timber, stuff (*hulē*) in the wake of the Aristotelian interpretation. This interpretation of the chora as resistant matter is based on the common experience of artists and craftsmen obliged to take into consideration the resistance of the material used in their productions. The divine craftsman of *Timaeus* is not free from this common preoccupation of all other *dēmiourgoi;* it is shown by the difficulty he has—after having bent the arms of the chiasm—in making the circles of the Same and of the Other coincide. But the demiurge of Timaeus's myth is not only an artist and artisan (architect, painter, potter, husbandman, weaver, sculptor), that is, a member of the third class, the class of workers and farmers, according to the legal division and the ideology of the *Republic.*[30] Some of the tasks performed by the demiurge, such as the settling of cities and colonies or political persuasion, belong to the competence of the members of the first class, philosopher-rulers, the "painters" of cities (500c–e), the "founding fathers" who perform, according to the Socrates of the *Republic,* the function of *patres familiarum* "on a large scale." In this perspective, the chora, compared by Timaeus to a mother and nurse, stands for all that the patriarchal order encounters in its task of "formation": the irreducible materiality of a gendered matrix, *mat(t)er.*[31]

The ideal medium of the demiurgic production of images might be compared to the "canvas," the tablet (*pinax, tabula*) of the philosopher-painters, the founders of the state in the *Republic,* who are indeed characterized by Socrates as "artificer[s] [*dēmiourgoi*] of justice, temperance, and every civil virtue" and thus are imitators who constantly refer to the divine model (500c–e).[32] They are allowed to purify their medium (*katharan poiēseian an*), that is, to perform the "catharsis" of the city-state so as to be perfectly able to trace on it the schema of the constitution and of the characters of men (501a). In fact, any foreign interference should be eliminated before the proper act of "mimetic" constitution begins. The result is to be a homogeneous picture without even traces of otherness. The "clean slate," a purified medium, should allow for an

30. Cf. Luc Brisson, *Le Même et l'Autre,* 35–54.

31. See Irigaray, *Speculum of the Other Woman,* 265 and passim (French: *Speculum de l'autre femme,* 195 and passim), and Judith Butler, *Bodies that Matter: On the Discursive Limits of "Sex"* (New York: Routledge, 1993), 31ff. On the problematic notion of "irreducible" materiality in particular, see Butler, *Bodies that Matter,* 27–31. I return to the question of chora and gender below.

32. *The "Republic" of Plato,* trans. Benjamin Jowett, 3:200.

exact reproduction of the forms and schemata of the paradigm, eliminating any possible margin of play between the same and the other.

The philosopher and his demiurge in the *Timaeus* make the same attempt at a "cathartic mimesis." The first part of Timaeus's discourse is an attempt to make mimesis the principle of differentiation between created things, the principle of generic and specific identification. According to Timaeus's closing statement at the beginning of the *Critias,* it will eventually become the principle of knowledge concerning the generation of the gods, creation of the world, of man, and so forth. Mimesis thus functions, paradoxically, as a supplement to an antidote (science as *pharmakon*), which, as a poison (*pharmakon*), it was supposed to require in the first place. Here, the logic of *pharmakon* threatens to upset the whole demiurgic operation.[33] To counter this threat, a rigorous separation (*khōrismos*) of the two kinds of mimesis—the bad and the good one—a sort of scientific catharsis, is needed.[34] The good, homogeneous, pictorial, or iconic, mimesis does not seem to interfere directly with the ideology of class division in the *Republic.* The same cannot be said, however, of the bad—heterogeneous, hypocritical, rhapsodic—mimesis.

Such mimesis is to be rejected not only as useless in the process of creation but as a threat to its result, the established order of identities and differences of character. Indeed, the main task of demiurgic action is strictly to delimit the boundaries of created things, to sort them out, to define them. The theoretical, philosophical purification of mimesis is a prerequisite of cosmic and political purification. But it is an uncertain operation, since one of its terms, rhapsodic mimesis, may in fact question the very possibility of such a strict separation. In the *Timaeus,* the difficulty is manifest in the treatment of the so-called chiasm of the same and the other. When shaping the soul of the world, the demiurge fuses, in a complex way, the indivisible and divisible substance, and he "sliced this entire compound [*sustasis*] in two along its length, joined the two halves together center to center like a khei (X)" (36b–c).[35] Subsequently, however, a violent action by the demiurge neutralizes this initial chiasm. The arms of the *khei* are forcibly bent to form two circles, and then the circle of the other is subjugated to the circle of the same (36c–d). For the second time the dialogue questions mimesis as otherness or errancy, embodied in the open arms of the

33. On the "logic of *pharmakon,*" see Derrida, "Plato's Pharmacy," 61–171, in Jacques Derrida, *Dissemination,* trans. Barbara Johnson (Chicago: University of Chicago Press, 1981), 61–171 (French: "La pharmacie de Platon," in *La dissémination* [Paris: Seuil, 1972], 79–213), and the discussion of this essay in chapter 2.

34. See Paul Ricoeur, *Être, essence, et substance chez Platon et Aristote* (Paris: Société d'édition d'enseignement supérieur, 1982), 108.

35. *Timaeus,* trans. Donald J. Zeyl, in *Plato: Complete Works,* ed. John M. Cooper and D. S. Hutchison (Indianapolis, Ind.: Hackett, 1997), 1240.

khei. The first time, even before Timaeus's narration (and in order to make it possible), Socrates played the representative of all marginal and wandering tribes and withdrew from the conversation (19d–e). He left the place to those who are firmly established in the cities, in a sense mimetically disposing of mimesis. In the "theater of the sky," by contrast, the subterfuge being unavailable, the violence of the demiurge seems necessary.[36] However, a chiasm, the figure of opening up, is not easily made into a circle, the sign of closure. Timaeus will have a hard time defining, limiting, the erratic, heterogeneous motions of the wandering stars (*planētai*) in terms of the perfectly regular, homogeneous course of the fixed ones.

The question of the original emplacement of the world, of a medium capable of receiving the images of demiurgic, mimetic (re)production, continues and deepens this theme of deviation or errancy. Indeed, the name of "errant cause" (*planōmenē aitia*) introduces the whole section on the chora in the middle of the *Timaeus* (48a). It will also point to the same/other polarity when it comes to considering the problem of essential identification of the elements, in the form of the Socratic question, "*Ti esti?*" ("What is?"). Only the reference to the paradigm of the Intelligible Forms can preserve the identity of fire and other elements that, when considered outside of this eidetic/mimetic identification, remain in constant transition. As in the *Republic,* resemblance (*homoiōsis*) becomes the very principle of the appellation *toiouton*—"such as," "of such sort," "of such character"—and thus the only principle of identity applicable to the fleeting, although recurrently appearing, images. The chora functions as the supplement of this mimetic identification.[37]

For Timaeus, the notion of chora is ambiguous and perplexing: it is difficult to think a "characterless" and "neutral" ground of phenomenal representation that is at the same time an effect of representation. The chora "itself" is "difficult and obscure" (*khalepon kai amudron* [49a]). When trying to elucidate it, one is in danger of being entangled in "strange and unfamiliar considerations," out of place and out of character (*atopos kai aēthēs* [48d]). It receives impressions in a "wonderful manner that is hard to express" (*dusphraston kai thaumaston* [50c]), and it "partakes of the intelligible in the most puzzling way [*aporōtata*] and is very hard to apprehend [*dusalōtotaton*]" [51a–b])—in

---

36. The *cosmic mise en ordre* in the soul of the world corresponds to the catharsis in the soul of the philosopher as described in Plato's *Phaedo,* if one interprets, with Luc Brisson, the circle of the same and the circle of the other in terms of intellectual and sensible knowledge, respectively (*Le Même et l'Autre,* 527).

37. See Cornford, *Plato's Cosmology,* 177, Richard D. Mohr, *The Platonic Cosmology* (Leiden: E. J. Brill, 1985), 88, and Jean-François Mattéi, *Platon et le miroir du mythe: De l'âge d'or à l'Atlantide* (Paris: Presses Universitaires de France, 1996), 208–9.

fact, it can be apprehended only by "a sort of bastard reasoning" (*logismōi tini nothōi* [52b]).[38]

On the other hand, the "reality" of the chora is strongly maintained, notwithstanding its dreamlike mode of perception (52b). Its stable and permanent (*aei on* [51a; cf. 49e]) presence allows one to call it "this" or "that" (*touto, tode*), in contradistinction to the mere resembling, to the "such" (*toiouton*) of the images (49d–50a). It is, however, precisely the deictic reality of "this" chora that shows the fragility of the mimetic identification of *toiouton*. The very lack of a determined character of the medium makes room for all imaginable characters, shows their relative contingency, their demiurgic, *poietic* origin. The chora opens up a "leeway," a *Spielraum,* a space of play with the il-lusions of mimesis. The images received in the chora are likely to be marked by its indeterminacy, its ex-centricity (*atopia*), by the lack of clearly drawn lines, boundaries, by its aporia. When taken for granted, the demiurgic (re)production gives the impression of a natural process. But when questioned in its very foundation, it reveals the danger of displacement, of defamiliarization, of the loss of an *idia oikesis,* of a home, the effect of *Unheimlichkeit.* It is when (dis)placed in the chora that phenomena "appear" necessary and random at the same time (*ex anankēs* ["of necessity"] and *to tukhon* ["at random"] [46e]).[39] "Errant necessity" gives the chora the "character" of an "ungodly" playground for the divine artificer.

In Timaeus's account, the chora consists of a shaking motion compared to the movement of a winnowing basket. But the "purification" (*katharsis*) said to be its goal is never completed. "Regionalization," which is a step in that direction, seems to be accompanied by the opposite drive of "*de*-regionalization," which defies any possibility of a proper, essential assignment of place.[40] On the other hand, it is when read in this way that the chora, in its "ungodly" (*hotan apēi tinos theos* [53b]) condition, can be said to conserve the energy and the state of imbalance, of irregularity (*anōmalia* [52e]). The ungodly matter

---

38. Cornford, *Plato's Cosmology,* 177, 161, 182, 186, 192; translation modified.

39. Cf. Cornford, *Plato's Cosmology,* 172.

40. One might think here of the Platonic hint at the complex movement of deterritorialization and reterritorialization, as described in Gilles Deleuze and Félix Guattari's critique of the Oedipal identification through the agency of the familial (was it not Plato after all who first pointed out "[la] direction du renversement du platonisme?"); see *Anti-Oedipus,* vol. 1 of their *Capitalism and Schizophrenia,* trans. Robert Hurley, Mark Seem, and Helen R. Lane (Minneapolis: University of Minnesota Press, 1983) (French: *L'anti-oedipe,* vol. 1 of *Capitalisme et schizophrénie* [Paris: Minuit, 1972]), *A Thousand Plateaus,* vol. 2 of their *Capitalism and Schizophrenia,* trans. Brian Massumi (Minneapolis: University of Minnesota Press, 1987) (French: *Mille plateaux,* vol. 2 of *Capitalisme et schizophrénie* [Paris: Minuit, 1980]), and *Kafka: Toward a Minor Literature,* trans. Dana Polan (Minneapolis: University of Minnesota Press, 1986) (French: *Kafka: Pour une littérature mineure* [Paris: Minuit, 1975]). Cf. Casey's view of *khōra* as "regionalization" in *The Fate of Place,* 34.

resists the *logos* incarnated by the demiurge. Lack of properties, of characters, far from rendering a medium pure and flexible, is rather like the void for Kant's dove: it thwarts flight, resists by not resisting, by not offering any point of resistance, any resting place. Receiving all characters without exception, the chora lets them play against each other, displaying the contradictions of the order of images and simulacra: *kosmos* and ideology.

The word by which, in his perplexity, Timaeus characterizes the thought that leads to the chora—his second beginning in Plato's dialogue, the second beginning, the second principle (*arkhē*), which has to supplement the first principle of the production of the world—is *khalepon*. Sallis renders the word as "severe, difficult, troublesome, dangerous," and he relates this characteristic of the thought of "displacing emplacement" to its troublesome intervention in the production as governed by the model/copy schema; the necessity of "chora," as the "beginning before the beginning," interrupts this simple representational structure.[41] In this process, the specular or painterly schema of mimesis in the tenth book of the *Republic,* a schema that yields itself to inclusion in the overall eidetic order, eventually comes undone as well.

The chora is certainly not an ideal canvas for the rational painter.[42] "Imagine the shock of the Demiurge," writes Edward Casey, "that eminently rational creator who intends to model the world on the pattern of an unchanging Form, when he confronts [its, her] crazy-quilt, irregular motions."[43] The chora apparently offers an irresistible resistance of play on a cosmic scale, a resistance to the ordering and stabilizing *poiēsis* of the demiurge. It is thus perhaps not so much the canvas of a painting as the stage that would be the best image for the chora as a support of images, if one still can speak of images here.[44] A

---

41. John Sallis, "Χαλεπόν," in *Double Truth* (Albany: State University of New York Press, 1995), xi.

42. The demiurge is literally a painter of constellations; see *Timaeus* 55c; cf. Cornford, *Cosmology,* 219.

43. *The Fate of Place,* 37.

44. *Khōra*—perhaps related etymologically to χορός, "emplacement for the dance, chorus," and thus to the origin of Attic drama (see Pierre Chantraine, *Dictionnaire étymologique de la langue grecque: Histoire des mots* [Paris: Klincksieck, 1984], 1269–70; cf. Jean-François Mattéi, *Platon et le miroir du mythe,* 200ff., who, following Albert Rivaud, evokes the ground for the performance of the ancient theater and suggests an interpretation of the chora and its/her myth in terms of estrangement [ἄτοπος καὶ ἀήθης διήγησις] *Timaeus* 48d). It is not without reason that the "epic theater" has been called "Platonic" and its emblematic hero compared to Socrates. Walter Benjamin might have been thinking of the χώρα in the *Timaeus* when he noted in Brechtian characters a lack of "fidelity to any single essence of one's own" and "a continual readiness to admit a new essence" (in the first version of "What is Epic Theatre?" in Walter Benjamin, *Understanding Brecht,* trans. Anna Bostock [London: Verso, 1983], 9) [German: "Was ist das epische Theater?" in *Versuche über Brecht* (Frankfurt am Main: Suhrkamp, 1966), 25]); cf. the introduction to this book. In Plato's dialogue itself, the discourse of the chora seems to animate a textual resistance, a resistance to the narrator of this story, to the interpreters of the dialogue, to the philosophical recuperation of mimesis; I will return to this aspect of the chora.

third genre that questions the model/image dichotomy, an other that questions the same/other dichotomy, a "scene of emplacement," the chora disrupts Timaeus's discourse and displaces the simple pattern of the demiurgic attempt at an eidetic mimesis.[45] A name for a strictly delimited social role and a defended range of political power in *Critias* (e.g., 110c–e) and at the beginning of *Timaeus* (19a), the chora becomes in the middle of the latter a name for an irregular movement that questions all strict boundaries. The chiasm of the same and the other, which the demiurge attempted to circumscribe and submit to the perfect circle of the same in the first part of the dialogue, is here mis en abyme by the apparently characterless and nameless chora. If the chora is a third kind, it is in fact a kind beyond all kind (*eidos*). If it is a third kind of being, it "is" in fact beyond all being (*on, ousia*). The names with which it/she is dubbed by Timaeus ("mother," "nurse," "receptacle," "gold") are not *proper* in any sense that would conform to the eidetic logic of sense. In a dialogue with Derrida, Sallis characterizes this unstable status of the chora with the Socratic (and Lévinasian) phrase, *epekeina tēs ousias*.[46] But if Socrates refers to the idea of the good (*idea tou agathou*), the idea of the ideas, as the supreme guarantee of the eidetic order (and Lévinas marks with the same phrase the absolute transcendence of the ethical), Sallis characterizes Timaeus's chora as the ungrounding of being in its very foundation "as inaugural emplacement outside being, in the outside of being, as submission to the dispersal that holds apart from being."[47] "Chorology," that is, the thought provoked by the chora, by the original abyss or the abysmal origin, would thus contain both the condition of Western (Platonic) metaphysics and the seeds of its exhaustion: "the beginning of metaphysics will have been already the end of metaphysics."[48]

The word "chorology" seems contradictory, since there can hardly be a metaphysical, "logical" account of the chora. But for Sallis, Plato's *logos* is always already entangled in this so-called second sailing (*deuteros plous*), as for example in the *Phaedo* (99d–e), where, unable to look at things (*ta pragmata*), the sun, directly, Socrates decides to seek refuge in *logoi*. He thus behaves like those prudent men who do not look at the sun directly, even during an eclipse, but turn to its image (*eikōn*). The doubling of *ta pragmata* by *logoi* is thus a mimetic

45. Casey, *The Fate of Place*, 34.

46. Sallis, *Chorology: On Beginning in Plato's "Timaeus"* (Bloomington: Indiana University Press, 1999), 113–14, and Derrida, "Tense," in *The Path of Archaic Thinking: Unfolding the Work of John Sallis*, ed. Kenneth Maly (Albany: State University of New York Press, 1995), 49–74; cf. Sallis, *Double Truth*, 2.

47. Lévinas, *Otherwise Than Being; or, Beyond Essence*, trans. Alphonso Lingis (The Hague: Martin Nijhoff, 1981), 3 (French: *Autrement qu'être; ou, Au-delà de l'essence* [Paris: Kluwer Academic, 1978], 13); Sallis, *Platonic Legacies*, 43.

48. Sallis, *Chorology*, esp. 91–124 and 123.

doubling as well.[49] And the "paradigmatic" case of such doubling is the chora of the *Timaeus*. Of course, "paradigmatic" cannot be used in a proper sense here, since what the chora introduces into the schema of eidetic/mimetic determination of being is precisely the transcendence of both being and the proper, transcendence in the sense of *epekeina* and of *heteron* in a radical sense, that is, "in a sense irreducible to a difference of sense."[50]

The most paradoxical, and most disturbing, character of the chora is thus its "senselessness," its "neutrality," its lack of a precise inscription. How should we square this "lack of character" with its effectiveness? If the chora were just an insipid medium of demiurgic production, a tabula rasa of inscription, there would be no reason for such unease, for calling it *khalepon*. On the other hand, the status of the chora would remain an intellectual curiosity rather than a serious "matter" if it quietly remained on the margin of philosophical and political discourse. But perhaps the effectiveness of the chora resides precisely in this lack of actual eidetic determination, in its "radical passivity" and its readiness to receive all possible determinations. At the level of logos as a mode of discourse, as a mode of a mimetic *dia-logos*, it is a *mimētēs*, a rhapsode, an actor, that would play the role of the cosmic chora as an abyssal foundation of the (im)proper inscription of characters. And the unease of Timaeus and his audience, including the dialogue's readers, would result from the fact that the chora, and the dialogue that both inscribes it and is inscribed by it, might communicate the potentiality of their dispossession to the world of becoming and the images and characters for which they are an abyssal ground. The chora and the rhapsodic dialogue would undermine the strict determination of all characters projected in the process of (cosmological, political, artistic, etc.) representation.

The Rhapsodic Indeterminacy of Chora

In this theatre of irony, where the scenes interlock in a series of receptacles without end and without bottom, how can one isolate a thesis or a theme that could be attributed calmly to the "philosophy-of-Plato," indeed to *philosophy* as the Platonic thing?

—JACQUES DERRIDA

. . . And Derrida's own essay might suffer the same indetermination, the same impossibility of isolating "a thesis or a theme that could be attributed calmly" to the "philosophy-of-Derrida" or deconstruction.[51] Except that Derrida, contrary

---

49. See Sallis's account of Nietzsche's reading of the *deuteros plous* in the *Phaedo* in *Crossings: Nietzsche and the Space of Tragedy* (Chicago: University of Chicago Press, 1991) 122ff., and *Double Truth*, 2.

50. Sallis, *Platonic Legacies*, 43.

51. The epigraph to this section comes from "*Khōra*," 119 (French: "Dans ce théâtre de l'ironie où les scènes s'emboîtent dans une série de réceptacles sans fin et sans fond, comment isoler une thèse ou un

to most readers of Plato, does not bemoan this fact but rather celebrates it. In fact, the strength of "his" deconstruction would reside in its nonexistence as a "philosophie comme la chose platonicienne," in its nonexistence as "*a* deconstruction or *simply* deconstruction as if there were only one, as if the word had a (single) meaning outside of the sentences which inscribe it and carry it within themselves."[52] Perhaps there is no Platonic or Derridean thing in itself, that is, outside of the discourse that is supposed to contain them, just as there is no world outside of the chora in the *Timaeus*. In fact, for Derrida— and this would be a thesis or theme that one would be tempted to isolate as "his," were it not for the fact that it is just what forbids one to do so— the chora functions in Plato's dialogue as receptacle of both the world and discourse, and it cannot do this without placing both of them *en abyme*, in the representational abyss of mirrors, scenes, the abyss of stories within stories and of those who tell them, perform them: authors, actors, readers—rhapsodes. Indeed, the cosmological myth cannot give even a probable (*eikos*) validity to the discourse on the chora, situated beyond the opposition *muthos/logos,* and the uncertainty, undecidability, of the chora is communicated to any discourse concerning the world. Ideal Being cannot enter the world of representation without losing its purity, yet it would be sterile without the possibility of producing images.

The dialogue *Timaeus* is itself abysmal, frustrating the reader's effort to locate a single thread, a single trace that would traverse the text and that would unify its subject matter. The dialogue in general, a rhapsodic genre par excellence, functions like the chora, that is, situates, but en abyme, its various themes and topics. The best example of this unsettling emplacement is the political history of Athens, the "cinematic" picture of the ideal republic in action. It will be told by Critias, who heard it from his grandfather, Critias as well, who heard it from Solon, who might have heard it from an Egyptian priest during his travels but might also have read it in the Egyptian archives when told by the priest that the history of Athens was preserved there. The fact that this series of narratives is embedded in Plato's dialogue, which is itself mimetic, and that eventually the story is not really told after all, certainly unsettles the representation of the city in action that was supposed to be its main theme. What remains is the potential transmission, a transmissivity of discourse, a rhapsodic performance of the other's voice that is always in danger of frustration because of the failure of its literal and literary support.

---

thème qu'on attribuerait paisiblement à la 'philosophie-de-Platon,' voire à *la* philosophie comme la chose platonicienne?" [*Khôra,* 80]).

52. *Memoires: For Paul de Man* (1986; rpt., New York: Columbia University Press, 1989), 17.

The dominant theme that has been extracted from *Timaeus* in the history of its interpretation is Platonism, Platonic ontology, the philosophy of Plato, and it is the legitimacy of this extraction that Derrida's reading of the dialogic genre as its support eventually questions. In spite of what one would think, Derrida does not reject such an operation. It is legitimate, as long as its character as one abstraction among others has been recognized. "Platonism" or philosophy as "Platonic thing" has to be seen as a necessary effect of the text transmitted under the name of "Plato," its dominant effect in the history of Western thought, the one that, turning against the heterogeneous text that produced it, tends to obliterate all other effects.[53] And philosophy will always be "Platonic" in the sense of this tendency to abstract a dominant thesis that would present itself as unique. But at the same time, it will also always contain the potential for its unsettling through the return to the rhapsodic and ventriloquist text that produced it. There will always be "forces" within the text that will "maintain a certain disorder, some potential incoherence, and some heterogeneity," some "parasitism, clandestinity, ventriloquism" that threatens to erupt from within the text and disrupt the philosophical system it helps to found.[54]

The relationship between the discourse on chora and philosophy is analogous to the one between chora and cosmos: *chora* comes *before* the cosmos (and thus before any order, any determination) yet is described with the help of figures drawn from that cosmos, and so this description, this figuration, necessarily lacks the clarity and exactness required by philosophy. Thus, philosophy is unable to speak philosophically of that which comes before it. Just as chora is situated on a deeper level than the opposition of model and copy, the discourse on chora must be situated beyond the standard philosophical discourse with all its binaries, and especially the *normal couple* at its origin.[55] This "origin" precisely cannot be a "normal couple," since chora is beyond genre, categories, and categorical oppositions, and thus, even as a mother, chora (a third gender or kind) does not join sexually with the father but remains apart—a "strange mother who gives place without engendering."[56] A philosophical treatise cannot give full account of such a mother of emplacement without imposing on her the norms of authorial, authoritative—even authoritarian—discourse. Perhaps a dialogue is the only genre, a genre beyond

53. "*Khōra*," 120 (French: *Khôra*, 82).

54. "*Khōra*," 121 (French: *Khôra*, 84). On the notion of ventriloquism, see Nancy's essay "Le ventriloque," discussed in chapter 3.

55. "[L]et us go back behind and below the assured discourse of philosophy, which proceeds by oppositions of principle and counts on the origin as on a *normal couple*" ("*Khōra*," 125–26 [French: "[R]evenons en deçà du discours assuré de la philosophie qui procède par oppositions principielles et compte avec l'origine comme avec un *couple normal*" (*Khôra*, 94)]).

56. "*Khōra*," 90 (French: *Khôra*, 17); "*Khōra*," 124 (French: *Khôra*, 92).

the rule of the separation of genres, that is able to receive and give without authorship/authority, to transmit rhapsodically the voice of an other, thus questioning the identity, the distinctive, proper essence, of the same.

Such a discourse corresponds to the essential dispossession of chora "it/ herself." Derrida's phrase marking this dispossession, "singular impropriety," could thus be extended from cosmology to the theory of rhapsodic discourse.[57] In this regard, his gesture of dropping the article ("definite," that is, determining, or "indefinite," that is, at least potentially determining) that usually accompanies the transliteration *khōra,* or chora, is crucial, and in fact reflects Timaeus's hesitation between determination and indetermination of (the) chora: *hē khōra, khōra tis, khōra* (52a–d). An article would determine chora on the level of language and thus inscribe it within a determinate system of signs. The lack of article, on the other hand, would make chora into a proper name, designating a singular being, indetermined but not indifferent. But is not such a singular lack of determination a form of determination after all? Does not tabula rasa consist of *rasum tabulae?*[58] And would not this indeterminate quality, this quality of indetermination in a writing tablet, then be transmitted to the being inscribed in it?[59]

In that case even the political system of Plato's *Republic* would not escape an undermining effect. The guardians of the city "themselves," those who are supposed to regulate its order, supposed to have all power and regulate the system of proper social roles, have nothing proper to themselves, and Derrida asks whether this is not precisely the status of chora. The guardians would, in some sense, even if only a "playful" one, belong to the same category (*genos*) as the sophists and poets who are excluded from the republic and, indeed, the same category as Socrates himself—unless Socrates is something else altogether. Socrates, after all, excludes himself from speaking in the *Timaeus* precisely because he has no fixed residence, no established position within the political structure of the city, and thus, as we already noted, is *like* the sophists and poets. But in saying this, Socrates "pretends to rank himself among those who feign. He affects to belong to the *genos* of those whose *genos* consists in affecting"; he *"pretends to belong to the genus of those who pretend to belong to the genus of those who have (a) place, a place and an economy that are their own."*[60]

57. *"Khōra,"* 97 (French: *Khôra,* 33).

58. Cf. Giorgio Agamben, *Potentialities: Collected Essays in Philosophy,* ed. and trans. Daniel Heller-Roazen (Stanford, Calif.: Stanford University Press, 1999), 215.

59. This transmission will have a particular importance in both the formation of the community and its questioning; I take up this problematic in the conclusion.

60. *"Khōra,"* 108 (French: "Socrate feint de se ranger parmi ceux qui feignent. Il affecte d'appartenir au *genos* de ceux dont le *genos* consiste à affecter . . . [il] *fait donc semblant d'appartenir au genre de ceux qui font semblant d'appartenir au genre de ceux qui ont lieu, un lieu et une économie propre"* [*Khôra,* 55–56]).

If Socrates, having excluded himself from the category of philosophers and politicians, only *pretends* to belong to that other category, that of the poets and sophists, then in fact he introduces another level of pretending and thereby belongs to a "third genus," "like" chora does. Socrates is thus in a sense more "like" chora than the sophists or the philosophers, the guardians or the poets are; precisely because he is less like anything else. The resemblance involved here is then of a particular, paradoxical type in which absolute resemblance approaches otherness or absolute difference, and thus the category of resemblance is here again, just as in the *Sophist,* called into question. It is decidedly a most slippery genus (*olisthērotaton gat to genos* [*Sophist* 231a]).

The "Characterless Femininity" of (the) Chora

> I'll show you what this unintelligible receptacle can do to your system.
> —JUDITH BUTLER

Socrates' "own" marginality, which in the *Timaeus* parallels that of chora, is often associated with femininity: his "midwifing" (the *Theaetetus*), his association with women-teachers (Diotima in the *Symposium,* Aspasia in the *Menexenus*), his constant reference to weaving, his being courted (for example, by Alcibiades in the *Symposium*), even his usual "feminine" oath: "by Hera" (*nē tēn Hēran* [*Phaedrus* 230b]).[61] But it is mostly his "all-receiving" mode of discourse, a discourse that we have called "rhapsodic," that closely associates Socrates with the feminine character of chora and the play of juxtaposition between the "literal" and the "literary" emplacement of the world. Feminist writers have adopted this character and this mode as a particularly "feminine" type of discourse, although they rarely refer to Socrates or to the mode of Plato's dialogues.

In Plato's *Timaeus,* the femininity of the emplacement in chora seems to impose itself linguistically in spite of the temptation to refer to chora as "it." Indeed, chora's absolute indetermination would perhaps require a neutral word to designate "it." Timaeus may have such a requirement in mind when referring to chora as "this" (neutral thing): *touto.* But the gender of the noun *khōra* is feminine (just as that of *dēmiourgos* is masculine), and Timaeus recognizes this. Indeed, he stresses the femininity of the chora by comparing "her" to a mother and nurse (49a, 50d). Toward the end of the dialogue, he introduces the erratic (*planōmenon*), "choric" movement of matrix or womb (*mētra kai hustera*) in order to explain the inconstancy of the feminine soul (91c). The hesitation between "she" and "it" is perhaps responsible for the particular "status"

---

61. The epigraph to this section comes from *Bodies That Matter,* 45; Butler is "giving voice" to Irigaray.

of (the) chora in the dialogue, its being a "site of ambivalence," in Butler's phrase.[62] Mother, nurse, virgin, in the rhetoric of Timaeus and the interpreters of the dialogue, (the) chora, as an "all accepting" (*pandekhēs*) receptacle (*hupodokhē*), is also the space of marginal indeterminacy, of the effacement of all character, a space beyond kind, genre, or gender (*exō genous*), to use the Sophoclean designation of excluded heroes or monsters.[63]

For feminist writers the paradoxical nature of (the) chora—characterless and yet feminine—is not nearly as perplexing as it is for Timaeus and some readers of the dialogue. Its indeterminacy can be read first of all as the effect of the common image of femininity as the other, the foil against which the image of dominant masculinity in the West has been determined. The paradox of "characterless femininity" or "feminine neutrality" is not paradoxical in face of the common, masculine "doxa," since this neutrality is necessary to secure the identity of the masculine.[64] Irigaray characterizes the feminine in Western thought in a way that evokes the characterless chora, especially with respect to the masculine impression of the subject: it is "never here and now of being that everywhere else where the 'subject' continues to draw his reserves, his re-sources."[65] The subject cannot exist without this emplacement, which, however, is not a stable emplacement at all: it is "already scattered into *x* number of places that are never gathered together into anything she knows of herself, and these remain the basis of (re)production—particularly of discourse—in all its forms."[66] The scattering (*dispersion*) of the place of the feminine is thus the background for the imposition of the masculine order, and yet it is always already a "source" of the potential scattering of the world, a potential that manifests itself in discourse. Grosz is even more explicit in bringing together femininity and its function in the "Platonic" West with the "characterless character" of chora in the *Timaeus,* its malleability and suppleness. She draws our attention to several "features" of Platonic chora, such as self-obliteration for the sake of others, engendering without possession, receiving without giving and giving without receiving, evading "all characterization including the

---

62. *Bodies That Matter,* 49.

63. On the gender of (the) chora see Derrida, *"Khôra,"* 95 (French: *Khôra,* 33); on the space of indeterminacy see René Girard, *Violence and the Sacred,* trans. Patrick Gregory (Baltimore, Md.: Johns Hopkins University Press, 1977), 49ff. and passim (French: *La violence et le sacré* [Paris: B. Grasset, 1972], 77ff. and passim).

64. As Butler puts it, discursive systems of intelligibility require "a domain of radical *unintelligibility*" to be excluded from themselves in order to function (*Bodies That Matter,* 35).

65. *Speculum of the Other Woman,* 227; translation modified (French: "Jamais ici maintenant d'être ce partout ailleurs où le 'sujet' continue de puiser ses réserves, ses re-sources" [*Speculum de l'autre femme,* 282]).

66. *Speculum of the Other Woman,* 227; translation modified (French: "déjà dispersée en x lieux qui n'ont leur rassemblement en rien qu'elle se sache et qui restent le support de la (re)production—notamment du discours—sous toutes ses formes" [*Speculum de l'autre femme,* 282]).

disconcerting logic of identity, of hierarchy of being, the regulation of order."
She concludes that one should not be surprised if chora "resembles the characteristics the Greeks, and all those who follow them, have long attributed to femininity, or rather, have expelled from their own masculine self-representations and accounts of being and knowing (and have thus *de facto* attributed to the feminine)."[67]

The production of masculine order out of feminine chaos has been analyzed in psychoanalytic terms by Kristeva. She implicitly questions the logos imposed by the demiurge, opposing the motility of the maternal chora to the violent, hardening effect of the oedipal mechanism that initiates the process of consolidation of the paternal symbolic order. In Kristeva's view, language is born within the semiotic chora or rather within the movement of *signifiance,* which consists of the "unceasing operation of the drives toward, in, and through language; toward, in, and through the exchange system and its protagonists—the subject and his institutions."[68] This would correspond to the constructive aspect of the Platonic chora. But just as in Irigaray's notion of the feminine source of becoming and of (masculine) discourse, the generating process of the subject in Kristeva's theory is unlimited and unbounded and as such contains the potential for revolutionary disruption. Thus, the semiotic chora becomes the key notion of Kristeva's theory of language, designating the space of a preoedipal and prespecular, unmediated relationship between mother and child, which can be recovered in the experience of poetic language.[69] Such an experience might lead to "the outer *boundaries* of the subject and society" and thus open the space of unlimited and unbounded potentialities.[70] The enigmatic, feminine motility of the chora thus designates the potentiality for rupture with the established political, religious, and aesthetic order of discursive representation.

Even though Kristeva does not offer a direct reading of Plato, her theory of poetic language does belong to the history of the interpretation of the Platonic

67. Elizabeth A. Grosz, "Women, *Chora,* Dwelling," in Elizabeth A. Grosz, *Space, Time, and Perversion: Essays on the Politics of Bodies* (New York: Routledge, 1995), 116. The portrayal of the feminine as the "dumping ground" of the masculine representation of the world constructed by the demiurge is certainly present in Timaeus's phallogocentric discourse —for example, in the last section of the dialogue, where women are said to be the result of the transformation of the second generation of cowardly and unjust men (90e–91a).

68. *Revolution in Poetic Language,* 17 (French: "Ce que nous désignons par *signifiance* est précisément cet engendrement illimité et jamais clos, ce fonctionnement sans arrêt des pulsions vers, dans et à travers le langage, vers, dans et à travers l'échange et ses protagonistes: le sujet et ses institutions" [*La révolution du langage poétique,* 15]).

69. *Revolution in Poetic Language,* 29–30 (French: *La révolution du langage poétique,* 28–29).

70. *Revolution in Poetic Language,* 29–30 (French: "passage à la *limite* subjective et sociale" [*La révolution du langage poétique,* 28–29]).

chora and to the modern overturning of Platonism.[71] She has decisively transferred the focus of "chorology" from the single moment of cosmological foundation by the demiurge to the constant experience of discourse: "Our discourse—all discourse—moves with and against the *chora* in the sense that it simultaneously depends upon her and refuses."[72] The principle of this double movement of semiotic chora is play—for example the rhythmic play of gestures and sounds in the development of language, a play that in its turn is circumscribed by the biological, familial, and political constraints belonging to the symbolic order. In fact, there is no pure region of the semiotic chora, just as there is no symbolic order completely free from the choric play of rhythmic motility. The two are always thrown or stitched together, even though the potentialities of semiotic chora are incomparably better revealed in poetry (Kristeva analyzes the poetic process of Gérard de Nerval, Lautréamont, Stéphane Mallarmé, James Joyce, and Artaud, among others) than in traditional philosophical discourse.[73]

Irigaray, whose *Speculum of the Other Woman* was published in the same year as *Revolution in Poetic Language,* reads Plato's text more directly, which is not to say conventionally. Her reading and her translation would be considered misreading and mistranslation in conventional Plato scholarship and would elicit a chorus of disapproval there—in fact, it did, in those rare cases when it was considered at all. For example, Irigaray translates the key passage on chora in the *Timaeus* in the following way: "Unstable, inconsistent, fickle, unfaithful, she seems ready to receive all beings into herself. Keeping no trace of them. Without memory. She herself is without figure or face or proper form, for otherwise '(she) would take the impression badly because (she) would intrude (her) own shape'" (50e).[74] This is not a faithful translation of Plato, not

---

71. On Kristeva's reconceptualization of the "Platonic" chora, see Linda Kintz, "Plato, Kristeva, and the Chora: Figuring the Unfigurable," in *Plato and Postmodernism,* ed. Steven Shankman (Glenside, Pa.: Aldine Press, 1994), 153–54.

72. *Revolution in Poetic Language,* 26; translation modified (French: "Notre discours—le discours—chemine contre elle, c'est-à-dire s'appuie sur elle en même temps qu'il la repousse" [*La révolution du langage poétique,* 23]).

73. See, besides *Revolution in Poetic Language, Desire in Language: A Semiotic Approach to Literature and Art,* trans. Thomas Gora, Alice Jardine, and Leon S. Roudiez (New York: Columbia University Press, 1980) (French: *Polylogue* [Paris: Seuil, 1977] and *Sēmeiōtikē* [Paris: Seuil, 1969]); *Black Sun,* trans. Leon S. Roudiez (New York: Columbia University Press, 1987) (French: *Soleil noir; Dépression et mélancholie* [Paris: Gallimard, 1987]), and *Powers of Horror: An Essay on Abjection,* translated by Leon S. Roudiez (New York: Columbia University Press, 1982) (French: *Pouvoirs de l'horreur: Essai sur l'abjection* [Paris: Seuil, 1980]).

74. *Speculum of the Other Woman,* 307 (French: "Instable, inconsistante, versatile, infidèle, elle se prêterait également à recevoir en soi tous les êtres. N'en gardant pas de traces. Sans mémoire. Elle-même sans figure, sans visage, sans forme propre, sous peine d' 'offusquer de son propre aspect' certains des êtres qui y entrent, 'les reproduisant mal' [*Timée* 50e] [*Speculum de l'autre femme,* 383]); see also "Volume-Fluidity," in *Speculum of the Other Woman,* 227–40 (French: "L'incontournable volume," in *Speculum de*

in a traditional sense. Nor is it an interpretation; at least, it would be difficult to evaluate it according to the standards of Plato scholarship.[75] It is, indeed, a confrontation (*Auseinandersetzung*) with this tradition, the tradition of Western thought that speaks of the unfaithfulness, inconsistency, fickleness of woman— "la donna è mobile." Irigaray's discourse leaves it undecided whether she simply rejects this characterization or also celebrates it. The confrontation and undecidability are present in Timaeus's rhapsodic voice, in such a way that he would be hard put to protest. For is he not "himself" perplexed by chora, whose only possible determination, "her" feminine character, does not remedy the threat of the abyss, since femininity is itself associated with chasm, abyss, a fluidity and errancy of immeasurable motion? Woman is confusing, dissembling, seducing. But so is the discourse that is supposed to contain her: Timaeus's, Plato's, even Irigaray's.

It is true that, for all the "femininity" of its/her characterization, the particularity of chora resides in its/her marginal position in respect to all binaries, including that of masculine/feminine. In Irigaray's view, chora is nevertheless associated with woman, since, contrary to her common portrayal in Western culture, woman, like chora, in fact exists in a "third place," the place beyond the exclusive "neither/nor" and the inclusive "both/and" that is supposed to serve at once to enable and to undermine the terms of the "either/or." Indeed, the binary system that ostensibly *includes* the feminine as a subordinate term must, in order to function, *exclude* the feminine. Woman "herself" is "neither open nor closed," Irigaray writes. "She is before all pairs of opposites, where the attribution of all distinctions between active and passive or past and future is drawn."[76] The borders of philosophy and politics are secured by this "constitutive exclusion" of the feminine, which becomes for Western logocentric

---

l'autre femme, 282–98), *This Sex Which Is Not One,* trans. Catherine Porter and Carolyn Burke (Ithaca, N.Y.: Cornell University Press, 1985), esp. 26ff., 108ff., 122, 214–15 (French: *Ce sexe qui n'en est pas un* [Paris: Minuit, 1977], 26ff., 121, 106ff., 213–14), and "Place, Interval: A Reading of Aristotle, *Physics* IV," in *An Ethics of Sexual Difference,* translated by Carolyn Burke and Gillian C. Gill (Ithaca, N.Y.: Cornell University Press), 34–55 (French: *Ethique de la différence sexuelle* [Paris: Minuit, 1984], 41–59).

75. Drew Hyland's critique of Irigaray's scholarship—of her neglect of Plato's real and apparent intentions ("the *intention* of the *author*" [*Questioning Platonism,* 125; his emphasis; cf. 132–33]), of Plato's authorship and authority ("the author here is *authoritative*" [125; his emphasis]), of the well-established historical and dramatic context (132ff.), and so forth—seems to be missing the point of Irigaray's rhapsodic play; see Elizabeth Weed's perceptive characterization of this play in her "Question of Style," in *Engaging With Irigaray: Feminist Philosophy and Modern European Thought,* ed. Carolyn Burke, Naomi Schor, Margaret Whitford (New York: Columbia University Press, 1994), 79–109; to paraphrase Weed, Irigaray does not write *on* Plato, she *writes* Plato.

76. *Speculum of the Other Woman,* 229–30; translation modified (French: "Or la femme n'est ni fermée, ni ouverte . . . En deçà de toute opposition dans un couple où se dessine l'attribution de l'actif et du passif, ou du passé et du futur" [*Speculum de l'autre femme,* 284, 286]).

discourse "the illegible condition of its own legibility," as Butler writes, speaking in Irigaray's voice and thus entering the space of rhapsodic discourse.[77]

Irigaray recognizes the representational structure of Western philosophical and political thought. Theater—"Plato's Hystera" is a theater—is the model of this structure.[78] Its "scenography," "its props, its actors, their respective positions, their dialogues," strictly determine this thought. The only way to disturb it consists in rhapsodic mimicry. Like the characterless support of chora, woman will threaten to disrupt the order of the city by refusing to remain contained within a single identity, a single category. Indeed, this is, in Irigaray's view, the role reserved for woman in the history of the West and thus, paradoxically, the role woman must also play in order to undermine the system that assigned her that role in the first place: all that takes place on the scene of philosophy and politics must be "reenacted" in order to be exposed and disrupted.[79] Woman cannot *argue* against logos; this would be to retain the "onto-theo-logic" model; rather, she must *reiterate* the manner in which the feminine is defined in discourse in order to make manifest a *disruptive excess* in such a discourse.[80] This excess will in turn threaten the masculine philosophical and political order, and call into question the very notion of the proper, including the propriety of discourse.

When Irigaray writes of woman (and chora) that "she (is) pure mimicry," she refers of course to her own status as a writer as well.[81] The radical nature of Irigaray's work has to do not just with what she says but with how she says it: she engages in the play of mimicry, a rhapsodic performance, giving voice to the philosopher, but only in order to undermine his discourse from within (we could think here, again, of the ventriloquous Eurycles, the rhapsode Ion, and Socrates "himself"). It is the abyssal playground of chora and the *hystera,* or womb, in Plato's *Timaeus* and the *Republic* that provides Irigaray with the stage for miming—and undermining—the representational setting of the patriarchal speculative system of Western philosophy. At its most radical, this miming takes the form of sheer quotation, such as, for example, the

77. Butler, *Bodies That Matter,* 36–37; In this sense, on Butler's reading, Irigaray's work goes beyond that of Kristeva, whose emphasis on the rhythmic space of the semiotic seems to leave unproblematized the conflation of chora and maternal body; see *Bodies That Matter,* 41; cf. Judith Butler, *Gender Trouble: Feminism and the Subversion of Identity* (New York: Routledge, 1990), 79ff.

78. Irigaray, "Plato's Hystera," in *Speculum of the Other Woman,* 244–45 (French: "L'ὑστέρα de Platon," in *Speculum de l'autre femme,* 302–3).

79. Irigaray, "The Power of Discourse and the Subordination of the Feminine," in *This Sex Which Is Not One,* 75–76 (French: "Pouvoir du discours, subordination du féminin," in *Ce sexe qui n'en est pas un,* 73–75).

80. "The Power of Discourse," 78; her emphasis (French: "Pouvoir du discours, subordination du féminin," 75–76).

81. *Speculum of the Other Woman,* 307 (French: "Elle (est) pur mimétisme" [*Speculum de l'autre femme,* 383–84]).

section of *Speculum of the Other Woman* entitled "On the Index of Plato's Works: Woman," a collection of quotations from Plato's texts, and the similar section "Une mère de glace," a collection of quotations from Plotinus—dealing (in)appropriately with the question of matter, and of chora, in Plato.[82] On the other hand, the long final section of *Speculum,* "Plato's *Hystera,*" a critical rereading of the allegory of the cave in the *Republic,* combines citation, paraphrase, and critical interpretation in a continuous narrative whose style makes it nearly impossible to determine, at certain points, who is "really" speaking— Socrates, Plato, Irigaray, Irigaray in the voice of Socrates or Plato, Socrates or Plato in the voice of Irigaray? As Butler notes, Irigaray cites Plato not in deference to his authority but as an act of "insubordination," exposing what is excluded from his text and at the same time calling into question the very notions of origination and of propriety.[83]

Irigaray performs the dangerous play of mimesis that threatens the discourse on the republic and the cosmos. And it is again Butler who in turn gives voice to Irigaray's performance: "I will not be a poor copy in your system, but I will resemble you nevertheless by *miming* the textual passages through which you construct your system."[84] We might continue: "Will I be a simulacrum then?" No, because this would be to yield to the distinctions of philosophical discourse. "I will resemble you precisely in order not to resemble you." There is not a locatable frontier between philosophical discourse and Irigaray's own voice, only a disruptive gesture, mimicry as a sort of "overreading" that exposes the limits and excesses of the philosophical text.[85] To play with mimesis is, for Irigaray "to resubmit herself—inasmuch as she is on the side of the "perceptible," of "matter"—to "ideas," in particular to ideas about herself, that are elaborated in/by a "masculine logic" but so as to make "visible," by an effect of playful repetition, what was supposed to remain invisible: the cover-up of a possible operation of the feminine in language."[86] Again, "Platonic theater," in

82. Sallis's critique of this passage from "Une mère de glace," pertinent within the framework of traditional rigorous scholarship, overlooks the rhapsodic play of Irigaray precisely with the tradition of rigorous Platonic and neo-Platonic scholarship (*Chorology,* 151 n. 9).

83. *Bodies That Matter,* 45; One of the curious effects of this method, parallel to the reinscription of the chora discussed by Sallis, is that Butler, in discussing "Une mère de glace," refers to "Irigaray's essay" and argues that "her reading establishes the cosmogony of the Forms in the *Timaeus* as a phallic phantasy of a fully self-constituted patrilineality," although the essay seems to be nothing other than citations from Plotinus.

84. *Bodies That Matter,* 45; Butler also notes at least one troubling consequence of Irigaray's "tactical" mimicry, namely that "her terms tend to mime the grandiosity of the philosophical errors that she underscores" (36).

85. *Bodies That Matter,* 36.

86. Irigaray, "The Power of Discourse," 76 (French: "Pouvoir du discours, subordination du féminin," 75). Butler argues that matter does not come prior to signification but is rather produced as an effect

Brecht or in Plato, would be the model for such a rhapsodic display of ideological cover-up. Aspasia or Diotima through the voice of Socrates, or Shui Ta
through the voice of Shen Te, like "Plato" through the voice of Irigaray, would
only apparently submit to the exigencies of the dominant discourse; in fact, it
would lead it to its limits.[87] *La mystérique* is Irigaray's word for "the trap of
mimesis" set by feminine writing for all that claims to be "self-as-same."[88] It
opens up "the abyss of her prodigality, her madness, expansion and dissipation
of self," a space of infinite difference, of "a-typical, a-topical mysteria."[89] The
objective of "mimicry" and "masquerade," of the play of repetition with the
paternal symbolic order of the same, is to dis-play the chasm of the—necessary
and dangerous—chora by frustrating the ideological operation of camouflage.

   The notion of a constitutive exclusion of the feminine from the very philosophical system that figures the feminine as one of its subordinate terms is
echoed in Irigaray's understanding of a sort of materiality, excluded from the
ostensive opposition "form/matter," itself an *excessive* materiality, an inscriptional space that the opposition is unable to contain or to thematize.[90] This
inscriptional space remains as a "remnant" of unintelligible femininity within
ontology, "the specular surface which receives the marks of a masculine signifying act."[91] There are thus, for Irigaray, two ways of understanding "matter":
as a conceptual support of the phallogocentric system, and, more importantly,

---

of signification (since the very priority of its materiality is itself *signified,* the material shaped and delimited by signification), by a discourse that must be understood as *performative* rather than *representational.*
In this reading, Irigaray's miming may take on an additional signification: it may not just reenact the
performance of chora, but "constitute" chora through its very performance. Yet to understand matter as
posited by signification does not negate the fact that it is posited *by* signification *as exterior* to signification; indeed, this (posited) exteriority remains the necessary condition for the continuation of the (effect
of) the "coherent systematicity" of philosophical discourse, that which must be excluded "in order to sus-
tain and secure the borders of philosophy" (*Bodies That Matter,* 30–32).

   87. Plato, *Symposium* and *Menexenus;* Bertolt Brecht, *The Good Person of Szechwan,* in Bertolt Brecht,
Collected Plays, vol. 5, ed. John Willet and Ralph Manheim (London: Eyre Methuen, 1970).

   88. I do not take up here Hélène Cixous's notion of *l'écriture féminine,* as formulated in *The Newly
Born Woman,* trans. Betsy Wing (Minneapolis: University of Minnesota Press, 1986) (French: *La jeune née*
[Paris: Union générale d'éditions, 1975]), and *"L'heure de Clarice Lispector,"précédé de "Vivre l'orange"/ "To
Live the Orange,"* French/English text, trans. Ann Liddle and Sarah Cornell (Paris: Éditions des femmes,
1979), but I would like to quote a passage from "The Laugh of the Medusa" where the feminine voice
seems particularly rhapsodic: "Listen to a woman speak at a public gathering. . . . She doesn't "speak," she
throws her trembling body forward; she lets go of herself, she flies; all of her passes into her voice, and it's
with her body that she vitally supports the "logic" of her speech" (*Norton Anthology of Theory and Criticism,* ed. Vincent B. Leitch [New York: Norton, 2001], 2044).

   89. *Speculum of the Other Woman,* 191ff. (French: "l'abîme où elle se prodigue, se déploie et se dissipe
dans sa folie" [*Speculum de l'autre femme,* 238 ff.]); *Speculum of the Other Woman,* 192 (French: "atypique,
atopique, mystérie" [*Speculum de l'autre femme,* 239]).

   90. Butler, *Bodies That Matter,* 38.

   91. Butler, *Bodies That Matter,* 39.

as an "ungrounded figure . . . that marks for her the possible linguistic site of a critical mime."[92] The excess of this second sort of matter is what erupts within and disrupts the repetition of phallogocentric discourse. In this context, it is important to note that, although chora's (non)characterization has been read productively vis-à-vis the notion of woman, the same procedure could be employed in the case of any being marginalized in the history of Western culture; indeed, Butler suggests that a weakness of Irigaray's critique is her failure to pursue the wider implications of chora, not just in terms of woman but in terms of other "Others"—slaves, children, even animals, the exclusion of whom is equally important to philosophy's "scenography."[93] The threat to the scene of representation results from the voicing of beings within the essential indetermination of chora. For, "if the copies speak, or if what is merely material begins to signify, the scenography of reason is rocked by the crisis on which it was always built," thus collapsing into the abyss that was there from the start.[94]

Philosophical and/or Rhapsodic Discourse

It is inevitable, I suppose, that everything we all say is a kind of representation and attempted likeness.

—CRITIAS

The long third part of the *Timaeus* is an example of an attempt to cover up the abyss opened by chora in the ontological/representational system of Platonism.[95] Does it succeed? Can the result of this effort by Timaeus and his demiurge, as well as by most interpreters of the dialogue, be found in the ostensible conclusion of the dialogue, "Here at last let us say that our discourse (*logos*) concerning the universe has come to its end (*telos*)" (92c?)[96] This self-satisfaction of the philosophical *logos* seems to be refuted by the opening of the *Critias,* which seems a more reliable conclusion to the *Timaeus* that points out the unreliability of absolute philosophical discourse, separated from its mode of presentation. In the *Critias,* mimesis is reaffirmed as universal, but its representational character is questioned. In the *Republic,* the consternation of Socrates before the "injustice" of dissemblers, of those who do not respect the

92. In Butler's felicitous formulation (*Bodies That Matter,* 47).
93. Butler, *Bodies That Matter,* 48–49.
94. Butler, *Bodies That Matter,* 52.
95. The epigraph to this section comes from Plato, *Critias* 107b (trans. Diskin Clay, in *Plato: Complete Works,* 1293) [Greek: "μίμησιν μὲν γὰρ δὴ καὶ ἀπεικασίαν τὰ παρὰ πάντων ἡμῶν ῥηθέντα χρεών που γενέσθαι"].
96. Cornford, *Plato's Cosmogony,* 359. Cf. Derrida's assessment of the conclusion of the dialogue ("*Khôra,*" 104 [French: *Khôra,* 49]).

rigorous separation of functions (*erga*) and of places (*khōrai*), resembled the shock of the demiurge and the narrator before the "characterless" chora in the *Timaeus*. The spectacle of false doctors, false shepherds, false politicians, and especially of those who make a profession of falsifying in defiance of "ergonal" boundaries—sophists, rhapsodes, actors, and so forth—launched the investigation into the nature of justice and remained constantly behind the formation of the (ideal) Republic as the philosopher Socrates' nightmare. But even there Socrates was not absolutely separated from the tribe of pretenders, since it was eventually his own rhapsodic discourse that welcomed all the other characters as he "pretended" to be each one in turn.

The Socrates of the *Timaeus* is another, different character, a character of an other, a wanderer, a vagrant (*planētēs*), characterless like chora "itself/herself"; and just like chora, he tends to resist the demiurgic, paternal logos, eventually receiving those who receive him, his hosts: Timaeus, Critias, Hermocrates, philosophers and politicians par excellence, readers perhaps, in the ranks of "poets and performers," rhapsodes moved by the spirit of theater (*hē tou theatrou dianoia* [*Critias* 108b]). Is this all-receiving (*pandekhēs*) character the same as the philosopher of the *Republic* and other dialogues? He *is* the same if we understand "the same Socrates" in the way of chora, the receptacle (*hupodokhē*) of the *Timaeus,* as the (im)proper *this* (*touto*), a rhapsode capable of "performing difference," of receiving all properties, all characters, and thus able to display the mimetic play-ground of the chiasm of the same and the other or radically different. (Dis)placed (*anakhōrētēs*) on the margin of philosophical and political discourse in the company of the poets and sophists, Socrates as chora is better "placed" to question the topology, the politics, and ideology of places, which the philosophers and the politicians of the *Republic* tried rigorously to establish by eliminating all traces of rhapsodic mimesis.

The chasm of chora, then, cannot be entirely covered over, regulated, or contained in Plato's dialogue. It is not the cosmological category by itself, however, that makes this resistance possible but rather its implication in the play of mimesis, its interaction with the other elements of the rhapsodic mode (such as characters, especially that of Socrates), with the myth and the complex historical narrative, with the repetition of an "absolute beginning," and so forth. The importance of all these elements—often taken for stylistic effects, separable from the real "matter" of the dialogue—can be seen when Plato's dialogue is compared with a paraphrasis in a later philosophical treatise. *On the Nature of the World and the Soul,* supposed to be the original work of Timaios of Locri, was in fact probably composed in the first century BCE or the first century CE.[97]

---

97. Timaios of Locri, *On the Nature of the World and the Soul,* ed. and trans. Thomas H. Tobin (Chico, Calif.: Scholars Press, 1985).

The cosmological discourse of the *Timaeus* is almost entirely transcribed there, including the passage on the third genre of chora, but none of the rhapsodic traits of Plato's dialogue survive. The effect is the illusion of an author in perfect possession of his knowledge and communicating it apodictically. Not rhapsodic enthusiasm but cool reason, not a Socratic desire for wisdom but wisdom itself, marks the treatise. This attempt to "translate" chora into a rational discourse runs the risk of domesticating chora "itself"/"herself," of transforming it into something more manageable, less dangerous. The revolutionary potential of chora is indissociable from rhapsodic performance.[98] Not just the essays of Irigaray and Derrida but Plato's dialogue itself are examples of such a performance. The dialogue produces a kind of impersonation of philosophy or philosophical myth, and in this way, it helps to found that philosophy called "Platonism," but at the same time, it enables its questioning. Even before a miming of Plato's text such as Irigaray's mimique, Plato's text would already mime itself. And the very "characteristic" that allows that text to found Platonism would at the same time prevent it from being itself "Platonic."

98. Sallis does include all these rhapsodic elements in his complex notion of "chorology," but he seems to underestimate the functioning of the rhapsodic mode in other dialogues of Plato, without a direct reference to chora, as well as in the work of contemporary continental philosophers, such as Irigaray or Derrida; see especially *Chorology*, 146–54.

Rhapsodic Conclusion
"The Dialogue That We Are" in Plato, Heidegger, and Nancy

J (Japanese): But then, not every talk between people could be called a dialogue any longer . . .

    I (Inquirer): . . . if we from now on hear this word as though it named for us a focusing on the reality of language.

    J: In this sense, then, even Plato's *Dialogues* would not be dialogues?

    I: I would like to leave the question open.

—MARTIN HEIDEGGER

But beyond Heidegger himself, and although on account of him, it will be necessary to take up once again the most ancient philosophical document concerning *hermēneia*, Plato's *Ion*: that is to say, as will be seen, it will be necessary once more to take up the sharing and the dialogue of philosophy and poetry.

—JEAN-LUC NANCY

"The dialogue of thinking with poetry is long. It has barely begun." Heidegger does not think here of Plato's "old quarrel" between poetry and philosophy. The dialogue in question should circumvent philosophy, at least "Platonic" philosophy, which is interested in the domination of, rather than a genuine

---

The first epigraph to this chapter is drawn from Heidegger's 1954 "A Dialogue on Language (Between a Japanese and an Inquirer)" (in Martin Heidegger, *On the Way to Language,* trans. Peter D. Hertz [New York: Harper and Row, 1971], 52 [German: "Aus einem Gespräch von der Sprache (Zwischen einem Japaner und einem Fragenden)," in *Unterwegs zur Sprache* (Stuttgart: Neske, 1959), 151]). In German, it reads:

> J (ein Japaner): Dann dürften wir aber nicht mehr jedes Miteinanderreden ein Gespräch nennen.
> F (ein Fragender): . . . falls wir diesen Namen fortan so hörten, daß er uns die Versammlung auf das Wesen der Sprache nennt.
> J: In diesem Sinne wären dann auch Platons Dialoge keine Gespräche?
> F: Ich möchte die Frage offenlassen.

The second epigraph comes from Nancy's "Sharing Voices," trans. Gayle L. Ormiston, in *Transforming the Hermeneutic Context: From Nietzsche to Nancy,* ed. Gayle L. Ormiston and Alan D. Schrift (Albany: State University of New York Press, 1990), 211 (French: "Mais par-delà Heidegger lui-même, et bien qu'à cause de lui, il faudra remonter au plus ancien document philosophique de l'*hermeneia*: au *Ion* de Platon. C'est-à-dire, on le verra, une fois de plus au partage et au dialogue de la philosophie et de la poésie" [*Le partage des voix* (Paris: Galilée, 1982), 11]).

dialogue with, poetry. I have postulated the need for a confrontation with the legacy of Western philosophy, that is, with "Platonism," as a condition of the dialogue called for by Heidegger. If in a sense philosophy will always be "Platonic," as the philosophers discussed in this book claim, the major task of philosophical thought has to be such a confrontation or dialogue—a particular dialogue that I have called "rhapsodic"—with Plato's texts rather than an attempt to circumvent them. And I hope to have shown that certain key notions of Western metaphysics—such as the true and the false, identity and difference, speech and writing, the same and the other, rigor and play—need to be set into play again and referred back to Plato, where they were first rigorously formulated and where they eventually remained in a state of aporia. Only such a questioning of its basic notions would allow philosophy to enter the dialogue with poetry, considered as a partner rather than an object of analysis and interpretation to be mastered. The very notion of "interpretation," which the philosophical tradition has used as a means of confining poetry, must be put at stake in order to open the way toward a genuine dialogue between philosophy and poetry.

Even though Plato's own texts call into question such masterful interpretation, those texts themselves have most often been read according to reifying hermeneutic standards. Indeed, the main currents in Plato scholarship are united in their maintenance of the ideal of a univocal interpretation, and they achieve this goal through a strict separation of seriousness and play in their reading.[1] In the introduction, I argued that representatives of two apparently opposed ways of interpreting Plato actually adhere to the same hermeneutic principle: the assured self-identity of the author or his mouthpiece, his ultimate seriousness, his univocal, rigorously defined meaning.

In the chapters that followed, I traced a contemporary break with the tradition of a scholarly, "authorized" interpretation that had neglected this rhapsodic and "writerly" textual aspect of Plato's dialogues.[2] I suggested, with Derrida

---

1. See, for example, Charles L. Griswold Jr., *Self-Knowledge in Plato's "Phaedrus"* (1988; rpt., University Park, Pa.: Pennsylvania State University Press, 1986), 239, and Rosemary Desjardins, "Why Dialogues? Plato's Serious Play," in *Platonic Writings/Platonic Readings*, ed. Charles L. Griswold Jr. (New York: Routledge, 1988), 110–25. Hans-Georg Gadamer, in his early essay on the old quarrel between philosophy and poetry, interprets Plato's position in the following way: "The theme voiced continually in Plato's critique of the poets is that they take seriously what is not worth being taken seriously. Here and there Plato gives us indications that his own creations, because they are in jest and are only meant to be in jest, are the true poetry" ("Plato and the Poets," in Hans-Georg Gadamer, *Dialogue and Dialectics: Eight Hermeneutical Studies on Plato*, trans. Christopher Smith [New Haven, Conn.: Yale University Press, 1980], 71 [German: *Plato und die Dichter* (1934; rpt., in Hans-Georg Gadamer, *Platos dialektische Ethik* [Hamburg: Meiner, 1968], 203–4)]).

2. For a discussion of textuality in Plato's dialogues and its relation to the magnetic or Heraclean chain in the *Ion*, see Harry Berger Jr., "Levels of Discourse in Plato's Dialogues," in *Literature and the Question of Philosophy*, ed. Anthony J. Cascardi (Baltimore, Md.: Johns Hopkins University Press, 1987), 82ff.

and others, that there is an undecidability and play in Plato's text—a play of (re)semblance, of *pharmakon,* of *khōra,* of *mimēsis* as play "itself"— frustrating any particular interpretation that would claim exclusivity or even priority over different interpretations. In this concluding chapter, I would like to problematize the very notion of *interpretation,* taken to be the translation of the Greek *hermēneia,* which underlies most traditional readings of the dialogues and thus also underlies the "Platonic" desire of philosophy and of literary theory (though not, perhaps, "Plato's" desire) to reduce any text, be it philosophical or poetical, to a rigorous, univocal meaning.

Modern hermeneutics has been associated with the interpretation of Plato since Schleiermacher, the founder of romantic hermeneutics and a prominent Plato scholar.[3] But in the work of Gadamer, Plato's dialogues become the very model for hermeneutic experience. The problematic of Platonic dialectic and of dialogue had been a constant object of Gadamer's studies from his early *Plato's Dialectical Ethics* to *The Idea of the Good in Platonic-Aristotelian Philosophy* and "Plato as Portraitist," and it is taken up at the critical moment in his *Truth and Method,* "the bible of present day German ('hermeneutic') philosophy."[4] The paradigm of the dialogue is introduced just after the elaboration of the notion of "historically effected consciousness" (or rather "consciousness of the history of effects" [*wirkungsgeschichtliches Bewußtsein*]) and of hermeneutic experience (*hermeneutische Erfahrung*), which in turn have consolidated the fact of "belonging to tradition" (*Zugehörigkeit zur Überlieferung*) and of authority (*Autorität*).[5] A thorough analysis of dialogue (*Gespräch*) and of the interpretation of texts then leads directly to the "lingual" (*sprachlich*) determination

    3. Friedrich D. E. Schleiermacher, *Kritische Gesamtausgabe,* 14 vols. to date, ed. Hans-Joachim Birkner et al. (Berlin: de Gruyter, 1980–).

    4. *Plato's Dialectical Ethics: Phenomenological Interpretations Relating to the "Philebus,"* trans. Robert M. Wallace (New Haven, Conn.: Yale University Press, 1991) (German: The text was originally a *Habilitationsschrift,* written with Heidegger in Freiburg in 1929; it appeared in revised form in 1931 as *Platos dialektische Ethik* [Leipzig: Meiner, 1931]); Hans-Georg Gadamer, *The Idea of the Good in Platonic-Aristotelian Philosophy,* P. Christopher Smith (New Haven, Conn.: Yale University Press, 1986) (German: *Idee des Guten zwischen Plato und Aristoteles* [Heidelberg: Winter, 1978]); Hans-Georg Gadamer, "Plato as Portraitist," trans. Jamey Findling and Snezhina Gabova, *Continental Philosophy Review* 33, no. 3 (2000): 245–74 (German: "Platon als Porträtist," in Hans-Georg Gadamer, *Gesammelte Werke,* 10 vols. [Tübingen: Mohr, 1985–95], 7:228–57). Hans Albert describes *Truth and Method* as the bible of present-day German philosophy in a letter to Paul Feyerabend dated 20 February 1967, quoted in Jean Grondin, *Hans-Georg Gadamer: A Biography,* trans. Joel Weinsheimer (New Haven, Conn.: Yale University Press, 2003), 283.

    5. Hans-Georg Gadamer, *Truth and Method,* trans. Joel Weinsheimer and Donald G. Marshall (1975; rpt., New York: Continuum, 2002), 362 (German: *Wahrheit und Methode: Grundzüge einer philosophischen Hermeneutik* [Tübingen: Mohr, 1960], 344); cf. Paul Ricoeur, *Hermeneutics and the Human Sciences,* trans. John B. Thompson (Cambridge: Cambridge University Press, 1981), 61; *Truth and Method,* 262–63, 328–29 (German: *Wahrheit und Methode,* 247–48, 312); *Truth and Method,* 277ff. (German: *Wahrheit und Methode,* 261ff.)

of hermeneutic experience, the emphasis on and the examination of which is considered the culmination of Gadamer's work.[6]

Platonic dialogue is taken up at this critical juncture in *Truth and Method* as the enactment of the Socratic dialectic, which, through the refutation of those who pretend to a certain knowledge, allows for questioning—questioning that in turn is able to open up a genuine hermeneutic experience. Indeed, the knowledge of not-knowing, the *docta ignorantia,* is for Gadamer the condition of the "logical structure of openness" (*die logische Struktur der Offenheit*).[7] And it is the latter that might allow a "variety of voices" (*eine Vielzahl von Stimmen*), voices that ultimately constitute our historical consciousness, to be heard.[8] However, the logic of the question is not only the logic of openness but also the logic of limitation (*Begrenzung*).[9] Indeed, Socratic dialogues achieve their questioning openness through a conscious art (*bewußte Handhabung*).[10] Even though this art is not a *tekhnē* in a strict (Greek, Platonic) sense, it does preserve some of its essential traits, first of all the directionality of meaning in its questioning, its *Richtungssinn*.[11] Thus, Platonic dialectic is not only the art of conducting a conversation but also an art of "seeing things in the unity of an aspect" (*sunoran eis hen eidos*)—that is, it is the art of forming concepts through working out the common meaning (*das gemeinsam Gemeinte*).[12] It is in fact this "unidirectionality" within a conversation that, according to Gadamer, makes of Plato's dialogues a perfect model for hermeneutics ("In dialogue[,] spoken language . . . performs the communication of meaning that, with respect to the written tradition, is the task of hermeneutics") and at the same time seems to allow it to be brought together with Hegelian dialectics ("The primacy of dialogue, the relation of question and answer, can be seen in even so extreme a case as that of Hegel's dialectic as a philosophical method. To elaborate the totality of the determinations of thought, which was the aim of Hegel's logic, is as it were the attempt to comprehend within the great monologue of modern "method" the continuum of meaning that is realized in every particular instance of dialogue.")[13] This rapprochement—the reflection

6. See, for example, Ricoeur, *Hermeneutics and the Human Sciences,* 62, and Jean Grondin, *Introduction à Hans-Georg Gadamer* (Paris: Cerf, 1999), 213ff.; cf. Drew A. Hyland, *Questioning Platonism: Continental Interpretations of Plato* (Albany: State University of New York Press, 2004), 171–72.

7. *Truth and Method,* 362 (German: *Wahrheit und Methode,* 344).

8. *Truth and Method,* 284 (German: *Wahrheit und Methode,* 268).

9. *Truth and Method,* 363 (German: "Fragestellung setzt Offenheit voraus, aber zugleich eine Begrenzung" [*Wahrheit und Methode,* 346]).

10. *Truth and Method,* 366 (German: *Wahrheit und Methode,* 348).

11. *Truth and Method,* 362 (German: *Wahrheit und Methode,* 345).

12. *Truth and Method,* 368 (German: *Wahrheit und Methode,* 350).

13. *Truth and Method,* 362 (German: *Wahrheit und Methode,* 345); *Truth and Method,* 369 (German: "Die Ursprünglichkeit des Gesprächs als des Bezugs von Frage und Antwort zeigt sich aber selbst noch in

of which we have already seen in Griswold's dialectical reading of Plato's dialogues—results from the tendency to preserve the authority of the tradition
even while including the largest possible variety of compatible voices (voices
that would not, however, interrupt its continuity).[14] Thus the openness created by the question is only a station on the way to the all-inclusive "rightness
and truth" (*Recht und Wahrheit*) of what is said (*das Gesagte*).[15] In fact, the (real)
task of hermeneutics, especially in the case of the written text, consists in the
"transformation back" (*Rückverwandlung*) of what has been alienated (*entfrem-
dete Rede*) into "the clear unambiguity of the intended meaning" (*die Eindeutig-
keit des gemeinten Sinnes*).[16] This is what, for Gadamer, defines "hermeneutic
success" (*hermeneutisches Gelingen*).[17]

Dialogue can perform this function of the determination of meaning only
if it is dialectical also in a modern, Hegelian sense. Gadamer often emphasizes
this modern aspect of the dialogue that governs his hermeneutic: "The true
depth of the dialogical principle first enters philosophical consciousness in the
twilight of metaphysics, in the epoch of German romanticism, and then is re-
habilitated in our century in opposition to the subjective bias that characterized idealism."[18] Gadamer has indeed contributed greatly to countering the
preponderance of the modern Cartesian subject by inscribing the individual
within the tradition as the "history of effects." But he eventually had to trans-
form the latter into another subject, the true subject of history, in order to
maintain the authority of the tradition. If for Gadamer the phenomenological
notion of the "horizon" *limits* the power of the individual subject, the related

---

einem so extremen Fall, wie ihn die Hegelsche Dialektik als philosophische Methode darstellt. Die Total-
ität der Gedankenbestimmung zu entfalten, wie es das Anliegen von Hegels Logik war, ist gleichsam der
Versuch, im großen Monolog der neuzeitlichen 'Methode' das Sinnkontinuum zu umgreifen, dessen je
partikulare Realisierung das Gespräch der Sprechenden leistet" [*Wahrheit und Methode*, 351]).

14. See the introduction and chapter 2 in this book; cf. Charles L. Griswold Jr., "Style and Philosophy: The Case of Plato's Dialogues," *Monist* 63, no. 4 (1980): 530–46, and Charles L. Griswold Jr., "Reflection on 'Dialectic' in Plato and Hegel," *International Philosophical Quarterly* 22, no. 3 (1982): 115–30. Drew
Hyland, who presents Gadamer's work with constant reference to Heidegger and his supposedly Aristotelian reading of Plato, misses the Hegelian side of his hermeneutic; see his *Questioning Platonism*, 174, 180,
and passim.

15. *Truth and Method*, 367–68 (German: *Wahrheit und Methode*, 349–50)

16. *Truth and Method*, 393 (German: *Wahrheit und Methode*, 371); *Truth and Method*, 394 (German:
Wahrheit und Methode, 371).

17. *Truth and Method*, 394 (German: *Wahrheit und Methode*, 371).

18. Gadamer, "Text and Interpretation," trans. Dennis J. Schmidt and Richard E. Palmer, in *Dialogue and Deconstruction: The Gadamer-Derrida Encounter*, ed. Diane P. Michelfelder and Richard E.
Palmer (Albany: State University of New York Press, 1989), 27 (German: "Die Tiefe des dialogischen
Prinzips ist . . . erst in der Abenddämmerung der Metaphysik, im Zeitalter der deutschen Romantik, zu
philosophischem Bewußtsein gelangt und in unserem Jahrhundert erneut gegen die Subjektsbefangenheit
des Idealismus geltend gemacht worden" ["Text und Interpretation," in *Gesammelte Werke*, 2:336]).

notion of the "fusion of horizons" reestablishes to some extent the subject in its historical dimension.

Even before introducing the notion of the "history of effects" and of the "fusion of horizons" in the second part of *Truth and Method,* at the end of the first part Gadamer appeals to Hegel and his notion of "interiorizing recollection" (*Er-innerung*) as a model for his own interpretation of works of art of the past, opposing this approach to Schleiermacher's vain attempt to recover the "original setting" of such works. Only through an internalizing "thoughtful mediation" (*denkende Vermittlung*) can we approach the truth of art. Thus for Gadamer, Hegel's "idea of hermeneutics is fundamentally superior to Schleiermacher's."[19] In the second part of *Truth and Method,* it is again in reference to Hegel that the key notion of *wirkungsgeschichtliches Bewußtsein* is formulated: it "is an element in the act of understanding itself and . . . is already effectual in *finding the right questions to ask.*"[20] The Hegelian notion of substance as what is historically pregiven will determine both the possibility and limits of the historical understanding of tradition, and this is what for Gadamer "almost defines the aim of philosophical hermeneutics."[21] The task of asking the right questions in order to display the historical substance of the tradition is entrusted to the hermeneutical dialogue marked by the historically effected consciousness that is instrumental in achieving the eventual "fusion of horizons" (*Horizontverschmelzung*).[22]

But is such a fusion possible at all? Gadamer himself insists on "the one great horizon," on a "single horizon" (*ein einziger Horizont*), insists that we belong to one heritage and tradition.[23] Is not such a single outlook the result of a domination of one horizon, just as in an attempt to have a dialogue in two different languages, "one of the languages always tries to establish itself over the other as the medium of understanding" as if "impelled by the higher force"?[24] In Manfred Frank's view, not a fusion of horizons but rather a subordination of one form of subjectivity to another characterizes Gadamer's hermeneutics, and "the speculative dialogue of effective history ultimately becomes a version

19. *Truth and Method,* 169 (German: *Wahrheit und Methode,* 161).
20. *Truth and Method,* 301 (German: *Wahrheit und Methode,* 285).
21. *Truth and Method,* 302 (German: *Wahrheit und Methode,* 286).
22. *Truth and Method,* 306–7 (German: *Wahrheit und Methode,* 289).
23. *Truth and Method,* 304 (German: *Wahrheit und Methode,* 288).
24. *Truth and Method,* 384 (German: "Bekanntlich ist nichts schwieriger als ein Dialog in zwei fremden Sprachen, von denen der eine die eine, der andere die andere Sprache gebraucht, weil jeder der beiden die andere Sprache zwar versteht, aber nicht zu sprechen weiß. Wie durch eine höhere Gewalt sucht sich alsdann die eine der Sprachen vor der anderen als das Medium der Verständigung durchzusetzen" [*Wahrheit und Methode,* 362]).

of the speculative monologue of the dialectic."[25] In the same vein, Philippe
Forget speaks of Gadamer's "illusion of dialogue" and John Caputo of his
"creeping Hegelianism."[26] The fusion of horizons is for Caputo comparable to
such Hegelian notions as *Aufhebung* (overcoming and preserving, "sublation")
and *Erinnerung* (interiorizing recollection), and it is supposed to maintain a
certain mastery of the tradition.[27] In his reading, Gadamer always tries to find
a common ground that would allow the fusion of horizons, as for example in
his "Amicus Plato Magis Amica Veritas" and "The Proofs of Immortality in
Plato's *Phaedo*," and he is most frustrated when such a common ground is
eluded, as in the famous (non)encounter with Derrida in 1981 in Paris.[28]

But perhaps, as Derrida himself has suggested, it is just such an interrupted
dialogue that reserves the greatest potential for an exchange that respects the
difference, the otherness of the interlocutors.[29] Plato's dialogue *Ion*, which

25. "Limits of the Human Control of Language: Dialogue as the Place of Difference Between Neo-
structuralism and Hermeneutics," trans. Richard Palmer, in *Dialogue and Deconstruction*, 158; but see already
Jürgen Habermas, "A Review of Gadamer's *Truth and Method*," trans. Fred R. Dallmayr and Thomas A.
McCarthy, in *Understanding and Social Inquiry*, ed. Fred R. Dallmayr and Thomas A. McCarthy (South
Bend, Ind.: University of Notre Dame Press, 1977), 335–63 (German: "Zu Gadamers *Wahrheit und Meth-
ode*," in Jürgen Habermas, *Zur Logik der Sozialwissenschaften* [Frankfurt am Main: Suhrkamp, 1970],
251–90); cf. Paul Ricoeur, "Hermeneutics and the Critique of Ideology," in his *From Text to Action*, trans.
Kathleen Blamey and John B. Thompson (Evanston, Ill.: Northwestern University Press, 1991), 270–307
(French: "Herméneutique et critique des idéologies," in *Du texte à l'action* [Paris: Seuil, 1986], 333–77).

26. Phillipe Forget, "Argument(s)," trans. Diane Michelfelder, in *Dialogue and Deconstruction*, 143;
John D. Caputo, *More Radical Hermeneutics: On Not Knowing Who We Are* (Bloomington: Indiana Uni-
versity Press, 2000), 46; see also Catherine H. Zuckert, *Postmodern Platos: Nietzsche, Heidegger, Gadamer,
Strauss, Derrida* (Chicago: University of Chicago Press, 1996), 70 and 72.

27. "Gadamer's hermeneutics is traditionalism and the philosophy of eternal truth pushed to its historical limits. He offers us the most liberal form of traditionalism possible. He introduces as much change
as possible into the philosophy of unchanging truth, as much movement as possible into immobile ver-
ity" (Caputo, *Radical Hermeneutics: Repetition, Deconstruction, and the Hermeneutic Project* [Bloomington:
Indiana University Press, 1987], 113; cf. 111).

28. Gadamer, *Dialogue and Dialectic*, 194–218 and 21–38 (German: "Amicus Plato magis amica veritas,"
in Hans-Georg Gadamer, *Platos dialektische Ethik und andere Studien zur platonischen Philosophie* [Ham-
burg: Meiner, 1968], 251–68, and "Die Unsterblichkeitsbeweise in Platos *Phaidon*," in *Wirklichkeit und
Reflexion: Walter Schulz zum 60. Geburstag*, ed. Helmut Fahrenbach [Pfullingen: Neske, 1973], 145–61). On
the famous (non)encounter, see Philippe Forget, ed., *Text und Interpretation: Eine deutsch-französische
Debatte* (Munich: Fink, 1984).

29. Responding to the reproaches of having interrupted the Paris encounter, and evoking his lifelong
"partage" and "partnership" with Gadamer, Derrida says that this missed encounter "succeeded so well at
being missed that it left an active and provocative trace, a promising trace, with more of a future ahead
than if it had been a harmonious and consensual dialogue" and "far from signifying the failure of the dialogue, such an interruption could become the condition of comprehension and understanding" (*Sovereignties in Question: The Poetics of Paul Celan*, ed. Thomas Dutoit and Outi Pasanen [New York: Fordham
University Press, 2005], 137 and 139) [French: "(Cette rencontre) réussi si bien à être manquée qu'elle laissa
une trace active et provocante, promise à plus d'avenir que ne l'eût été un dialogue harmonieux ou con-
sensuel" and "loin de signifier l'échec du dialogue, telle interruption pouvait devenir la condition de la
compréhension et de l'entente" (*Béliers: Le dialogue ininterrompu; Entre deux infinis, le poème* [Paris: Galilée,

Gadamer has never analyzed in detail, constitutes the model of such an inter-rupted—here most appropriately called rhapsodic—dialogue. *Hermēneia* is indeed the key word in the *Ion*—a dialogue that has recently become the focus of a dialogue and confrontation with Platonism and with the hermeneutical tradition. But the translation of *hermēneia,* taken for granted in this tradition, needs to be and indeed has been questioned. It is not certain that the word can be taken in the rigorous sense of modern hermeneutics as the theory (in the sense of *tekhnē*) of interpretation and then carried back, retranslated into Plato's dialogue. In other words, the word *hermēneia* in *Ion* perhaps requires an "interpretation" different from the one to which it has supposedly given rise in the Western hermeneutic tradition. Heidegger himself seems to have such a reinterpretation in mind in the context of the dialogue between poetry and thought; he explicitly refers to Plato's *Ion* in his "Dialogue on Language."[30]

Indeed, the *Ion* comes the closest to constituting a bridge from the *palaia diaphora* in Plato to the contemporary *Zwiesprache des Denkens mit dem Dichten.*[31] In a concise form, the *Ion* rehearses the terms of the quarrel between philosophy and poetry. If a rhapsode is here the interlocutor of Socrates, it is not only, as is usually maintained, in the role of a modest representative of great (in particular, Homeric) poetry, but also—especially—as the epitome of the whole culture of oral performance and of performative reading, the rhap-sodic mode of both poetry and philosophy. It is in reading the *Ion* that we shall bring together all the discussions of contemporary dialogues with Plato in this book while at the same time gesturing toward an authentic dialogue between poetry and thought.

The Truth of Ion's Rhapsodic Wisdom

Ion: Indeed, I love to hear you wise men talk.
     Socrates: I wish that were true, Ion. But wise? Surely you are the wise men, you rhapsodes and actors, you and the poets whose work you sing. As for me, I say nothing but the truth . . .
                                                                                    —PLATO

The *Ion* is often presented as a companion piece to the *Republic,* in particular to book 10. Most anthologies of literary theory and criticism begin with these

2003], 14 and 21)]). The notion of interrupted dialogue is central to Maurice Blanchot's *The Infinite Con-versation,* trans. Susan Hanson (Minneapolis: University of Minnesota Press, 1993), xxii (French: "Parlant à quelqu'un, il lui arrive de sentir s'affirmer la force froide de l'interruption. Et, chose étrange, le dialogue ne s'arrête pas, il devient au contraire plus résolu, plus decisive, cependant si risqué qu'entre eux deux dis-paraît à jamais l'appartenance à l'espace commun" [*L'entretien infini* (Paris: Gallimard, 1969), xxiv]).

    30. "A Dialogue on Language," in *On the way to Language,* 29 (German: "Aus einem Gespräch von der Sprache," in *Unterwegs zur Sprache,* 122).

    31. "The dialogue of thinking with poetry is long. It has barely begun" (Martin Heidegger, "Language

two texts.[32] The strict opposition between philosophy and poetry clearly formulated in the *Republic* seems also to obtain in the *Ion,* and it governs most
traditional readings of the *Ion* as well. Nickolas Pappas's essay on *Ion* is an
example of such a reading that opposes the philosopher Socrates to Ion, a representative of poetry. Pappas emphasizes this polarity (there is "the most un-
resolvable opposition" between poetry and philosophy) and argues against a
view that might allow one to bring them together; for him, the dialogue "offers
no hope for a reconciliation between poetry and philosophy."[33]

One might well agree with this conclusion of Pappas, except for the note of
regret that it sounds. Indeed, I have maintained all along that "reconciliation
between poetry and philosophy" always involves a subordination of the former
to the latter. Poetry comes out "purified," "sublated," relegated to the irrele-
vance of a "thing of the past." On the other hand, the apparent harshness of
banishment or the dread of a discordance may be considered tokens of distance
and respect, a refusal to understand the other on one's own terms, in other
words, a refusal to "interpret." In the *Ion,* it is the apparently ironic dismissal of
the rhapsode as "divinely inspired" that may be read as a form of such respect-
ful refusal of "masterful" interpretation.

Roochnik, a "dramatic" reader, insists even more on the irreconcilability of
the opposition between poetry and philosophy, although his formulation of the
"old dispute" seems to alter its original Socratic formulation: not only poetry
but also sophistry, rhetoric, and a certain kind of thought are set against philosophy, rather narrowly defined as their other. Roochnik places characters
such as Cleitophon and Callicles on poetry's side, together with a whole line
of Western thinkers: Descartes and Baruch Spinoza, Heraclitus and Nietzsche,
Richard Rorty and Derrida, whom otherwise one would expect to find on the
philosophy side of the dispute. It is apparently because of this broad understanding of the ancient dispute that Roochnik can say that it has not lost its
relevance today; it is "alive and well" and still "frames our most pressing debates."[34] But is this extension and transformation of the meaning of the dispute
legitimate? What about mimesis as a part of the original Socratic formulation?

---

in the Poem: A Discussion on Georg Trakl's Poetic Work," in *On the Way to Language,* 161 [German: "Die
Sprache im Gedicht: Eine Erörterung von Georg Trakls Gedicht," in *Unterwegs zur Sprache,* 39]).

32. The epigraph to this section comes from Plato, *Ion* 532d (trans. Paul Woodruff, in *Plato: Complete
Works,* ed. John M. Cooper and D. S. Hutchison [Indianapolis, Ind.: Hackett, 1997], 940 [Greek: "ΙΩΝ.
χαίρω γὰρ ἀκούων ὑμῶν τῶν σοφῶν. ΣΩ. Βουλοίμην ἄν σε ἀληθῆ λέγειν, Ἷ ...ὦ Ἴων· ... ἀλλὰ σοφοὶ μέν
πού ἐστε ὑμεῖς οἱ ῥαψῳδοὶ καὶ ὑποκριταὶ καὶ ὧν ὑμεῖς δετε τὰ ποιήματα, ἐγὼ δὲ οὐδὲν ἄλλο ἢ τἀληθῆ
λέγω"]).

33. "Plato's *Ion:* The Problem of the Author," *Philosophy* 64, no. 249 (1989): 382–89.

34. *The Tragedy of Reason: Toward a Platonic Conception of Logos* (New York: Routledge, 1990), 205
and 125.

It is after all "the poetry that aims at pleasure and imitation" (*hē pros hēdonēn poiētikē kai hē mimētikē*) that is opposed to *philosophia* in the *Republic* 607b–c.[35]

It is this consideration of mimesis that is lacking in Roochnik's reading of Plato's *Ion*. The profession of Ion, *hermēneia*, is hardly taken into account. He is just a representative of all those who make a claim to *tekhnē* without sufficient credentials, and are thus easily refuted by Socrates ("quite easily refuted").[36] Ion's character appears as particularly naïve and stubborn since he is given a clear chance to "carve for himself an inviolable space, one immune to Socratic refutation."[37] This space would be marked by a refusal to enter "Socrates' game," to abide by the rules of logic, and in particular the principle of non-contradiction, and to enter the world of rigorous distinctions between fields of knowledge.[38] It would be a space of silence, as in Cleitophon's case, or the Muse's inspiration, as in Hesiod's. It is the Muse's inspiration that Socrates offers to Ion in the form of a *theia moira* or divine dispensation, that is, participation in the magnetic chain of enthusiasts, suspended on the power of the Muse herself (534c).[39]

For Roochnik, there is an unbridgeable gap between philosophy and poetry and any attempt to cross over from one realm to the other has disastrous consequences. Roochnik calls Ion foolish ("Ion is made to look extremely foolish") because he ignores this gap.[40] But a rigorous reader of *The Tragedy of Reason* calls its author foolish in his turn. Indeed, C. C. W. Taylor judges Roochnik's argument "confused," "fatally flawed," and "breathtaking in its fatuity."[41] Does Roochnik deserve to be call foolish? As little as Ion, and for the same reasons: the rhapsodic character of his work.

Indeed, Roochnik's book is perhaps, of all the "dramatic" readings we have considered, the one that has the strongest claim to a rhapsodic, dialogic style; Roochnik announces his approach as rhapsodic, even if he doesn't use the word. His project is to exhibit the "Platonic conception of logos" by "giving voice to a competing set of views and forcing them to confront one another." Such a competition, he claims, is "of the essence in Plato's thought."[42] What are these

35. *The Republic*, trans. G. M. A. Grube, rev. C. D. C. Reeve (Indianapolis, Ind.: Hackett, 1992), 278.
36. *The Tragedy of Reason*, 177, 186.
37. *The Tragedy of Reason*, 177.
38. *The Tragedy of Reason*, 183. "Socrates' game" is one of the most common phrases in Roochnik's book; it is instructive to compare it to his notion of an athletic game, which he opposes to the Heraclitean *pais paizōn* ("child's play" [frag. 52]).
39. *The Tragedy of Reason*, 179.
40. *The Tragedy of Reason*, 184
41. C. C. W. Taylor, review of *The Tragedy of Reason: Toward a Platonic Conception of Logos*, by David Roochnik, *Classical Review* 42, no. 1 (1992): 205–6.
42. *The Tragedy of Reason*, xii.

competing views? First of all, Logos (always capitalized), the main character
in his drama, sometimes translated as "reason" but more complex than mere
reason, especially since it is divided into an unconditionally good and condi-
tionally good Logos, the good Logos being aware of its limits. The book's title,
The Tragedy of Reason, refers to the painful progression of Logos, passing from
a hubristic belief in its unconditional goodness to the self-awareness of the
Platonic Logos "knowing itself," that is, knowing its limits. Like Sophocles'
proud king Oedipus, Logos is humbled in its hubristic claims by all those other
characters in Roochnik's book, the "relativists": ancient rhetors, like Protagoras,
Thrasymachus, or the latter's disciple Cleitophon, poets, like Hesiod and Agathon but also the rhapsode Ion, "technicians," like the physician Eryximachus,
appearing in the *Symposium,* and finally the contemporary counterparts of
the ancient relativists, such as Rorty and Derrida.[43] Roochnik, taking his cue
from Socrates in the *Phaedo,* calls them all "mysologists." But they are not only
"haters"; they are successful arguers, able to shake Logos's self-confidence and
lead "him" to a tragic crisis. Here is Logos's outburst in Roochnik's text:

> Logos: "My mind begins to wander, to whirl; I think I may go mad. Can
> this be? I no better than Thrasymachus because I cannot refute Cleito-
> phon? I cannot break beyond this fact. I . . . *one voice among many* and
> not a king who with only his words shapes the world? I . . . not uncon-
> ditionally good? I am but a desire and all desires emanate from the same
> source, the human beings who desire; and this source, this vast mass of
> struggle, cannot possibly sustain the claim of being unconditionally good.
> I fear the old prophet had eyes; I fear I have said too much. Am I guilty
> of the very crime of which I accused others?"
>   Logos trembles . . . and well it should.[44]

What is the status of this and many other "rhapsodic" passages in Roochnik's
book? Do they really reduce Logos to "one voice among many"? Or did the
old critic "have eyes" when, referring to the shared standard of logical coherence, he held Roochnik responsible for the "logical" incoherence in *The Tragedy of Reason?* It seems that the only way to defend Roochnik would be to
challenge his reading of the *Ion.* Only then would his standard of self-reference
be respected: "Throughout this book self-reference has been a standard used
to criticize others. (The relativist, for example, was accused of failing to refer
to himself coherently.) Therefore, the same standard should be used to measure

---

43. Roochnik's hasty coupling of these two last names and his arguing as if the two men represented
a common view is disconcerting; we have seen it already in Griswold (see chapter 2).

44. *The Tragedy of Reason,* 108; my emphasis.

any position this book would advocate."[45] In other words, the validity of Roochnik's mode stands or falls with that of Ion's (or Socrates', or Plato's) when the
Ion is (im)properly read.

The beginning of such a reading is provided by Jacob Klein in the form of
a suggestion to include Socrates among the rhapsodes.[46] Referring to the same
key passage as Roochnik and to the same problematic of truth, Klein goes
beyond its narrowly logical understanding and questions not only Ion's but
also Socrates' claim to truth (*alēthē*). Indeed, after his famous speech explain-
ing the nature of poetry, Socrates asks Ion: "Don't you think that I'm right,
Ion?" and Ion enthusiastically assents: "Lord yes, I certainly do. Somehow you
touch my soul with your words, Socrates, and I do think it's by divine gift that
good poets are able to present these poems to us from the gods" (535a).[47] Thus,
contrary to Roochnik, for whom the truth of the poets can only be defined in
reference to a rational account ("By describing themselves poetically as winged
bees [the poets] relinquish all pretense to a rational justification for themselves"), Klein extends the notion of truth to include poetry: "We *do* assume
that Socrates speaks the truth. But is his long speech a truthful speech? How
can he *know* that beautiful poems are the work of gods? How can he *know* that
this claim of the poets is a true claim?"[48] Yet we do feel that Socrates is right to
suggest the truth of his account, even if this truth cannot be "logically" defined.
Indeed, Socrates *performs* the truth of poetic rhapsody: "Is not [Socrates']
speech, which reaches poetic heights and touches not only Ion's soul, but also
our souls, dictated by a Muse? Or rather, isn't Socrates playing the Muse himself? Indeed, and this is the point, he is."[49] "He is" playing the Muse? Or he
is the Muse? The ambiguity here points toward a dangerous play, apparently
dismissed by Socrates in the *Republic* in favor of a "playful game" and dismissed by Roochnik as child's play in favor of a well-ordered athletic game.[50]
But, in truth, it is precisely this ontological insecurity that marks the seriousness of the rhapsodic play.

45. *The Tragedy of Reason*, 201.
46. "Plato's *Ion*," in *Lectures and Essays*, ed. Robert B. Williamson and Elliott Zuckerman (Annapo-
lis, Md.: St. John's College Press, 1985).
47. *Ion*, trans. Paul Woodruff, 942.
48. *The Tragedy of Reason*, 180; Klein, "Plato's *Ion*," 351; his emphasis.
49. Klein, "Plato's *Ion*," 351; his emphasis.
50. "Without serious and goal-directed activity, we lose ourselves and cannot play well. Heraclitus'
pais paizōn is a distortion" (*The Tragedy of Reason*, 173); see also Drew Hyland, "Athletic Angst: Reflections
on the Philosophical Relevance of Play," in *Sport and the Body: A Philosophical Symposium*, ed. Ellen W.
Gerber (Philadelphia: Lea and Febiger, 1972), 87–94; and Drew Hyland, *The Question of Play* (Lanham,
Md.: University Press of America, 1984). On the other hand, see Fink's notion of a "play without a player"
in Eugen Fink, *Das Spiel als Weltsymbol* (Stuttgart: Kohlhammer, 1960), and his understanding of Heraclitus and Nietzsche in "The Ontology of Play," in *Sport and the Body*, 86.

Rhapsodic play is also compromised in Mihai Spariosu's reading, which, in the spirit of Nietzsche, situates the opposition between poetry or art (*mousikē*) and philosophy in its historical context.[51] The archaic culture of poetry and of the rhapsodic performance was being supplanted in Socrates' and Plato's time by serious, "logo-rational" thought: the rhapsode, writes Spariosu, should have appeared in the fourth century BCE as a "living fossil of archaic times."[52] It is this change that is reflected in the *Ion*. Spariosu maintains, and even emphasizes, a doctrinal opposition between the serious and the playful, which supports his view of the historical break with rhapsody. Rhapsody is playful, whereas philosophy is serious: "Socrates does not have time for play, he is engaged in a serious business." This is why he refuses to attend Ion's performance: "The rhapsode's performance would end all serious (philosophical) discourse, opening up the world of play, in which one participates without reflection or criticism."[53] This radical opposition is operative, according to Spariosu, not only in this but in other dialogues of Plato as well. Now, to maintain such an opposition is to ignore the fact that in the *Ion,* and, as we saw in the first chapter, in the *Republic* as well, Socrates "himself" takes the role of a rhapsode and that from this perspective Plato's own "authorial perspective" might suffer.[54]

It is true that at first sight, this dialogue resembles the other dialogues that dismiss or subjugate the supposed arts or crafts (*tekhnai*) to the rule of a rational philosophical method. Ion appears similar to those other pretended craftsmen who are unable to justify their competence, such as Gorgias, Protagoras, Euthyphro, or Hippias. Just like they, he has some difficulties delimiting his field of competence, the object of his *tekhnē*, of his supposedly rigorous art or craft. And it is again *ergon* (function or job) that appears as the criterion of exactness necessary to constitute the competence of Ion's *tekhnē*. Even the models of such competence are the same as in the first book of the *Republic:*

51. "Plato's *Ion: Mimesis, Poetry, and Power,*" in *Mimesis, Semiosis, and Power,* vol. 2 of *Mimesis in Contemporary Theory: An Interdisciplinary Approach,* ed. Ronald Bogue (Philadelphia: John Benjamins, 1991), 13–26. For an account of the rhapsodic mode in Nietzsche, see chapter 2 of this book.

52. "Plato's *Ion,*" 14.

53. "Plato's *Ion,*" 15.

54. "Plato's *Ion,*" 23. When Spariosu complains that "not many modern philosophers seem to take this dialogue seriously," he overlooks the "blend of play and seriousness" that in "Plato's" view, but also in that of contemporary thought, marks a "true philosopher" ("Plato's *Ion,*" 14). It is to this philosophical blend that we need to be attentive in "interpreting" the dialogues, and in particular the *Ion,* which sets into play the very notion of *interpretation.* Here, Spariosu's neglect of Jean-Luc Nancy's playfully serious text on the *Ion,* "Sharing Voices," is significant. The only author Spariosu critically refers to is Edith Hamilton ("Plato's *Ion,*" 14). *Ion* apparently also resists other readings in light of the thesis of the transition from the oral to the written tradition in Plato. Havelock, in his attempt to reduce Homer to an imposing encyclopedia, later resisted by Plato, does not refer even once to *Ion* in his chapter "Plato on Poetry," where one would expect to find it as a crucial text; the whole chapter is based on the *Republic* and *Laws* (*Preface to Plato* [1963; rpt., Cambridge, Mass.: Harvard University Press, 1982], 3–19).

the art of navigation and medicine. Socrates asks Ion rhetorically: "Then to each profession a god has granted the ability to know a certain function [*ergon*]. I mean the things navigation teaches us—we won't learn them from medicine, will we?" And Ion agrees: "Of course not" (537c).[55] The method of clear distinctions, of rigor, and of the proper *ergon,* seems to be carried over from the *Republic.* It even appears to be established more securely here, since the gentle, apparently naive Ion does not offer a resistance comparable to that of the fierce Thrasymachus and sophisticated Protagoras. Over and over again, he disclaims any pretension to competence in the professional fields that Socrates points out in Homer's text. He is neither a seer, nor a charioteer, nor a doctor. Any of those real craftsmen would be better prepared to judge the appropriateness of Homer's description when he talks about the performance of their peers: prophesizing, racing, preparing medicines.

And yet, Ion does claim to be able to talk about Homer in general and about any particular passage in the epics better than anyone. His first prize at the festival in Epidamnus and his high hopes as to the competition in Athens—never really questioned or derided in the dialogue—make him an honest representative of the profession of rhapsodes (rather than a delusional eccentric), that is to say, if there were such a profession (*tekhnē*). And this is precisely the point. The competence of a craftsman is general and well determined but that of Ion is singular and unlimited: everything that pertains to Homer.

When pressed by Socrates to declare what it is that he is able to spell out in Homer, to put in words better than anyone, Ion says: "What it's fitting [*ha prepei*] for a man or a woman to say—or for a slave or a freeman, or for a follower or a leader" (540b).[56] This is an important divergence from the theory of the rigorous separation of types in the *Republic,* which aligned political with professional status. Here, Ion clearly distinguishes the words proving people's expert knowledge from the words expressing their very being (gender, free status, and so forth), and he claims to be a good judge only as to the latter. Thus a field seems to open where professional competence would no longer obtain, where the rhapsode (and the poet) might want to establish his/her "competence." *Hermēneuein* would be the word marking this paradoxically noncompetent competence in the domain of discourse appropriate to each person's existence in the world of Homer and hence in the world in which Homer's world plays an important role.

With respect to the problem of professional competence, the dramatic attitude of Ion is different from that of Socrates' interlocutors in, for example,

---

55. *Ion,* trans. Paul Woodruff, 945.
56. *Ion,* trans. Paul Woodruff, 947.

Gorgias, Euthyphro, or *Protagoras.* Ion does not follow the philosopher into his supposed domain of logical argument but remains firmly on the rhapsodic terrain of mimetic presentation. He very much admires Socrates' "performance," and he may be more sincere in his admiration than Socrates is when he praises Ion's costume. Is it not, in fact, this amused attitude of Ion that entices Socrates actually to venture into the field of rhapsody and to try to circumscribe it from within? The function of the "theory" of inspiration (*enthusiasmos*) and the divine share (*theia moira*) that together connect a long series of followers (from the Muse down to us, the spectators) would be in this case to "give an account" of this particular field. But rhapsody, which as mediation epitomizes the whole series of artistic processes, does not constitute a rigorously delimited field comparable to those of arts and crafts (*tekhnai*). A rhapsode such as Ion cannot display any strictly professional identity except for being, as rhapsode, precisely "beside himself," always outside of himself, in a constant ec-stasy. And it is because of this becoming-another that he participates in poetic experience and is able to dis-play as *hupokritēs* and judge the behavior of those he impersonates or into whom he almost metamorphoses himself. Rhapsody is thus the apparent contrary of professional sobriety and distance from one's object of expertise, the opposite of expert specialization and objectification. Socrates is right to compare Ion to Proteus, a mythical figure capable of taking all kinds of shapes.

But Ion is also, like Proteus, not exactly out of his mind. He knows very well what he is doing when he monitors the reaction of his spectators: "I look down at them every time from up on the rostrum, and they're crying and looking terrified, and as the stories are told they are filled with amazement. You see, I must keep my wits and pay close attention to them: if I start them crying, *I* will laugh as I take their money, but if *they* laugh, I shall cry at having lost money" (535e).[57] Just like the imperfect craftsmen in the *Republic,* who combined moneymaking with the proper *ergon* of their craft, Ion cares about his salary and thus about the effects of his performance.

How should we reconcile these two apparently opposed motives in Ion's attitude? Is he not sincere when he says that when he "tell[s] a sad story, [his] eyes are full of tears" and that when he "tell[s] a story that is frightening or awful, [his] hair stands on end with fear and [his] heart jumps" (535c)?[58] In fact, the play between sincerity and simulation is another characteristic of both a rhapsode and an artist. It is only the logician displayed, and thus exposed, by Socrates that would require such a strict separation between absolutely

---

57. *Ion,* trans. Paul Woodruff, 943; his emphasis.
58. *Ion,* trans. Paul Woodruff, 943.

sincere and absolutely insincere behavior. But a rhapsode, like Denis Diderot's actor, would incarnate the very being of an artist: a combination of rapture and calculation.[59] He could also be compared to the actor in Brecht's epic theater, who has some of these "rhapsodic" characteristics; he should at once narrate (*erzählen*) and represent, impersonate, dis-play (*darstellen*) a character.[60]

But does not this double characterization apply to Socrates as well—not only, in an obvious way, to the inspired Socrates of the *Phaedrus* but also to the Socrates of *Ion?* Was it not, in fact, because of this common, rhapsodic mode of display that Brecht decided to call his theater "epic" and that it was later called "Socratic" and "Platonic" theater?[61] We have observed in all the preceding chapters a constant rapprochement between poetry and philosophy, in spite of their radical separation in Socrates' formulation of the old quarrel and the efforts of modern interpreters to uphold it.[62] We noticed the rhapsodic form of the *Republic,* with Socrates as a narrator. We saw Socrates' rhapsodic palinode or recantation in the *Phaedrus.* In the *Sophist,* one could hardly miss the resemblance between the Socrates familiar from Plato's other dialogues and the sophist/rhapsode.[63] And in the *Timaeus,* the all-receiving chora was compared to Socrates as the (feminine) host of (rhapsodic) discourse. In the *Ion,* there is a direct association between the rhapsode, representing the culture of poetic presentation and display, and the philosopher, whose attitude toward this culture is ambiguous. Indeed, Socrates' fascination with Homer here goes past a formal declaration of love, in the tenth book of the *Republic.* He seems to take pleasure in quoting the *Iliad* and the *Odyssey* at length, well beyond the necessity of exemplifying his points in the argument (or is it "Plato" who

59. "The Paradox of Acting," trans. Walter Herries Pollock, in *"The Paradox of Acting" by Denis Diderot and "Masks or Faces?" by William Archer* (New York: Hill and Wang, 1957), 11–74 (French: "Le paradoxe sur le comédien," in Denis Diderot, *Oeuvres esthétiques* [Paris: Garnier, 1968], 299–381).

60. "A Short Organum for the Theatre," ed. and trans. John Willett, in *Brecht on Theater* (New York: Hill and Wang, 1964), 194 (German: "Kleines Organon für das Theater," in Bertolt Brecht, *Schriften zum Theater* 2: *Gesammelte Werke,* vol. 16 [Frankfurt am Main: Suhrkamp, 1963–64], 684–85).

61. It was so called by Walter Benjamin in "What is Epic Theater?" and "The Author as Producer," and by Stanley Mitchell in his introduction to the English translation of Benjamin's essays on Brecht: *Understanding Brecht,* trans. Anna Bostock (London: Verso, 1983), 1–13 and 85–103 (German: "Was ist das epische Theater?" (first version) and "Der Autor als Produzent," in *Versuche über Brecht* [Frankfurt am Main: Suhrkamp, 1966], 17–29 and 101–19]).

62. See, for example, Paul Ricoeur's insightful comments on the relation between philosophy and poetry in his *The Rule of Metaphor: Multidisciplinary Studies of the Creation of Meaning in Language,* trans. Robert Czerny (Toronto: University of Toronto Press, 1977), 18, 280ff., and passim (French: *La métaphore vive* [Paris: Seuil, 1975], 18, 356ff., and passim), and compare it with Roochnik's insistence on the lack of common ground between the two (*The Tragedy of Reason* 139, 182, 192, and passim).

63. The sophists often dressed like rhapsodes in order "to emphasize their continuation of the function of the poets in earlier days," writes G. E. R. Lloyd in *The Revolutions of Wisdom: Studies in the Claims and Practice of Ancient Greek Science* (Berkeley: University of California Press, 1987), 83ff.

decides to give this rhapsodic part to Socrates?). But why is Ion not given more
of a chance to display his skills here? Why are his offers to make a presentation frustrated? The traditional explication—that Socrates (and Plato) is not
interested in performance but in argument about it—doesn't hold in the face
of Socrates' own performance. The only justification for this fact seems to
be "Plato's wish" to make a philosopher impersonate a rhapsode. Only in such
becoming-another would Socrates be able to "talk best" about what is proper
to a rhapsode, about his/her "nature."

We have already noticed, however, that there is no such a thing as the rhapsode's proper *ergon* (function, task, defining nature). The rhapsode is a Proteus,
able to take on all shapes. To be sure, this does not prevent him, any more than
it did Proteus, from displaying a particular, prophetic wisdom. And it is perhaps this wisdom (*sophia*) that philosophy needs to acquire in order to be able
to claim its universal competence. For is not philosophy as hard put as rhapsody to legitimate a pretension to rigorous competence in a well-delimited
field or, even more so, a pretension to govern all knowledge? Ion's incompre-
hensible but certain mastery of the Homeric world might be in fact what
Socrates envies him.

The "theory" of *hermēneia* as *theia moira*, of the series of rings, and of *enthusiasmos* would then be less an ironic rebuttal of Ion's pretensions, as most interpreters take it to be, than a serious questioning of the enigma within both
rhapsodic and philosophical competence. *Hermēneuein* would not mean "to
interpret," in the sense of translating into the plain language of a univocal, or
at least rigorously polysemic, meaning, but rather "to announce," "to bring
tidings," "to share a certain knowledge." At the very beginning of the dialogue,
Socrates, praising the profession of the rhapsode, insists on the fact that a
rhapsode knows not only the verses of the poet but his thought (*dianoia*
[530b–c]) as well. In order to become a good rhapsode, one has to understand
(*sunein*) "what is said by the poet" (*ta legomena hupo tou poiētou*): "A rhapsode
must come to present the poet's thought to his audience" (*ton gar rhapsōidon
hermēnea dei tou poiētou tēs dianoias gignesthai tois akouousi* [530c])—more literally, a rhapsode has to generate for his audience *hermēnea* of the poet's
thought— and he can't do that beautifully unless he knows (*gignōskonta*) what
the poet says (*hoti legei*).[64] The translation of *ta legomena* as "what is meant"

---

64. *Ion*, trans. Paul Woodruff, 938; translation modified; by translating "τὰ λεγόμενα" as "what is
meant" and "ὅτι λέγει" as "what the poet means," Woodruff suggests the necessity of interpretation in the
ordinary sense; the verb "συνείη," translated by "understand," can be the third person aorist optative active
of both "σύνειμι" ("to be with") and "συνίημι," which means first of all "to bring" or "to set together" (also
in a fight) and only second ("metaphorically") "to perceive, hear, be aware of, observe, understand" (from
"ἵημι," "to let go, utter, throw").

and *hoti legei* as "what the poet means" strongly suggests the necessity of interpretation in the ordinary sense. But to be acquainted with what the poet says is different from understanding exactly what he means. The latter implies placing the poet's words in a fixed and rigorous conceptual system. The former leaves open the question of meaning, allowing for the *legomena* by the poet to be presented as something *pollakhōs legomena*, or "said in many ways."[65] In this case, a certain polysemy or even "dissemination" of the poet's saying would be preserved rather than reduced in the process of interpretation.

The central passage on *hermēneia* as the essential task of both rhapsody and poetry confirms this view. In the "chain" of enthusiasts suspended by the magnet or the Heraclean stone of divine inspiration, the poets occupy the first ring; they are the "hermeneuts" of the god:

> Socrates: . . . poets are nothing but representatives of the gods [*hermēnēs eisin tōn theōn*], possessed by whoever possesses them. To show *that,* the god deliberately sang the most beautiful lyric poem through the most worthless poet. Don't you think I'm right, Ion?
> Ion: Lord yes, *I* certainly do. (534e–535a)[66]

The rhapsodes are in the middle of the chain of magnetic rings, conveying the poet's message to the audience. They are mediators par excellence:

> Socrates: And you rhapsodes in turn present what the poets say.
> Ion: That's true too.
> Socrates: So you turn out to be representatives of representatives.
> Ion: Quite right. (535a)[67]

Paul Woodruff's translation of *hermēnēs* as "representatives" rather than, for example, "interpreters" seems to reintroduce here the representational structure of the *Republic*. Indeed, the designation of rhapsodes as "representatives of representatives" might evoke the critique of the poets in the tenth book of the *Republic* as imitators of imitators, thrice removed "from the king and the truth." But the *hermēneia* in the *Ion* is not exactly equivalent to *mimēsis*, certainly not in the sense of representation or imitation as copying, and far

---

65. Aristotle refers this formula to being as such qua being ("τὸ δὲ ὂν λέγεται μὲν πολλαχῶς"), but he immediately feels the need to unify those multiple ways ("ἀλλὰ πρὸς ἓν καὶ μίαν τινὰ φύσιν" [*Metaphysics* 1003a33–34]).

66. *Ion,* trans. Paul Woodruff, 942.

67. *Ion,* trans. Paul Woodruff, 942.

from being distanced from being and political truth, *hermēneuein* would in fact be the truth of communal being.

The Dialogical Play of Being and Thinking

[The Greek verb] *hermeneuein* is related to the noun *hermeneus,* which is referable to the god Hermes by a play of thinking that is more compelling than the rigor of science.

—MARTIN HEIDEGGER

Much, from the morning onwards,
  Since we have been a dialogue and have heard from one another
  Has human kind learnt; but soon we shall be song.

—FRIEDRICH HÖLDERLIN

Heidegger, who quotes the passage on poets and rhapsodes from the *Ion* in his "Dialogue on Language," translates *hermēnēs* as "messengers" (*Botschafter*).[68] His English translator interprets this as "interpreters," thus, again, bringing Heidegger's reading back within the hermeneutical tradition of Plato scholarship. To be sure, in what precedes this passage, Heidegger does bring together *hermēneuein* and *Auslegen,* a word usually translated as "interpretation" and interpreted within the context of traditional hermeneutics. But the point is not, perhaps, to bring this notion into conformity with that tradition but, on the contrary, to question it from the perspective of the Platonic notion of *hermēneuein* and of a view of poetry different from the one obtained in the most common reading of the *Republic.* The very notions of *Auslegung* and of *interpretation* will then need to undergo a reexamination.

The context of the reference to Plato's dialogue in Heidegger's own dialogue makes it clear that this is not a casual remark but rather an essential inscription of the theme of *hermēneuein* within the text—and perhaps within the whole previous development of Heidegger's thought, which it sketches. Indeed, "A Dialogue on Language" begins with the question of hermeneutics; Heidegger mentions the tradition of Schleiermacher and Wilhelm Dilthey and refers to his own position in *Being and Time* regarding this question, but this is not the end of it.[69] Later in the "Dialogue," he (or rather the Inquirer—*ein*

---

68. The first epigraph to this section comes from "A Dialogue on Language," 29; translation modified (German: "[Das griechische Zeitwort ἑρμηνεύειν] bezieht sich auf das Hauptwort ἑρμηνεύς, das man mit dem Namen des Gottes Ἑρμῆς zusammenbringen kann in einem Spiel des Denkens, das verbindlicher ist als die Strenge der Wissenschaft" ["Aus einem Gespräch von der Sprache," 121]). The second epigraph comes from Hölderlin's poem "Celebration of Peace," in Friedrich Hölderlin, *Poems and Fragments,* trans. Michael Hamburger (London: Anvil Press Poetry, 1994), 523 (German: "Viel hat von Morgen an, / Seit ein Gespräch wir sind und hören voneinander, / Erfahren der Mensch; bald sind wir aber Gesang" ["Friedensfeier," *in Gedichte.* (Stuttgart: Philipp Reclam, 2000), 319]).

69. "A Dialogue on Language," 10, 11 (German: "Aus einem Gespräch von der Sprache," 96–98).

Fragender, who explicitly appears here as the author of *Being and Time* and some of Heidegger's other writings) and the Japanese return to the notion of hermeneutics, and Heidegger emphasizes the inadequacy of his previous treatment of the question; he only "told stories . . . showing how [he] came to employ the word [hermeneutics]."[70] He is willing, though, to continue his reflection on the question of hermeneutics, reemphasizing his earlier opposition to the way this question has been understood within the tradition: "I emphasized that 'hermeneutics' [*das Hermeneutische*], used as an adjunct word [*Beiwort*] to 'phenomenology,' did not have its usual meaning, methodology of interpretation [*Methodenlehre des Auslegens*], but the interpretation [*Auslegen*] itself."[71]

This is not, however, an exact account of what was said in the beginning. There, the Inquirer claimed that in *Being and Time,* "hermeneutics mean[t] neither the theory of the art of interpretation [*die Lehre von der Auslegungskunst*], nor interpretation itself [*das Auslegen selbst*], but rather the attempt first of all to define the nature of interpretation [*das Wesen der Auslegung*] from the hermeneutic experience [*aus dem Hermeneutischen*]."[72] Why this apparent discrepancy between the initial statement and its later "reformulation," or rather, how does that discrepancy function within the dialogue? An obvious result is the attention drawn to the notion of *Auslegen* and *Auslegung* and, most importantly, the difficulty of conceiving an *Auslegen* itself, in other words, the difficulty of formulating a rigorous concept of interpretation. Both *"Auslegen* itself" and the "nature of *Auslegung"* convey the problematic character of "interpretation," which seems to resist definition.[73]

The very notion of methodological rigor, however, perhaps needs to be reconsidered. When the Japanese requests "a more precise explanation of the terms 'hermeneutics' and 'hermeneutic,'" the Inquirer responds by hinting at Plato's playful etymology linking *hermēneus* to the messenger of the gods, Hermēs, pointing out the more compelling, more binding (*verbindlicher*) character of "a play of thought" (*ein Spiel des Denkens*), perhaps even more "rigorous" than the "rigor of science" (*die Strenge der Wissenschaft*).[74] And the

70. "A Dialogue on Language," 28 (German: "Aus einem Gespräch von der Sprache," 120).

71. "A Dialogue on Language," 28; translation modified (German: "Aus einem Gespräch von der Sprache," 120). The translation of "das Hermeneutische" is difficult; "hermeneutic experience" is meant to bring up the parallel with the "experience with language," discussed in the next text within the collection: "Das Wesen der Sprache."

72. "A Dialogue on Language," 11 (German: "Aus einem Gespräch von der Sprache," 97–98).

73. There doesn't seem to be an essential difference between "die Auslegung" and "das Auslegen"; the latter, a nominalized verb, might suggest more strongly the progressive character of the process of "interpretation."

74. "A Dialogue on Language," 29 (German: "Aus einem Gespräch von der Sprache," 121). Not exactly "playful thinking," in Hertz's translation, which might suggest a possibility of a partnerless *Erörterung.*

play of *hermēneuein,* the "play of thought," in turn becomes inseparable from poetry, once the poets are designated as the initial messengers of the divine (*hermēnēs . . . tōn theōn, Botschafter . . . der Götter*).[75] The play of *hermēneuein* in Plato thus becomes an opening of the dialogue between poetry and thought, which presupposes the equal status of both participants.

This is why the translation of *Botschafter* as "messengers" is so crucial. Peter Hertz's translation-interpretation of both *hermēnēs* and *Botschafter* as "interpreters," as I noted, brings Socrates' statement within the purview of traditional hermeneutics, disregarding Heidegger's attempt to undermine this tradition. But *Botschafter* are hardly "interpreters," and their task is explicitly distinguished from interpretation by the Inquirer: "Hermeneutics [*das Hermeneutische*] does not mean in the first place the interpretation [*nicht erst das Auslegen*] but, even before it, the bearing of message and tidings [*das Bringen von Botschaft und Kunde*]."[76]

Heidegger's reading of Hölderlin's poem "In Lovely Blueness . . ." in " . . . Poetically Man Dwells . . ." supplements these reflections on *hermēneuein* and makes the role of poetry even more prominent. If, for Heidegger, the human being (*der Mensch*) herself or himself is eventually defined as the hearer of the message (*die Botschaft*) of the twofold of presence and present beings (*die Zwiefalt vom Anwesen und Anwesendem*), it is perhaps because she or he is always engaged in the hermeneutic series that begins with the poets as the messengers of the divine.[77] It is in terms of this participation in the endless process of *hermēneia*—that is, eventually, in the experience with the nature of language—that one may say with Hölderlin that the human being "dwells poetically on this earth."

Poetic dwelling—which can only be achieved in conjunction with others, through an insertion in the process of hermeneutic "communication"—is here shown to be an existential condition of every human being rather than the exceptional activity of a few individuals. In terms of *Being and Time,* this poetic condition grounds the authentic existence of human Dasein. At the same time, the concessive "yet" (*doch*), which separates the "full of merit" (*Voll Verdienst*) from "poetically man dwells" in Hölderlin's poem (*Voll Verdienst, doch*

---

75. "A Dialogue on Language," 29 (German: "Aus einem Gespräch von der Sprache," 122).

76. "A Dialogue on Language," 29; translation modified (German: "Aus einem Gespräch von der Sprache," 122).

77. "A Dialogue on Language," 40; translation modified (German: "Aus einem Gespräch von der Sprache," 135). As the hearer of the message, the human being stands in "the hermeneutical relation" ("hermeneutischer Bezug") bringing the tidings of the message of the twofold: "Man is the message-bearer of the message which the two-fold's unconcealment speaks to him ("A Dialogue on Language," 40 [German: "Der Mensch ist der Botengänger der Botschaft, die ihm die Entbergung der Zwiefalt zuspricht" ("Aus einem Gespräch von der Sprache," 136)]).

dichterisch / wohnet der Mensch), indicates the strangeness of *dichterisches Wohnen* in respect to the common notion of dwelling. The role of the poet is to measure this dwelling in all its strangeness, to measure the dimension, the span between sky and earth that contains human existence: "Poetry is this measure-taking— its taking, indeed, for the dwelling of man."[78] This is a "strange measure" (*ein seltsames Maß*), says Heidegger, and it is undoubtedly also the measure of the strangeness of the human being.

Such strangeness, and its measure, are to be found in language itself, pro- vided one is able to hear it. Thus poetry as a measure taking becomes at the same time an apprenticeship to hearing the strangeness of language. Indeed, if the ("highest and everywhere the first") "appeal of language" (*Zuspruch der Sprache*) is that to which the human being responds when she or he speaks, poetry is the primary instance of such a response.[79] The measure taking of poetry does not consist in a "clutching" (*Zugriff*) or a "grasping" (*Greifen*) of the thing according to a received standard, in other words, in a conceptual (*begrifflich*) interpretation, but rather in the "letting come of what has been dealt out, shared out" (*Kommen-lassen des Zu-Gemessenen*).[80] The same kind of receptivity is required for *hearing* poetry. Again, as opposed to a "conceptual grasping" and an interpretation of the poet's meaning, this hearing belongs to the experience of "enthusiasm" and the "inspiration" of the *theia moira,* or divine sharing, in the process of *hermēneuein,* that is, the process of receiving and transmitting a message, an "announcement."

Heidegger sees the eventual fulfillment of this process of reception and transmission in the dialogue between poetry and thought. This is apparent both in " . . . Poetically Man Dwells . . ." and in the "Dialogue on Language." In the former, an important "parenthetical remark" (in fact essential to Heideg- ger's reading) reveals his view on the nature of the dialogue in question, despite the fact that he does not use the word "dialogue" here. Poetry and thinking (*das Dichten und das Denken*), he writes, encounter each other (*begegnen sich*) in the same (*im selben*) rather than being subsumed under an empty overall concept: an "empty indifferent oneness of what is merely identical" (*das leere*

78. " . . . Poetically Man Dwells . . . ," in Martin Heidegger, *Poetry, Language, Thought,* trans. Albert Hofstadter (1971; rpt., New York: HarperCollins, 2001), 221 (German: " . . . Dichterisch wohnet der Mensch . . . ," in *Vorträge und Aufsätze* [Stuttgart: Neske, 1954], 192). "The nature of the dimension is the meting out—which is lightened and so can be spanned—of the between: the upward to the sky as well as downward to earth" (" . . . Poetically Man Dwells . . . ," 218 [German: "Das Wesen der Dimension ist die gelichtete und so durchmeßbare Zumessung des Zwischen: des Hinauf zum Himmel als des Herab zur Erde" (" . . . Dichterisch wohnet der Mensch . . . ," 189)]).

79. " . . . Poetically Man Dwells . . . ," 214 (German: " . . . Dichterisch wohnet der Mensch . . . ," 184).

80. " . . . Poetically Man Dwells . . . ," 222 (German: " . . . Dichterisch wohnet der Mensch . . . ," 193).

Einerlei des bloß Identischen).[81] In fact, only what is essentially different (*verschieden*) can be brought together as the same.[82] Sameness and difference do not exclude each other; on the contrary, they belong (have to "be thought") together: "We can only say 'the same' (*das Selbe*) if we think difference (*der Unterschied*). It is in the carrying out and settling (*im Austrag*) of differences that the gathering nature of sameness comes to light. The same banishes all zeal always to level what is different into the equal and identical."[83] The terms of the encounter between poetry and thought here return to Heidegger's rethinking of Nietzsche's notion of the raging discordance between art and truth, one that might eventually turn into a felicitous discordance (*ein beglückender Zwiespalt*) both in Plato and in Nietzsche.[84] In these encounters there is an essential play between sameness and difference that points to the essence of the true dialogue, ultimately a dialogue on the nature of language.

In the text just quoted, Heidegger uses the word *Austrag*—translated by Albert Hofstadter as "carrying out and settling"—in order to mark the essential relationship between poetry and thinking. It is remarkable that in another text, the essay "Language," the same word *Austrag* translates the Greek *diaphora*—"difference" but also "quarrel" or "dispute."[85] We are indeed familiar with the *palaia diaphora,* the old quarrel between philosophy and poetry. Heidegger's translation and interpretation itself thus suggests the rapprochement between Plato's old quarrel and the dialogue between poetry and thought.

In "Language," *diaphora* or *Austrag* refer to the intimacy (implied in both the Latin and the English *inter* and in the German *unter*) *between* the thing and the world. The German word *Unter-schied,* which Heidegger hyphenates in this text, combines this intimacy with separation (*Scheidung*). The *diaphora* or *Austrag* of the dif-ference is in the case under discussion the "carrying out that carries through" (*dia-phorein* or *aus-tragen*) of the "world in(to) its worlding" and of "things in(to) their thinging."[86] World and things do not exist separately before the dif-ference, nor are they in fusion (*Verschmelzung*). They are first

81. ". . . Poetically Man Dwells . . . ," 216 (German: ". . . Dichterisch wohnet der Mensch . . . ," 187). In "the same" rather than in "one and the same," as the translator has it; the same or united (*einig*) is precisely never one (*Einer or Eines*), as Hölderlin's epigram "Root of All Evil" ("Wurzel allen Übels"), quoted by Heidegger (". . . Poetically Man Dwells . . . ," 217 [German: ". . . Dichterisch wohnet der Mensch . . . ," 187]), emphasizes.

82. On the originary metaphysical position of the same and of difference itself, see Martin Heidegger, *Identity and Difference,* trans. Joan Stambaugh (1969; rpt., Chicago: University of Chicago Press, 2002) (German: *Identität und Differenz* [Pfullingen: Neske, 1957]).

83. ". . . Poetically Man Dwells . . . ," 216 (German: ". . . Dichterisch wohnet der Mensch . . . ," 187).

84. See chapter 2 in this book.

85. "Language," in *Poetry, Language, Thought,* 200 (German: "Die Sprache," in *Unterwegs zur Sprache,* 25).

86. "Language," 200; translation modified [German: "Die Sprache," 25).

brought to presence and manifested in their nature (*Wesen*), that is, "in their "being toward one another" (*ihr Zueinander*), precisely in the medium of difference. The latter is neither a distinction nor a relation but rather a dimension (*Dimension*), since it "measures out and apportions" (*er-mißt*) world and thing.[87] It is in fact this measuring and apportioning of the difference that, through an opening (das *Eröffnen*), allows the "separateness and towardness [*Aus- und Zueinander*] of world and thing [*Welt und Ding*]" to come to presence.

It is Georg Trakl's poem "A Winter Evening" ("Ein Winterabend") that, in "Language," is said to bid (*heißen*) things and the world to come to presence, to come together at the point of their encounter, that is, in the middle (*die Mitte*) as the "carrying out of intimacy" (*der Austrag der Innigkeit*).[88] This carrying out that carries through of the middle is itself called for in the third stanza of the poem. The second line—"Pain has turned the threshold to stone" (*Schmerz versteinerte die Schwelle*)—has for Heidegger a particular significance in establishing the ground for world and things to appear. Indeed, pain as the dif-ference itself—rending and separating and at the same time drawing everything to itself—secures the between of the encounter between world and things. It is Trakl's poem that names pain, as well as the petrified threshold, and, in the preceding stanzas, calls for things and world to come. But for us, the readers of the poem and of Heidegger's essay, the medium of the *Unterschied* as well as the encounter between world and things, between earth and sky, between humans and divinities only fully emerges from the dialogue between Trakl and Heidegger, one that perhaps corresponds to Heidegger's own notion of a dialogue between poetry and thought.

But, one might object, how does Heidegger's reading differ from the kind of ordinary interpretation that we so firmly rejected at the outset of this chapter? To be sure, there is no criterion that would allow an easy distinction; however, one would certainly have to consider the question of the reader's/interpreter's mastery over her or his text. The notion of a meaning that is to be determined or at least approached always entails a subordination of the text to an interpretive act. Perhaps the only way to preserve the text's autonomy, on the other hand, is to do what a rhapsode does: to recite the text almost verbatim and then, eventually, to respond to it in another, different voice. Heidegger acknowledges this necessity in the case of his response to Hölderlin; they don't speak of poetic dwelling in the same way, he says, but nevertheless he is "thinking the same thing that Hölderlin is saying poetically."[89] Certainly,

---

87. "Language," 199–200 (German: "Die Sprache," 24–25).
88. "Language," 201 [German: "Die Sprache," 26].
89. ". . . Poetically Man Dwells . . . ," 216 (German: "denken wir das Selbe, was Hölderlin dichtet" [". . . Dichterisch wohnet der Mensch . . . ," 187]).

one cannot deny Heidegger's patience in reciting the poet's "own" words. On the other hand, it would be difficult not to recognize Heidegger's "own" voice when, in response to Trakl's poem, he names, for example, the fourfold of earth and sky and of humans and divinities as well as the dif-ference (*Unterschied* or *Austrag*) as the medium of their emergence. Is this not, then, a form of the "intimate separation," the *Unter-schied* that would obtain in the case of the "quarrel" (*diaphora*) between philosophy and poetry, of the dialogue (*Gespräch*) between poetry and thought, or of the discordance (*Zwiespalt*) between art and truth? We have seen (in chapter 2) that Heidegger, in his dialogue/confrontation with Nietzsche and Plato, suggested such a characterization of the discordance in terms of the intimate separation of dif-ference. And there is just such an intimate separation between what is in fact emerging as Heidegger's "own" thought and the text of the poems that he reads, one in which he asks not what the poem means but rather what the poet's saying uncovers, makes appear—something that, as the poet Ingeborg Bachmann says, can only "emerge from an exchange with the poem."[90]

The Rhapsodic Community of Shared Voices

Being is that which we announce to each other; unless it is the very fact of announcing ourselves to each other, in a "long chain"—poetic, magnetic, rhapsodic.

—JEAN-LUC NANCY

Two questions that punctuate Heidegger's "Dialogue on Language," the question of hermeneutics and interpretation, on the one hand, and the question of language, on the other, are finally suspended there.[91] The character of the "Inquirer" is not in a hurry to give conclusive answers. Both questions eventually lead to the question of dialogue (*Gespräch*), which, rather than designating every sort of talk between people (*jedes Miteinanderreden*), would be restricted to a "focusing on the reality of language" (*die Versammlung auf das Wesen der Sprache*).[92] It is at this moment that the Japanese visitor considers the question of whether Plato's dialogues, the epitome of this genre in the West,

90. Ingeborg Bachmann, *Werke*, 4 vols., ed. Christine Koschel, Inge von Weidenbaum, and Clemens Münster (1978; rpt., Munich: Piper, 1982), 4:202, cited in Sabine I. Gölz, "Reading in the Twilight: Canonization, Gender, the Limits of Language—and a Poem by Ingeborg Bachmann," *New German Critique* 47 (1989): 29–52.

91. The epigraph to this section comes from Nancy's "Sharing Voices," 244, translation modified (French: "L'être est ce que nous nous annonçons les uns aux autres. A moins que l'être ne soit *que* nous nous annonçons les uns aux autres, en une 'longue chaîne' poétique, magnétique et rhapsodique" [*Le partage des voix*, 83]).

92. *Unterwegs zur Sprache*, 151; *On the Way to Language*, 52.

would be dialogues by the Inquirer's lights (*In diesem Sinne wären auch Platons Dialoge keine Dialoge?*). If one accepts the strict requirements of the "Inquirer," then perhaps Plato's dialogues would not be dialogues, not in the true sense of the word, not dialogues sui generis (*ganz eigener Art*).[93]

In these concluding remarks, I would like to take up for the last time the problematic suggested by the visitor's question, which is in fact the problematic underlying this whole book: are Plato's dialogues real dialogues? And what are dialogues sui generis? Heidegger himself wishes to leave this question open (*die Frage offenlassen*), and one cannot escape the impression that it is this very openness that would mark the *eigene Art* of the dialogue.[94] It is suggested that such a dialogue would arise from the experience of language and would question rather than affirm the identity of the speakers. The Inquirer requires "that the kind of dialogue is determined by the provenance of the address to those who seemingly are the only speakers [can seemingly speak by themselves]— men, human beings" (*daß sich die Art eines Gespräches aus dem bestimmt, von woher die dem Anschein nach allein Sprechenden, die Menschen, angesprochen sind*).[95] And what addresses men in a true dialogue is "the nature of language" (*das Wesen der Sprache*), which is perhaps itself dialogical. Presented in this way, the argument might appear circular. What the Inquirer says is only that "wherever the nature of language were to speak, to say [*ansprüche, ansagte*] to men as saying [*als die Sage*], *it*, Saying, would bring about the real dialogue [*das eigentliche Gespräch*]," and the Japanese completes the thought by distinguishing between speaking "about" (*über*, also "above") and "of" (*von*, also "from") language; only speaking "of" or "from" qualifies as true dialogue.[96] The emphasis is here on passive receptivity rather than on the intentional act of a speaking subject with its corresponding object. Hearkening to the nature of language, then, rather than attempting to objectify it, would be a true dialogic—or, one might say, rhapsodic—attitude.

The questioning of an intended semantic univocity is what distinguishes Heidegger's notion of dialogue not only from the ordinary "dramatic" interpretation but also from the hermeneutic tradition both before and after his

---

93. "A Dialogue on Language," 52 (German: "Aus einem Gespräch von der Sprache," 151). Drew Hyland's declaration that "Plato is never mentioned" (*Questioning Platonism*, 18) in "A Dialogue on Language" is puzzling since it is precisely the reference to Plato's dialogues that launches the investigation into the nature of dialogue sui generis; Plato's *Ion* is explicitly mentioned in Heidegger's dialogue some thirty pages earlier, and it is Socrates' definition of the poets and rhapsodes as "ἑρμηνῆς" or "Botschafter" (messengers) that reintroduces the discussion of hermeneutics ("das Hermeneutische") in this text ("A Dialogue on Language," 28ff. [German: "Aus einem Gespräch von der Sprache," 120ff.]).

94. "A Dialogue on Language," 52 (German: "Aus einem Gespräch von der Sprache," 151).

95. "A Dialogue on Language," 52 (German: "Aus einem Gespräch von der Sprache," 151).

96. "A Dialogue on Language," 52 (German: "Aus einem Gespräch von der Sprache," 152).

own intervention in its history. And his dialogue with Plato is, in Jean-Luc Nancy's view, the best example of the rhapsodic exchange that listens and announces rather than interprets: "By no means does Heidegger interpret Plato: he allows him to be his hermeneut. They announce the same thing; they make the same *hermēneia:* that *logos* is a sharing, our sharing, which brings us together only in dividing."[97] Nancy's *partage,* or sharing, supplements here the "intimate separation" of Heidegger's *Unter-schied* with the idea of destiny (*moira, Geschick*) and perhaps the idea of "playing a *part*" in the actor's and rhapsode's sense. Our share is to play a part in the chain of *hermēneuein,* in the exchange of messages, of announcements, epitomized by the magnetic, rhapsodic chain of the *Ion.*

A true dialogue, or rather dia-logue, would thus be a *partage du logos* ("sharing of the logos") rather than an exchange of opinions in pursuit of an agreement, reasonable consensus, and so forth—a common understanding of the word "dialogue." The logos brings us together in dividing us, connects, "stitches" the parts. The German *Gespräch* of Hölderlin and Heidegger, Nancy suggests, "implies *Ge-flecht* (interlacing) or is caught within *Ge-flecht.*"[98] "Perhaps one should say that the *Geflecht* is what provides the order or the nature of the *Ge* of *Gespräch:* that is to say, a 'collective' (that is the ordinary nature of the *Ge-*) yet with the function of 'inter' (*entre-,* interlacement, dialogue) and finally of a *dia-* that is not dialectical (*ne dialectise pas*) but that shares and divides (*partage*). What interlaces us divides us, what divides us interlaces us."[99] Nancy's play with etymology is remarkable here, comparable in its rigor to that of Heidegger's play with the god-messenger Hermes and *hermēneia.*[100]

97. "Sharing Voices," 245; translation modified (French: "Heidegger n'interprète nullement Platon: il le laisse être son herméneute. Ils annoncent la même chose, ils font la même *hermeneia:* que le *logos* est un partage, notre partage, ce qui ne nous rassemble qu'à nous partager" [*Le partage des voix,* 84]). Ormiston's "he always allows himself to be Plato's hermeneut" is an unwarranted interpretation that refuses to take into account the radical transformation of the "hermeneutic context."

98. On Plato's notion of *sumplokē* and its Heideggerian translation *Geflecht,* see chapter 2 of this book.

99. "Sharing Voices," 259 n. 57; translation modified. Ormiston's "correction" of the passive voice ("What we interlace we share, what we share we interlace") is particularly inappropriate here (French: "Le *Gespräch* implique un *Ge-flecht,* ou est pris dans le *Geflecht.* Peut-être faudrait-il dire que le *Geflecht* est ce qui donne le régime ou la nature du *Ge* du *Gespräch:* c'est-à-dire un 'collectif' (c'est dans la nature ordinaire du *Ge-*), mais avec la fonction d'un *entre-* (entrelancement, entretien), et finalement d'un *dia-* qui ne dialectise pas, mais qui partage. Ce qui nous entrelace nous partage, ce qui nous partage nous entrelace" [*Le partage des voix,* 86–87]).

100. Cf. Bakhtin's play on the Russian word событие ("sobytie"), or "event," composed of the prefix co- or c- ("with," Greek συν-) and бытие, or "being" (from быть, "to be")—a rapprochement made by Lacoue-Labarthe and Nancy in "Le dialogue des genres." Bakhtin constantly uses the word "sobytie" to designate the dialogical nature of truth (истина, "istina"). Truth is perhaps, in Bakhtin's view, by its very nature (по природе) communal, rhapsodic (событийна), and only a genuine dialogue (существтенный диалог) is likely to reveal it; see *Problems of Dostoevsky's Poetics,* trans. Caryl Emerson (Minneapolis:

Of course, logos itself can carry this meaning of assembling, as in col-lecting (from *cum* and *legere*), for example in *anthologia,* or "collection of flowers." It was certainly the principal trait of Heraclitus's *logos,* to the listening of which he enjoined his contemporaries.[101] It is this logos that divides and interlaces us (*nous partage et nous entrelace*) according to Nancy. Its dynamic role is partic-ularly important; the being-with or *logos* is there before "we" are. And it is itself being divided, without the possibility of being "dialectized," *aufgehoben,* sub-lated. It is only to be read—*legendum est.*

Indeed, the rhapsodic community is first of all a community of readers. The essential incompleteness of (the human) being—the *principe d'insuffisance, d'incomplétude,* which Blanchot elaborates in a dialogue with Bataille as the answer to the question "Why 'community'?"—is that of the essential lacunae in any text.[102] They do not imply a necessity for completion. On the contrary, the "principal" incompleteness and finitude of (human) being has to be preserved in the community, just as the lacunary character of the text is to be preserved in the rhapsodic *hermēneia.* This is particularly apparent in those dialogues of Plato that ostensibly present *hupomnēmata* or *memorabilia,* designed to refresh the memory of another event.

The narration in such dialogues does not seem all that reliable; we saw this when analyzing Socrates' account of the conversation reported in the *Repub-lic.* In some dialogues other intermediaries are introduced, rendering the chain of rhapsodic voices longer and even less reliable. This structure is relatively simple in *Parmenides,* where the encounter between a very old Parmenides and very young Socrates is recounted by Pythodorus, who witnessed it, to Anti-phon, who memorized it as a young man and now, a long time after having

---

University of Minnesota Press, 1984), 81, cf. 279-80 and passim (Russian: Михаил Михаилович Бахтин, Проблемы поэтики Достоевского [Москва: Советский Писатель, 1963], 107, cf. his Эстетика Словесного Творчества, 2nd ed. [Москва: Издательство "Искусство,"1986], 196-97). Bakhtin's view on Plato's dialogues and their relationship to Dostoevsky's dialogic mode underwent a remarkable change in this respect from the first (1929) to the second (1963) edition of his Dostoevsky book.

101. Heraclitus frag. 50, in Hermann Diels, *Die Fragmente der Vorsokratiker,* 6th ed., 3 vols., ed. Walther Kranz (1952; rpt., Zurich: Weidman, 1985), 1:161.

102. "The existence of every being thus summons the other or a plurality of others. . . . It therefore summons a community: a finite community, for it in turn has its principle in the *finitude* of the beings which form it and which would not tolerate that it (the community) forget to carry the *finitude* consti-tuting those beings to a higher degree of tension" (Blanchot, *The Unavowable Community,* trans. Pierre Joris [New York: Station Hill Press, 1986], 6 [French: "Ainsi, l'existence de chaque être appelle l'autre ou une pluralité d'autres. . . . Il appelle, par là, une communauté: communauté finie, car elle a, à son tour, son principe dans la *finitude* des êtres qui la composent et qui ne supporteraient pas que celle-ci (la com-munauté) oublie de porter à un plus haut degré de tension la *finitude* qui les constitue" (*La communauté inavouable* [Paris: Minuit, 1983], 16-17)]). Cf. Jacques Derrida, "Plato's Pharmacy," in Jacques Derrida, *Dissemination,* trans. Barbara Johnson (Chicago: University of Chicago Press, 1982), 63 (French: "La phar-macie de Platon," in *La dissémination* [Paris: Seuil, 1972], 79) and chapter 2 above.

lost all interest in philosophy, tells it from memory to Cephalus; we the readers participate in this dialogue between Antiphon and Cephalus. The chain of
voices/witnesses is longer and more complex in the *Symposium,* where the dialogue and the speeches at the party of Agathon are narrated by Aristodemus to
Apollodorus, who tells it to a friend in the dialogue that we are witnessing as
readers; besides this, at the party, Diotima, one of the chief characters, speaks
in the voice of Socrates. But the supposed eyewitness Aristodemus doesn't remember all the speeches—how could he, since he falls asleep during the event
he narrates? In *Theaetetus,* the series of levels is further complicated by the
use of writing. The conversation between Socrates, Theodorus, and young
Theaetetus had been narrated to Euclides, who wrote down a memoir (*hupomnēmata*) of it (the accuracy of which he then checked with Socrates). We are
not reading these *hupomnēmata,* however, but a report of their reading by a
rhapsode/reader. The account follows the dialogue between Euclides and his
friend Terpsion, who has just met the dying Theaetetus. Euclides explains that
he somewhat simplified the narration by suppressing the constant intervention
of the rhapsode Socrates:[103]

> Euclides: This is the book, Terpsion. You see, I have written out the con-
> versation like this: I have not made Socrates narrate [*diēgoumenon*] it
> as he did, but as talking directly [*dialegomenon*] with the persons with
> whom he said he had this conversation. . . . I wanted, in the written ver-
> sion, to avoid the bother of having the bits of narrative in between the
> speeches [*hai metaxu tōn logōn diēgēseis*]—I mean, when Socrates, when-
> ever he mentions his own part in the discussion, says "And I maintained"
> or "I said," or, of the person answering, "He agreed" or "He would not
> admit this." That is why I have made him talk directly to them [*diale-
> gomenon*] and have left out these formulae.
> Terpsion: That is quite fitting [*ouden ge apo tropou*], Euclides.
> Euclides: Come boy, take the book and read [*lege*]. (143b)[104]

103. See my introduction, p. 14 and chapter 1, pp. 52–54.
104. *Theaetetus,* trans. by M. J. Levett, rev. Myles Burnyeat, in *Plato: Complete Works,* ed. John M.
Cooper and D. S. Hutchison (Indianapolis, Ind.: Hackett, 1997), 159. Ruby Blondell seems to describe
rhapsodically the "ventriloquation of a ventriloquation" in the *Theaetetus,* referring to Socrates' impersonation of Protagoras (the words are "put into the dead Protagoras' mouth by Socrates, into Socrates'
mouth by the fictitious author Eukleides, and into *his* mouth by Plato, then read aloud many years later,
in the dialogue's preamble, by Eukleides' slave"), and she concludes that "Protagoras is . . . unimaginably
far from speaking 'for himself'" (*The Play of Characters in Plato's Dialogues* [Cambridge: Cambridge University Press, 2002], 21). However, she uses this and other similar texts to oppose speaking for another
to speaking in one's own voice; and later in her book, she will insist on Plato's ultimate control of the situation, arguing that such ventriloquation "forcefully reminds us that it is the power of Plato's imagination

Thus, Plato "himself" is perhaps hinting at the keyword to authentic *hermē-neia*—*lege,* read. What does it mean to "read" here? For the "boy" (*pais*)—a euphemism for a slave—it means to be a rhapsode and thus to play a free man for a while, to impersonate and to become, in turn, a mathematician, a philosopher, a young student. In other words, it means to upset, at least to a point—but precisely the point feared by Socrates in the *Republic*—the established social order, established "typology." The reader, however, should imagine another reader, another "boy-rhapsode," reading and playing the parts of Terpsion and Euclides, playing the part of the "author" in the process of composing her or his text. For indeed, in its original context, the whole dialogue, including the frame, had to be read, that is, at least to a point, performed. For the readers of the dialogue, aware of the complex process of writing and of its mode of delivery, reading thus has to be rhapsodic, that is, "writerly" and "performative," marked by spacing, absence, distance, and *partage*.[105]

Such *partage,* or sharing, has always already been inscribed in the mimetic/rhapsodic process of its transmission. The transitivity of the "dia-" of *dia-logos* is always already in the process of *hermēneuein,* which is the essence of both the logos and the human being as *logon ekhōn,* or "having, possessing logos," in the Aristotelian definition. However, contrary to the common interpretation of Aristotle's formula, this characterization of human being in terms of *hermēneuein,* as sharing her or his voice within the community, divests her or him of the (illusion of) certain "possessive" mastery over the message (the text). It would be, rather, the divine logos of human destiny (the *theia moira* of the *Ion*) that "possesses" human being: the poet, the rhapsode, the reader. This rhapsodic-hermeneutic mediation constitutes, in Nancy's words, the finitude of "the endless end to the end of the dialogue." It is the perfect model for the limitation of the mono-logical understanding of logos (as in Western logocentrism).[106] If the human being "possesses" logos in any way, it would always be the divided/dividing and shared/sharing logos of the dialogue.

Nancy carries out this extension of the poetic and rhapsodic condition to the human condition as such—an extension that the length of the hermeneutic chain in *Ion* (it could become "a very long chain" [533e]) had already

---

that is conjuring and controlling all the characters . . . and hence that his representations too are inescapably colored by a personal perspective and agenda" (309).

105. The names of Roland Barthes and John L. Austin have to be mentioned here, even though a discussion of their work is beyond the scope of this study.

106. See also Heidegger's own understanding of the Platonic dialogue as "breaking through the prattle" ("das Durch-brechen des Geredes") in his early 1924–25 lecture course, *Plato's "Sophist,"* trans. Richard Rojcewicz and André Schuwer (Bloomington: Indiana University Press, 1997), 135 (German: *Platon: "Sophistes"* [Frankfurt am Main: Klostermann, 1992], 195).

suggested and that Heidegger articulated in terms of Hölderlin's "poetic dwelling"—elaborating a thought of human finitude and communal life based on
the sharing (*partage*) of singular voices.[107] Singularity is, indeed, the major
characteristic of the rhapsode, but perhaps also inherent to human being as
such. Ion's attachment to Homer epitomizes this singularity. There is no science of the universal that would not require being partitioned into singular
voices, those of Homer, of Ion, of Socrates, of the boy-reader in the *Theaetetus*.
The so-called universal logos that Socrates often credits in Plato's dialogues with
the merit of refuting the arguments of his opponents would be nothing without being transmitted through Socrates' own singular voice and through the
voice of the rhapsode-reader. And in the end, it is the singular voice that determines not only the mode of the dialogues but also the rhapsodic and dialogic
nature of human beings. Contrary to traditional hermeneutics, the rhapsodic
dia-logos is not directed toward the appropriation of a "meaning" or "logos"
but rather toward the realization of its inappropriability.[108]

This dia-logic inappropriability of a definite meaning corresponds to the
finitude of human beings. A singular voice is essentially incomplete, always
divided and directed toward another being or other beings. In the rhapsodic dialogue of singular voices "[n]o meaning originates . . . , nor is any
achieved . . . , but an always other announcement is delivered there: precisely
that of the other."[109] And Nancy is careful not to capitalize the "other," so as
not to suggest a general, essentialized meaning, to the knowledge of which the
singular voices in the dialogues would contribute.[110]

Nor would the other of the rhapsodic dialogues be, in Plato's terms, the
Other (*thateron*) of *Timaeus*—entangled in the chiasm with the Same and at
risk of being submitted to it in the demiurge's bending of the chiasm into a
circle (a hermeneutic circle?)—but rather the chora as a third genre, which
would prevent such a bending by enabling, but at the same time frustrating,
the mimetic foundation of the world: a generous, all-receiving medium of
cosmic inscription. Such generosity should be that of the hermeneut in a rhapsodic hermeneutics, a generosity that responds to the generosity of meaning—
perhaps the only meaning of, or direction of, meaning (*sens du sens*)—which

107. *Ion*, trans. Paul Woodruff, 941.

108. Cf. Giorgio Agamben's definition of criticism as the safeguarding of the "inappropriability" (of
the sense) "as its most precious possession" (*Stanzas: Word and Phantasm in Western Culture*, trans. Ronald
L. Martinez [Minneapolis: University of Minnesota Press, 1993], xvii [Italian: *Stanze: La parola e il fan-
tasma nella cultura occidentale* (Torino: Einaudi, 1977), xiv]).

109. "Sharing Voices," 245 (French: *Le partage des voix*, 85).

110. In this respect, Gadamer's rapprochement between hermeneutics and semantics in his *Philosophical Hermeneutics*, trans. and ed. David E. Linge (Berkeley: University of California Press, 1976),
82–94, is significant.

gives and exposes itself ("Meaning gives itself, abandons itself"; *Le sens se donne, il s'abandonne*).[111] And the participants in the dialogue that we have encountered in the preceding chapters—Socrates and the Stranger, Plato and Nietzsche, the sophist and the voice of Eurycles, woman and chora, Euclides and his boy-reader, Heidegger and Nancy, Derrida, Irigaray, and others—will also have participated in this hermeneutic generosity of meaning/direction (*sens*), which is also that of language itself. Like Ion, like his archetype Proteus, like the boy-reader, they all are "able to play all the parts, and also able to confound the parts, so as not to allow their distinction [*ne plus permettre de les départager*]."[112] Nancy's *partage des voix*, or sharing voices, expresses such a potentially double effect of the dialogical rhapsody: dividing and joining, stitching together and tearing asunder.

Will this omnipresence of the rhapsodic mode result in the subordination of philosophy to its old rival, poetry? Indeed, Nancy's "sharing" explicitly refers to what we have analyzed in terms of the old quarrel: "This sharing is also that of philosophy and poetry."[113] But, as he hastens to add, "it does not assign them either place or meaning."[114] Indeed, mimesis, the rhapsodic mimesis first introduced in the third book of the *Republic,* is fundamentally an-archic. Poets, actors, and rhapsodes to a certain extent escape the sanctioned order, the hierarchy, of the state and of the philosophical system that is supposed to uphold it. When extended beyond the domain of poetry and art, the rhapsodic mode will not be able to assume the position of power. The origin of the hermeneutic "order," the Muse, should itself be understood as a gift, a dia-logic address, an origin without compulsion, a divine dispensation of *theia moira:* "The *dia-logue* can only be, perhaps, another name for the *theia moira,* that is to say, *hermē-neia,* this dialogue in which Plato himself is Proteus, in turn Socrates and Ion, in turn Ion and Homer, in turn Homer and Plato. This sharing, this dia-logy, does not allow itself to be seized—and the mastery of Socrates is, in a sense, nothing more than, if one can speak in this way, the mastery of this recognition."[115]

111. "Sharing Voices," 244 (French: *Le partage des voix,* 83).

112. "Sharing Voices," 245; translation modified (French: *Le partage des voix,* 84). On the protean character of mimesis and of language itself, see Dennis J. Schmidt, *On Germans and Other Greeks: Tragedy and Ethical Life* (Bloomington: Indiana University Press, 2001), 31, and his reference to Hölderlin and Foucault in chapter 1, n. 25.

113. "Sharing Voices," 245 (French: "Ce partage est aussi celui de la philosophie et de la poésie" [*Le partage des voix,* 84]).

114. "Sharing Voices," 245 (French: "Il ne leur assigne pas de place ni de sens" [*Le partage des voix,* 84]).

115. Nancy, "Sharing Voices," 242; translation modified (French: "Le *dia-logue* n'est peut-être qu'un autre nom de la *theia moira,* c'est-à-dire de *l'hermēneia,* ce dialogue dans lequel Platon lui-même est le Protée, tour à tour Socrate et Ion, tour à tour Ion et Homère, tour à tour Homère et Platon. Ce partage, cette dia-logie ne se laisse pas saisir—et la maîtrise de Socrate n'est en un sens rien de plus, si on peut dire, que la maîtrise de cet aveu." [*Le partage des voix,* 79–80]).

194   Rhapsody of Philosophy

"Rhapsodic mastery" would be the acknowledgment of the impossibility and unwillingness, of the "incompetence," that belongs not only to the rhapsode Ion but also to Socrates, to the Stranger, and to others, including the often perplexed readers of Plato's dialogues. A potential confusion of roles, statuses, genres, and genders in such a mode—of which the resemblance between the sophist and Socrates in the *Sophist* appeared as the most striking example— will never lead to a monological identity of rigorously defined types. The aporetic character of Plato's dialogues, even of those that ostensibly end in the unity of an agreement, results from this rhapsodic nonauthority.

It is not surprising that, considered from the point of view of this renunciation of mastery, the rhapsodic mode will later constitute for Nancy the point of departure for a thought of community that will challenge the common view of Plato's politics. The thought of the "inoperative community" (*communauté désœuvrée*) begins with sharing (*partage*), although a radicalized sharing, said to precede the voices that might otherwise be taken as autonomous. "Being in common," an expression that in *The Inoperative Community* explicates the sharing of voices, is "absolutely" originary, if that is, one can speak of an originary an-archy or lack of origin. Such being-in-common makes the individual paradoxically, irreducibly divisible and divided (*partagé*) and for this reason finite and transcendent, that is, open to sharing (*partage*) with others.

This opening to others, a quintessentially rhapsodic stance, is not an essential characteristic. In fact, the lack of work, of the opus in the inoperative community (of the oeuvre in *la communauté désoeuvrée*), designates precisely the lack of essence, of the *ergon* that, as we have seen in the first chapter, defined rigor (*akribeia*) as the principle of justice in Plato's *Republic*. There, the poets, actors, and rhapsodes were blamed for promoting "injustice," that is, lack of rigorously defined type or function (*ergon*), and as such became sacrificial victims (*pharmakoi*) to be sacrificed for the sake of the perfect community. Here, in this most radical version of community, the inoperative community, the community without types, *erga,* or *opera,* the *par-ergonal* rhapsode becomes the epitome of the finite singular being, marked by nothing other than the turning toward others in language, thus allowing the language of being-in-common to come through, to open the way to a rhapsodic community—not a future community (*communauté d'avenir*) but a community to come (*communauté à venir*), always in the process of coming, a finite community of finite beings, incomplete but without hope of completion, engaged in a dialogue without end, a dialogue that we are.[116]

116. A comparable vision of an an-archic rhapsodic community is offered by Giorgio Agamben, *The Coming Community*, trans. Michael Hardt (Minneapolis: University of Minnesota Press, 1993) (Italian: *La comunità che viene* [Torino: Einaudi, 1990])—a community that is always in the making since it is always

The apparent reversal of the "Platonism" of the *Republic* in the model of the inoperative community should be viewed within the context of the play of/with representation that we analyzed in the preceding chapters. The danger of the hypnotically persuasive force of, say, Wagner's theater, of the empire of simulacra, or of the mythical, forceful ordering of chaos according to the ideal model is always present in the form of the ideological effects of representation, interdependent with the dominant political order.[117] It is only the serious play in the rhapsodic mode of reading, which we found both in Plato's dialogues and in the contemporary dialogue with Plato, that, constantly touching the limits of representation without pretending to cross them or to conclude, allows for the continual questioning of the order of rigorously fixed identities and divisions.

Plato's dialogues, like the dialogues with Plato analyzed in this book, are "dialogues sui generis" (*ganz eigener Art*) not because they stage conversations between dramatic characters in a "dialogue form" but because they are able to initiate a "very long chain" of rhapsodic voices, singular voices without rigorously fixed (semantic, political, ethical, aesthetic) identities, voices able in their turn not only to "stitch" together diverse messages but also to cut through (*dia-*) the *logos* or *muthos* of the language that would sanction the established hier-archy—and thus to engage in an an-archic dia-logos.

---

threatened by conservative inertia toward (political, familial, national, professional) belonging and identity. This community is formed around "[t]ricksters or fakes, assistants or 'toons'" (*The Coming Community*, 11 [Italian: "tricksters o perdigiorno, aiutanti o toons" (*La comunità che viene*, 14)]), in other (Platonic) words, "mimetic gentlemen" or rhapsodes; see my essay "The Matter of Language: A Dialogue Between Poetry and Philosophy in Agamben's Critical Thought," *Rivista di Studi Italiani* 22, no. 2 (2004): 198–220. "A dialogue that we are" modifies the phrase "we have become a discourse" (Hamburger's translation) from Hölderlin's poem "Celebration of Peace," quoted by Heidegger in "The Way to Language," in *On the Way to Language*, 135 (German: "ein Gespräch wir sind," in "Der Weg für Sprache," in *Unterwegs zur Sprache*, 266).

117. In Nancy's *Inoperative Community*, it is the play between the invention of myth and its interruption through literature that averts such a danger.

Selected Bibliography

Agacinski, Sylviane, et al. *Mimésis des()articulations.* Paris: Aubier-Flammarion, 1975.

Agamben, Giorgio. *The Coming Community.* Translated by Michael Hardt. Minneapolis: University of Minnesota Press, 1993. (*La comunità che viene* [Torino: Einaudi, 1990].)

———. *Means Without End: Notes on Politics.* Translated by Vincenzo Binetti and Cesare Cesarino. Minneapolis: University of Minnesota Press, 2000. (*Mezzi senza fine: Note sulla politica* [Torino: Bollati Boringhieri, 1996].)

———. *Potentialities: Collected Essays in Philosophy.* Edited and translated by Daniel Heller-Roazen. Stanford, Calif.: Stanford University Press, 1999.

Allison, David B. *The New Nietzsche: Contemporary Styles of Interpretation.* Cambridge, Mass.: MIT Press, 1985.

———. *Reading the New Nietzsche.* Lanham, Md.: Rowman and Littlefield, 2001.

Althusser, Louis. "Ideology and Ideological State Apparatuses." In Louis Althusser, *Lenin and Philosophy and Other Essays.* Translated by Ben Brewster. New York: Monthly Review Press, 1971. ("Idéologie et appareils idéologiques d'état," in Louis Althusser, *Sur la reproduction.* Edited by Jacques Bidet, 269– 314 [Paris: Presses Universitaires de France, 1995].)

———. "On Brecht and Marx." Translated by Max Statkiewicz. In Warren Montag, *Louis Althusser,* 136–49. New York: Palgrave Macmillan, 2003.

———. *Sur la philosophie.* Paris: Gallimard, 1994.

Ammianus Marcellinus. *Rerum gestarum libri qui supersunt.* Latin/English text. Translated by John C. Rolfe. 1939. Reprint, Cambridge, Mass.: Harvard University Press, 1972.

Annas, Julia. *An Introduction to Plato's "Republic."* Oxford: Clarendon Press, 1981.

———. "Plato on the Triviality of Literature." In *Plato on Beauty, Wisdom, and the Arts.* Edited by Julius Moravcsik and Philip Temko, 1–28. Totowa, N.J.: Rowman and Littlefield, 1982.

Arieti, James A. *Interpreting Plato: The Dialogues as Drama.* Savage, Md.: Rowman and Littlefield, 1991.

Aristophanes. *The Acharnians, The Knights, The Clouds, The Wasps.* Translated by Benjamin Bickley Rogers. 1924. Reprint, Cambridge, Mass.: Harvard University Press, 1982.

Aristotle. *The Metaphysics.* Greek/English text. Translated by Hugh Tredennick. 1933–35. Reprint, Cambridge, Mass.: Harvard University Press, 1990.

———. *The Nicomachean Ethics.* Greek/English text. Translated by Harris Rackham. 1926. Reprint, Cambridge, Mass.: Harvard University Press, 1982.

———. *The Poetics.* Greek/English text. Edited and translated by W. Hamilton Fyfe. 1927. Reprint, Cambridge, Mass.: Harvard University Press, 1982.

————. *The Poetics.* Translated by Stephen Halliwell. Chapel Hill: University of North Carolina Press, 1987.

Artaud, Antonin. *The Theater and Its Double.* Translated by Mary Caroline Richards. New York: Grove Weidenfeld, 1958. (*Le théâtre et son double* [1938]. In Antonin Artaud, *Œuvres complètes,* vol. 4:9–137 [Paris: Gallimard, 1978]).

Ashbaugh, Anne Freire. *Plato's Theory of Explanation.* Albany: State University of New York Press, 1988.

Aubenque, Pierre. *Le problème de l'être chez Aristote.* Paris: Presses Universitaires de France, 1962.

Ausland, Hayden W. "On Reading Plato Mimetically." *American Journal of Philology* 118, no. 3 (1997): 371–416.

Babich, Babette E. "*Mousikē Technē:* The Philosophical Practice of Music in Plato, Nietzsche, and Heidegger." In *Between Philosophy and Poetry: Writing, Rhythm, History.* Edited by Massimo Verdicchio and Robert Burch, 171–80. New York: Continuum, 2002.

Bachmann, Ingeborg. *Werke.* 4 vols. Edited by Christine Koschel, Inge von Weidenbaum, and Clemens Münster. 1978. Reprint, Munich: Piper, 1982.

Bakhtin, Mikhail. *Problems of Dostoevsky's Poetics.* Translated by Caryl Emerson. Minneapolis: University of Minnesota Press, 1984. (Проблемы поэтики Достоевского [Москва: Советский Писатель, 1963].)

Barish, Jonas. *The Anti-Theatrical Prejudice.* Berkeley: University of California Press, 1981.

Barker, Stephen, ed. *Signs of Change: Premodern—Modern—Postmodern.* Albany: State University of New York Press, 1996.

Barnes, Jonathan. "Heidegger spéléologue." *Revue de Metaphysique et de Morale* 95, no. 2 (1990): 173–96.

Barthes, Roland. *The Pleasure of the Text.* Translated by Richard Miller. New York: Hill and Wang, 1975. (*Le plaisir du texte* [Paris: Seuil, 1973].)

————. *The Rustle of Language.* Translated by Richard Howard. 1986. Reprint, Berkeley: University of California Press, 1989. (*Essais critiques IV: Le bruissement de la langue* [Paris: Seuil, 1984].)

————. *S/Z.* Translated by Richard Miller. New York: Hill and Wang, 1974. (*S/Z* [Paris: Seuil, 1970].)

Baudrillard, Jean. *Illusion, désillusion esthétiques.* Paris: Sens and Tonka, 1997.

————. *Simulacra and Simulation.* Translated by Sheila Faria Glaser. Ann Arbor: University of Michigan Press, 1994. (*Simulacres et simulation* [Paris: Galilée, 1981].)

————. *Simulations.* Translated by Paul Foss, Paul Patton, and Philip Beitchman. New York: Semiotext[e], 1983.

Benardete, Seth. *The Argument of the Action: Essays on Greek Poetry and Philosophy.* Chicago: University of Chicago Press, 2000.

————. *Socrates' Second Sailing: On Plato's "Republic."* Chicago: University of Chicago Press, 1989.

Benjamin, Walter. *Illuminations: Essays and Reflections.* Translated by Harry Zohn. New York: Schocken, 1969. (*Illuminationen* [Frankfurt: Suhrkamp, 1955].)

————. *Understanding Brecht.* Translated by Anna Bostock. London: Verso, 1983. (*Versuche über Brecht* [Suhrkamp, 1966].)

Berger, Harry, Jr. "Levels of Discourse in Plato's Dialogues." In *Literature and the Question of Philosophy.* Edited by Anthony J. Cascardi, 75–100. Baltimore, Md.: Johns Hopkins University Press, 1987.

———. "The Origins of Bucolic Representation: Disenchantment and Revision in Theocritus' Seventh *Idyll.*" *Classical Antiquity* 3, no. 1 (1984): 1–39.

———. "*Phaedrus* and the Politics of Inscription." In *Textual Fidelity and Textual Disregard.* Edited by Bernard P. Dauenhauer, 81–103. New York: Peter Lang, 1990.

———. "Plato's Flying Philosopher." *Philosophical Forum* 18, no. 4 (1982): 385–407.

Blanchot, Maurice. *The Infinite Conversation.* Translated by Susan Hanson. Minneapolis: University of Minnesota Press, 1993. (*L'entretien infini* [Paris: Gallimard 1969].)

———. *The Space of Literature.* Translated by Ann Smock. Lincoln: University of Nebraska Press, 1982. (*L'espace littéraire* [Paris: Gallimard 1955].)

———. "Traces." *La Nouvelle Revue Française* 10, no. 129 (1963): 472–80.

———. *The Unavowable Community.* Translated by Pierre Joris. New York: Station Hill Press, 1988. (*La communauté inavouable* [Paris: Minuit, 1983].)

Blondell, Ruby. *The Play of Character in Plato's Dialogues.* Cambridge: Cambridge University Press, 2002.

Bogue, Ronald., ed. *Mimesis, Semiosis, and Power.* Vol. 2 of *Mimesis in Contemporary Theory: An Interdisciplinary Approach.* Philadelphia: John Benjamins, 1991.

Böhler, Dietrich. "Zu einer philosophischen Rekonstruktion der 'Handlung.'" In *Logik, Ethik, Theorie der Geisteswissenschaften.* Edited by Günther Patzig, Erhard Scheibe, Wolfgang Wieland, 306–17. Hamburg: Meiner, 1977.

Boundas, Constantin V., and Dorothea Olkowski, eds. *Gilles Deleuze and the Theater of Philosophy.* New York: Routledge, 1994.

Boutot, Alain. *Heidegger et Platon: Le problème du nihilisme.* Paris: Presses Universitaires de France, 1987.

Brecht, Bertolt. *The Good Person of Szechwan.* Translated by John Willett. New York: Arcade, 1994. (*Der Gute Mensch von Sezuan* [1955. Reprint, Frankfurt am Main: Suhrkamp, 1964].)

———. "A Short Organum for the Theatre." In *Brecht on Theatre.* Edited and translated by John Willett, 179–206. New York: Hill and Wang, 1964. ("Kleines Organon für das Theater." In Bertolt Brecht, *Schriften zum Theater* 2: *Gesammelte Werke*, vol. 16 [Frankfurt am Main: Suhrkamp, 1963–64].)

Brisson, Luc. *Le même et l'autre dans la structure ontologique du "Timée" de Platon: Un commentaire systématique du "Timée" de Platon.* 1974. Reprint, Sankt Augustin: Academia, 1994.

———. *Plato the Myth Maker.* Translated by Gerard Naddaf. Chicago: University of Chicago Press, 1988. (*Platon, les mots et les mythes: Comment et pourquoi Platon nomma le mythe?* [Paris: Éditions la Découverte, 1994].)

Brown, Lesley. Review of *Plato's "Sophist,"* by Stanley Rosen. *Classical Review* 35, no. 1 (1985): 69–70.

Bruns, Gerald L. *Hermeneutics Ancient and Modern.* New Haven, Conn.: Yale University Press, 1992.

———. *On the Anarchy of Poetry and Philosophy: A Guide for the Unruly.* New York: Fordham University Press, 2006.

Buber, Martin. *Between Man and Man.* Translated by Ronald Gregor-Smith. 1947. Reprint, London: Routledge, 2002. (*Das dialogische Prizip* [Heidelberg: Schneider, 1962].)

Burger, Ronna. *The "Phaedo": A Platonic Labyrinth.* New Haven, Conn.: Yale University Press, 1984.

———. *Plato's "Phaedrus": A Defense of a Philosophic Art of Writing.* Alabama: University of Alabama Press, 1980.

Burke, Carolyn, Naomi Schor, and Margaret Whitford, eds. *Engaging With Irigaray: Feminist Philosophy and Modern European Thought.* New York: Columbia University Press, 1994.

Butler, Judith. *Bodies that Matter: On the Discursive Limits of "Sex."* New York: Routledge, 1993.

———. *Gender Trouble: Feminism and the Subversion of Identity.* New York: Routledge, 1990.

Caputo, John D. *More Radical Hermeneutics: On Not Knowing Who We Are.* Bloomington: Indiana University Press, 2000.

———. *Radical Hermeneutics: Repetition, Deconstruction, and the Hermeneutic Project.* Bloomington: Indiana University Press, 1987.

Cascardi, Anthony J., ed. *Literature and the Question of Philosophy.* Baltimore, Md.: Johns Hopkins University Press, 1987.

Casey, Edward S. *The Fate of Place: A Philosophical History.* Berkeley: University of California Press, 1997.

Cassin, Barbara, ed. *Nos Grecs et leurs modernes: Les stratégie contemporaines d'appropriation de l'antiquité.* Paris: Seuil, 1992.

Celan, Paul. *Collected Prose.* Translated by Rosmarie Waldrop. New York: Sheep Meadow Press, 1986. (Paul Celan, *Gedichte, Prosa, Reden.* Vol. 3 of *Gesammelte Werke.* Edited by Beda Allemann and Stefan Reichart [Frankfurt am Main: Suhrkamp, 1983].)

Chantraine, Pierre. *Dictionnaire étymologique de la langue grecque: Histoire des mots.* Paris: Klincksieck, 1968–1980.

Cixous, Hélène. *"L'heure de Clarice Lispector," précédé de Vivre l'orange/To Live the Orange.* French/English text. Translated by Ann Liddle and Sarah Cornell. Paris: Éditions des femmes, 1979.

Cixous, Hélène, and Catherine Clément. 1986. *Newly Born Woman.* Translated by Betsy Wing. Minneapolis: University of Minnesota Press, 1986. (*La jeune née* [Paris: Union générale d'éditions, 1975].)

Clark, Timothy. *Derrida, Heidegger, Blanchot: Sources of Derrida's Notion and Practice of Literature.* Cambridge: Cambridge University Press, 1992.

Clay, Diskin. "Reading the *Republic.*" In *Platonic Writings/Platonic Readings.* Edited by Charles L. Griswold Jr., 19–33. New York: Routledge, 1988.

———. *Platonic Questions: Dialogues with the Silent Philosopher.* University Park, Pa.: Pennsylvania State University Press, 2000.

Collingwood, R. G. "Plato's Philosophy of Art." *Mind* 34, no. 134 (1925): 154–72.

Corlett, J. Angelo. *Interpreting Plato's Dialogues.* Las Vegas, Nev.: Parmenides Publishing, 2005.

Cornford, Francis M. *Plato's Cosmology: The "Timaeus" of Plato, Translated with a Running Commentary.* 1937. Reprint, London: Routledge, 1966.

Corrigan, Kevin, and Elena Glazov-Corrigan. *Plato's Dialectic at Play: Argument, Structure, and Myth in the "Symposium."* University Park, Pa.: Pennsylvania State University Press, 2004.

Cossutta, Frédéric, and Michel Narcy, eds. *La forme dialogue chez Platon: Évolution et réceptions.* Grenoble: Editions Jérôme Millon, 2001.

Cross, R. C., and A. D. Woozley. *Plato's "Republic": A Philosophical Commentary.* London: Macmillan, 1964.

Dannhauser, Werner J. *Nietzsche's View of Socrates.* Ithaca, N.Y.: Cornell University Press, 1974.

Danto, Arthur C. "Philosophy as/and/of Literature." In *Literature and the Question of Philosophy.* Edited by Anthony J. Cascardi, 1–23. Baltimore, Md.: Johns Hopkins University Press, 1987.

Debord, Guy. *The Society of the Spectacle*. Translated by Donald Nicholson-Smith. New York: Zone Books, 1995. (*La société du spectacle* [Paris: Gallimard, 1992].)

Deleuze, Gilles. *Difference and Repetition*. Translated by Paul Patton (New York: Columbia University Press, 1994. (*Différence et répétition* [Paris: Presses Universitaires de France, 1968].)

————. *Francis Bacon: Logique de la sensation*. Paris: Éditions de la différence, 1984.

————. *The Logic of Sense*. Translated by Mark Lester. New York: Columbia University Press, 1990. (*Logique du sens* [Paris: Minuit, 1969].)

————. *Nietzsche and Philosophy*. Translated by Hugh Tomlinson. New York: Columbia University Press, 1983. (*Nietzsche et la philosophie* [Paris: Presses Universitaires de France, 1962].)

Deleuze, Gilles, and Félix Guattari. *Kafka: Toward a Minor Literature*. Translated by Dana Polan. Minneapolis: University of Minnesota Press, 1986. (*Kafka: Pour une littérature mineure* [Paris: Minuit, 1975].)

De Man, Paul. *Allegories of Reading: Figural Language in Rousseau, Nietzsche, Rilke, and Proust*. New Haven, Conn.: Yale University Press, 1979.

Derrida, Jacques. *Dissemination*. Translated by Barbara Johnson. Chicago: University of Chicago Press, 1981. (*La dissémination* [Paris: Seuil, 1972].)

————. "Economimesis." Translated by Richard Klein. *Diacritics* 11, no. 2 (1981): 3–25. ("Économimésis." In Sylviane Agacinski et al., *Mimesis des()articulations*, 57–93 [Paris: Aubier-Flammarion, 1975].)

————. "Khōra." In Jacques Derrida, *On the Name*. Translated by David Wood, John P. Leavey Jr., and Ian McLeod. Edited by Thomas Dutoit, 89–127. Stanford, Calif.: Stanford University Press, 1995. (*Khôra* [Paris: Galilée, 1993].)

————. "Otobiographies." Translated by Avita Ronell. In Jacques Derrida, *The Ear of the Other: Otobiography, Transference, Translation*. Edited Christie McDonald, 1–37. Lincoln: University of Nebraska Press, 1985. (*Otobiographies: L'enseignement de Nietzsche et la politique du nom propre* [Paris: Galilée, 1984].)

————. *Sovereignties in Question: The Poetics of Paul Celan*. Edited by Thomas Dutoit and Outi Pasanen. New York: Fordham University Press, 2005. (*Béliers: Le dialogue ininterrompu; Entre deux infinis, le poème* [Paris: Galilée, 2003].)

————. *Spurs: Nietzsche's Styles*. Translated by Barbara Harlow. Chicago: University of Chicago Press, 1979. (*Éperons: Les styles de Nietzsche* [Paris: Flammarion, 1978].)

————. "Tense." In *The Path of Archaic Thinking: Unfolding the Work of John Sallis*. Edited by Maly Kenneth, 49–74. Albany: State University of New York Press, 1995.

————. *Writing and Difference*. Translated by Alan Bass. Chicago: University of Chicago Press, 1978. (*L'écriture et la différence* [Paris: Seuil, 1967].)

Descombes, Vincent. *Modern French Philosophy*. Translated by L. Scott-Fox and J. M. Harding. Cambridge: Cambridge University Press, 1980. (*Le Même et l'Autre* [Paris: Minuit, 1979].)

Desjardins, Rosemary. "Why Dialogues? Plato's Serious Play." In *Platonic Writings/Platonic Readings*. Edited by Charles L. Griswold Jr., 110–25. New York: Routledge, 1988.

Diderot, Denis. "The Paradox of Acting." Translated by Walter Herries Pollock. In *"The Paradox of Acting" by Denis Diderot and "Masks or Faces?" by William Archer*, 11–74. New York: Hill and Wang, 1957. ("Le paradoxe sur le comédien." In Denis Diderot, *Œuvres esthétiques*, 291–381 [Paris: Garnier, 1968].)

Diels, Herman. *Die Fragmente der Vorsokratiker*. 6th ed. 3 vols. Edited by Walther Kranz. 1952. Reprint, Zurich: Weidmann, 1985.

Dixsaut, Monique, ed. *Contre Platon: Le platonism dévoilé*. Paris: J. Vrin, 1993.

———. *Métamorphoses de la dialectique dans les dialogues de Platon*. Paris: J. Vrin, 2000.

———. *Platon et la question de la pensée*. Paris: J. Vrin, 2001.

DuBois, Page. *Sappho Is Burning*. Chicago: University of Chicago Press, 1995.

Dünkelsbühler, Ulrike Oudée. *Reframing the Frame of Reason: "Trans-Lation" in and Beyond Kant and Derrida*. Translated by Max Statkiewicz with preface by Jacques Derrida. New York: Humanity Books, 2002. (*Kritik der Rahmen-Vernunft* [Munich: Fink, 1991].)

Dupréel, Eugène. *La légende socratique et les sources de Platon*. Bruxelles: Sand, 1922.

Dürrenmatt, Friedrich. *Turmbau, Stoffe 4–10*. Zurich: Diogenes, 1994.

Edmundson, Mark. *Literature Against Philosophy, Plato to Derrida: A Defence of Poetry*. Cambridge: Cambridge University Press, 1995.

Else, Gerald F. *Plato and Aristotle on Poetry*. Chapel Hill: University of North Carolina Press, 1986.

Euripides. *Les Troyennes, Iphigénie en Tauride, Électre*. Greek/French text. Translated by Léon Parmentier and Henri Gregoire. Paris: Société d'Édition "Les Belles Lettres," 1982.

Ferrari, Giovanni R. F. *Listening to the Cicadas: A Study of Plato's "Phaedrus."* Cambridge: Cambridge University Press, 1987.

———. Review of *Self-knowledge in Plato's "Phaedrus,"* by Charles L. Griswold Jr. *Philosophical Review* 97, no. 3 (1988): 408–11.

Festugière, André Jean. *Commentaire sur le "Timée" [par] Proclus*. Paris: J. Vrin, 1966.

Fine, Gail J. "Knowledge and Logos in the *Theaetetus*." *Philosophical Review* 88, no. 3 (1979): 368–86.

Fink, Eugen. *Spiel als Weltsymbol*. Stuttgart: W. Kohlhammer, 1960.

Ford, Andrew. "The Classical Definition of PAΨΩIΔIA." *Classical Philology* 83, no. 4 (1988): 300–307.

Foucault, Michel. *The Archaeology of Knowledge and the Discourse on Language*. Translated by A. M. Sheridan Smith. New York: Pantheon Books, 1972. (*L'archéologie du savoir* [Paris: Gallimard, 1969].)

———. *The Order of Things: An Archeology of the Human Sciences*. New York: Random House, 1970. (*Les mots et les choses* [Paris: Gallimard, 1966].)

———. "Theatrum Philosophicum." *Critique* 26, no. 282 (1970): 885–908.

———. *This Is Not a Pipe*. Translated by James Harkness. Berkeley: University of California Press, 1982. (*Ceci n'est pas une pipe* [Montpellier: Fata Morgana, 1973].)

Friedländer, Paul. *Plato: The Dialogues, First Period*. Vol. 2 of *Plato*. Translated by Hans Meyerhoff. Princeton, N.J.: Princeton University Press, 1964. (*Die platonischen Schriften, erste Periode*. Vol. 2 of *Platon* [Berlin: de Gruyter, 1964].)

———. *Plato: The Dialogues, Second and Third Periods*. Vol. 3 of *Plato*. Translated by Hans Meyerhoff. Princeton, N.J.: Princeton University Press, 1969. (*Die platonischen Schriften, zweite und dritte Periode*. Vol. 3 of *Platon* [Berlin: de Gruyter, 1975].)

———. *Plato: An Introduction*. Vol. 1 of Paul Friedländer, *Plato*. Translated by Hans Meyerhoff. Princeton, N.J.: Princeton University Press, 1958. (*Seinswahrheit und Lebenswirklichkeit*. Vol. 1 of *Platon* [1935. Reprint, Berlin: Gruyter, 1964].)

Gadamer, Hans-Georg. *Dialogue and Dialectic: Eight Hermeneutical Studies on Plato*. Translated by P. Christopher Smith. New Haven, Conn.: Yale University Press, 1980.

———. *The Idea of the Good in Platonic-Aristotelian Philosophy*. Translated by P. Christopher Smith. New Haven, Conn.: Yale University Press, 1986. (*Die Idee des Guten zwischen Plato und Aristoteles* [Heidelberg: Winter, 1978].)

———. *Literature and Philosophy in Dialogue*. Translated by Robert H. Paslick. Albany: State University of New York Press, 1994.

———. *Plato's Dialectical Ethics: Phenomenological Interpretations Relating to the "Philebus."* Translated by Robert M. Wallace. New Haven, Conn.: Yale University Press, 1991. (*Platos dialektische Ethik* [1931. Reprint, Hamburg: Meiner, 1983].)

———. "Plato as Portraitist." Translated by Jamey Findling and Snezhina Gabova. *Continental Philosophy Review* 33, no. 3 (2000): 245–74. ("Platon als Porträtist." In Hans-Georg Gadamer, *Gesammelte Werke.* 10 vols., 7: 228–57 [Tübingen: Mohr, 1991].)

———. "Text and Interpretation." Translated by Dennis J. Schmidt and Richard E. Palmer. In *Dialogue and Deconstruction: The Gadamer-Derrida Encounter*. Edited by Diane P. Michelfelder and Richard E. Palmer, 21–51. Albany: State University of New York Press, 1989. ("Text und Interpretation." In Hans-Georg Gadamer, *Gesammelte Werke,* vol. 2. [Tübingen: Mohr, 1986].)

———. *Truth and Method.* Translated by Joel Weinsheimer and Donald Marshall. New York: Continuum, 1975. (*Wahrheit und Methode: Grundzüge einer philosophischen Hermeneutik* [Tübingen: Mohr, 1960].)

Gaiser, Konrad. *Protreptik und Parenese bei Platon: Untersuchungen zur Form des platonischen Dialogs* (Stuttgart: W. Kohlhammer, 1959).

Gebauer, Gunter, and Christian Wulf. *Mimesis: Culture—Art—Society.* Translated by Don Reneau. Berkeley: University of California Press, 1995. (*Mimesis: Kultur—Kunst—Gesellschaft* [Reinbek bei Hamburg: Rowohlt, 1992].)

Genette, Gérard. *Figures of Literary Discourse.* Translated by Alan Sheridan. New York: Columbia University Press, 1982. (Selection from *Figures 1, 2,* and *3* [Paris: Seuil. 1966–72].)

———. *Introduction à l'architexte.* Paris: Seuil, 1979. ("Genres, 'types,' modes," *Poétique* 32 [November 1977]: 389–421).

———. *Mimologics.* Lincoln: University of Nebraska Press, 1995. (*Mimologiques* [Paris: Seuil, 1976].)

Gerber, Ellen W., ed. *Sport and the Body: A Philosophical Symposium.* Philadelphia: Lea and Febiger, 1972.

Girard, René. *The Scapegoat.* Translated by Yvonne Freccero. Baltimore, Md.: Johns Hopkins University Press, 1986. (*Le bouc émissaire* [Paris: Grasset, 1982].)

———. *A Theater of Envy: William Shakespeare.* New York: Oxford University Press, 1991.

———. *Violence and the Sacred.* Translated by Patrick Gregory. Baltimore, Md.: Johns Hopkins University Press, 1977. (*La violence et le sacré* [Paris: Grasset, 1972].)

Golden, Leon. "The Clarification Theory of *Katharsis.*" *Hermes* 104 (1976): 437–52.

———. "Mimesis and Katharsis." *Classical Philology* 64, no. 3 (1969): 145–53.

Goldschmidt, Victor. *Platonisme et pensée contemporaine.* Paris: Aubier, 1970.

Gölz, Sabine I. "Reading in the Twilight: Canonization, Gender, the Limits of Language—and a Poem by Ingeborg Bachmann." *New German Critique* 47 (1989): 29–52.

Gordon, Jill. *Turning Toward Philosophy: Literary Device and Dramatic Structure in Plato's Dialogues.* University Park, Pa.: Pennsylvania State University Press, 1999.

Gonzalez, Francisco J., ed. *The Third Way: New Directions in Platonic Studies.* Lanham, Md.: Rowman and Littlefield, 1995.

Gould, Josiah B. "Klein on Ethnological Mimes, for Example, the *Meno.*" *Journal of Philosophy* 66, no. 9 (1969): 253–65.

Gould, Thomas. *The Ancient Quarrel Between Poetry and Philosophy.* Princeton, N.J.: Princeton University Press, 1990.

Griswold, Charles L., Jr. "*E Pluribus Unum?* On the Platonic 'Corpus.'" *Ancient Philosophy* 19, no. 2 (1999): 361–97.

———. "*E Pluribus Unum?* On the Platonic 'Corpus': The Discussion Continued." *Ancient Philosophy* 20, no. 1 (2000): 185–97.

———. "The Idea and the Criticism of Poetry in Plato's *Republic*, Book 10." *Journal of the History of Philosophy* 19, no. 2 (1981): 135–50.

———, ed. *Platonic Readings/Platonic Writings.* New York: Routledge, 1988.

———. "Plato's Metaphilosophy: Why Plato Wrote Dialogues." In *Platonic Readings/Platonic Writings.* Edited by Charles L. Griswold Jr., 143–67. New York: Routledge, 1988.

———. "Reflections on 'Dialectic' in Plato and Hegel." *International Philosophical Quarterly* 22, no. 3 (1982): 115–130.

———. *Self-Knowledge in Plato's "Phaedrus."* New Haven, Conn.: Yale University Press, 1986.

———. "Style and Philosophy: The Case of Plato's Dialogues." *The Monist* 63, no. 4 (1980): 530–46.

———. "Unifying Plato: Charles Kahn on Platonic *Prolepsis.*" *Ancient Philosophy* 10, no. 2 (1990): 243–62.

Grosz, Elizabeth A. "Women, *Chora*, Dwelling." In Elizabeth A. Grosz, *Space, Time, and Perversion: Essays on the Politics of Bodies*, 111–24. London: Routledge, 1995.

Guthrie, W. K. C. *A History of Greek Philosophy.* 6 vols. Cambridge: Cambridge University Press, 1962–81.

Habermas, Jürgen. "A Review of Gadamer's *Truth and Method.*" Translated by Fred R. Dallmayr and Thomas A. McCarthy. In *Understanding and Social Inquiry.* Edited by Fred R. Dallmayr and Thomas A. McCarthy, 335–63. South Bend: University of Notre Dame Press, 1977. ("Zu Gadamers *Wahrheit und Methode.*" In Jürgen Habermas, *Zur Logik der Sozialwissenschaften*, 251–90 [Frankfurt am Main: Suhrkamp, 1970].)

Halliwell, Stephen. *Aristotle's Poetics.* 1986. Reprint, Chicago: University of Chicago Press, 1998.

Halperin, David M. "Plato and the Erotics of Narrativity." In *Methods of Interpreting Plato and His Dialogues.* Edited by James C. Klagge and Nicholas D. Smith, 93–150. Oxford: Clarendon Press, 1992.

Hart, Richard, and Victorino Tejera, eds. *Plato's Dialogues: The Dialogical Approach.* Lewiston, N.Y.: Edwin Mellen, 1997.

Hartman, Geoffrey. *Saving the Text: Literature/Derrida /Philosophy.* Baltimore, Md.: Johns Hopkins University Press, 1981.

Havelock, Eric A. *Preface to Plato.* 1963. Reprint, Cambridge, Mass.: Harvard University Press, 1982.

Hegel, Georg Wilhelm Friedrich. *Phenomenology of Spirit.* Translated by A. V. Miller. Oxford: Oxford University Press, 1977. (*Phänomenologie des Geistes.* 1807 [Reprint, Hamburg: Meiner, 1988].)

Heidegger, Martin. "The Age of the World Picture." In Martin Heidegger, *The Question Concerning Technology and Other Essays.* Translated by William Lovitt, 115–54. New York: Harper and Row, 1977. ("Die Zeit des Weltbildes." In *Holzwege*, 69–104 [Frankfurt am Main: Klostermann, 1950].)

———. *Being and Time.* Translated by Joan Stambaugh. Albany: State University of New York Press, 1996.

———. *Being and Time.* Translated by John Macquarrie and Edward Robinson. New York: Harper and Row, 1962. (1927. Reprint, *Sein und Zeit* [Tübingen: Niemeyer, 1979].)

———. *Nietzsche.* Translated by David Farrell Krell. San Francisco: Harper and Row, 1979–
87. 4 vols. (*Nietzsche* [Pfullingen: Neske, 1954].)

———. *Off the Beaten Track.* Edited and translated by Julian Young and Kenneth Haynes.
Cambridge: Cambridge University Press, 2002. (*Holzwege* [Frankfurt am Main:
Klostermann, 1950].)

———. *On the Way to Language.* Translated by Peter D. Hertz. San Francisco: Harper and
Row, 1971. (*Unterwegs zur Sprache* [Stuttgart: Neske, 1959].)

———. "Plato's Doctrine of Truth." Translated by Thomas Sheehan. In Martin Heidegger,
Pathmarks. Edited by William McNeill, 155–82. Cambridge: Cambridge University
Press, 1998. (*Platons Lehre von der Wahrheit* [Bern: Francke, 1947].)

———. *Plato's "Sophist."* Translated by Richard Rojcewicz and André Schuwer. Bloomington:
Indiana University Press, 1997. (*Platon: "Sophistes"* [Frankfurt am Main: Klostermann,
1992].)

———. *Poetry, Language, Thought.* Translated by Albert Hofstadter. 1971. Reprint, New York:
HarperCollins, 2001.

———. *The Principle of Reason.* Translated by Reginald Lilly. Bloomington, Indiana University Press, 1991. (*Der Satz vom Grund* [Stuttgart: Neske, 1957].)

———. "The Question Concerning Technology." In Martin Heidgger, *The Question Con-
cerning Technology and Other Essays.* Translated by William Lovitt, 3–35. New York:
Harper and Row, 1977. ("Die Frage nach der Technik." In *Vorträge und Aufsätze.*
[Stuttgart: Neske, 1954], 9–40).

Hermeias of Alexandria. *In platonis phaedrum scholia.* Edited by P. Couvreur. 1901. Reprint,
Hildesheim: Olms, 1971.

Hirzel, Rudolf. *Der Dialog: Ein literarhistorischer Versuch.* Leipzig: S. Hirzel, 1895.

Hölderlin, Friedrich. *Poems and Fragments.* Translated by Michael Hamburger. London: Anvil
Press Poetry, 1994.

Howland, Jacob. "Re-reading Plato: The Problem of Platonic Chronology." *Phoenix* 45, no. 3
(199): 189–214.

Hyland, Drew A. *Finitude and Transcendence in the Platonic Dialogues.* Albany: State University of New York Press, 1995.

———. *The Question of Play.* Lanham, Md.: University Press of America, 1984.

———. *Questioning Platonism.* Albany: State University of New York Press, 2004.

———. "Why Plato Wrote Dialogues." *Philosophy and Rhetoric* 1, no. 1 (1968): 38–50.

Irigaray, Luce. *An Ethics of Sexual Difference.* Translated by Carolyn Burke and Gillian C. Gill.
Ithaca, N.Y.: Cornell University Press, 1993. (*Éthique de la différence sexuelle* [Paris:
Minuit, 1984].)

———. *Speculum of the Other Woman.* Translated by Gillian C. Gill. Ithaca, N.Y.: Cornell
University Press, 1985. (*Speculum de l'autre femme* [Paris: Minuit, 1974].)

———. *This Sex Which Is Not One.* Translated by Catherine Porter and Carolyn Burke.
Ithaca, N.Y.: Cornell University Press, 1985. (*Ce sexe qui n'en est pas un* [Paris: Minuit,
1977].)

Irwin, Terence. *Plato's Moral Theory: The Early and Middle Dialogues.* Oxford: Clarendon Press,
1977.

Johnson, William A. "Dramatic Frame and Philosophic Idea in Plato." *American Journal of
Philology* 119, no. 4 (1998): 577–98.

Joly, Henri. *Études platoniciennes: La question des étrangers.* Paris: J. Vrin, 1992.

———. *Le renversement platonicien.* Paris: J. Vrin, 1974.

Judovitz, Dalia. "Philosophy and Poetry: The Difference Between Them in Plato and Descartes."
    In *Literature and the Question of Philosophy*. Edited by Anthony J. Cascardi, 24–51. Bal-
    timore, Md.: Johns Hopkins University Press, 1987.
Kant, Immanuel. *Critique of Pure Reason*. Translated by Norman Kemp Smith. Rev. 2nd ed.
    New York: St. Martin's Press, 2003. (*Kritik der reinen Vernunft*. 2 vols. [Frankfurt am:
    Suhrkamp, 1956].)
Klagge, James C., and Nicholas D. Smith, eds. *Methods of Interpreting Plato and His Dialogues*.
    Oxford: Clarendon Press, 1992.
Klein, Jacob. *A Commentary on Plato's "Meno."* Chapel Hill: University of North Carolina
    Press, 1965.
———. *Lectures and Essays*. Edited by Robert B. Williamson and Elliott Zuckerman. Anna-
    polis, Md.: St. John's College Press, 1985.
———. *Plato's Trilogy: "Theaetetus," the "Sophist" and the "Statesman."* Chicago: University of
    Chicago Press, 1977.
Kofman, Sarah. *Nietzsche and Metaphor*. Translated by Duncan Large. London: Athlone Press,
    1993. (*Nietzsche et la métaphore* [Paris: Galilée, 1983].)
———. *Nietzsche et la scène philosophique*. Paris: Galilée, 1979.
———. *Socrate(s)*. Paris: Galilée, 1989.
Kosman, Aryeh L. "Silence and Imitation in the Platonic Dialogues." In *Methods of Interpret-
    ing Plato and His Dialogues*. Edited by James C. Klagge and Nicholas D. Smith, 73–92.
    Oxford: Clarendon Press, 1992.
Kott, Jan. *Shakespeare Our Contemporary*. Translated by Boleslaw Taborski. New York: W. W.
    Norton, 1974. (*Szkice o Szekspirze* [Warsaw: Państwowe Wydawnictwo Naukowe, 1964].)
Kowzan, Tadeusz. *Hamlet, ou; Le miroir du monde*. Paris: Éditions Universitaires, 1991.
Kristeva, Julia. *Desire in Language: A Semiotic Approach to Literature and Art*. Translated by
    Thomas Gora, Alice Jardine, and Leon S. Roudiez. New York: Columbia University
    Press, 1980. (*Polylogue* [Paris: Seuil, 1977] and *Sēmeiōtikē* [Paris: Seuil, 1969].)
———. *Revolution in Poetic Language*. Translated by Margaret Waller. New York: Columbia
    University Press, 1984. (*La révolution du langage poétique* [Paris: Seuil, 1974].)
Lacoue-Labarthe, Philippe. *The Subject of Philosophy*. Edited by T. Trezise. Minneapolis: Uni-
    versity of Minnesota Press, 1993. (*Le sujet de la philosophie* [Paris: Aubier-Flammarion,
    1979].)
———. "Typography." In Philippe Lacoue-Labarthe, *Typography: Mimesis, Philosophy, Politics*.
    Edited and translated by Christopher Fynsk, 43–138. Cambridge, Mass.: Harvard Uni-
    versity Press, 1989. ("Typographie." In Sylviane Agacinski et al., *Mimesis des()articula-
    tions*, 165–270 [Paris: Aubier-Flammarion, 1975].)
Lacoue-Labarthe, Philippe, and Jean-Luc Nancy. "Le dialogue des genres." *Poétique* 21, no. 1
    (1975): 148–75.
Laertius, Diogenes. *Lives of Eminent Philosophers*. Translated by R. D. Hicks. Cambridge,
    Mass.: Harvard University Press, 1925.
Lafrance, Yvon. "Autour de Platon: Continentaux et analystes." *Dionysius* 3 (1979): 17–37.
———. *Pour interpreter Platon*. Montreal: Bellarmin, 1987.
Lane, Melissa. *Plato's Progeny: How Plato and Socrates Still Captivate the Modern Mind*. Lon-
    don: Duckworth, 2001.
Lattimore, Richmond, ed. and trans. *Greek Lyrics*. Chicago: University of Chicago Press, 1955.
Levin, Susan B. *The Ancient Quarrel Between Philosophy and Poetry Revisited: Plato and the
    Greek Literary Tradition*. Oxford: Oxford University Press, 2001.

Lévinas, Emmanuel. *Ethics and Infinity: Conversations with Philippe Nemo.* Translated by Richard A. Cohen. Pittsburgh, Pa.: Duquesne University Press, 1985. (*Ethique et infini: Dialogues avec Phillipe Nemo* [Paris: Fayard, 1982].)

———. *Otherwise Than Being; or, Beyond Essence.* Translated by Alphonso Lingis. Boston: Kluwer, 1991. (*Autrement qu'être; ou, Au delà de l'essence* [Martinus Nijhoff, 1978].)

———. *Proper Names.* Translated by Michael B. Smith. Stanford, Calif.: Stanford University Press, 1996. (*Noms propres* [Montpellier: Fata Morgana, 1976] and *Sur Maurice Blanchot* [Montpellier: Fata Morgana, 1975].)

Lord, Albert B. *The Singer of Tales.* Cambridge, Mass.: Harvard University Press, 1960.

Lyotard, Jean-François. *The Differend: Phrases in Dispute.* Translated by Georges Van Den Abbeele. Minneapolis: University of Minnesota Press, 1988. (*Le différend* [Paris: Minuit, 1983].)

Maly, Kenneth, ed. *The Path of Archaic Thinking: Unfolding the Work of John Sallis.* Albany: State University of New York Press, 1995.

Mattéi, Jean-François. *L'Étranger et le simulacre: Essai sur la fondation de l'ontologie platonicienne.* Paris: Presses Universitaires de France, 1983.

———. *L'ordre du monde: Platon, Nietzsche, Heidegger.* Paris: Presses Universitaires de France, 1989.

———. *Platon et le miroir du mythe: De l'âge d'or à l'Atlantide.* Paris: Presses Universitaires de France, 1996.

Melling, David J. *Understanding Plato.* Oxford: Oxford University Press, 1987.

Miller, Mitchell H., Jr. *Plato's "Parmenides": The Conversation of the Soul.* Princeton, N.J.: Princeton University Press, 1986.

Mittelstrass, Jürgen. "On Socratic Dialogues." Translated by Steven Gillies. In *Platonic Writings/ Platonic Readings.* Edited by Charles L. Griswold Jr., 126–42. New York: Routledge, 1988. ("Versuch über den Sokratischen Dialog." In *Das Gespräch.* Edited by Karlheinz Stierle and Rainer Warning, 11–27 [Munich: Fink, 1984].)

Moravcsik, Julius, and Philip Temko, eds. *Plato and Platonism.* Oxford: Blackwell, 1992.

———. *Plato on Beauty, Wisdom, and the Arts.* Totowa, N.J.: Rowman and Littlefield, 1982.

Mohr, Richard D. *The Platonic Cosmology.* Leiden: E. J. Brill, 1985.

Murdoch, Iris. *Acastos: Two Platonic Dialogues.* London: Penguin Books, 1986.

———. *The Fire and the Sun: Why Plato Banished the Artists.* Oxford: Clarendon Press, 1972.

Nancy, Jean-Luc. *La communauté affrontée.* Paris: Galilée, 2001.

———. *The Creation of the World or Globalization.* Translated by François Roffoul and David Pettigrew. Albany: State University of NewYork Press, 2007. (*La création du monde ou la mondialisation* [Galilée, 2002].)

———. *The Inoperative Community.* Edited and translated by Peter Connor. Minneapolis: University of Minnesota Press, 1991. (*La communauté désœuvrée* [Paris: Christian Bourgois, 1986].)

———. *Sharing Voices.* Translated by Gayle L. Ormiston. In *Transforming the Hermeneutic Context: From Nietzsche to Nancy.* Edited by Gayle L. Ormiston and Alan D. Schrift. Albany: State University of New York Press, 1990. (*Le partage des voix* [Paris: Galilée, 1982].)

———. "Le ventriloque." In Sylviane Agacinski et al., *Mimesis des()articulations.* Paris: Aubier-Flammarion, 1975.

Nancy, Jean-Luc, and Jean-Christophe Bailly. *La comparution (politique à venir).* Paris: Christian Bourgois, 1991.

Narcy, Michel. 2001. *Platon: L'amour du savoir.* Paris: Presses Universitaires de France.

Nehamas, Alexander. "Plato on Imitation and Poetry in *Republic* 10." In *Plato on Beauty, Wisdom, and the Arts.* Edited by Julius Moravcsik and Philip Temko, 47–78. Totowa, N.J.: Rowman and Littlefield, 1982.

———. "Self-Predication and Plato's Theory of Forms." *American Philosophical Quarterly* 16 (1979): 93–103.

Nietzsche, Friedrich. *Basic Writings of Nietzsche.* Translated and edited by Walter Kaufmann. New York: The Modern Library, 1966.

———. *Kritische Studienausgabe.* 15 vols. Edited by Giorgio Colli und Mazzino Montinari. 1967–77. Reprint, Berlin: de Gruyter, 1988.

———. *Philosophy in the Tragic Age of the Greeks.* Translated by Marianne Cowan. Washington, D.C.: Regnery, 1962. (*Philosophie im tragischen Zeitalter der Griechen* [1923. Reprint, Leipzig: Reclam, 1931].)

———. *The Portable Nietzsche.* Translated and edited by Walter Kaufmann. New York: Viking Penguin, 1954.

———. *Twilight of the Idols.* Translated by Duncan Large. Oxford: Oxford University Press, 1998. (*Götzen-Dämmerung.* In Friedrich Nietzsche, *Kritische Studienausgabe.* Vol. 6. Edited by Giorgio Colli and Mazzino Montinari [Berlin: de Gruyter, 1969].)

———. *Untimely Meditations.* Translated by R. J. Hollingdale. Edited by Daniel Breazeale. Cambridge: Cambridge University Press, 1997. (*Unzeitgemässe Betrachtungen* [Leipzig: Fritzsch, 1873–76].)

———. *The Will to Power.* Translated by Walter Kaufmann and R. J. Hollingdale. New York: Vintage Books, 1996. (In *Nachgelaßene Fragmente, 1884–1885.* In Friedrich Nietzsche, *Kritische Studienausgabe.* Vol. 11. Edited by Giorgio Colli and Mazzino Montinari [Berlin: de Gruyter, 1974].)

Nussbaum, Martha C. *The Fragility of Goodness: Luck and Ethics in Greek Tragedy and Philosophy.* Cambridge: Cambridge University Press, 1986.

O'Meara, Dominic J., ed. *Platonic Investigations.* Washington, D.C.: Catholic University of America Press, 1985.

Ormiston, Gayle L., and Alan D. Schrift, eds. *The Hermeneutic Tradition: From Ast to Ricoeur.* Albany: State University of New York Press, 1990.

———. 1990. *Transforming the Hermeneutic Context: From Nietzsche to Nancy.* Albany: State University of New York Press.

Pappas, Nickolas. "Plato's *Ion:* The Problem of the Author." *Philosophy* 64, no. 249 (1989): 382–89.

Partenie, Catalin, and Tom Rockmore, eds. *Heidegger and Plato: Toward Dialogue.* Evanston, Illinois: Northwestern University Press, 2005.

Patočka, Jan. *Plato and Europe.* Translated by Petr Lom. Stanford, Calif.: Stanford University Press, 2002. (*Platon et l'Europe [Platón a Evropa].* Translated by Erica Abrams [Lagrasse: Verdier, 1983].)

Patzer, Harald. "ΡΑΨΩΙΔΟΣ." *Hermes* 80, no. 3 (1952): 314–25.

Pavese, Carlo Odo. "The Rhapsodic Epic Poems as Oral and Independent Poems." *Harvard Studies in Classical Philology* 98 (1998): 63–90.

Peperzak, Theodor. *Platonic Transformations: With and After Hegel, Heidegger and Levinas.* Lanham, Md.: Rowman and Littlefield, 1997.

Plato. *Complete Works.* Edited by John M. Cooper and D. S. Hutchison. Indianapolis, Ind.: Hackett, 1997.

————. *The Dialogues of Plato.* 5 vols. Translated by Benjamin Jowett. 3rd rev. ed. New York: Macmillan, 1892.

————. *Laws.* Translated by R. G. Bury. 1926. Reprint, Cambridge, Mass.: Harvard University Press, 1984.

————. *Oeuvres complètes.* Translated by Léon Robin. Paris: Gallimard, 1950.

————. *Phaedrus.* Translated by Alexander Nehamas and Paul Woodruff. Indianapolis, Ind.: Hackett, 1995.

————. *Phèdre.* Translated by Luc Brisson. Paris: Flammarion, 1989.

————. *Plato in Twelve Volumes.* Translated by Harold N. Fowler. Cambridge, Mass., Harvard University Press, 1921.

————. *Platonis opera.* Edited by John Burnet. 1902. Reprint, Oxford: Oxford University Press, 1989.

————. *Plato's "Phaedrus."* Translated by Reginald Hackforth. Cambridge: Cambridge University Press, 1952.

————. *The Republic.* Edited by G. R. F. Ferrari. Translated by Tom Griffith. Cambridge: Cambridge University Press, 2000.

————. *The "Republic" of Plato.* Translated by Allan Bloom. 2nd ed. New York: Basic Books, 1991.

————. *The "Republic" of Plato.* Translated by Francis M. Cornford. 1941. Reprint, London: Oxford University Press, 1961.

————. *Theaetetus, Sophist.* Greek/English text. Translated by Harold N. Fowler. 1921. Reprint, Cambridge, Mass.: Harvard University Press, 1996.

————. *Timaeus, Critias.* Translated by R. G. Bury. 1929. Reprint, Cambridge, Mass.: Harvard University Press, 1989.

————. *Two Comic Dialogues: "Ion" and "Hippias Major."* Translated by Paul Woodruff. Indianapolis, Ind.: Hackett, 1983.

Plutarch. *Lives.* Translated by Bernadotte Perrin. Cambridge, Mass.: Harvard University Press, 1914.

Poulakos, Takis. Review of *"Self-knowledge in Plato's "Phaedrus,"* by Charles L. Griswold Jr. *Quarterly Journal Of Speech* 75, no 2 (1989): 299–31.

Press, Gerald A., ed. *Plato's Dialogues: New Studies and Interpretations.* Lanham, Md.: Rowman and Littlefield, 1993.

————, ed. *Who Speaks for Plato? Studies in Platonic Anonymity.* Lanham, Md.: Rowman and Littlefield, 1999.

Proimos, Constantinos. "Martin Heidegger on Mimesis in Plato and Platonism." In *Neoplatonism and Western Aesthetics.* Edited by Aphrodite Alexandrakis, 153–63. Albany: State University of New York Press, 2001.

Puchner, Martin. "The Theater in Modernist Thought." *New Literary History* 33, no. 3 (2002): 521–32.

Quine, Willard Van Orman. *From a Logical Point of View.* New York: Harper and Row, 1963.

Raeder, Hans. *Platons Philosophische Entwicklung.* Leipzig: Druck and Teubner, 1905.

Renaud, François. *Die Resokratisierung Platons.* Sankt Augustin: Academia, 1999.

Ricoeur, Paul. *Être, essence, et substance chez Platon et Aristotle.* Paris: Société d'enseignement supérieur, 1982.

————. 1991. *From Text to Action.* Translated by Kathleen Blamey and John B. Thompson. Evanston, Ill.: Northwestern University Press. (*Du texte à l'action* [Paris: Seuil, 1986].)

Robin, Léon. "Notice." In Plato, *Oeuvres complètes: "Phèdre,"* vol. 4, pt. 3. Edited by Claudio Moreschini. Translated by Paul Vicaire. Paris: Société d'Édition "Les Belles Lettres," 1985.

———. *Théorie platonicienne de l'amour.* 1908. Reprint, Paris: Presses Universitaires de France, 1933.

Robinson, Richard. *Plato's Earlier Dialectic.* Oxford: Clarendon Press, 1953.

Rogers, Pat. "Shaftesbury and the Aesthetics of Rhapsody." *British Journal of Aesthetics* 12, no. 3 (1972): 244–57.

Roochnik, David. *Beautiful City: The Dialectical Character of Plato's "Republic."* Ithaca, N.Y.: Cornell University Press, 2003.

———. *Of Art and Wisdom: Plato's Understanding of "Techne."* University Park, Pa.: Pennsylvania State University Press, 1996.

———. "Socrates' Rhetorical Attack on Rhetoric." In *The Third Way: New Directions in Platonic Studies.* Edited by Francisco J. Gonzalez, 81–94. Lanham, Md.: Rowman and Littlefield, 1995.

———. *The Tragedy of Reason: Toward a Platonic Conception of Logos.* New York, London: Routledge, 1990.

Rorty, Richard. *Contingency, Irony, and Solidarity.* Cambridge: Cambridge University Press, 1989.

———. *Philosophy and the Mirror of Nature.* Princeton, N.J.: Princeton University Press, 1979.

Rosen, Stanley. "Platonic Hermeneutics: On the Interpretation of a Platonic Dialogue." *Proceedings of the Boston Area Colloquium on Ancient Philosophy* 1 (1986): 271–97.

———. *Plato's "Republic": A Study.* New Haven, Conn.: Yale University Press, 2005.

———. *Plato's "Sophist": The Drama of the Original and Image.* New Haven, Conn.: Yale University Press, 1983.

———. *Plato's "Statesman": The Web of Politics.* New Haven, Conn.: Yale University Press, 1995.

———. *Plato's "Symposium."* New Haven, Conn.: Yale University Press, 1968.

———. *The Quarrel Between Philosophy and Poetry: Studies in Ancient Thought.* New York: Routledge, 1988.

———. *The Question of Being. A Reversal of Heidegger.* South Bend, Ind.: St. Augustine's Press, 2002.

Ross, David. *Plato's Theory of Ideas.* Oxford: Clarendon Press, 1951.

Rudolph, André. "Kontinuum der Rhapsodie: Herder–Hamann–Shaftesbury." In *Der frühe und der späte Herder: Kontinuität und/oder Korrektur.* Edited by Sabine Groß and Gerhard Sauder, 269–84. Heidelberg: Synchron, 2007.

Sallis, John. *Being and Logos: Reading the Platonic Dialogues.* 1975. Reprint, Bloomington: Indiana University Press, 1996.

———. *Chorology: On Beginning in Plato's "Timaeus."* Bloomington: Indiana University Press, 1999.

———. *Crossings: Nietzsche and the Space of Tragedy.* Chicago: University of Chicago Press, 1991.

———. *Double Truth.* Albany: State University of New York Press, 1995.

———. *Platonic Legacies.* Albany: State University of New York Press, 2004.

Schaerer, René. *La question platonicienne: Étude sur les rapporte de la pensée et de l'expression dans les Dialogues.* 1938. Reprint, Paris: J. Vrin, 1969.

Schlegel, August Wilhelm, and Friedrich Schlegel, eds. *Athenaeum, 1798–1800.* 1798–1800. Reprint, Stuttgart: Cotta, 1960.

Schleiermacher, Friedrich. *Introductions to the Dialogues of Plato.* Translated by William Dobson. 1836. Reprint, New York: Arno Press, 1973.

Schmidt, Dennis J. *On Germans and Other Greeks: Tragedy and Ethical Life.* Bloomington: Indiana University Press, 2001.

Schmidt, Hermann Josef. *Nietzsche und Sokrates.* Meisenheim: Anton Hain, 1969.

Schuhl, Pierre-Maxime. *La fabulation platonicienne.* Paris: J. Vrin, 1968.

———. *Platon et l'art de son temps.* Paris: Presses Universitaires de France, 1952.

Schweitzer, B. "Mimesis und Phantasia." *Philologus* 89 (1934): 286–300.

Seeskin, Kenneth. "Socratic Philosophy and the Dialogue Form." *Philosophy and Literature* 8, no. 2 (1984): 181–94.

Shankman, Steven, ed. *Plato and Postmodernism.* Glenside, Pa.: Aldine Press, 1994.

Shorey, Paul. *What Plato Said.* 1933. Reprint, Chicago: University of Chicago Press, 1965.

Smith, P. Christopher. "Orality and Writing: Plato's *Phaedrus* and the *Pharmakon* Revisited." In *Between Philosophy and Poetry: Writing, Rhythm, History.* Edited by Massimo Verdicchio and Robert Burch, 73–90. New York: Continuum, 2002.

Sophocles. *Antigone, The Women of Trachis, Philoctetes, Oedipus at Colonus.* Greek/English text. Translated by Hugh Lloyd-Jones. Cambridge, Mass.: Harvard University Press, 1994.

Spariosu, Mihai. *Literature, Mimesis, and Play: Essays in Literary Theory.* Tübingen: Narr, 1982.

———. "Plato's *Ion*: Mimesis, Poetry, and Power." In *Mimesis, Semiosis, and Power.* Vol. 2 of *Mimesis in Contemporary Theory: An Interdisciplinary Approach.* Edited by Ronald Bogue, 13–26. Philadelphia: John Benjamins, 1991.

Sprinker, Michael. *Imaginary Relations: Aesthetics and Ideology in the Theory of Historical Materialism.* London: Verso, 1987.

Statkiewicz, Max. "Brecht's (Non-)Philosophical Theater." *The Brecht Yearbook* 26 (2001): 276–93.

———. "The Matter of Language: A Dialogue Between Poetry and Philosophy in Agamben's Critical Thought." *Rivista di Studi Italiani* 22, no. 2 (2004): 198–220.

———. "On the Truth and Lie of Illusion in the Theatrical Sense." *Analecta Husserliana* 87 (2005): 43–53.

———. "Platonic Theater: Rigor and Play in the *Republic.*" *Modern Language Notes* 115, no. 5 (2000): 1019–51.

Stenzel, Julius. *Plato's Method of Dialectic.* Translated by D. J. Allan. 1940. Reprint, New York: Arno Press, 1973. (*Studien zur Entstehung der platonischen Dialektik von Sokrates zu Aristoteles* [1931. Reprint, Stuttgart: B. J. Teubner, 1961].)

Stokes, Michael C. *Plato's Socratic Conversations: Drama and Dialectic in Three Dialogues.* Baltimore, Md.: Johns Hopkins University Press, 1986.

Strauss, Leo. *The City and Man.* Chicago: University of Chicago Press, 1964.

———. *Studies in Platonic Political Philosophy.* Chicago: University of Chicago Press, 1983.

Szymborska, Wiesława. "Plato, or Why?" Translated by Clare Cavanagh and Stanislaw Barańczak. *Poetry* 185, no. 5 (2005): 352. ("Platon, Czyli Dlaczego." In Wiesława Szymborska, *Chwila* [Kraków: Wydawnictwo Znak, 2002].)

Taminiaux, Jacques. *Le théâtre des philosophes: La tragédie, l'être, l'action.* Grenoble: Jérôme Millon, 1995.

Tate, J. "Imitation in Plato's *Republic.*" *Classical Quarterly* 22, nos. 3–4 (1928): 16–23.

———. "Plato and 'Imitation.'" *Classical Quarterly* 26, nos. 3–4 (1932): 161–69.

Taylor, A. E. *A Commentary on Plato's "Timaeus."* 1928. Reprint, New York: Garland, 1987.

Taylor, C. C. W. Review of *The Tragedy of Reason: Toward a Platonic Conception of Logos,* by David Roochnik. *Classical Review* 42, no. 1 (1992): 205–6.

Tejera, Victorino. *Plato's Dialogues One by One: A Dialogical Interpretation.* Lanham, Md.: University Press of America, 1991.

———, ed. *Plato's Dialogues: The Dialogical Approach.* Lewiston, N.Y.: Edwin Mellen, 1997.

Thesleff, Holger. "Platonic Chronology." *Phronesis* 34, no. 1 (1989): 1–26.

Tigerstedt, E. N. *Interpreting Plato.* Uppsala: Almqvist and Wiksell International.

Timaios of Locri. *On the Nature of the World and the Soul.* Edited and translated by Thomas H. Tobin. Chico, Calif.: Scholars Press, 1985.

Van Eck, Job. "Falsity without Negative Predication." *Phronesis* 40, no. 1 (1995): 20–47.

Verdenius, W. J. *Mimesis: Plato's Doctrine of Artistic Imitation and Its Meaning to Us.* Leiden: E. J. Brill, 1949.

Verdicchio, Massimo, and Robert Burch, eds. *Between Philosophy and Poetry: Writing, Rhythm, History.* New York: Continuum, 2002.

Vernant, Jean-Pierre. *Myth and Thought Among the Greeks.* London: Routledge and Kegan Paul, 1983. (*Mythe et pensée chez les Grecs: Études de psychologie historique* [1965. Reprint, Paris: Éditions la Découverte, 1996].)

———. *Myth and Tragedy in Ancient Greece.* Translated by Janet Lloyd. New York: Zone Books, 1988. (*Mythe et société en Grèce ancienne* [Paris: François Maspero, 1974].)

Vernant, Jean-Pierre, and Pierre Vidal-Naquet. *Myth and Tragedy in Ancient Greece.* Translated by Janet Lloyd. New York: Zone Books, 1990. (*Mythe et tragédie en Grèce ancienne* [Paris: Maspero, 1979].)

Vlastos, Gregory. *Platonic Studies.* Princeton, N.J.: Princeton University Press, 1973.

———. *Socrates, Ironist and Moral Philosopher.* Ithaca, N.Y.: Cornell University Press, 1991.

Vries de, G. J. Review of *Self-knowledge in Plato's "Phaedrus,"* by Charles L. Griswold Jr. *Mnemosyne* 41, nos. 1–2 (1988): 161–64.

Weed, Elizabeth. "Question of Style." In *Engaging With Irigaray: Feminist Philosophy and Modern European Thought.* Edited by Carolyn Burke, Naomi Schor, and Margaret Whitford, 79–109. New York: Columbia University Press, 1994.

Weidle, Wladmir. "Der Sinn der Mimesis." *ERANOS-Jahrbuch* 31 (1963): 249–73.

Wieland, Wolfgang. *Platon und die Formen des Wissens.* Göttingen: Vandenhoeck and Ruprecht, 1982.

Wilamowitz-Moellendorff, Ulrich. *Platon—Sein Leben und seine Werke.* Berlin: Weidmann, 1929.

Willett, John. *Brecht in Context: Comparative Approaches.* London: Methuen, 1984.

Wood, David, ed. *Philosophers' Poets.* London: Routledge, 1990.

Wood, Kelsey. *Troubling Play: Meaning and Entity in Plato's "Parmenides."* Albany: State University of New York Press, 2005.

Xenophon. *"Memorabilia" and "Oeconomicus."* Greek/English text. Translated by E. C. Marchant. 1923. Reprint, Cambridge, Mass.: Harvard University Press, 1979.

Zuckert, Catherine H. *Postmodern Platos: Nietzsche, Heidegger, Gadamer, Strauss, Derrida.* Chicago: University of Chicago Press, 1996.

Index

Aeschylus, 88

Agamben, Giorgio, 61, 150 n. 58, 192 n. 108, 195 n. 116

agōn, 37, 40, 43, 89, 93

akribeia. See rigor

allegory of the cave, 16, 18–20, 28, 55, 57, 157

altēheia. See truth

Althusser, Louis, 54 n. 69, 54

ambiguity, 30, 42, 61, 69, 73, 84, 92–93, 114, 143, 152, 173

ambivalence, 54, 65, 67, 84, 100, 137, 152

anarchy, 50, 95, 111 n. 26, 116, 195

Annas, Julia, 55 n. 74, 55, 58

aporia, 60, 100, 117–19, 123, 127, 144, 163, 194

appearance, 128, 140, 143, 185

mere appearance, 43, 49, 89, 114, 117, 125. *See also* illusion

appearing, 18–20, 30, 73, 76, 83, 105. *See also* shining

Arieti, James A., 23 n. 91, 25

Aristophanes, 128 n. 80

arkhē (beginning, origin), 30, 48, 145, 195

art. *See tekhnē* and *poiēsis*

Artaud, Antonin, 7 n. 21, 30, 111 n. 26

Aubenque, Pierre, 36 n. 4, 125 n. 68

Bacon, Francis, 31, 111, 115–16, 131

Bakhtin, Mikhail, 188

Barthes, Roland, 1, 51, 191

Baudrillard, 2 n. 3, 125 n. 69

beauty (*kallos*), 70–101

Benjamin, Walter, 94 n. 102, 177 n. 61

Berger, Harry, Jr., 13 n. 53, 13–16, 61 n. 98, 163 n. 2

Bildung. See education

Blanchot, Maurice, 169 n. 29, 189

Blondell, Ruby, 23, 119 n. 51

border. *See* margin

boundary. *See* margin

Brecht, Bertolt, 22–23, 53 n. 64, 158 n. 87, 177

Burger, Ronna, 14 n. 56, 79

Burnet, John, 1, 11

Butler, Judith, 134, 141 n. 31, 151, 157–59

Caputo, John, 168

Casey, Edward S., 140 n. 26, 144 n. 40, 145

catharsis (purification), 20, 22, 64–69, 107, 118, 138, 141–42, 144

character, 66, 73, 135, 139, 143, 145, 147, 151–52, 160

role (*ēthos*), 7–10, 13, 18, 22–23, 47–48, 52–54, 99

type (*kharakter*), 18–20, 39, 44–45, 48, 62, 136 n. 10, 140–41

chora, 31–33, 132–61, 164

chorology, 146, 154

Clay, Diskin, 18 n. 72

closure, 2–4, 143

community, 12, 33, 38, 130, 138, 150 n. 59, 180

genres of, 31, 129

rhapsodic, 31, 60, 189, 194–95

confrontation (*Auseinandersetzung*), 24, 27, 74–75, 89, 90, 119. *See also* dialogue; conversation

conversation, 1, 19, 27, 33, 80 n. 41, 111, 130, 136–39, 165, 189, 190, 195

Cornford, Francis M., 25, 47 n. 43

Dasein (There-being), 73, 103, 117–19, 122, 128, 182

Debord, Guy, 2–3

deconstruction, 16, 57, 92–93, 96, 100–101, 147–48

Deleuze, Gills, 1–2, 4, 19, 30–31, 104–16, 144 n. 40

Difference and Repetition, 2 n. 3, 18 n. 72, 106–10

The Logic of Sense, 1 n. 2, 26 n. 102, 105 n. 6, 107–9

demiurge, the, 141–47, 151, 154, 159–60
Derrida, Jacques, 3 n. 7, 4–5, 29–30, 46 n. 40, 61
    n. 98, 62, 70–73, 90–101, 133–61, 168
    "*Khôra*," 5 n. 13, 133–37, 147, 150, 152, 159
    "Plato's Pharmacy," 39, 40, 70–72, 90–100, 142
    n. 33, 189 n. 102
    Spurs, 90 n. 82, 91–92
dia-logos, 2, 33, 123, 147, 191–92, 195
dialogue, 2–10, 21, 23–24, 27, 33, 39, 52, 56, 72, 75,
    186–95. *See also* confrontation
    "dialogue proper," 13–15
dianoia, 22, 59, 160, 178
diaphora. See quarrel
diēgēsis. See narration
discordance (*Zwiespalt*), 29, 35–36, 70, 73–79,
    83–85, 90–93, 97, 101, 184–86
displacement, 14, 57, 110, 116, 136, 140, 144
dissemination, 37, 93, 96–97, 100, 104, 108,
    115–17, 127–29
distance, 11, 50, 76–77, 90–91, 107, 170, 191
division (*diairesis*), 31, 104, 106–8, 116, 121–22
doctrinal interpretation (reading), 5, 25–26, 34,
    103, 119
doctrine, 11, 13 n. 48, 16, 45, 75, 128, 134 n. 5
drama, 1, 51, 63, 68, 106, 120, 129
    dramatic, 28, 45–46, 63, 129
    dramatic interpretation, 1–35, 58, 80, 82, 119,
    134, 170, 187
    dramatis personae, 12, 139
Dürrenmatt, Friedrich, 7 n. 20

education (*paideia, Bildung*), 16–20, 27, 44–46,
    49, 54, 64–69, 106, 138–39
eidōlon. See image
eikōn. See image
emplacement, 31, 132, 140, 143, 145–52
ergon (work, function), 41–42, 46–49, 160,
    174–78, 194
Euripides, 9 n. 30, 29, 37 n. 6, 54 n. 68, 64 n. 105,
    86–87, 89
ex-centricity, 133, 144

femininity, 31–32, 90, 92, 151–58
Ferrari, G. R. F., 70, 80
Fine, Gail, 15
Foucault, Michel, 30–31, 104, 110 n. 25, 111–14

Gadamer, Hans-Georg, 33, 80 n. 42, 163 n. 1,
    164–68
game, 24, 45, 70, 90, 93, 95, 100, 117, 135, 173
gender, 27, 48, 67, 91, 141, 149, 151–52, 175, 194
Genette, Gérard, 27, 51–53, 62 n. 99

genre, 4 n. 10, 23, 27, 47, 50–55, 61, 64–65, 132,
    129, 149–52
    community of, 31, 129
    separation of, 24, 28, 150
genus (*genos*), 69, 106–7, 129, 150–51
Girard, René, 27–28, 56, 61, 64–65, 67, 152
    n. 63
Godard, Jean-Luc, 111
Gordon, Jill, 21–22
Gorgias, 8, 87, 99, 174
Griswold, Charles L., 5 n. 12, 6 n. 17, 15–18, 23,
    29, 79–82
Grosz, Elizabeth A., 152–53
Grube, G. M. A., 17
Guthrie, W. K. C., 42 n. 31

Hackforth, Reginald, 82
Halliwell, Stephen, 21
Halperin, David M., 14 n. 56
Hamann, Johann Georg, 4 n. 10
Havelock, Eric, 39, 174 n. 54
Hegel, G. W. F., 165, 167
Heidegger, Martin, 3–4, 8, 20 n. 78, 28, 55–58, 61,
    70–76, 83–85, 90–92, 103, 117–20, 162–63,
    169, 180–88, 192
    "A Dialogue on Language," 33, 75 n. 16, 162,
    180, 187
    "Language in the Poem," 8 n. 23, 170 n. 31
    Nietzsche: The Will to Power as Art, 20 n.
    77–78, 29, 57 n. 78, 72–76, 84, 92
    "Plato's Doctrine of Truth," 3 n. 7, 16–20, 75,
    120 n. 53
    ". . . Poetically Man Dwells . . . ," 183–86
Heraclitus, 19, 24 n. 97, 189 n. 101
Herder, Johann Gottfried, 4
hermēneia, 4, 27, 33, 162, 164, 169–71, 178–82,
    188–93
hermeneutics, 4, 10–11, 33, 119, 164–71, 180–82,
    186, 192. *See also* interpretation
Hippias, 87, 174
Hölderlin, Friedrich, 19, 180, 185
Horizontverschmelzung (the fusion of horizons),
    167–68
Hyland, Drew A., 4 n. 11, 6 n. 17, 10, 13, 22, 80
    n. 42, 117 n. 44, 134 n. 6

Idea (*ideal eidos*), 2, 10, 15, 18, 20, 56, 58–61,
    76–77, 107–9, 126, 130, 133
ideology, 2, 11–12, 18, 20, 22–24, 27, 29, 38–42,
    48–49, 54–59, 66–69, 125, 136–45, 158–60
identity, 3, 20, 30, 43, 52, 62, 89, 93, 114, 184 n. 82
    formation of, 22, 93, 120, 126, 133, 152, 195 n. 116

questioning of, 38, 91, 102, 109, 111–12, 150, 156, 187
illusion, 67, 130, 161, 168, 191
image (*eidōlon, eikōn, Bild*), 17, 20, 24, 30, 73, 79, 104–17, 121–31, 137, 146–48, *See also* simulacrum; picture
imitation, 10, 20, 24, 26, 38, 45–48, 51–54, 66, 120, 137, 171. *See also* mimesis
interpretation, 2, 4, 8, 27, 33, 80, 104, 117, 141, 163–86
Ionesco, Eugene, 111
Irigaray, Luce, 4, 133–34, 141 n. 31, 153–58
Speculum of the Other Woman, 133, 141, 154–58
This Sex Which is not One, 156

Janko, Richard, 22
Johnson, Barbara, 95
Johnson, William A., 14 n. 56
justice, 40–43, 46, 50, 60, 139

Kabuki, 23
kallipolis, 59–60
Kant, Immanuel, 4
khōra. See chora
Klein, Jacob, 12–14, 173
knowledge (*epistēmē, to eidenai*), 15, 20, 25, 44, 58, 66, 77, 100, 118, 137, 165, 171, 178
Kristeva, Julia, 133, 136 n. 11, 153–54

Lacoue-Labarthe, Philippe, 4, 7 n. 19, 23 n. 95, 28, 50, 56–57, 61–63
Lévinas, Emmanuel, 71
likeness (resemblance, similarity), 30–31, 68–69, 104–16, 120–21, 125–31, 137, 143, 151, 159, 164
logos (ratio, rational element, argument), 2–3, 6, 77, 85, 96, 146–48, 156, 171–72
logography, 97–98
rhapsodic, 188–89, 191–92, 195
rhetorical, 13, 65, 78, 93, 99, 159
Lord, Albert B., 39
Lucas, F. L., 21

Magritte, René, 31, 112–15, 125–26
margin, 132–33, 136, 146, 153, 155, 160
Mattéi, Jean-François, 145 n. 44
metaphysics, 2, 56, 70, 74, 77, 94, 104, 146, 163, 166. *See also* Platonism
mimesis, 6, 8, 24, 36–44, 47, 51–55, 61, 65–69, 106, 120–22, 129–31, 138, 179
dissimulation of, 29–30, 90–91
eidetic, 143, 145–47

impersonation of, 38, 45, 49–50, 55, 122, 140, 161
play of, 26–28, 63, 116, 164
rhapsodic, 19–20, 32, 36, 100, 117, 129–30, 142, 160
theatrical, 66, 135
Mitchell, Stanley, 36 n. 2
mousikē, 49, 69, 174
Müller, Heiner, 23
Murdoch, Iris, 44
muthos (myth, legend, plot), 21–22, 48, 77, 96, 100, 135, 148, 195

Nancy, Jean-Luc, 1, 4, 23 n. 95, 30–31, 33, 102–4, 116–24, 162, 186–95
"Sharing Voices," 1, 33, 128, 162–74, 186, 193
"Le ventriloque," 30, 32, 102–4, 117–24, 130, 149 n. 54
narration, 8, 14, 28, 50–54, 131, 143, 189
Nehamas, Alexander, 58
Nietzsche, Friedrich, 1, 4, 29–30, 35–36, 69, 71, 74–75, 85–92, 110 n. 23
Nussbaum, Martha C., 21

opinion (*doxa*), 13, 98–99, 110 n. 23, 152, 188
orality (vs. literacy), 39–40
otherness, 31–32, 97, 128–30, 141–43, 146, 148, 152, 160–63, 167–68, 192

palaia diaphora, 24, 27, 70, 100, 110, 169, 184
palinode, 29, 77–83, 98
Pappas, Nikolas, 170
parergon (bye-work), 45–47, 49, 63, 93, 194
Parry, Milman, 39
pharmakon (drug), 27, 30, 58, 64–69, 81, 90, 93–94, 96–100, 137, 142, 164
picture, 2–3, 18–19, 114–15, 138, 141, 148
Platonism, 8, 27, 40, 103, 103–6, 109–10, 134, 149, 161, 163. *See also* metaphysics
deconstruction of, confrontation with, 92, 100, 104, 169
overturning of, reversal of, 1, 26, 29–30, 35, 70–71, 84, 92, 112, 195
Plato and, 76, 83, 92
representation and, 103, 105, 109, 159
play (*paidia, jeu, Spiel*), 7, 35–69, 70–101, 121, 129, 131, 135, 164, 181
abyssal play (mise en abyme), 24, 120, 146, 148, 155–56
education and play, 19–20, 24, 44–50, 106, 117
mimetic play, 5, 14, 24, 114, 116, 123, 157

play (*continued*)
seriousness and, 27, 135, 173–74
theatrical play, 5, 29
woman and play, 30, 156
poiēsis, 55, 57, 93, 145
polemos, 8–9, 24
polis (city-state, republic), 41, 47, 49, 63, 67, 133,
138–39, 141, 148, 157, 186–95
Press, Gerald A., 5 n. 12, 9 n. 25, 27
Protagoras, 15, 87, 172, 174–75
protreptic function, 9–10, 12, 22

quarrel (dispute), 6–8, 23–26, 35–37, 57–61, 73–88,
90–93, 100–101, 169, 184, 193
Quine, Willard Van Orman, 15

Raeder, Hans H., 71
recognition, 22, 24, 26, 28, 111, 193
representation, 2–3, 13, 18–21, 28–31, 57–62,
109–17, 130–31, 147–48, 195. *See also* eidetic
mimesis
resemblance. *See* likeness
rhapsody. *See also* rhapsodic play
etymology of, 3–4
rhapsodic community, 60, 186, 189, 194
rhapsodic dialogue, 3, 8, 24, 192
rhapsodic mode, 2, 4–7, 11–15, 17, 20–21, 24,
26, 28–32, 50–55, 60, 69, 73, 77, 119, 123, 136,
169, 193
rhapsodic performance (the rhapsode), 89,
120–22, 124, 134, 138–40, 147–48, 169–70,
174–79, 190–93
Ricoeur, Paul, 115, 177 n. 62
rigor (*akribeia*), 3–4, 6–8, 20, 27–32, 35–69, 75,
88, 93–96, 110, 119–23, 135–36, 159, 163, 175,
181, 188, 194
Robin, Leon, 41, 71
Romilly, Jacqueline de, 21 n. 82
Roochnik, David, 6 n. 17, 9, 24 n. 97, 37 n. 7,
170–73
Rorty, Richard, 6 n. 17, 172
Rosen, Stanley, 8–9, 20 n. 80, 28, 30, 35, 58–61, 66
n. 114, 102, 126–27
Rowe, C. J., 103
Russell, Bertrand, 102

Sallis, John, 32, 83 n. 57, 119 n. 51, 134, 146, 157
n. 82, 161 n. 98
Schleiermacher, Friedrich D. E., 164, 167
Schuhl, Pierr-Maxime, 7 n. 18
seriousness (vs. play), 6–7, 24–29, 36, 42, 45, 50–
55, 73–74, 91, 96, 98–99, 117, 131, 135, 163,
173–74, 195

Shaftesbury, Anthony A. C., 4
Shakespeare, 23
sharing (*partage*), 33, 128, 188–94
shining, 76, 82–83
similarity. *See* likeness
simulacrum (*phantasma*), 2–3, 30–31, 91, 104–10,
113, 116–17, 121, 124–31, 157
singularity, 27, 31, 60, 82–83, 150, 175, 194
singular voices, 33, 192, 195
Socratism (aesthetic, logical), 85, 87
Sophocles, 19, 87 n. 72, 88
Spariosu, Mihai, 174
Stesichorus, 78, 98
Stoppard, Tom, 23
Strauss, Leo, 11 n. 41, 12 n. 46, 15 n. 62, 23
sumplokē (intertwining), 31, 127–28, 130–31
Szymborska Wieslawa, 132

Tejera, Victorino, 5 n. 14, 9
tekhnē (art, craft), 29–31, 37, 57, 82, 98, 121,
126–27, 165, 167, 171, 174–76
theia moira (divine share), 33, 171, 176, 178, 183,
191, 193
therapeutic function, 11–12, 29, 80–81
Thrasymachus, 37–44, 53–54, 68–69, 172, 175
Trakl, Georg, 8 n. 23, 33, 170 n. 31, 185–86
translation, 17, 30, 78, 94–96, 100–101, 105, 154,
164
treatise, 2–5, 8–10, 32, 91, 123, 134, 149, 160–61
truth, 10, 16, 18–19, 26, 28, 55–57, 70–101, 103,
107, 166, 173, 179
art and, 8, 26, 29–30, 35, 55, 57, 69–101, 167,
184, 186
education and, 13, 18, 55
justice and, 67, 180
play and, 26, 29, 55, 70–101
rigor and, 6, 36, 63, 169
unconcealment (*alētheia*), 19, 30, 57, 83
type (*tupos*), 48, 50, 62–63, 65, 67, 139
typography, 28–29, 48, 69, 122
See also rigor and justice

uncanny, the (the unhomely), 19, 115, 133

ventriloquist, the, 7, 31, 119, 122, 128, 149, 156
Vernant, Jean-Pierre, 6 n. 17

Wagner, 29, 89
Warhol, Andy, 112
womb (*hystera*), 151, 156–57
Wulf, Christoph, 36 n.4

Zarathustra, 29, 75